U0105559

中國特色話語：

——陳安論國際經濟法學 第四卷 下冊

陳安 著

第四卷

第五編　國際經濟法熱點學術問題長、短評　001

第一章　改進我國國際法教育的「他山之石」
——歐美之行考察見聞　003

第二章　從難從嚴訓練成果人才並出　019

第三章　「博士」新解　031

第四章　是「棒打鴛鴦」嗎？
——就「李爽案件」評《紐約時報》報導兼答美國法學界同行問　041

第五章　小議對外學術交流的「大忌」　089

第六章　向世界展現中國理念　093

第七章　朝著合作共贏方向發展推動國際經濟法理念變革　097

第八章　建構中國特色國際法學理論　101

第九章　「左公柳」、中國魂與新絲路
——「七七事變」七十週年隨筆　105

第六編　有關陳安學術論著和學術觀點的書評等 115
第一章　《陳安論國際經濟法學》書評薈萃 117
第二章　《中國的吶喊》書評薈萃 203
第三章　陳安早期論著書評薈萃（1981-2008） 563
第四章　群賢畢至，少長咸集，坐而論道，暢敘舊情 609

第七編　有關陳安學術活動的報導、函件等 637
第一章　媒體報導 639
第二章　學界來函 669
第三章　陳安學術小傳及歷年主要論著目錄（以倒計年為序） 735
第四章　陳安論著、業績獲獎一覽（以倒計年為序／2016-1960） 747

後　記 751

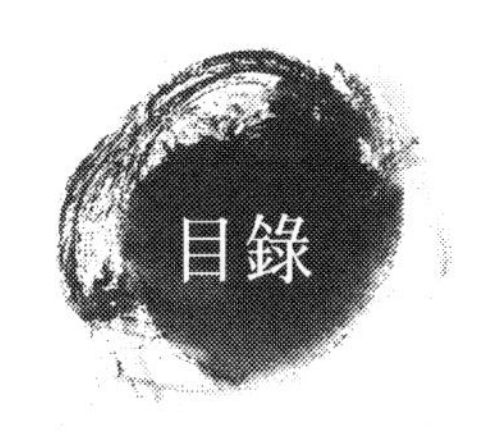

第四卷

第五編　國際經濟法熱點學術問題長、短評

第一章　改進我國國際法教育的「他山之石」
——歐美之行考察見聞　003
一、關於國際法專業人才的培養　005
二、關於國際法資料中心的建立　014
三、關於國際法專業力量的合作　015
第二章　從難從嚴訓練成果人才並出　019
一、實行「大運動量」訓練，過法學專業英語關　020
二、多學科交叉滲透，建立合理的知識結構　023
三、理論聯繫實際，提高實務工作能力　025
四、充分信賴，畀以「重擔」，嚴密組織，嚴格把關　026
五、賦予較大「成才自留權」，加速形成「人才生產力」　029
第三章　「博士」新解　031
附錄一　官員與老闆：心儀博士帽　033
附錄二　「教授」貶值為哪般　035

附錄三　該擠擠「學術泡沫」了　038

第四章　是「棒打鴛鴦」嗎？

——就「李爽案件」評《紐約時報》報導兼答美國法學界同行問　041

一、李爽是何許人？「李爽案件」的背景如何？　043

二、李爽觸犯了什麼法律？犯了什麼罪？　046

三、是打擊「鴛鴦」的無情棒，還是拯救沉淪的救生圈？　049

附錄一　中國拘禁了法國男人的情婦　057

附錄二　法國外交官說中國拘留了他的未婚妻　059

附錄三　小題大做

——評白天祥等人在所謂「李爽案件」上的喧嚷　060

附錄四　The Li Shuang Case: A Wet Blanket over Romantic Love?　062

附錄五　《紐約時報》報導英文原文　078

第五章　小議對外學術交流的「大忌」　089

第六章　向世界展現中國理念　093

第七章　朝著合作共贏方向發展推動國際經濟法理念變革　097

第八章　建構中國特色國際法學理論　101

第九章　「左公柳」、中國魂與新絲路

——「七七事變」七十週年隨筆　105

第六編　有關陳安學術論著和學術觀點的書評等

第一章　《陳安論國際經濟法學》書評薈萃　117

一、陳安：知識報國，壯心不已　117

二、中國國際經濟法學的基石之作

——評陳安教授的《論國際經濟法學》　123

三、試論秉持第三世界共同立場的中國特色國際經濟法學派的形成及其代表性成果 125
四、從陳安教授辛勤探索的結晶中感悟其治學之道 143
五、中國特色國際經濟法學的理念與追求
——《陳安論國際經濟法學》的學術創新與特色貢獻 148
六、中國參與經濟全球化管理的戰略思考
——評《陳安論國際經濟法學》的主導學術理念 171
第二章 《中國的吶喊》書評薈萃 203
一、中國吶喊　發聾振聵 204
The Enlightening and Thought-provoking Voice from China 207
二、晨起臨窗坐　書香伴芳菲
——喜覽《中國的吶喊：陳安論國際經濟法》 211
By the Casement at Dawn, in the Fragrance of New Book
—A Joyful Browse of *The Voice from China: An CHEN on International Economic Law* 212
三、弘中華正氣　為群弱發聲 214
Spreading China's Justice, Voicing for the Global Weak 217
四、老艄公的鏗鏘號子　發出時代的最強音
——《中國的吶喊：陳安論國際經濟法》讀後的點滴感悟 221
The Sonorous Work Song of an Old Helmsman of International Economic Law
—Some Reflections and Thoughts After Reading *The Voice from China: An CHEN on International Economic Law* 225

五、天下視野　家國情懷　公平秉守
——讀《中國的吶喊：陳安論國際經濟法》 231
Global Perspective, State Position and Equity Pursuance
—Introducing *The Voice from China: An CHEN on International Economic Law* 238
六、「提出中國方案、貢獻中國智慧」的先行者
——評《中國的吶喊：陳安論國際經濟法》 246
A Pioneer in "Providing China's Proposal and Contributing China's Wisdom"
—Review on *The Voice from China: An CHEN on International Economic Law* 252
七、追求全球正義　抵制國際霸權 260
Pursuing Global Justice Resisting International Hegemony 268
八、國家主權等國際經濟法宏觀問題的深刻反思
——評《中國的吶喊：陳安論國際經濟法》 278
Reflections on State Sovereignty and Other Grand Themes o15f International Law 283
九、精當透徹的論證　盡顯大師的風采
——簡評《中國的吶喊：陳安論國際經濟法》 293
Precise and Thorough Analyses—Illustrating a Guru's Profound Knowledge
—A Brief Commentary on *The Voice from China: An CHEN on International Economic Law* 300
十、獨具中國風格氣派　發出華夏學術強音
——評《中國的吶喊：陳安論國際經濟法》 311

Academic Voice with Chinese Characteristics
—A Commentary on *The Voice from China: An CHEN on International Economic Law* 320
十一、把准南方國家共同脈搏的學術力作
——評《中國的吶喊：陳安論國際經濟法》 332
A Highly Recommendable Monograph that Senses the Pulse of the South 334
十二、國際經濟法研究的「中國立場」
——讀《中國的吶喊》有感 337
A Chinese School of Jurisprudence on International Economic Law 342
十三、不為浮雲遮眼　兼具深邃堅定
——評《中國的吶喊：陳安論國際經濟法》 347
Never Covered by Cloud, Insisting Profound Insight
—Comments on *The Voice from China* 350
十四、任你風向東南西北　我自巋然從容不迫
——國際經濟新秩序的重思：以陳安教授的國際經濟法研究為視角 354
Disregarding Whither the Wind Blows, Keeping Firm Confidence of His Owns
——A Revisit to Prof. Chen's Research on NIEO 360
十五、老戰士新吶喊　捍衛全球公義
——評《中國的吶喊：陳安論國際經濟法》 369

An Old Warrior's New Defense of Global Justice
—Comments on *The Voice from China* 372
十六、二十五年實踐顯示了一九九一年陳安預言的睿智　中美國際經貿關係需增進互補、合作和互相依存
——評《中國的吶喊》專著第十四章 376
Twenty-Five Years of Experience Show the Wisdom of An Chen's 1991 Prediction of Increasing Complementarity, Cooperation and Interdependence of Sino-American International Busines Relations
—Comments on Chapter 14 of Chen's Monograph 380
十七、評陳安教授英文專著《中國的吶喊》：聚焦ISDS和二〇一五中美BIT談判 384
Review on Prof. Chen's English Monograph
—Focusing on the ISDS & 2015 China-U.S. BIT Negotiation 392
十八、矢志不渝倡導南南聯合自強與國際經濟新秩序
——評陳安教授專著《中國的吶喊：陳安論國際經濟法》 400
A Tireless Advocate for S-S Coalition and NIEO: Comments on Prof. Chen's Monograph 406
十九、中國呼聲　理應傾聽
——評陳安教授專著《中國的吶喊》 413
China's Voice Deserves Hearing
——Comments on Prof. Chen's *The Voice from China* 418
二十、魅力感召、法治理念與愛國情懷之和諧統一
——讀陳安教授《中國的吶喊》有感 424
Harmonization of Charisma, Jurisprudence and Patriotism

—The Inspiration from *The Voice from China: An CHEN on International Economic Law* 436

二十一、駁「中國威脅」論——史學、政治學與法學的視角

——讀陳安教授《中國的吶喊》第四章 452

Rebutting "China's Threat" Slander from the Perspectives of History, Politics and Jurisprudence

—On Chapter 4 of Professor Chen's Monograph *The Voice from China* 457

二十二、論國際經濟法的普遍性

——評《中國的吶喊：陳安論國際經濟法》 464

On the Universality of International Economic Law

—Comments on *The Voice from China: An CHEN on International Economic Law* 477

国際経済法の普遍性について

—An Chen, *The Voice from China: An CHEN on International Economic Law*, Berlin / Heidelberg: Springer, 2013を素材に 495

二十三、一部深邃厚重的普及讀物

——評陳安教授對「中國威脅」讕言的古今剖析 502

A Profound but Popular Reading Material

—On the Anatomy of the "China Threat" Slander by Professor Chen 507

二十四、揭露「中國威脅」論的本質：三把利匕剖示美霸讕言真相 515

"China Threat" Slander's Ancestors & Its US Hegemony Variant: Disecting with Sharp Daggers 518

第三章　陳安早期論著書評薈萃（1981-2008）　563
一、立意新穎務實　分析縝密深入　理論實踐交融
——對陳安主編《國際投資法的新發展與中國雙邊投資條約的新實踐》一書的評價　563
二、內容豐富　系統完整　洵是佳作
——《美國對海外投資的法律保護及典型案例分析》評介　564
三、評陳安主編的國際經濟法系列專著（1987年版）　565
四、新視角：從南北矛盾看國際經濟法
——評陳安主編的《國際經濟法總論》　571
五、獨樹中華一幟　躋身國際前驅
——評陳安主編的《MIGA與中國》　579
六、深入研究　科學判斷
——《「解決投資爭端國際中心」述評》簡介　581
七、國際投資爭端仲裁研究的力作
——評《國際投資爭端仲裁——「解決投資爭端國際中心」機制研究》　583
八、俯視規則的迷宮
——讀陳安教授主編的《國際經濟法學專論》　588
九、「問題與主義」中的「問題」
——讀《國際經濟法學專論》　594
十、高屋建瓴　視角獨到
——推薦《晚近十年來美國單邊主義與WTO多邊主義交鋒的三大回合》　600
十一、以史為師　力排「眾議」　說理透闢

——推薦《南南聯合自強五十年的國際經濟立法反思》 602
十二、緊扣學科前沿　力求與時俱進
——推薦《國際經濟法學》（第三版） 604
第四章　群賢畢至，少長咸集，坐而論道，暢敘舊情 609
一、在「中國國際經濟法的研究方法暨陳安教授學術思想」研討會上的致辭 609
二、我與陳安教授 612
三、誨人不倦　師道悠悠 614
四、陳安老師與中國國際經濟法事業 615
五、知識報國　後學師範 618
六、春分化雨育新人 622
七、八十感懷 623
八、高山仰止
——寫於陳安老師八十壽誕之際 627
九、五「嚴」源自一「愛」 633

第七編　有關陳安學術活動的報導、函件等

第一章　媒體報導 639
一、在哈佛的講壇上
——訪廈門大學政法學院副院長陳安 639
二、他把法的目光投向世界與未來
——訪廈門大學法律系陳安教授 643
三、適應對外開放和發展外向型經濟需要，國際經濟法系列專著問世 648

四、為對外開放鋪路

——記廈門大學法學教授陳安 648

五、就閩臺兩省結拜「姊妹」一事，廈門大學法學教授發表看法 651

六、理性務實的學術交流盛會

——一九九三年兩岸法學學術研討會綜述 653

七、春風吹拂紫梅　白鷺振翅騰飛

——陳安教授談廈門獲得立法權 657

八、第十二屆「安子介國際貿易研究獎」頒獎大會圓滿結束（摘要）660

九、第十二屆「安子介國際貿易研究獎」頒獎 661

十、中國特色國際經濟法學的探索者和開拓者

——陳安教授 663

十一、十位廈大學者入選中國傑出社會科學家 665

第二章　學界來函 669

一、來函概述 669

二、來函選輯 681

第三章　陳安學術小傳及歷年主要論著目錄（以倒計年為序） 735

一、陳安學術小傳 735

二、陳安歷年主要論著 737

第四章　陳安論著、業績獲獎一覽（以倒計年為序／2016-1960） 747

一、國家級、省部級一等獎 747

二、國家級、省部級二等獎 748

三、國家級三等獎 749

四、廈門大學最高榮譽獎 750

後　記 751

十五、老戰士新吶喊　捍衛全球公義

——評《中國的吶喊：陳安論國際經濟法》

王江雨*

《中國的吶喊：陳安論國際經濟法》的出版，是國際經濟法發展過程中一個里程碑性的標誌。事實上，這本書是近年來論述國際經濟新秩序問題最重要的著作。這本巨著八百多頁，從陳安教授過去三十年取得的大量的學術成果中，遴選二十四篇代表性文章，匯輯而成。

該英文專著獲得「國家社會科學基金中華學術外譯專案」的立項。據悉，這是中國國際經濟法學界獲此立項的第一例。依據全國社科規劃辦公室檔解釋，「中華學術外譯專案」是二〇一〇年由全國哲學社會科學規劃領導小組批准設立的國家社科基金新的主要類別之一，旨在促進中外學術交流，推動中國哲學社會科學優秀成果和優秀人才走向世界。它主要資助中國哲學社會科學研究的優秀成果以外文形式在國外權威出版機構出版，進入國外主流發行傳播管道，增進國外對當代中國、對中國哲學社會科學以及傳統文化的了解，推動中外學術交流與對話，提高中國哲學社會科學的國際影響力。[314]

「專家評審意見」認為，陳安教授的這部英文專著「**對海外讀者全面了解中國國際經濟法學者較有代表性的學術觀點和主流思想具有重要意義。全書結構自成一體，觀點新穎，具有中國風格和中國氣派，闡釋了不同於西方發達國家學者的創新學術理念和創新學術追求，致力於初步創立起以馬克思主義為指導的具有**

中國特色的國際經濟法理論體系，為國際社會弱勢群體爭取公平權益鍛造了法學理論武器」[315]

《中國的吶喊：陳安論國際經濟法》是陳安教授站在中國和國際弱勢群體的共同立場，踐行知識報國夙志，投身國際學術爭鳴之力作，也是其命名為「中國的吶喊」之由來。

《中國的吶喊》全書分為六個部分，不僅分析國際經濟法重大的理論問題，而且也從學理上討論國際經濟法的實際應用。它首先探討國際經濟法的一般理論原則，有力地論證了國際經濟法的內涵。陳安教授認為，國際經濟法乃是一門獨立的學科，而不應僅僅被視為國際公法的一個分支。這部著作第一部分最有價值、猶如皇冠珠寶的地方，是針對當代經濟主權的「大辯論」所作的精闢剖析。陳安教授批評了美國的單邊主義，並將其與他所贊同的WTO多邊主義加以比較，論證熱烈而極具感染力。該著作還就中國對國際秩序諸多問題所持的各種主張加以仔細分析並進行辯護。它是迄今針對中國在國際秩序中所持態度最好的陳述。《中國的吶喊》第四、第五和第六部分，分別探討了中外雙邊投資條約、中國的涉外經濟立法以及中國參與國際經濟爭端解決等方面的法律問題。

《中國的吶喊》一書中的所有文章，都是陳安教授過去在各國發表的論文，它們具有三個共同特點。第一，從歷史、政治和經濟綜合的角度對法律問題進行探討。雖然該書較少對國際經濟法中的具體規則和案例進行學理分析，因此不能成為實務律師的參考書，但這本書的獨到智慧在於深入探討剖析國際上聚訟紛紜的各種問題，如國家主權、管理體制、經濟民族主義、美國單邊主義、「中國威脅」論等等。第二，陳安教授從南方國家的視角來分析和論證各種問題，也就是說，在南北兩類國家有關國際經濟秩序的分歧中他支持發展中國家的觀點。但是，和某些持有「第三世界思路」的國際法學者的僵硬觀點不同，陳安教授贊同多邊主義，並認為國際經濟秩序可以由諸如WTO之類的各種國際組織來驅動和引導。他似乎並不認為新自由主義是一種具有「原罪」的理念，它代表發達國家富豪們的利益壓迫發展中國家窮苦大眾。陳安教授主要是反對一些西方國家，特別是美國鼓吹和實行單邊主義。第三，陳安教授顯然是一位愛國主義者，甚至是思想開明、毫無偏見的民族主義者。[316]他為維護中國在國際舞臺上的既定立場和行動舉止進行辯護，其滿腔熱忱，令人印象深刻。

本書作者陳安教授是中國最傑出的法律學者之一，他帶頭宣導從南方國家的視角（當然更多是從中國的視角）看待國際經濟法問題。陳安教授出生於一九二九年，經歷和見證了中國和全球在二十世紀發生的許多最重要的事件。他在一九四九年之前的民國時代就接受了正規的法學教育，在一九七九年之後自學了中華人民共和國的法律體系和國際法。據報導，他在「文化大革命」之後，從一九八一至一九八二年開始致力於國際經濟法的研究，並應邀到哈佛大學進行學術訪問。[317]他在五十多歲才開始接觸國際經濟法卻能夠成為該領域全球最著名的學者之一，可謂奇跡。更難能可貴的是，除了從事學術研究，他在重建廈門大學法學院中發揮了重大作用。廈門大學法學院在一九五三年全國性「院系調整」中被撤銷，中斷二十七年之後，直到一九八〇年才重新組建，但現在已發展成為中國最頂尖的法學院之一。總之，陳安教授堪稱一位既博學多才又勤奮不息的天才人物。

An Old Warrior's New Defense of Global Justice

—Comments on *The Voice from China*

Wang Jiangyu*

The publication of *The Voice from China*: An CHEN *on International Economic Law* represents a landmark development in the discourse of international economic law. As a matter of fact, it is the single most important book on the New International Economic Order (NIEL) published in recent years. This enormous book, featuring almost 800 pages, is a collection of 24 representative articles selected from the voluminous scholarship authored by Professor An Chen that spanned the past 30 years.

This English monograph has successfully won the support from the Chinese Academic Foreign Translation Project (CAFTP), making itself the first of such kind within the academic circle of International Economic Law in China. According to the official specifications〔318〕 from the National Social Science Fund of China (NSSFC), CAFTP is one of the major categories of projects set by the NSSFC and approved by the National Philosophy and Social Science Planning Leading Group of China in 2010. This Project aims to promote Sino-foreign academic exchanges, and to facilitate the outstanding works as well as prominent scholars in the field of philosophy and social science towards the world's academic stage. For this purpose, a major part of such funding is allocated to sponsor the aforesaid achievements to be published in foreign language through authoritative publishers abroad. It is expected that, by such way of accessing and participating in foreign **mainstream** distribution channels, foreigners could have a better understanding of contemporary China, its philosophy and social sciences and its traditional culture. It is also expected that Sino-foreign academic exchange and dialogue would hence be more active, and the overseas influence of Chinese philosophy and social science would be enhanced.

In the Expert Review Report, some of the most professional peers opine that Prof. Chen's book "contributes vastly in the sense of introducing onto the world arena a series of typical academic views and mainstream ideas of Chinese International Economic Law scholars. The whole book is well and uniquely structured, and loaded with creative points of views. With its obvious Chinese character and style, this book has illustrated various innovational academic ideals and pursuits that are different from those voices & views preached by some authoritative scholars from Western developed powers. The author has endeavored to create a specific Chinese theoretical system of International Economic Law under the guidance of Marxism, to further serve as a theoretical weapon for the weak groups of international society to fight for their equitable rights and interests." [319]

The Voice from China: An CHEN on International Economic Law is a masterpiece of Prof. An Chen to practice his lifetime will of serving the home country with knowledge and participating in the international competition of academic views. The whole book is based on the common stand of China and other international weak groups, and is indeed a strong & just Voice from China.

Divided into six parts, this magnificent book discusses both grand theories as well as practical doctrinal issues in international economic law. It starts with discussions on the general theories of international economic law, including a vigorous effort to define the international economic law so that it can be an autonomous academic discipline and so that it should not be regarded as merely part of public international law according to Prof. Chen. However, the examination of the "Great Debates" on contemporary economic sovereignty forms the crown's jewels of this first part of the book. Prof. Chen's critique of U.S. unilateralism, contrasted with his praise of multilateralism represented by the WTO, is powerful and passionate. The book also carefully examines and defends China's position on various issues concerning the international order. It offers by far the best account of China's attitude in this regard. Parts IV, V and VI examine, respectively, legal issues concerning Sino-foreign bilateral investment treaties (BITs), Sino-foreign legislation and China's participation in the settlement of international economic disputes.

All the chapters, originally journal articles published by Prof. Chen in various places, have three common features. First, they all put legal issues in their historical, political and economic contexts. Although the book does not work much on doctrinal analysis of specific rules and cases in international economic law and hence it cannot be treated as such a reference book by practicing lawyers, its wisdom lies more in the examination of international controversial issues such as sovereignty, regulatory space, economic nationalism, U.S. unilateralism, the China threat theory, etc. Second, it reasons from Southern perspective, meaning it sides with the developing countries in the North-South division in the international economic order. However, unlike many of the diehards in the camp of the Third World Approaches to International Law, An Chen favors multilateralism as well as an international economic order driven and led by international institutions such as the WTO. He does not seem to view neoliberalism as an idea with the original sin of oppressing the poor people in the developing countries on behalf of the billionaires in the developed world. Rather, he is mainly opposed to the employment of unilateralism by some Western countries, especially the U.S. Third, Prof. Chen is obviously also a patriot and even an open-minded nationalist.[320] His passion to defend China's relevant positions and behaviors at the international level is remarkably impressive.

The author of the book, Prof. An Chen, is one of China's most prominent legal scholars and a leading advocate of the southern view of international economic law, of course more from a Chinese perspective. Born in 1929, Prof. Chen has experienced or witnessed many of the most important events in China and the world in the 20th century. His legal education walks from formal legal education during the Republic of China period before 1949 to self-education of the PRC legal system and international law after 1979. Reportedly, he started to devote his energy to international economic law during 1981-1982, when, after the disastrous and lawless Cultural Revolution, he was invited to be a visiting scholar at Harvard University.〔321〕It is however a miracle that he was able to turn himself into one of the world's most distinguished scholars in this field given that he only started to learn and work on international economic law after he was 50 years old. More mysteriously, besides his research, he also played a major role in reestablishing the school of Law, Xiamen University, which was once interrupted and dismantled for 27 years since the 1953 nationwide "School Adjustments" until 1980, and developed it into one of the very best law schools in China. By all means, Prof. Chen deserves to be called a genius who is both talented and hardworking.

（翻譯、編輯：陳　欣）

十六、二十五年實踐顯示了一九九一年陳安預言的睿智　中美國際經貿關係需增進互補、合作和互相依存

——評《中國的吶喊》專著第十四章

〔美〕斯蒂芬·坎特*

我收到陳安院長新近出版的英文專著《中國的吶喊》[322]一書，並且有機會撰寫書評，對此我感到特別高興。這部重要著作包含二十四篇專論，彙集了陳安過去三十多年來研究中國與國際經濟法的代表作，具有重大學術價值。中國自一九八〇年開始對外開放，如今已經發展成為全球舉足輕重的經貿強國之一。對於任何希望了解中國上述發展進程的人們來說，陳安這部著作乃是重要的資訊來源。

陳安是一位傑出的學者，一個具有前瞻思維的教育家。他在中國重新融入世界經濟和實行法治的三十多年進程中，始終發揮著至關重要的作用。他是許多中國年輕一代法學專業人才的導師，這些人才在過去三十多年中積極參與了令人振奮的全部發展進程。同時，他也一直是眾多國際同行的好朋友，我自己也有幸身列其中。

我特別樂意重新閱讀《中國的吶喊》一書的第十四章，即《是重新閉關自守？還是擴大對外開放？——論中美兩國經濟上的互相依存以及「1989年政治風波」後在華外資的法律環境》。[323]這一章的基本內容是基於在「1989年政治風波」之後一年多（即1990年秋）陳安在一次國際學術會議上發表的演講，見解深刻，而且富有洞察力。那次國際學術會議即由路易士與克拉克西北法學院主辦，而當時我正在擔任該法學院的院長一職。

「1989年政治風波」曾經導致中美兩國關係十分緊張，並且引起許多人懷疑中美兩國之間開展的合作和經濟互動能否持久。在這種環境下，陳安敢於大膽地、正確地提出自己的見解，雄辯滔滔，他斷言：儘管問題多多，時時出現，今後中美兩國間的經貿合作互動關係勢必經久持續，而且日益增強。他明確指出中美交往已經給中美兩國人民帶來互惠互利的許多事實，並且列舉當時中國正在進一步實行的六個方面的改革，它們勢必為中美經濟互相依存關係的進一步深化創造更加有利的基礎。這些改革包括：修訂了一九七九年的《中外合資經營企業法》，賦予外商更多權益；制定了適用於經濟特區的《外商投資開發經營成片土地暫行管理辦法》，放寬了土地使用權的轉讓，便於外商投資成片開發土地；開放和拓展上海浦東地區，擴大了外商投資極其重要的平臺；統一了外商投資企業和外國企業所得稅，使之對外商更為優惠；實施了《行政訴訟法》，使外商有權依法「民告官」接受了ICSID體制，使外商可以把投資爭端提交ICSID進行國際仲裁。[324]

陳安在一九九一年提出的關於中美關係的上述預言，現在已被證實是正確的。可是，在二十世紀八〇年代和九〇年代，我們美國大多數人士即使是最樂觀的人也很難預見中國經濟竟然會如此非同凡響地快速發展，而陳安這篇論文中所強調的上述這些改革措施，在中國經濟如此快速發展的進程中確實起到了關鍵的作用。

回首前塵，自一九七九年中美全面恢復外交關係，迄今三十多年以來，中國和美國一直在民生的各個方面不斷地發展更加密切的關係。除了在經濟方面建立了互惠互利和互相依存關係之外，在文化、教育以及其他諸多人文領域，兩國人民也一直分享著美好的互相交流成果。

在當今世界，我們正面臨著許多嚴重的問題。這些問題，只能通過各國人民和各國政府之間的互相合作、互相尊重和共同努力，特別是各個大國人民和大國政府之間的互相合作、互相尊重和共同努力，才能成功地加以解決。中國和美國是全球最重要大國之中的兩個。有幸的是，近幾十年來我們兩國的各屆領導人都致力於建立這種關係，並不斷取得進展。政府與政府之間不斷接觸、舉行會談以及解決各種層次的實質問題，這已經成為兩國關係的常態特徵。我們兩國的首腦，美國總統奧巴馬和中國國家主席習近平之間，已經建立起緊密的工作關係和個人關係，經常互相邀請和互相訪問。二〇一五年九月，習近平主席即將對美國進行重要的國事訪問。這種友好和坦誠的氛圍相當有利於逐步解決範圍廣泛的各種爭議問題，包括國際衝突和世界和平問題、淨化環境問題、能源安全問題、改善嚴重威脅人類的氣候變化問題、加強互相理解和坦誠討論各種分歧問題、改進健康和消滅貧困問題。這種不斷接觸和加強溝通的模式，完全符合一九九一年陳安預言中提出的見解，是當前我們應當採取的正確途徑，也是造福全球的必不可少的關鍵舉措。

最後，在書評末尾我想談談個人的訪華經歷。一九八四至一九八五年，我曾經以美國富布萊特基金法學教授的身份，在中國的南京大學法律系講學。我經常愉快地回憶起一九八五年春天，在陳安院長的盛情邀請下，我帶著八歲的兒子到廈門訪問，很高興在廈門大學做了幾場學術演講，會見了陳安指導的許多才俊學生，而其中一些人隨後赴美留學成為我的學生，並在美國路易士與克拉克西北法學院獲得法學博士學位。在廈門期間，承蒙陳安及其家人和廈門大學法學院同行們的盛情款待。後來，陳安在一九九一年回訪美國，我們共同在路易士與克拉克西北法學院非常愉快地相處了一段美好時光。

陳安是我的老朋友。中美兩國都有不少人士其職業生涯中始終致力於在中美之間確立建設性的和友好相處的關係，陳安是其中的重要人物之一。在他撰寫的這部精彩著作出版之際，我向他表示祝賀，並且向讀者們鄭重推薦此書。

（翻譯：楊　帆）

Twenty-Five Years of Experience Show the Wisdom of An Chen's 1991 Prediction of Increasing Complementarity, Cooperation and Interdependence of Sino-American International Busines Relations

—Comments on Chapter 14 of Chen's Monograph

Stephen Kanter*

It is with special pleasure that I received and have had the chance to review Dean An Chen's recent volume, *The Voice from China.* [325] This important work contains twenty-four articles that represent a portion of An Chen's significant scholarship over thirty years on China and International Economic Law. It is an important source for anyone wishing to understand China, and the development of her initial opening to the wider world from 1980 to China's critical position as one of the most important economic and international trading powers today.

An Chen played a vital role throughout this period of China's reintegration into the world economic and rule of law systems as a prominent scholar, as a forward-thinking educational leader, and as a mentor to so many of China's young lawyers who have participated in all of the exciting developments of the last thirty years. He has also been a good friend to countless international colleagues. I consider myself fortunate to be among their number.

I am particularly pleased to revisit Chapter 14, To Close Again or to Open Wider: The Sino-US Economic Interdependence and the Legal Environment for Foreign Investment in China After Tian' anmen.[326] This chapter is based upon an insightful talk that An Chen gave as part of an International Law Conference held in Autumn 1990 and hosted at Lewis and Clark Law School, where I was serving as Dean, just over one year after the disturbing 1989 events in Tiananmen Square. These events created great tension in the Sino-American relationship and raised doubts about the durability of cooperation and economic interaction between our two countries.

An Chen boldly and correctly argued that the relationship would endure and grow stronger despite problems (even serious ones) that would arise from time to time. He pointed to the mutual benefits already accruing to both countries and noted six recent further reforms in China that he knew would provide the basis for deeper economic interdependence. These included revision of the 1979 Joint Venture Law, granting more rights and benefits to foreign investors; easing of land use transfer rights within Special Economic Zones, promoting foreign investors to land-tract development; simplification of the tax structure and improved tax incentives for foreign investors; the opening and development of Shanghai's Pudong district, extending a significant key platform for foreign investors; improved enforcement of the Administrative Procedure Law, allowing foreign investors easier to bring suits aganst Chinese governments; and accession to the ICSID international dispute resolution mechanism, allowing foreign investors to submit the investor-state disputes to ICSID for international arbitration. [327]

His predictions have been proven correct. Even the most optimistic among us in the 1980s and 1990s would have been hard pressed to envision the extraordinary pace of further development of the Chinese economy, and the reforms he highlighted in his article played crucial roles.

From the first days of the Shanghai Communiqué in 1972 and the restoration of full diplomatic relations in 1979 to the present, China and the United States have continued to develop closer relations in every aspect of life. In addition to mutually beneficial economic interdependence, our two peoples have shared cultural, educational and many other wonderful human experiences.

Our world faces many serious problems that can only be successfully addressed through mutual cooperation, respect and effort among peoples and governments, especially those of the world powers. China and the

United States are two of the most important of these powers, and it is fortunate that the leaders of both of our countries are committed to building on the progress that has been achieved in recent decades. Government-to-government contacts, meetings and substantive problem solving at all levels have become a regular feature of our nations' relationship. Our two Presidents, Barack Obama and Xi Jinping, have a close working and personal relationship and they have exchanged invitations and visits. President Xi will be making an important state visit to the United States in September 2015. This friendly and candid atmosphere is conducive to progress on a wide range of issues from international conflicts and peace, to a cleaner environment and energy security while ameliorating the threat of severe climate change, to mutual understanding and open discussion of differences, and to improved health and the reduction of poverty. This model, consistent with Chen An's 1991 prediction, is the right one for our new century and is essential for the well-being of the whole world.

I want to close with a personal note. I served as Fulbright Professor of Law at Nanjing University Law Department in 1984-1985, and will always fondly remember the visit my eight-year-old son and I made to Xiamen at Dean Chen's kind invitation in the spring of 1985. I greatly enjoyed giving some visiting lectures, meeting a number of An Chen's talented students (some of whom subsequently were my students and obtained their J.D. degrees from our law school at Lewis and Clark), and experiencing the kindness and hospitality of An Chen and his family and law department colleagues. It is wonderful that he was able to return the visit and spend time with us at Lewis and Clark in 1991.

An Chen is a lao pengyou (old friend) of mine, and one of the important people who worked throughout his career for constructive and friendly Sino-American relations. I congratulate him on the publication of this fine volume and commend it to readers' attention.

十七、評陳安教授英文專著《中國的吶喊》：聚焦 ISDS 和二〇一五中美 BIT 談判

〔加拿大〕格斯・范・哈滕*

陳安教授是中國國際經濟法學領域資歷最深的學者之一，他撰寫的英文專著《中國的吶喊》一書，針對中國與國際經濟法學之間的互動關係，提出了議題廣泛、學識精深的一系列看法。本書匯輯了陳安教授自二十世紀八〇年代初期以來撰寫的二十四篇專題論文，闡述了中國對有關問題的見解和看法，視角獨到、引人入勝，涉及眾多議題，既包括中國對國際經濟法的總體看法和價值理念、概述中國遭受外國列強多次入侵和占領的慘痛歷史，也包括對各種具體問題的探討，諸如「安全閥」在投資條約中的作用問題、中國涉外商事合同爭端解決問題、中國經濟特區的法律法規問題、美國單邊主義與WTO多邊主義之間的緊張關係和矛盾衝突問題，等等。整體看來，陳教授的這些論文猶如一幅絢麗多彩的織錦掛毯，向我們展示了中國「重新崛起」（re-emergence）的總體理念和具體決策，以及中國與國際經濟法律架構之間的互

動關係。

全書的一個新穎獨到之處在於：針對占據國際投資法論壇主導地位的有害觀點，本書是一劑解毒良藥，反對嚴重偏袒西方資本輸出國的主導看法。這些主導觀點竭力鼓吹：應當優先考慮跨國公司的利益；投資者與東道國爭端仲裁中的律師們和仲裁員們所扮演的角色，應當是這些跨國公司利益的支持者；保護外國投資者享有的特權應當被視為一項全球化的指導性規範。與此同時，民主、民族自決和國家主權的價值觀，卻被輕描淡寫，不受重視；或被橫加誹謗詆毀，有時候甚至到了這種程度，即胡說什麼民主、民族自決和國家主權的價值觀會對人類福祉構成威脅，其負面作用甚至超過了跨國公司濫用權力、寡頭政體、殖民主義。至少從這些主導看法中，人們幾乎聽不到批判殖民主義歷史流毒的聲音，也幾乎聽不到評論、剖析殖民主義歷史流毒與當今「投資者東道國爭端解決機制」（Investor-State Dispute Settlement，以下簡稱「ISDS」）之間因果關聯的聲音。這種機制，歸根到底就是由ISDS這一法律行業的從業者們以及北美和西歐各強國政府所積極推動的。

在此種占主導地位的大量國際法文獻背景下，認真思考、鑒別來自飽受歷代形形色色殖民主義禍害國家的考察家們的看法，顯得尤為重要。陳教授的專著之所以被稱作是「一劑解毒良藥」，是因為他不僅深入洞察並強烈譴責肆虐於中國和其他國家的殖民主義，同時還頌揚中國人民在反對帝國主義和法西斯占領的鬥爭中取得的成就。基於此，他致力於將這一源於中國歷史的價值理念引入國際經濟法。例如，對中國飽受殖民主義荼毒的歷史，陳教授不但沒有諱言回避，反而大聲疾呼：「自臭名昭著的1840年鴉片戰爭以後，中國飽受西方列強欺凌和殘暴日寇入侵，喪權辱國。」正是這種歷史使命感激勵他具有「強烈的民族自豪感和愛國主義情懷」，並「立志為本國和廣大發展中國家弱勢群體的正義要求，吶喊和鼓呼」。銘記殖民主義歷史並致力於國際主義事業，尤其是為廣大弱勢群體大聲疾呼，這種理念，迥異於那些專為豪富強勢精英們的利益而粉飾殖民主義的大量學術文獻。

同時觸動我的是，陳教授這本專著也給中國學者們帶來了挑戰。我不想對另一個擁有獨特歷史和文化的國度作過多評論，但我想說的是，我看到了在中華民族自豪感和明顯由西方規則主導的遊戲戰略之間存在的衝突，即希望西方強國被擊敗在他們自己設計的遊戲裡。陳教授強調「我們不能盲目地附和遵從西方學者的觀點」，「應該以求真務實的態度，獨立思考，明辨是非」，對此我十分贊同。但是，我認為中國目前面臨的直接挑戰是：必須機智地決定接受什麼和拒絕什麼，尤其是在西方強國的壓力之下，該何去何從。

遺憾的是，我的母國——加拿大，當今的聯邦政府是一個極度「右翼」且非常「不理智」的政府。正因為此，面對中國遭受的來自西方軍國主義的誹謗詆毀，加拿大當局一直表現得更像是一個煽動者而非公正調停人。陳教授將西方軍國主義對中國的中傷稱為「中國威脅」讕言。晚近，這一讕言在北美被頻頻援引，目的是推動由美國主導的跨太平洋夥伴關係談判（Trans-Pacific Partnership，以下簡稱「TPP」）項下處於保密狀態的ISDS條款的達成，然而，美國國會和美國人民對該談判卻持懷疑態度。TPP的支持者們並沒有解釋其中的ISDS機制是如何運行的，外國投資者享有的特權包含哪些內容，怎樣做到在ISDS機制下優先保障公眾利益而避免仲裁缺乏獨立性、公正性、平衡性等問題；也沒有對該機制所耗費的總成本以及給公眾帶來的風險作出說明。他們一心一意專注於將TPP塑造成「反華」的工具，以此滿足自身的需要。

面對TPP項下以美國範本為藍本的ISDS條款的擴張和其聚焦「反華」的宣傳，特別是考慮到中國自己在過去十五年時間裡已經採納的強有力ISDS機制基本上是參照美國範本建立的，此時，我們該如何應對？此外，中國賦予外國投資者的寬泛特權也有進一步擴張，諸如在「公平公正待遇」之類的靈活性術語的設置上，只給外國投資者設定有限的例外，便將本國的國家主權讓渡給ISDS機制下那些往往依附成性、並非真正獨立的仲裁員，這些仲裁員往往以國際法院的法官們顯然不會採取的某種方式，依附於跨國公司和行政官員；相比其他國家的政府，跨國公司和行政官員與美國政府當局之間的聯繫要更為密切。這樣看來，中國和美國開始同步並行，對權力讓渡加以認可，使得權力從國家機構（包括立法、行政、司法機構）手中，轉移至外國投資者以及那些以仲裁員身份坐堂審案的私家律師手中。儘管中美之間還存在差異，但在ISDS機制問題上中國卻趨向於仿效美國的做法。然而，ISDS依舊被當作西方強國的工具，用以對抗那些不滿ISDS給本國民主和主權構成威脅的弱小國家，也用以「反華」以滿足自身的需要。就這一矛盾悖論（paradox）問題我還不能作出明確的闡釋，但我相信它是一個值得關注的問題，不論對中國學者還是西方學者，都是如此。

我一向批判ISDS機制反對民主，在制度設計上存有偏袒，偏向於支持大型的公司和豪富的個體。接下來我想以學者的身份進行評論。從陳教授關於ISDS的論證中引發的一個最為迫切的問題是：中國在同美國談判締結雙邊投資條約（Bilateral Investment Treaty，以下簡稱「BIT」）時該作何選擇？中美BIT談判將是繼歐盟和美國「跨大西洋貿易與投資夥伴協議」（Transatlantic Trade and Investment Partnership，以下簡稱「TTIP」）談判以及上述TPP談判之後最為緊要的談判。正是因為ISDS的不斷擴張，已經使其從之前一個微不足道的角色發展到如今在全球治理中占據絕對的優勢地位。換言之，中美BIT與TTIP、TPP三者是相輔相成的，特別是TPP，不只是「反華」，更主要是對國家主權的全盤否定。

中國在中美BIT談判中面臨的主要挑戰是什麼？中國會因為ISDS存在缺陷，而基於我前述的任何一項理由拒絕接受嗎？我認為答案很可能是否定的。以中加投資條約為例，在我看來，加拿大在某種程度上扮演著犧牲品的角色，就像是「一隻被獻祭給華盛頓的羔羊」。中加投資條約中涉及的一些主要問題同樣也是中美BIT談判所面臨的挑戰。其中最為關鍵的就是市場準入問題。中國迄今既有的投資條約從未給予外國投資者以準入前的國民待遇（pre-establishment national treatment），中加投資條約也不例外。值得注意的是，中國卻向美國表達了同意以準入前國民待遇為基礎進行談判的意願。就美國而言，根據其所締結的BIT來推測，它希望為本國投資者在中國爭取到一個擴大版的市場準入權，但對中國投資者在美國享有的市場準入卻施加諸多限制條件。一個最好的例證，就是美國和厄瓜多爾簽訂的BIT中就市場準入作出的例外規定，美國將涉及本國經濟運行的主要行業部門均排除在準入前國民待遇的清單之列；相比之下，厄瓜多爾對準入前國民待遇所作的保留幾乎等於零。[328]從某種意義上講，市場準入問題應被視為中美BIT談判真正開始之前的首要問題，其中的關鍵在於中國願意在市場準入方面對美國作出多大讓步？而作為回報，中國願意在市場準入方面接受美國作出的讓步又是多麼微乎其微？

陳教授在其專著中評論了十九世紀美國和其他西方強權國家把不平等條約強加於中國的歷史目的。他寫道：「根據不平等條約，列強以苛刻的條件貸款給中國政府，並在中國開設銀行，從而壟斷了中國的金融和財政。」如今，美國這一目標改變了嗎？儘管BITs和不平等條約在很多方面不能等同，但其基本主旨目標是永恆不變的，即通過層層加碼的方式訂立各種條款，使美國企業享有各種優惠，藉以促進它們對中國經濟的滲透。然而，這些優惠條件是怎樣層層加碼設置起來的呢？最為重要的一點是，雙方同意將涉及條款的各種爭端都提交ISDS機制去仲裁解決，但其中仲裁員的選擇卻最終是由世界銀行（World Bank）的行政官員們決定的。試想想，如果仲裁員不是由世界銀行選定，而是由某一家亞洲開發銀行（an Asian Development Bank）來選定，而後者在投票權分配方面又相對有利於中國，那麼，美國會舉手贊成嗎？我估計，美國會覺得這一提議根本不值得考慮。現在，中國願意對美國作出讓步的範圍究竟有多大？可以探討的是，中國在與其他國家（包括加拿大）締結的BITs中，似乎已經朝著這一方向發展，在此類BITs中，中國通常處於資本輸出國的地位。但到目前為止，中國尚未對美國作出重大讓步。

中美BIT談判還面臨哪些其他挑戰呢？因為加拿大當前是保守黨執政，正如陳教授所講的那樣，「加拿大這些年跟美國一直如影隨形，亦步亦趨」，只有當石油行業的要求超過了美國政府優先關注的事項時才是例外。我們可以設想，二〇一二年中加BIT和一般北美範本在ISDS規定上的差別，體現的是中國而非加拿大的偏好。基於這樣的設想，除市場準入議題之外，中國曾經盡其所能地支援國內產業，似乎並不贊同北美範本中相對開放的ISDS訴訟程式，也不允許原住民享有履行要求的例外，並堅持使用比美國範本還要寬泛的「拒絕授益」條款（"denial-of-benefits" clause）〔329〕。

雖然陳教授對二〇一二年中加投資條約的剖析有著深刻的見解，但其中卻沒有論及中加投資條約和美國BIT模式的差異。可以探討的是，陳教授似乎過分強調了中國與北美在路徑上的差別。例如，陳教授認為中方在二〇一二年中加投資條約路徑方面的獨特性時，強調的是徵收「補償」兩種標準之間的差別，即「興旺發達企業的價值」與「公平市場價值」之間的區分。我不想完全否定這種區分方法，但我猜測，很多ISDS的仲裁員在適用這兩種標準時應該會採取在本質上相同的方式。再者，二〇一二年中加投資條約項下的「稅收例外」條款，實際上沿用了自《北美自由貿易協定》（Norh American Free Trade Agreement）以來北美模式中的規定；而「用盡當地救濟」條款規定提出ISDS仲裁請求前的「等待期」，也僅僅是四個月。這個等待期的長度實際上要短於其他採取北美模式的條約。

在最惠國待遇（Most-Favoured-Nation，以下簡稱「MFN」）問題上，陳教授指出中國對該條款採用的是更為縮限的版本，因為二〇一二年中加投資條約規定MFN條款不能適用於爭端解決機制。但是，對MFN條款加以限制早在二十一世紀初期就已存在，之後被廣泛運用於北美範本中。需要說明的是，二〇一二年中加投資條約允許MFN條款適用於一九九四年以來中加兩國所簽訂的許多其他投資條約，這不免是對該條款的一種擴大適用，這就意味著投資者可以選擇適用自一九九四年以來中加兩國所簽訂的許多其他投資條約中更為優惠的規定。然而，不論是中國還是加拿大，一九九四年之後締結的BITs並未包含在中加投資條約中出現的各種例外和保留規定，直到發現MFN條款存在漏洞，才開始對其範圍進行縮減，從而達到限制外國投資者權利的目的。就其本身而言，二〇一二年中加投資條約對MFN條款所作的規定，看來實際上是降低和削減了針對平衡外國投資者權利和東道國主權利益問題所作出的適度改進。

陳教授強調中加投資條約是雙方「利益互相妥協」的典例，這一點我非常贊同。不過，就ISDS條款的設置而言，中國似乎已經朝著ISDS西方範本的方向走得很遠。基於這一立場，現在中國直接和美國進行BIT談判時將會面臨更大的挑戰。尤其是在諸如市場準入、維護自己的國民經濟戰略規劃、抵制同美國企業有緊密關係的世界銀行對ISDS的管轄等問題上，中國都將被迫對美國作出各種讓步。

我本著欽佩和尊敬的精神寫了這篇書評。全球化給我們帶來了許多積極正面的事物，其中之一就是讓我這樣一個居住在安大略湖畔靜謐郊區的加拿大人，能夠享有「特權」閱讀一位來自被群山環繞的福建省的中國傑出學者所寫的專著。為此，我心懷感激。我衷心地希望，陳安教授對國際經濟法領域所做的貢獻和他本人對人文價值所做的努力，能夠有助於牽制中國輕率地走向西方強國設定的關於ISDS和給予外國投資者特權的遊戲規則。

（翻譯：谷婀娜）

Review on Prof. Chen's English Monograph

—Focusing on the ISDS & 2015 China-U. S. BIT Negotiation

Gus Van Harten*

The Voice from China, by An Chen, offers a wide-ranging record of intensive scholarship on China's relationship to international economic law. It provides access to a rare and intriguing perspective from China by one of the country's most senior academics in the field. The book collects 24 articles written by Professor Chen since the early 1980s. The articles cover broad topics such as Chen's proposed values to inform international economic law and an outline of China's bitter history in relation to foreign powers- invasions and occupations. The articles also examine specifics including the role of safeguards in investment treaties, dispute resolution in Chinese commercial contracts, legal aspects of special economic zones, and the tension between U.S. unilateralism and WTO multilateralism. As a whole, Chen's writings offer a rich tapestry of generalist ideals and specific decisions to represent China's re-emergence and interaction with the legal architecture of the international economy.

A refreshing feature of the book is its antidote to dominant themes of international investment law scholarship, which has a heavy bias toward a Western capital-exporting point of view. That dominant theme prioritizes interests of multinational companies—and the role of investor-state lawyers and arbitrators as supporters of those interests—by defending the privileging of foreign investors as a guiding norm of globalization. Meanwhile, values of democracy, self-determination, and sovereignty are downplayed or denigrated, sometimes to such an extent as to suggest these values are a greater threat to human welfare than corporate abuse of power, oligarchy, or colonialism. At least, one hears little about the legacy of colonialism, on the one hand, and on the other hand the links between that legacy and investor-state dispute settlement (ISDS) as promoted primarily by the ISDS legal industry and North American and Western European powerful governments.

In this context of such innumerable literature on international law, it is important to identify perspectives from observers in countries victimized by colonialism in its various iterations. Professor Chen's book offers a refreshing antidote because he acknowledges and condemns strongly colonialism in China and elsewhere and because he celebrates the achievements of the Chinese people in resisting imperialism and fascist occupation. In turn, he strives to introduce values emerging from China's history into international economic law. For example, he does not shy away from but rather calls out the "aggression and suppression by the Western powers and Japan for more than a century" as "a humiliation to all Chinese people". His historical awareness motivated him to have a "strong sense of national pride and patriotism" and a "determination... to strive for social justice" and "to contribute to [his] own country and to support all other weak countries". The connection between remembering colonialism and committing to internationalism, especially on behalf of the weak, is the flipside of air-brushing colonialism from academic literature in the interests of wealthy and powerful elites.

Yet it struck me that Professor Chen's approach also presents a challenge for scholars in China. I do not want to go far in commenting on another country with its own extraordinary history and culture but will say that I see a tension between Chinese national pride and the apparent strategy of playing by Western rules in the hope of beating the West at its own game. Chen stresses "we should not blindly follow and completely accept... Western opinions" but rather "contemplate independently and critically in order... to distinguish right from wrong". I could not agree more. However, I expect the immediate challenge in China is to decide what to accept knowingly and what to reject, especially under pressure from the West.

Regrettably, my own country of Canada—under an exceptionally right-wing and often tactless federal government—has been more an agitator than a moderator of Western militarism based in part on the vilification of China. Chen calls the latter the "China Threat Doctrine". This doctrine was often invoked most recently in North America to promote the secretive ISDS provisions in the U.S.-led Trans-Pacific Partnership (TPP) to a sceptical U.S. Congress and American people. Instead of explaining how ISDS—and the privileging of foreign investors it entails—offers a public benefit to outweigh the lack of independence, fairness, and balance in ISDS and its gross costs and risks for the public, the TPP's promoters instead focused on portraying the TPP as "anti-China" and desirable on that basis.

What are we to make of the expansion of a U.S. model of ISDS in the TPP and its advertisement as "anti-China", especially if viewed alongside China's own embrace over the last 15 years of a muscular version of ISDS based largely on the U.S. model? China has also extended extraordinary rights to foreign investors, has settled for limited exceptions to flexible concepts like "fair and equitable treatment" for foreign investors, and has conceded its national sovereignty to ISDS arbitrators who are dependent—in a manner that international judges clearly would not be—on multinational corporations and executive officials who are more closely connected to the U.S. Administration than any other country's government. It seems the joint approach of China and the U.S. is to endorse the transfer of power from national institutions—legislative, governmental, or judicial—to foreign investors and private lawyers sitting as arbitrators. There are differences in their approaches, but the Chinese way in ISDS tends to have followed the U.S. path. Even then, ISDS is still presented in the West—to counter those weaks upset by its threat to democracy and sovereignty—as anti-China and therefore desirable. I do not have a clear explanation for this paradox but I think it warrants attention from Chinese and Westerners alike.

I offer the next comment as an academic who has criticized ISDS as anti-democratic, institutionally biased, and lopsided in favour of large companies and wealthy individuals. I think the most pressing question to emerge from Chen's scholarship on ISDS involves China's choices in the proposed China-U.S. bilateral investment treaty (BIT). A China-U.S. BIT would be the most significant step, after the proposed Europe-U.S. Transatlantic Trade and Investment Partnership (TTIP) and TPP, in the expansion of ISDS from its minority role to a dominant position in global governance. In other words, a China-U.S. BIT complements the TTIP and TPP; inter alia, the TTP is not merely anti-China but rather anti-sovereignty altogether.

What are the key challenges for China in such a BIT and will China reject ISDS on any of the grounds I have identified? I think the answer is likely not. Drawing from the example of the 2012 Canada-China investment treaty—where I see Canada partly as having played the role of a sacrificial lamb for Washington—there are a few major issues on which China and the U.S. will face challenges in negotiating a BIT. The most prominent is market access. China has not given market access on the basis of pre-establishment national treatment to foreign investors in its investment treaties, including the 2012 Canada-China treaty, but has signalled a willingness to do so with the U.S. For its part, the U.S., judging from its BIT record, will want an expansive version of market access for U.S. investors in China combined with more limited market access by Chinese investors to the U.S. economy. As an illustration, one can review the market access exceptions in the Ecuador-U.S. BIT where the U.S. exempted practically all of the major sectors of its economy from pre-establishment national treatment and Ecuador exempted virtually none in its own economy. [330] Having gone some way to allowing market access before the BIT negotiations really began, a key question is how much market access China will be willing to give up and how little China will be willing to accept in return.

Chen comments on the historical aim of the U.S. and other Western powers as reflected by the unequal treaties imposed on China in the nineteenth century. Chen says: "By establishing banks in China [they] monopolized the banking and finance of China". Has the aim changed? BITs differ from unequal treaties in many ways but a basic goal is constant: to facilitate the penetration of China's economy by U.S. companies on terms that are stacked in favour of the latter. How are the terms stacked? Most importantly, they refer disputes about the terms to ISDS where the choice of whom serves as an arbitrator is made ultimately by World Bank officials. Imagine if the arbitrators were chosen instead by officials at an Asian Development Bank based on an allocation of voting power relatively favourable to China, would the U.S agree with that? It would be a non-starter in the U.S., I expect. Will China accept a comparable concession to the U.S.? Arguably, China has moved in this direction in other BITs, usually while occupying a capital-exporting position, with other countries including Canada. But the big concession to the U.S. is yet to come.

What about other challenges in a BIT with the U.S.? Because Canada, as Chen puts it, tends to follow the U.S. path "like a shadow to a person"—certainly under the present Conservative government, except when U.S. government priorities are trumped by those of the oil industry—we can assume that the differences between the 2012 Canada-China BIT and the usual North American model of ISDS reflect Chinese, not Canadian, preferences. On this assumption, besides the issue of market access, it appears that China held onto its existing ability to favour domestic companies, did not agree to the North American model of relatively open ISDS proceedings, did not accept exceptions allowing for performance requirements that would support aboriginal peoples, and appears to have insisted on a broader version of the "denial-of-benefits" clause [331] than in the U.S. model.

While Chen's analysis of the 2012 Canada-China treaty is insightful, it does not address these divergences from the U.S. model. Instead, Chen arguably over-states the degree to which China varied from the

North American approach. For example, in stressing the uniqueness of China's approach based on the 2012 Canada-China treaty, Chen emphasizes the distinction between standards of "going concern value" and "fair market value" in compensating for expropriation. I do not wish to dismiss the distinction outright, but I suspect many ISDS arbitrators will apply these standards in essentially the same way. Further, the taxation carve-out in the 2012 Canada-China treaty actually tracks the North American model since NAFTA, and the 2012 Canada-China treaty's provision for exhaustion of local remedies is little more than a four-month waiting period for ISDS claims. That length of waiting period is actually shorter than other treaties on the North American model.

On the topic of most-favoured-nation (MFN) treatment, Chen comments that China achieved a more limited version of this concept because MFN was not extended in the 2012 Canada-China treaty to dispute resolution procedures. But that limitation on MFN has been present in the North American model since the early 2000s. More telling is the 2012 Canada-China treaty's extension of MFN to past BITs since 1994. For Canada and China, there are post-1994 BITs that do not include various exceptions and reservations in the 2012 Canada-China treaty that appear—until one considers the MFN loophole—to limit the scope of foreign investor rights. As such, the approach to MFN in the 2012 Canada-China treaty appears actually to roll back the modest improvements in balancing foreign investor rights with sovereign interests.

I sympathize with Chen's emphasize on 2012 Canada-China treaty as an example of "mutual compromise". Yet it seems that China has moved far already in the direction of the Western model of ISDS and will now face a greater challenge to its position in direct negotiations with the U.S. In particular, China will be pressured to make concessions to the U.S. on market access, its preserve a national economic strategy, and its past resistance to ISDS—under the authority of the World Bank—in its close relationship with U.S. corporations.

I offer this assessment in a spirit of admiration and respectful criticism. One of the positive things about globalization is that a Canadian from a quiet suburb beside Lake Ontario can have the privilege to review the writings of an eminent Chinese scholar from the mountains of Fujian Province. For that, I am grateful. I do hope the strength of Professor Chen's contribution to the field and his commitment to humanistic values may help to check China's imprudent move toward Western rules on ISDS and the privileging of foreign investors.

十八、矢志不渝倡導南南聯合自強與國際經濟新秩序

——評陳安教授專著《中國的吶喊：陳安論國際經濟法》

陳輝萍*

《中國的吶喊：陳安論國際經濟法》是陳安教授的新作，二〇一三年由Springer出版社出版。陳安教授是廈門大學法學院資

深教授。三十多年來，陳安教授在國際知名期刊上發表了眾多中文和英文論文，從其中精選出二十四篇進行翻譯和改寫，彙聚成這部八五二頁的巨著。

二〇〇八年由復旦大學出版社出版的專著《陳安論國際經濟法》（以下簡稱「2008年專著」）含五卷，七十八篇論文，多數是用中文寫成，也有少部分是英文論文。二〇一三年新專著精選了二十四篇論文，其中五篇是在二〇〇八年至二〇一三年期間完成的。

這兩大專著可視為姊妹卷。新專著承繼了陳教授的一貫學術追求和理念，但又顯示出歲月沉澱下來的更為成熟和老練的立場和觀點。作為陳教授曾經指導過的博士生，以及二十來年的同事，我拜讀了他幾乎所有的論文和專著，對其學術水準和學術理念熟稔於心。二〇一一年，我曾為他二〇〇八年的專著寫過書評，[332]評論了陳教授的人品、獨特的研究視角和寫作風格以及他對國際經濟法的重大貢獻。二〇一三年Springer推出的這部英文版新作，體現了中華法學學術代表作「走出國門」、進一步弘揚中華文明的努力追求，因此，我很樂意為它再寫一篇書評。

新作全書分為六個部分，分別探討和論證若干學術前沿重大問題：（一）當代國際經濟法的基本理論；（二）當代國家經濟主權的「攻防戰」；（三）中國在構建當代國際經濟新秩序中的戰略定位；（四）當代國際投資法的論爭；（五）當代中國涉外經濟立法的爭議；（六）若干涉華、涉外經貿爭端典型案例剖析。

該新作有兩大特點：第一，它涵蓋了國際經濟法的諸多廣泛議題；第二，在探討這些議題時，作者是站在中國的立場，因而將中國的觀點推介給了世界。故此，該書命名為《中國的吶喊》。本篇書評主要評論第二個特點。

陳安教授是中國第一個旗幟鮮明地提出「南南聯合自強」理論的學者。陳教授看到中國和廣大發展中國家在歷史上遭遇的各種磨難，以及它們當前在世界上所處的不利處境和弱小的政治經濟地位，就積極宣導南方國家在建立國際經濟新秩序中要聯合起來，依靠整體的力量，共同奮鬥。「南南聯合自強」理論最早由陳教授在《南南聯合自強五十年的國際經濟立法反思：從萬隆、多哈、坎昆到香港》一文中率先提出並積極宣導。他認為，通過南南聯合自強，各國通力合作，促進法律改革，不僅會使這些弱小國家群體改善處境，獲得平權，也會促使當前的國際經濟法律制度朝著有利於全世界的方向發展。金磚五國（BRICS，是巴西、俄羅斯、印度、中國和南非五個國家英文名稱第一個字母的組合縮寫）這個聯合體的建立和承擔的使命，以及新近成立的金磚國家開發銀行和已經簽署成立協定的亞洲基礎設施投資銀行，正是南南聯合自強的典範。

對於中國在南南聯合自強中的作用，陳教授認為，中國作為主要的發展中大國之一，應該成為南南聯合自強的強有力支持者，以及今後建立國際經濟新秩序的積極推手和中流砥柱。這應該成為中國在當代國際經濟法律議題上的戰略定位。這一觀點主要體現在他的《論中國在建立國際經濟新秩序中的戰略定位——兼評「新自由主義經濟秩序」論、「WTO憲政秩序」論、「經濟民族主義擾亂全球化秩序」論》一文中。

本著「中華民族的愛國主義」和國際主義的有機結合，陳教授宣稱中國應該堅定地與廣大發展中國家站在一起。陳教授提出這一定位的原因是，二〇〇九至二〇一〇年，一些外國學者和盲目附和的中國學者認為，根據「新自由主義經濟秩序」論、「WTO憲政秩序」論、「經濟民族主義擾亂全球化秩序」論等新理論，中國應該採取經濟上更加「自由主義」的立場，俯首貼耳地完全接受西方「華盛頓共識」和全盤遵守WTO的各項規則。對這些「時髦」理論，陳教授並不苟同。相反，他認為，這些理論會誤導中國在建立國際經濟新秩序中的方向。本書的目的就是批判性地分析和抵制這些理論，從而澄清是非，保護中國的國家利益和國際聲譽，並保障眾多發展中國家的平等權利。

陳教授認為，中國在國際經濟新秩序中的定位，也同樣適用於WTO體制這一具體問題。他認為，中國與廣大發展中國家對現有的WTO法制，不能僅限於「遵守」和「適應」，而應當通過南南聯合，凝聚力量，尋求對其中某些不公平不公正的「遊戲規則」加以改變、改革和補救。陳教授認為，WTO爭端解決機構充滿了缺陷和不平衡。他認為，某些WTO體制本身在立法之初就存在不公平不合理，可概稱為「先天不足」，有一些是武斷制定的，口惠而實不至，專門欺負弱小國家。他指出，WTO的某些專家組在執法實踐中顯示出「不公平和無能」，採取「政治上很圓滑但法律上破綻百出」的方法，可概稱為「後天失調」。他認為，中國應與這類不公平和不利於發展中國家的WTO規則做鬥爭，發展中國家應該聯合起來，自助自立自強。這與他一貫倡導的南南聯合自強理論是一脈相承的。陳教授提出的這一戰略定位，獨樹一派，與西方學者和某些追隨西方「時髦」理論的中國學者涇渭分明，大相徑庭。

該書讓人印象深刻的一點，是作者有力地反駁了西方對中國和平崛起和支持南南聯合集體行動的偏見和攻擊，其典例之一就是一些美國政客、軍隊和學界頭面人物提出的「中國威脅」論。這一誤導大眾的說辭被許多發達國家甚至某些不明真相的發展中國家所接受，嚴重損害中國的國際聲譽，甚至影響中國今後的政治經濟發展。陳教授溯本追源，通過比較源遠流長的中國對外關係的真實歷史、十九世紀歐洲和亞洲的歷史以及當前美國的具體情況，他得出結論：當代「中國威脅」論是十九世紀曾經甚囂塵上的「黃禍」論的變種，「黃禍」論是俄國沙皇和德國皇帝威廉二世最先提出來的。陳教授指出，「中國威脅」論和「黃禍」論擁有相同的DNA，其目的都是為了曲解歷史，曲解中外交往關係的傳統主流，成為殖民主義和帝國主義的口號。在反擊這類錯誤學說時，陳教授一方面充分運用其豐富的知識，以及對中國和美國、世界歷史的全面而深刻的洞察；另一方面，運用其犀利的語言風格和「妙語連珠」的中國成語來強化自己的立場。這種風格在法律文獻中比較少見，但這就是陳教授的風格。

南南聯合自強學說受廣大發展中國家歡迎。發展中國家在瞬息萬變的國際政治和經濟環境中，在傳統上南方國家存在的正當性備受質疑的情況下，面臨諸多共同的挑戰，南方思想家提出針對「全球南方國家：50年回顧及今後走向」的議題，以國際論壇的方式加以討論。[333]南方委員會認為，努力爭取更加公平的國際體制已經使南方國家更為團結，也強化了它們採取聯合行動的決心。[334]聯合國前秘書長加利親自來信邀請陳教授為該論壇撰文。加利是以聯合國和平大學歐洲和平發展中心名譽委員會主席、全球法語區秘書長和南方中心委員會前主席的名義發出邀請的。陳教授欣然授受邀請，寫了一篇題為《南南聯合自強：年屆「知命」，路在何方？——國際經濟秩序破舊立新的中國之聲》的論文。[335]

陳教授的理論研究高屋建瓴，入木三分。他的著作新穎尖銳，雄辯滔滔，具有中國風範和中國氣派，闡釋了不同於西方發達國家學者關於經濟主權和國際經濟新秩序的創新學術理念和學術追求，為國際社會的弱勢群體爭取公平權益鍛造了法學理論武器。正因為如此，該書獲得中國「國家社會科學基金中華學術外譯項目」的資助，他是國際經濟法領域迄今唯一獲此殊榮的學者。該項目的順利完成，說明陳教授的學術水準已獲得國際認同；而薈萃其三十多年來主要學術成果的代表作《中國的吶喊》進入國外主流發行傳播管道，勢必大大促進各國對當代中國的了解和理解。故此，Springer出版社將該書列人「理解中國」系列叢書。

此書出版時，陳教授已年屆八十五，這正是一般人安逸頤養天年的時候，陳教授卻仍孜孜不倦，筆耕不輟。這對年輕學者們確是一種榜樣和鞭策。

（編輯：楊帆）

A Tireless Advocate for S-S Coalition and NIEO: Comments on Prof. Chen's Monograph

Chen Huiping*

The Voice from China: An CHEN on International Economic Law is a new monograph written by Prof. An Chen, published by Springer in 2013. Prof. An Chen is a senior eminent resident professor at Xiamen University Law School (China). This 852 page book is a collection and compilation of 24 carefully selected articles written by him in English and published in international leading journals over the past 30-odd years. This English book is partially based on and substantially updated from his previous monograph entitled *An CHEN on International Economic Law* published by Fudan University Press (China) in 2008 (hereafter referred to as "the 2008 monograph"). The 2008 monograph consists of five volumes with 78 articles published until 2008, most of which are in Chinese with some in English. The new monograph consists of 24 English articles, five of which were written and published during 2008 and 2013. These two monographs could be seen as sister books in the sense that this new monograph continues his consistent academic pursuit and ideas, but also goes further to show well-established, more sophisticated ideas and positions gained from his aged experience. As Prof. Chen's previous PhD student and colleague for 20 years, I read almost all his articles and books and thus quite familiar with his scholarship and academic pursuits. I wrote a book review for the 2008 monograph in 2011 [336] covering broad comments including his personality, his unique research and writing approaches as well as his important contribution to international economic law. The new English monograph published by Springer in 2013 shows Prof. Chen's further efforts to promote the international exchange of Chinese legal scholarship and the dissemination of Chinese civilization. Therefore, I am glad to write a sister review for this new book.

The 24 articles in this new monograph are organized under six subheadings: (1) Jurisprudence of Contemporary International Economic Law; (2) Great Debates on Contemporary Economic Sovereignty; (3) China's Strategic Position on Contemporary International Economic Order Issues; (4) Divergences on Contemporary Bilateral Investment Treaty; (5) Contemporary China's Legislation on Sino-foreign Economic Issues; (6) Contemporary Chinese Practices on International Economic Disputes (Cases Analysis).

This monograph has two features: first, the book covers a broad range of international economic law issues; second, the author is standing in the shoes of China when taking positions in these issues, and thus brings China's views to the world. Hence, this book is entitled *The Voice from China*. This book review focuses on the second feature.

Prof. An Chen is the first Chinese scholar who takes a clear-cut stand proposing the "South-South coalition doctrine". Realizing the historical suffers by China and the developing countries (the "South countries") and their current disadvantageous and weak political and economic positions in the world, Prof. Chen strongly advocates that the South countries should unite and rely on themselves as a whole in the establishment of a new international economic order (NIEO).This doctrine is first formulated and elaborated by him in his article "A Reflection on the South-South Coalition in the Last Half Century from the Perspective of International Economic Law-making: From Bandung, Doha and Cancún to Hong Kong". He suggests that through collaboration of individual power found in South-South coalition, and through the united promotion of legal reform, these disadvantaged groups will not only become stronger, but also impel the advancement of the current international economic legal system for the benefit of the whole world. The establishment and the mandate of the BRICS association (BRICS is the acronym for an association of five major emerging national economies: Brazil, Russia, India, China, and South Africa) and the newly founded Development Bank of BRICS and the Asian Infrastructure Investment Bank are examples of South-South coalition.

As to China's role in the South-South coalition, Prof. Chen suggests that China, as one of the major developing countries, should be a strong supporter of South-South coalition and a driving force for the establishment of NIEO currently and in the future. This should be China's strategic position on contemporary international economic legal issues. This suggestion is mainly embodied in his article "What Should Be China's Strategic Position in the Establishment of New International Economic Order? With Comments on Neoliberalistic Economic Order,

Constitutional Order of the WTO, and Economic Nationalism's Disturbance of Globalization".

Based on the organic combination of "patriotism of Chinese People" and internationalism, he argues that China should stand firmly together with the developing countries. The reason for Prof. Chen to raise this position is that, during 2009-2010, some foreign scholars and their Chinese followers suggested that China ought to adopt a more economically liberal position, fully accept "Washington Consensus" and comply fully with WTO rules based on doctrines such as the Neoliberal Economic Order, Constitutional Order of the WTO, and Economic Nationalism's Disturbance of Globalization. Prof. Chen does not agree with these "pop" doctrines, and instead believes that these doctrines would mislead China in the NIEO. The purpose of this book is to critically analyze and resist the application of these doctrines to China, so as to protect China's national interest and international reputation, as well as the equal rights of vast developing countries.

According to Prof. Chen, this position towards NIEO also applies in the specific context of the WTO regime. He argues that China and the international developing countries shall not be limited only to "abide by" and "adapt to" current WTO laws, but should also consolidate with each other under the "South-South Coalition" to strengthen the ability to seek changes, reforms and redress from some unfair and disadvantageous "rules of the game" among WTO laws. In his opinion, the WTO/DSB (dispute settlement body) is the embodiment of deficiency and imbalance. He claims that some of the WTO laws are deficient since they are unfair and unreasonable at the very beginning of their enactment, some of which are arbitrarily made, nominal promises and an accessory in bullying the weak. He also argues that these principles are imbalances since some specific DSB panels show "injustice and incapability", and take "politically astute but legally flawed" approaches in law-enforcement practices. He advocates that China should combat these unfair and disadvantageous WTO rules. He suggests, in this regard, that developing states unite and work together for collective self-help and self-reliance as a whole. This echoes his persistent ideas of the South-South Coalition doctrine. By keeping and suggesting the strategic position, he creates a separate school which is quite different from and probably unacceptable by some foreign scholars and their Chinese followers.

I am impressed with the book's strong and vigorous refutation and rebuttal to some biases and attacks on China's peaceful rise and support of collective action from the South. The current "China Threat" doctrine proposed by some American politicians, military leaders and academics is one example. This misleading idea is accepted by developed countries and even some developing countries which are ignorant of the facts. This misguided understanding will seriously damage China's international reputation and potentially further block its economic and political development. After tracing the history of China's foreign relations, the history of nineteenth century in Europe and Asia, and after conducting careful analysis of the current US situation, Prof. Chen determines that the current China Threat Doctrine is a variant of the once prevalent, yet problematic, "Yellow Peril" doctrine fabricated and advocated for by the Russian Tsar and German Emperor. Prof. Chen holds that these two doctrines share the same DNA in their goal to distort the historical understanding of Sino-foreign relations, and have been used as slogans of colonialism and imperialism. In the fight against these misguided doctrines, Prof. Chen employs his abundant knowledge and complex understanding of Chinese and world history including US history; on the other hand, he takes advantage of his excellent command and unique style of language, i.e., his sharp and incisive language, and series of Chinese idioms and allusions used to emphasize his position. This literature language style is quite rare in legal analysis articles. But this is his style.

This South-South coalition doctrine is inspiring and accepted especially among developing countries. A forum on the topic of "Global South: At 50 and Beyond?" is proposed to look at instances where "developing countries face many common challenges in a changed and rapidly evolving global political and economic environment, and when the traditional rationale of the South is being questioned and even doubted by some". [337] The South Commission concludes that "The struggle for a fairer international system has consolidated their cohesion and strengthened their resolve to pursue united action". [338] Prof. Chen was invited to contribute to the forum by H.E. Boutros Boutros-Ghali, in his capacity as the Chairman of the Honorary Council of the European

Centre for Peace and Development (ECPD) of the UN University for Peace, and as the former UN Secretary-General, Secretary General of the Francophonie, and Chairman of the South Centre Board. Prof. Chen happily accepted this invitation and wrote the article "Global South: At 50 and Beyond?—The Voice from China for Establishing NIEO". [339]

Prof. Chen has conducted research from a strategically advantageous and high position and expressed fully his penetrating opinion. His book contains creative viewpoints, critical analysis and an eloquent plea, with a unique Chinese character, splendor and style. This book illustrates and elaborates his original and novel academic research, ideas which are substantially different from those of western academia. He had endeavored to fight for the rights and interests of the weak by providing theoretical weapons. These features illustrate the necessity and value of expanding upon and spreading the book across the world. For this reason the book was financially supported by the Chinese Academic Foreign Translation Project (CAFTP) sponsored by the Chinese Fund for the Humanities and Social Sciences. He is the only person so far who won this sponsorship among those in the international economic law circle. Through the CAFTP his scholarship and this book which is a collection of the essence of his scholarship with the 30 plus years have gained international recognition and have entered the primary channels of academic dissemination. The aim of this project is to promote Sino-foreign academic exchange, and to facilitate the global dissemination of high-level research for scholars in the field of philosophy and social science, hence this book is included in the series books of "Understanding China" by Springer. This series commonly aims to spread the works regarding Chinese culture and civilization, so as to promote foreigner knowledge and understanding of modern China.

At the age of 85 when most people at the same age retire from work, Prof. Chen continues to work hard in research and teaching. This is a great encouragement to and acts as a driving force for young scholars.

（翻譯：陳輝萍）

十九、中國呼聲　理應傾聽

——評陳安教授專著《中國的吶喊》

〔美〕洛林・威森費爾德*

兩年前出版的一部鴻篇力作——《中國的吶喊》，時至今日，我才有機會拜讀。該書的作者陳安教授曾經多年擔任中國最好的學府之一——廈門大學的法學院院長，又是中國國際經濟法學會的創始人之一，並長期擔任該學會的會長。陳教授是中國國際經濟法學領域最負盛名、最為傑出的學者之一，也是碩果纍纍、最為多產的學者之一。《中國的吶喊》這部內容深邃的專著，彙集融合了他三十多年撰寫的二十四篇長篇學術專論，聚焦探討國際貿易法與國際投資法領域聚訟紛紜的各種熱點問題。

這部扛鼎之作應該收藏在亞太地區所有學界和政府部門的閱

覽室和圖書館，以供關注當前國際貿易與國際投資法律熱點問題的學者們和政府官員們參考。

陳教授將其最新的著述取名為《中國的吶喊》，用意深遠。在他的學術生涯當中，他一直積極學習研究西方學者們的原著，汲取其中有益的智慧，同時又質疑、批駁西方學界有關貿易與投資的某些主流觀點。陳教授非常謙虛，他稱自己的觀點只不過是「具有中國特色的個人視角」，但應該指出的是，他的建議——特別是那些可能被視為「離經叛道」的異議——是深深植根於中國過去一百五十年的苦難歷史，其中很大一部分是他親身經歷過的切膚之痛。

在閱讀專著中的專論時，西方的讀者將會領略到貫穿其中的廣泛主題。第一，闡述建設性的愛國主義精神，支持和擁護正在「和平崛起」的中國。中華文明可以追溯到五千多年前，有過燦爛輝煌的時期，也有過令人沮喪的衰落式微。一八四〇至一九四九年是這個國家特別不幸的歲月，整個晚清階段，正值西方帝國主義最囂張之際，中國頻頻橫遭屈辱，飽受欺淩，多次被迫投降，國家主權大部分淪喪。在二十世紀初期革命已經成熟，但是又遭野蠻兇殘的日本人入侵占領，二戰之後，國內戰爭又接踵而至。

這些經歷促使中國知識份子在接受西方學者提出的一系列經濟學和法學理論過程中，心存戒懼，這就理所當然，不足為奇了。例如，中國比較遲才加入建立「解決投資爭端國際中心」的《華盛頓公約》，就是其後果之一。基此，陳教授在上述專著中，反覆多次回顧中國遭到發達國家列強不公平待遇的種種事實，以論證他對那些條約措辭或者法律學說提出的質疑和異議，在他看來，這些條約的措辭和學說只會加重「全球經貿大政決策權力在國際分配中的嚴重不公」。

貫穿於陳教授這部專著的另一個主要議題是，探討如何糾正「南北之間」（即發達國家與那些被視為正在發展中的國家）之間的不平衡問題。陳教授所指控的不公平待遇，不僅中國身受其害，所有的發展中國家也都深受其害，它們在二戰結束、殖民時代終結之後，不得不與資本輸出國展開國際談判。陳教授談論「弱小民族」，證論「南南合作」，敦促貧窮國家聯合起來「逐步爭得經濟平權地位」。只有努力糾正「全球經貿大政決策權力在國際分配中的嚴重不公」，發展中國家才能有效抨擊和改變「全球財富分配的不公」。陳教授認為，「權力分配與財富分配之間往往存在著不可分割的因果關係」，因此，「必須改變權力分配的不公，以保證全球財富分配的公平」。

貫穿於陳教授這部專著的第三個主要議題便是探討發展中國家在當前的貿易和投資談判中應當持有的具體立場。概括起來說，《中國的吶喊》一書探討如何在發達國家和發展中國家之間的各個領域實行更公平的經濟權力分配，向發展中國家的學者們和政府官員們提供了各種具體建議。陳教授畢竟是一位博學的法學教授，他旁徵博引，論據充分，資料翔實，論證嚴謹。因此，那些正在參加國際貿易談判和正在就雙邊投資條約最新版本進行磋商的發展中國家的代表們，都可以從陳教授的見解中領悟到很好的忠告和教益。

陳教授認為，當經濟強國和弱勢國家兩方聚集在一起進行貿易和投資條約談判時，前者往往採取「雙重標準」。諸如，發達國家一邊強迫發展中國家取消對非農業產品的關稅，把這些國家進一步融入世界經濟中，另一邊卻反其道而行之，設立種種「環境」壁壘，阻礙來自發展中國家的農產品進口的貿易自由，這是很不公平的。

在投資激勵方面也有類似的問題。西方資本輸出國所推行的雙邊投資條約要求東道國給予海外投資進入東道國關鍵經濟部門的「自由準入」權以及「國民待遇」。然而，恰恰又是這些國家針對來自發展中國家的某些投資設置所謂的「國家安全」壁壘。

晚近的不少實踐中，西方國家屢屢以提高效率為名，主張將發展中國家的國有企業私有化。在很多情況下，這可能是個不錯的建議。但陳教授擔心的是，讓外資進入國民經濟的關鍵部門，會使得東道國容易受到「國際壟斷資本主義的盤剝」。

西方讀者可能只對陳教授的某些主張給予較大同情，對他的其餘主張則未必盡然。在有關徵收後的補償問題的探討中，陳教授主張應採用限制性的標準而不是許多西方國家準備採用的標準。當然，有關賠償的計算方法，發達國家的學者們也見仁見智而尚無定論，但一般情況下，大多數會傾向於在條約中納人「赫爾」原則（the Hull Standard）（「充分」補償）的措辭，而不是僅採用「適當」補償的措辭。

類似的問題也出現在陳教授關於「用盡當地救濟」原則適用於解決投資爭端的討論當中。在一個發展中國家的部分行為涉嫌徵收外資的情形下，數億美元投資可能面臨危險時，幾乎沒有哪個資本輸出國的律師會贊同首先到東道國偏遠的中小省份的法院去尋求當地行政救濟。他們不會認為，他們不願意向一個從未審過徵收案件的鄉下法院尋求救濟，實際上是在「變相地」剝奪東道國的「經濟主權和司法主權」。相反，他們認為，直接訴諸國際仲裁，才能保護自己避免受害於經驗不夠豐富的法官作出「偏袒本地的裁決」。

需要強調的是，陳教授的著述絕非在雞蛋裡挑骨頭，或者惡意攻擊他人觀點，甚至誇誇其談，不切實際。無疑，他看問題有自己的立場。但他的目的只是在引導讀者理解他所看到的國際經濟談判中的不平衡，這種不平衡一直存在於過去兩代人的國際經濟談判之中。他的觀點是樂觀和積極的。正如他援引本國箴言所說，「千萬別把娃娃與洗澡水一起潑掉」。他更願意看到發達國家與發展中國家能夠達成共識。例如，中國與加拿大新近締結的BIT，歷經十八年的漫長磋商才達成共識，便是如此。所有的努力都是值得的。

作為他這一代人中的中國國際經濟法學的頂尖學者之一，陳教授是個相當難得、罕有其匹的人物。他來自福建省農村的一個知識份子家庭，但前半生在中國變亂動盪的時局下飽經滄桑。直到年逾半百，他才得以重返法學領域刻苦鑽研，並開始認真學習英語，獲得一個進入哈佛大學學習、研修的機會。

留美回國後，陳教授很快便成為廈門大學法學院的院長，這是中國國內頂尖的法學院。他作為中國國際經濟法學會的創始人之一，歷任會長多年。陳教授還榮獲政府授予的「全國傑出資深法學家」稱號。這一榮譽代表中國法學界的最高學術水平，自一九四九年以來，全國僅有二十五人獲此殊榮。

在閱讀陳教授的學術專論匯輯時，西方讀者也許不能完全認同他的所有觀點，但他們會從《中國的吶喊》當中認識一位元治學嚴謹、富有思想的學者，其獨樹一幟、不同凡響的吶喊呼聲，源自於他的祖國過去一百五十年來在政治和經濟方面的拼搏奮鬥。對於發展中國家的人們來說，它是指明前路、鼓舞人心的吶喊。對於發達國家人們來說，它是一種要求公平待遇和互相尊重的呼聲。總之，它是人們理應認真傾聽的吶喊呼聲。

（翻譯：李慶靈，校對：陳輝萍）

China's Voice Deserves Hearing

——Comments on Prof. Chen's *The Voice from China*

Lorin S. Weisenfeld*

Although it was published two years ago, I have just had a chance to read Prof. An Chen's weighty volume, *The Voice from China*. Dean for many years of Xiamen University Law School, one of China's best, and a founder and long the head of the Chinese Society of International Economic Law, Prof. Chen is one of China's best known and most distinguished scholars in the field of international economic law. He is also one of its most prolific and productive. In *The Voice from China*, Prof. Chen has pulled together in one hefty volume 24 of his lengthy academic articles, written over the course of more than 30 years, on contentious issues in international trade and investment law.

The volume is a tour de force. It ought to be in the reference library of every scholar and government official in the Asia-Pacific Region concerned with current issues in the fields of international trade and investment law.

Prof. Chen calls his latest publication *The Voice from China* for good reason. Over the course of his career, he has taken issue with elements of the received wisdom on trade and investment law emanating from Western scholars. With modesty, he labels his ideas simply "personal views with Chinese characteristics", but it should be noted that his proposals—particularly those that might be seen as iconoclastic—are deeply rooted in the troubled history of China over the past 150 years, a good part of which he has lived through and experienced personally.

A Western reader will note several broad themes running through the articles incorporated in this volume. The first is a notion of constructive patriotism in support of a China that is "peacefully rising". Chinese civilization extends back more than five thousand years, embracing extended periods of brilliance and dispiriting periods of decline. The years 1840-1949 were particularly unhappy ones for the country. Humiliated throughout the late Qing dynasty, repeatedly bullied by Western powers at their most imperialistic, and forced to surrender significant sovereign rights under insulting conditions, China was ripe for revolution at the beginning of the last century. To this mix should be added the brutal Japanese occupation during World War II and the civil war that followed.

It is not surprising that these experiences left Chinese intellectuals leery of accepting without question a range of doctrines in the fields of economics and law propounded by Western scholars. As a consequence, for example, China was relatively late to adhere to the treaty establishing the International Center for the Settlement of Investment Disputes (ICSID). Time and again, Prof. Chen returns to the shabby treatment received by China at the hands of industrialized powers to justify his questioning of treaty language or legal doctrines that, in his eyes, only reinforce "the severe unfairness in international power allocation in [the formulation of] global economic and trade policy making".

Redressing that balance between "North" and "South", the developed countries and those seen as developing, is another major theme that runs through this volume. The unequal treatment of which Prof. Chen complains has been experienced not only by China but by all developing countries that, following the demise死亡，終結 of colonialism in the post-war period, have had to negotiate with capital-exporting states in international fora. Prof. Chen talks of "weak nations" and of "South-South cooperation", urging that poorer countries stand together to "gradually obtain equal economic rights". Only by seeking to redress the "severe unfairness in international power allocation in [the] global economic and trade policy-making processes" can developing countries attack "unfair global wealth distribution". Prof. Chen finds a "causality between the allocation of power and the allocation of wealth." Thus, "unfair allocation of power must be reformed to guarantee fair distribution of global wealth."

Taken together, the articles republished in *The Voice from China* offer scholars and government officials in developing countries concrete suggestions in multiple contexts for rendering more fair the distribution of economic power between industrialized and developing countries. Prof. Chen is, after all, a law professor, and he advances his views carefully and with voluminous support Specific positions that developing states might take in current trade and investment negotiations are, thus, a third major theme that emerges in this volume.

Those involved on behalf of developing countries in international trade negotiations and in negotiations over the latest versions of bilateral investment treaties would be well advised to have a good understanding of Prof. Chen's views.

Several examples will serve to illustrate the tensions that Prof. Chen sees—double standards, as he calls them—between economically powerful states and the weaker ones when the two sides gather to negotiate trade and investment treaties. It is not fair, he argues, that developing countries be pressed to eliminate tariffs on non-agricultural goods, to further the integration of these states into the world economy, when developed states turn around and erect "environmental" barriers that hamper free trade in agricultural commodities from developing countries.

A similar problem emerges with respect to investment encouragement. Western bilateral investment treaties demand "free access" to critical economic sectors in host countries and "national treatment" for their investments, but then these same states bar certain investments from developing countries for reasons of "national security".

There have been numerous examples in recent years of Western nations arguing for privatization of state-owned enterprises in developing countries in the name of efficiency. This may be a good idea in many cases, but Prof. Chen worries about the instances in which foreign investment in critical sectors has made the recipient state vulnerable to "the predations of international monopoly capitalism".

A Western reader will be more sympathetic to some of these arguments than to others. In discussing the issue of compensation following an expropriation, Prof. Chen argues for a narrower standard than many in the West are prepared to accept. Of course, the measure of compensation is by no means a settled issue among scholars in developed countries, but in general terms, most would probably favor treaty language embracing the Hull standard ("adequate") as opposed language talking only of "appropriate" compensation.

The same point can be made regarding Prof. Chen's discussion of the role of the "exhaustion of local remedies" doctrine in the context of resolving investment disputes. In the face of allegedly expropriatory action on the part of a developing country, few lawyers in the capital-exporting states would support a requirement to first seek administrative remedies, often in a modest and distant provincial tribunal, when hundreds of millions of dollars may be at stake. They would not view their reluctance to go before a rural court that has never seen an expropriation case as a "disguised" effort to deprive the host country of its "economic and judicial sovereignty". Rather, they would see direct recourse to international arbitration as a way to protect themselves against "hometown decisions" by insufficiently experienced judges.

It should be underscored that there is nothing mean-spirited or vindictive or even doctrinaire in Prof. Chen's writings. He has a point of view, to be sure, but his objective is to guide his readers to an understanding of the imbalances as he sees them in international economic negotiations over the past two generations. His is an optimistic and positive view. As he notes in one of his homey references, he does not want to "throw out the baby with the bath water". Rather he wants to see a convergence between the industrialized states and the developing countries. If it took Canada and China 18 years to negotiate a new bilateral investment treaty, so be it. The result was worth the effort.

Prof. Chen is an unlikely figure to have emerged as one of the leading Chinese international economic law scholars of his generation. He comes from a family of intellectuals in rural Fujian Province, but he lived through all of the vicissitudes suffered by China for the first half of his life. It was not until the relatively ripe age of 50 that he was able to dedicate himself seriously to his field, when he began to learn English and secured an opportunity to study at Harvard.

Returning to China, Prof. Chen quickly became the dean of the Xiamen University Law School, a leading law school in the country. He was one of the founders of the Chinese International Economic Law Society, and for many years its head. Prof. Chen was awarded the designation by the government as a "Nationally Eminent and Senior Jurist", the highest academic honor in Chinese legal circles, one of only 25 such honorees since 1949.

Western readers will not agree with all of Prof. Chen's arguments as they read this compilation of his articles, but they will recognize in *The Voice from China* a serious and thoughtful scholar, whose distinctive voice has been shaped by the political and economic struggles of his country over the past 150 years. For those in the developing world, it is a voice of guidance and encouragement. For those in the industrialized countries, it is a voice calling for fair treatment and respect. It is a voice that deserves to be heard.

二十、魅力感召、法治理念與愛國情懷之和諧統一

——讀陳安教授《中國的吶喊》有感

趙 雲*

二〇一三年，一本重要的國際經濟法專著誕生。〔340〕該書甫一出版立即引起來自世界各地的國際法學界人士的關注和興趣，尤其是那些對中國國際經濟法實踐特別感興趣的國際法學界人士。陳教授是國際經濟法領域的世界知名學者。由於特殊的歷史原因，他的專業研究工作只能在二十世紀七〇年代末才得以展開。〔341〕但從那時起陳教授撰寫了許多國際經濟法研究領域的優

秀學術文章和書籍，這些學術成果對中國國際貿易和投資相關的法律制度的發展產生了重大的影響。

陳教授從過去三十年間撰寫的學術論文中精選二十四篇，匯輯成為一部專著，[342]全面且充分地展示了其作為一名中國學者對國際經濟法的理解。這是中國學者首次向全世界全面表明中國在國際經濟事務上的立場。陳教授是談論這一事務最為合適的人選。實際上，這部專著的一個顯著的特點是它從中國的視角系統性地審查和研究了國際經濟事務。[343]這正好與此專著的書名——《中國的吶喊》相呼應。因此，對於想知道中國學者對國際經濟法持何種看法的讀者而言，此專著是一份寶貴資料。

這部專著的論述幾乎覆蓋了國際經濟法的所有領域，包括貿易、投資、區域經濟一體化以及經濟全球化之趨勢。[344]中國執行對外開放政策之後，首先面臨的一個主要挑戰是爭端解決機制。外商投資者尤為關注中國的司法體制以及司法程式的公正與透明。在二十世紀八〇年代，建立一套與國際實踐互相接軌的爭端解決機制，是極為迫切的任務。作為應對，中國迅速恢復商事仲裁制度，以在某種程度上減輕外商投資者的顧慮。[345]一九九五年施行的《中華人民共和國仲裁法》（以下簡稱《仲裁法》）是中國仲裁制度發展的一塊里程碑。[346]

但是，一九九五年《仲裁法》的內容引發了激烈的爭論與批判，尤其是適用於中國國內與涉外仲裁裁決的雙軌體制。[347]在一九九五年《仲裁法》施行僅兩年之後，陳教授及時地對該部法律作出評價。他在論文中審查了《仲裁法》施行之時雙軌制度的合理性問題。文章扼要總結了針對涉外仲裁裁決實施不同制度的四種解釋與理解，即與《中華人民共和國民事訴訟法》（以下簡稱《民事訴訟法》）互相接軌的必要性、[348]與一九五八年《紐約公約》以及一九六五年《華盛頓公約》互相接軌的必要性、[349]符合國際實踐[350]以及考慮中國特色[351]。陳教授有條不紊地剖析論爭中的基本問題，即有關中國《仲裁法》的涉外仲裁監督規定與下述四個方面的接軌問題：

首先，在關於《仲裁法》中的涉外仲裁監督規定是否與相關的民事訴訟法互相接軌的爭論上，陳教授認為，其核心問題就在於《仲裁法》中的雙軌制度對國內與涉外的仲裁監督區別對待。[352]具體而言，國內的仲裁裁決可以就程式運作和實質內容同時進行審查與監督，而涉外仲裁裁決則只限於程式運作。[353]在與《民事訴訟法》比較之後，陳教授指出一九九五年《仲裁法》的一個積極的方面是，它進一步擴大了管轄法院對國內仲裁裁決的監督權力範圍，並授權法院在必要時可以裁定應予撤銷仲裁裁決。[345]但是，陳教授同時也強調，《仲裁法》將涉外裁決的監督範圍限於程式範圍之內，這可能導致在現行的仲裁監督制度下引發矛盾以及不公正的裁決。[355]另外，《民事訴訟法》中明確規定的「公共利益」保護條款在《仲裁法》中毫未提及，因為在對涉外仲裁裁決的監督制度中並沒有此類實質性規定。[356]

其次，陳教授在分析一九九五年《仲裁法》是否與國際條約有關規定接軌這一爭論上審查了兩個國際條約，即一九五八年《紐約公約》和一九六五年《華盛頓公約》。儘管有學者主張，「一九五八年的《紐約公約》也只是允許作為裁決執行地的東道國的主管機關對程序上有錯誤或違法之處的外國仲裁裁決實行必要的審查和監督」[357]，但陳教授指出，根據《紐約公約》第五條第二款的規定，[358]部分實體性問題比如「公共政策」[359]還是在公約中有所列舉，這顯然表明《紐約公約》對國際仲裁裁決中實體性內容的監督。另外，一九六五年《華盛頓公約》促進了解決投資爭端國際中心（ICSID）的設立，並在第五十二條[360]規定了其國際仲裁裁決的監督機制。通過這一監督機制，對實體性內容和程式性規定進行必要的審查和監督，以處理仲裁裁決的「終局性」與「公正性」這一對矛盾。[361]同時，陳教授也指出，《華盛頓公約》第五十二條規定的，由ICSID對實體性內容進行監督，可以化解「南」與「北」之間的矛盾，因為弱勢的一方（通常是發展中國家）可以借助這一條規定進行自我保護，以避免不公正的裁決。[362]因此，鑒於中國一九九五年《仲裁法》在對涉外仲裁裁決的監督機制上並沒有包含實體性內容，這很難與國際條約在這一事項上所規定的精神與實踐相一致。

再次，在涉外裁決監督條款是否符合先進的國際慣例這一爭論上，陳教授言簡意賅地列舉了國外在涉外仲裁裁決監督上的實踐，如美國、英國、德國、日本和澳大利亞的仲裁立法。「他山之石，可以攻玉。」基於發達國家的仲裁立法，陳教授總結道，發達國家的仲裁監督機制以同一的、統一的標準及同等的必要性要求對待各自的國內仲裁裁決和涉外仲裁裁決。此外，陳教授亦指出發達國家的仲裁立法不僅賦權於管轄法院可以裁定「不予執行」裁決，而且在必要時可以裁定「應予撤銷」。[363]至於發展中國家的仲裁立法，陳教授表示其中許多是借鑑發達國家先進的仲裁實踐經驗，並同樣建立了仲裁監督機制對它們國內和涉外仲裁裁決實行「一視同仁」的監督。[364]另外，陳教授還援引了聯合國國際貿易法委員會《國際商事仲裁示範法》[365]以證明對國內和涉外仲裁裁決實行監督的國際趨勢應當是「單軌制」而非「雙軌制」。顯然，中國一九九五年《仲裁法》中關於涉外仲裁裁決監督的規定與發達國家和其他發展中國家的實踐相左。

最後，在中國特色以及地方保護主義這一爭論上，陳教授重申追求所謂的「一片淨土」論會導致「缺乏應有的清醒和足夠的警惕」。[366]他還提到黨和國家領導人的號召和指示以提醒人們一個事實，即一套有效的、健全的仲裁監督機制應當是打擊和杜絕仲裁程式中的一切不法行為的。[367]有些人可能認為當前涉外仲裁的仲裁員的素質相對較高，因此推測在審理仲裁案件期間很少會存在不法行為，[368]而管轄法院某些法官的素質卻不夠理想，不足以對這些案件形成有效的監督，且他們還可能受地方保護主義影響。對於涉外仲裁的「極少不法行為」的推斷，陳教授不否認涉外仲裁的仲裁員的素質整體上具有較高水準且在仲裁的過程中會嚴以自律。[369]然而，仲裁審理期間「極少失當行為」並不必然意味著據此就能否定對仲裁員在整個涉外仲裁過程中的不當行為實施監管的必要性。這種忽略審理涉外仲裁案件的仲裁員也可能會存在某些不法及舞弊行為的觀點，顯然不符合中國現代社會的法治思想以及深深地紮根在法律框架內的正義精神。陳教授不同意以「預防地方保護主義」作為維持目前的「單軌」仲裁監督機制的藉口或護盾。這展示了他負責任的態度以及意圖尋求一套有效的、健全的仲裁監督機制的決心，他也鼓勵法學界、司法界、仲裁界和商界更多的人投身到設計與完善當前的仲裁監督機制的洪流中。

在一九九五年《仲裁法》實施當時，存在對中國仲裁員素質的質疑以及涉外仲裁程式可能難以有效運行的諸多顧慮是可以理解的。因此，就仲裁制度在中國的正常運作以及排除外商投資者對中國爭端解決機制的疑慮而言，一套適當的監督機制顯得尤為重要。在這一背景下，陳教授繼續就如何加強涉外仲裁程式的監督機制提出建言。諸如設立自律委員會、仲裁研究中心和專家委員會的此類設想，不僅旨在確保仲裁員和仲裁程式的公平公正，[370]而且有利於中國仲裁的有序發展，促進仲裁這一領域的學術研究。

仲裁的概念在商業世界中已被廣泛認可，中國國際經濟貿易仲裁委員會每年處理大量的商業爭端案件。中國仲裁實務發展相當快速，其間也吸收了其他世界級仲裁機構的先進經驗，增強了本土仲裁機構在世界仲裁市場中的競爭力。陳教授提出的觀點和見解在指導中國仲裁的發展方面至今仍有借鑑意義。只有對仲裁理論與實務的不斷研究，方能確保仲裁機構改善自身的仲裁管理與爭端解決程式。研究機構等仲裁內部相關機構提供的支援，應當為相關的研究與合作提供一個有益的平臺。

在如今的商業世界中，我們強調不同類型的糾紛解決機制共同存在的重要性。陳教授對這一問題也持開放的態度，而沒有局限於傳統的訴訟程式和仲裁機制。本專著裡的論文也涉及解決投資爭端國際中心（ICSID）和WTO爭端解決機制分別針對國際投資和貿易爭端而設立的糾紛解決機制。這些論文的討論中，我們可以看到陳教授對待不同類型的糾紛解決機制採納務實而開明的做法。通過研究這些機制的運作方式，陳教授就如何利用這些機制實現中國的最佳效益提出了自己的見解。例如，在分析WTO爭端解決機構（DSB）這一法律執行機構時，陳教授提到，儘管WTO爭端解決機制在所有現有的國際經濟爭端解決機制當中地位顯著，但它仍然問題不少，「先天不足，後天失調」。[371]具體而言，陳教授指出，爭端解決機制的「先天不足」在於其所執之法中，如在農產品協議的「三大支柱」（即市場準入、國內支持和出口補貼）規則中均包含對國際弱勢群體不利的「劣法」或「惡法」的內容，它們仍然不合理地在WTO爭端解決機制中生效、運行。[372]此外，正如其他發展中國家在「入世」時遭受不公正的待遇一樣，中國作為世界最大的發展中國家，其已經基本建立了市場經濟體制，但這一「雙重經濟身份」並沒有得到WTO／DSB的考慮，還迫使中國接受一些「不利條款」。[373]與之相反，有些發達國家則通過制定和執行WTO規則受益。在301條款和201條款的相關案例中，陳教授指出美國在全球經濟體系和WTO下的優勢地位，如其在WTO守法方面的剛愎自用、霸權成癮，進一步阻礙WTO/DSB朝著更為公平與公正的爭端解決機制發展。上述兩方面案例進一步反映了WTO／DSB是「後天失調」的。[374]但是，陳教授強調，由於WTO主要由發達國家發起和構建，包括中國在內的發展中國家應該尋求更靈活的戰略，以適應WTO的規則體系。發展中國家不應畏懼承擔在現行WTO規則下所作出的不公正的承諾，而應共同努力以儘快熟悉WTO的各種「遊戲規則」，並在面臨WTO不公正的立法、守法、執法、變法之時，共同為弱勢群體鼓與呼。[375]陳教授指出，WTO

成員之間關係的核心特徵在於貫穿於規則的確立、執行、遵守與改變始末的這一「成員驅動」（WTO所有的決議都是由其成員方共同作出）功能特徵。因此，發展中國家作為「遊戲規則」中的弱勢一方，儘管力量有限但卻是國際經濟領域不可或缺的，它們應該凝聚集體力量，謀求更為公平的國際經濟秩序和國際經濟法大背景下經濟上的平權。

從本書體現出的學術貢獻來看，不難發覺陳安教授對於不同的司法體系都有深入的掌握及獨到的見解。比如，在本書第二十四章《一項判決三點質疑評香港高等法院1993年第A8176號案件判決書》〔376〕中，陳安教授批判性地評論了香港高等法院的第A8176號案件，並且嚴格遵循「以事實為依據，以法律為準繩」原則對中國內地與香港地區不同的法律和司法體系作了比較。〔377〕在本章中，陳安教授主要從三個方面，分析並質疑香港高等法院的這一判決，即該案管轄權、所謂的中國票據法自治原則以及訴訟程式中的被告答辯權等。〔378〕該案原被告雙方爭議的焦點，〔379〕是案中的匯票能否絕對地「獨立存在」，具有「自主性」，也就是所謂的「匯票自治原則」在國際法、中國國內法和一九九三年香港地區司法體系中是否具有法律依據。根據陳安教授的觀點，該案的審理法官卡普蘭（Kaplan）先生作出判決的依據卻是原告方律師狄克斯（Dicks）先生提供的子虛烏有的規則。

關於第一項質疑，即關於該案的管轄權，陳安教授提出了一個非常重要的有待回答的問題：該案的管轄權究竟應歸屬誰？它應由香港地區的高等法院通過訴訟方式處斷，抑或是應由中國內地的CIETAC通過仲裁方式解決？〔381〕陳安教授注意到，卡普蘭法官把該案管轄權判歸香港地區法院，無視合同當事人在該案中自願選擇了簽約地、履行地、合同的仲裁管轄機構、適用的準據法（A158號合同〔382〕）以及合同仲裁條款應當適用於10732C號匯票爭端這些事實，從根本上違反了「有約必守」以及當事人「意思自治」這兩大基本法理原則。〔383〕香港地區《仲裁條例》（第2條、第34A條和第34C條〔384〕）和英國參加締結的、對香港地區有法律約束力的一九五八年《紐約公約》〔385〕均認可當事人「意思自治」的實踐。〔386〕諸如此類，該案裁決對已與國際慣例接軌的中國內地法律法規缺乏應有的尊重。〔387〕對此，陳安教授總結為：「任何人，只要真心實意地尊重和遵循當事人『意思自治』和『最密切聯繫』這兩大法理原則，就當然會認定中國內地的法律是解決A158號合同一切有關爭端的唯一準據法；任何人，只要言行一致地承認中國內地的法律是解決本合同一切爭端的準據法，並對此準據法給予起碼的尊重，就絕不會對中國內地法律體制中有關涉外合同爭議及其管轄權的一系列具體規定，棄置不顧。」〔388〕因此，根據陳安教授對此問題的深入分析，該案審理中把匯票爭端管轄權判歸香港地區法院是缺乏法律依據的。

在第二項質疑，也就是關於中國內地法律「承認」該案匯票之「獨立性」問題中，陳安教授指出，狄克斯先生（原告的代表律師，香港律師）在論證其論點時所援引的論據，即他所謂的「中國內地在匯票以及其他票據方面實施的各項法律原則」，往往是「無中生有」，或「化有為無」，並不符合事實原貌或原文原意。〔389〕為了進一步指出狄克斯先生在此方面的「無中生有」或「化有為無」，陳安教授分別從五個角度進行了闡述：第一，中國內地法律中並不存在「匯票自治原則」這個生造出來的名詞，也不存在狄克斯先生所推崇的匯票至高無上的「獨立性」〔390〕第二，狄克斯先生援引中國內地的《銀行結算辦法》時，使用了斷章取義的方法；〔391〕第三，狄克斯先生在轉述郭鋒先生論文時，閹割前提，歪曲原意；〔392〕第四，狄克斯先生的見解與中國內地票據法學術著作中公認的觀點、有關的國際公約及中國內地票據法的具體規定，都是背道而馳的；〔393〕第五，狄克斯先生在援引《民事訴訟法》，以論證其所謂的「匯票自治原則」時，竟然篡改條文，無中生有。〔394〕根據以上的五點，可以很自然地得出結論：狄克斯先生所呈遞的虛假證詞，誘使審理法官卡普蘭先生落入對中國內地票據法律原則的誤判和陷阱中。〔395〕

在第三項質疑中，陳安教授對於該案被告答辯權問題提出了疑問。關於法官卡普蘭先生在判決中作出的闡釋：「我拒絕了被告的申請，不接受他們提交的陳安教授所寫的另外一份意見書，因為已經為時太晚，而且在特殊的環境下，對方的專家狄克斯御用大律師沒有機會在足夠的時間內作出答覆」，陳安教授指出此說法難以令人信服。〔396〕首先，這種「為時過晚」論是站不住腳的，特別是考慮到法官允許狄克斯先生為原告提供的專家意見書一拖再拖，逾期整整三個月，〔397〕而被告針對狄克斯意見的答辯書距離狄克斯意見書的提交僅僅二十六天卻被拒絕接受。從這個角度來說，法官卡普蘭先生的「為時過晚」論缺乏令人信服的解釋和足夠的法律依據。其次，不給予被告充分的答辯權，是違反公平原則，違反國際訴訟程式慣例的。〔398〕這一原則已經在眾多的國內和國際立法中有所體現，如英美訴訟法的理論和實踐中的

「自然公平準則」中國民事訴訟法中的「以事實為根據，以法律為準繩」以及體現在一九五八年《紐約公約》和一九八五年聯合國《國際商事仲裁示範法》中的「給予被訴人以充分答辯權」。〔399〕總之，此案的判決依據是卡普蘭先生和狄克斯先生擅自編造的規則，缺少法律依據，應當被認定為喪失其法律約束力。

在這一起案件判決的研究和分析中，陳安教授展現出了作為一名傑出的國際法學者應有的姿態，有力、有理、有節地抨擊了該判決中的非正義。在對此案件分析和對判決質疑中，陳安教授不僅熟練和系統地運用相關的法律原則、實體和程式法律、學術著作，以及國際慣例，來發掘和批判該案判決中不合理和缺乏依據的事項。更重要的是，陳安教授此種遵照「以事實為依據，以法律為準繩」原則來對任何司法體系中存在的不公正行為進行據理力爭的精神，體現了中國法律體制的核心價值理念，值得所有的法律學者去學習。

上述討論也正對應陳教授此部專著的基調和核心議題——主權。二戰之後，國際社會所重組的國際經濟秩序犧牲了發展中國家的利益。中國作為最大的發展中國家，應當扮演改變這種不公正經濟秩序的重要角色。以爭端解決為例，陳教授深諳相關理論，並能夠就如何重構一套國內的爭端解決體制，以及發展國際經濟並與其他國家保持貿易關係提出務實的見解。〔400〕對於當下國際經濟法立法、守法和變法的問題，陳教授堅持「正確的態度」〔401〕應當是公平公正地對待弱勢群體。因此，我們不應將改革現有的國際經濟秩序的呼聲僅僅視為一種政治標語，而應將其視為一個「法律」概念以切實促進法律改革上的成果。此外，國際法環境下的弱勢群體應當不斷努力地主張及呼籲以消除現行國際經濟法的不公平現象，因為正如現在的狀況所印證的，發達國家不願意兌現它們的承諾，即犧牲它們的經濟優勢去作法律的變革（如在WTO多哈回合談判中，WTO中的發達國家成員國拒絕在農業談判上妥協並邁出實質的步伐）。正是在這一嚴峻的國際經濟法環境下，陳教授強調「南南合作」勢在必行，因為「集體力量」是促進穩固和公正的法律變革的唯一可行和有效之途徑。〔402〕

本專著中收集的每篇論文都鮮明地蘊含了主權這一主旋律。在鼓勵國際交易與交流的同時，中國應該能夠捍衛自身的主權以及經濟自主。筆者個人在二〇一五年底受邀前往廈門大學開展系列講座，其間首次見到陳教授，他睿智的言辭就讓我印象深刻。陳教授申明了青年一代國際學者積極地參與國際學術交流以及熟悉國際學術討論的重要性。但是，他也指出中國的國際法學者不應該盲目地附和或順從其他學者鼓吹的觀點，而應當具有獨立的見解並基於對中國大背景的考量提出建議。文如其人，這便是我對陳教授這樣一位享有盛譽的學者的確切感受。因此，筆者在閱讀他的專著期間甚為愉悅，而通過此書，讀者們不僅可以獲得國際經濟法領域的中國學者視角，更為重要的是，擁有一個優良契機去欣賞陳教授這位國際知名學者的個人魅力感召與愛國情懷。

Harmonization of Charisma, Jurisprudence and Patriotism

—The Inspiration from *The Voice from China: An CHEN on International Economic Law*

Zhao Yun*

A major monograph on international economic law was produced in 2013,[403] immediately arousing the attention and interests from international lawyers around the world, in particular from those with special interest in the Chinese practice in the international economic field. Professor An Chen is a world-renowned scholar in the field of international economic law. Due to the special history, he could only start his research in late 1970s;[404] but since then, Prof. Chen has produced many excellent articles and books in the field, which exert a heavy influence on the development of the legal regime in China for international trade and investment.

Twenty-four carefully-selected articles written during the last three decades by Prof. Chen[405] effectively demonstrate the views of Prof. Chen, a Chinese scholar, on relevant issues on international economic law in a comprehensive manner. It is for the first time that a Chinese scholar comprehensively shows to the world China's position on international economic affairs.[406] Prof. Chen is exactly the right person to speak on the matter. Actually, one distinct feature of this monograph is its systemic review and study of international economic affairs from a Chinese perspective. This exactly corresponds to the title of this monograph—*The Voice from China*. Accordingly, this monograph is a valuable source for readers to know the Chinese views on international economic law.

This monograph touches on almost every aspects of international economic law, including trade, investment, regional economic integration and the trend of economic globalization.[407] One major challenge facing China after its implementation of the open-door policy was the dispute resolution mechanism at that time. Foreign investors were seriously concerned about the judicial system and the quality of judicial proceedings in China. The establishment of a dispute resolution framework to be in line with the international practice was an urgent task in the 1980s.[408] China was quick to respond by reinstating arbitration for commercial arbitration, which to a certain extent help to relieve the concerns of foreign investors. The milestone in the development of arbitration was the enactment of Arbitration Law in 1995.[409]

However, the contents in the 1995 Arbitration Law aroused heated discussions and criticism, especially the dual-track regime ("separate track")[410] for domestic and foreign-related arbitral awards. Prof. Chen was quick to make comments on the regime just two years after the enactment. He examined the reasonableness of the dual-track regime at the time when the Arbitration Law was enacted. Four types of interpretation and understanding for the separate regime for foreign-related arbitral awards were succinctly summarised in his paper, namely, the necessity of compliance with the Civil Procedure Law;[411] necessity of compliance with New York Convention of 1958 and Washington Convention of 1965; [412] following relevant international practices; [413] taking into consideration of the unique situation in China. [414] Prof. Chen methodically indicated the essential issues within the debates concerning the tallying provisions of Foreign-Related Arbitration Supervision of Arbitration Law with the four aspects below.

First, with regard to the debate over whether Arbitration Law provisions tallying with corresponding Civil Procedure Law in foreign-related arbitration supervision, the core issue mentioned by Prof. Chen concerning the separate track adopted by China's Arbitration Law is that it differentiates domestic arbitration supervision from foreign-related arbitration supervision. [415] That is to say, both procedural operation and substantive matters are allowed to be examined and supervised in the domestic awards, whereas in a foreign-related arbitral award, only its procedural operation is allowed to be examined and supervised. [416] In the comparison between the current Arbitration Law and the Civil Procedure Law of China, one positive aspect of the Arbitration Law, noted by Prof. Chen, is that it has further broadened the scope of the jurisdictional court's supervision power over domestic awards, thus empowering the court to set aside an arbitral award when necessary. [417] However, Prof. Chen also emphasized that this Arbitration Law limits the scope of the supervision over foreign-related arbitration awards to procedure operations only, and can lead to some contradictions and unjust awards under present arbitration supervision mechanism. [418]

Moreover, the "public interest" protection, which is expressly enumerated in the Civil Procedure Law, is not appropriately reflected in the Arbitration Law as no such substantive content is listed in the supervision over foreign-related awards. [419]

Second, two international treaties, i.e. New York Convention of 1958 and Washington Convention of 1965, have been involved in the analysis of Prof. Chen regarding the debate over whether Arbitration Law provisions tallying with those of international treaties correspondingly. Even though some people argued that "New York Convention of 1958 only allows the competent authority of a Contracting State where an enforcement is sought to carry out a necessary examination and supervision over foreign awards involving procedural errors or violations of law" [420], Prof. Chen indicated that based on the stipulation in Section 2, Article 5 [421] of the New York Convention, some substantive issues such as "public policy", [422] are enumerated in this Convention and thus obviously manifesting that New York Convention stipulates the supervision over substantive contents in international arbitral awards. On the other hand, the Washington Convention of 1965, which facilitates the establishment of International Centre for Settlement of Investment Disputes (ICSID), also enumerates its supervision mechanism on international arbitration in Article 52. [423] This supervision mechanism is employed to strike a balance in the contradiction between the"finality" and "justice" of an award by conducting necessary examination and supervision over both the substantive contents and procedural operations.

[424] Furthermore, Prof. Chen also indicated that including substantive matters to be supervised by ICSID in Article 52 can settle the contradiction between the "North" and the "South", based on the fact that the weaker party (frequently the developing countries) can resort to this article to protect themselves from unjust awards.[425] Therefore, considering the present Arbitration Law of China has not included the substantive matters into the supervision mechanism over foreign-related arbitral awards, it is unlikely that this mechanism is in compliance with the spirit and practice of international treaties in this regard.

Third, in the respect of debating whether foreign-related awards supervision provisions in compliance with advanced international practices, Prof. Chen precisely and concisely enumerates the instances of foreign practice in terms of foreign-related awards supervision, i.e. the arbitration enactments of United States, United Kingdom, Germany, Japan, and Australia. As "stones from other hills may serve to polish the jade of this one", in view of the developed countries' arbitration enactments, Prof. Chen concluded that the arbitration supervision mechanism in developed countries treat the domestic arbitration and foreign-related arbitration with identical and unified standard and corresponding necessary requirements. Moreover, Prof. Chen also indicated that the developed countries' arbitration enactments not only empower the jurisdictional court to make an order to refuse the enforcement of an award, but set aside it when necessary as well.[426] As to the developing countries' arbitration enactments, Prof. Chen indicated that many of them draw on the advanced arbitration practice experience from the developed countries, and also set up arbitration supervision mechanism to conduct identical supervision towards domestic and foreign-related awards.[427] Besides, Prof. Chen also referred to the UNCITRAL Model Law on International Commercial Arbitrationl[428] to demonstrate the "same track" international trend instead of "separate track" concerning the foreign-related arbitration supervision and domestic awards supervision. It is obvious that the present provisions concerning foreign-related arbitral awards supervision in the Arbitration Law of China are not in compliance with neither the developed countries' arbitration enactment practices, nor the practices in the developing countries.

Fourth, over the debate upon the uniqueness and local protectionism of China, Prof. Chen reiterated that pursuing the so-called "a piece of pure land" can lead to "lacking a clear head and due vigilance".[429] He also referred to the calls and instructions of party and state leaders[430] to remind people of the fact that an effective and perfective arbitration supervision mechanism is expected to prohibit and fight any misconducts[431] in the arbitral proceedings. Some people may argue that the current arbitrators in the foreign-related arbitration are at relatively higher levels and thus are expected to commit few misconducts during these arbitrational cases, whereas some judges from jurisdictional courts are not high enough to effectively conduct supervision over these cases and may be influenced by "local protectionism". With regard to the "few misconducts" in the foreign-related arbitration, Prof. Chen admitted that arbitrators in the foreign-related arbitration are at relatively high level and may behave themselves well during the arbitration courses. [432] However, "fewer misconducts" being discovered during the arbitration proceedings does not necessarily mean that the whole process of foreign-related arbitration should not be supervised in terms of misconducts by arbitrators. Obviously, neglecting the possibility that certain misconducts and malpractices may be exercised by arbitrators in the foreign-related arbitration, is not in line with China's modern social rule-by-law thought and the spirit of justice rooted deeply inside the law. Prof. Chen disagreed with the opinion to manipulate the "local protectionism" as an excuse or a guarding shield for maintaining the present "separate track" arbitration supervision mechanism, which identifies his responsible attitudes and determined mind-set towards an effective and perfective arbitration supervision system, and encouraged more people from law circles, judicial circle, arbitral circles, and business circles to engage into the designation and perfection of the current arbitration supervision mechanism.

It is understandable at the time of the enactment of the Arbitration Law, a lot of concerns existed in China over the quality of arbitrators and possible malfunctioning of the arbitration mechanism for foreign-related arbitration proceedings; consequently, a proper supervision mechanism appeared all the more important for the proper functioning of arbitration in China and dissipate the concerns of foreign investors over the dispute resolution system in China. Under this circumstance, Prof. Chen continued to make suggestions on how to strengthen the supervision mechanism for foreign-related arbitration proceedings. The ideas on the establishment of a Self-Disciplined Committee, Research Institute of Arbitration, and Expert Committee have their target to ensure the proper function of the arbitrators and the arbitration proceedings.[433] These ideas, moreover, support the smooth development of arbitration in China and promote academic research on the topic of arbitration.

The concept of arbitration has been widely accepted in the commercial world, with the CIETAC receiving large number of commercial cases annually. The arbitration practice has developed rather quickly, absorbing useful experience from other world arbitration institutions, adding in the competitiveness of the Chinese arbitral institutions in the world arbitration market. The ideas raised by Prof. Chen continue to be useful in guiding further development of arbitration in China. Only by continuous study of arbitration theory and practice, can the arbitration institutions improve on their arbitration administration and dispute resolution processes. The support of relevant internal organs, such as research institutes shall provide a useful platform for relevant research and cooperation.

In the commercial world nowadays, we emphasize the importance of the co-existence of different types of dispute resolution mechanisms. Prof. Chen was also open-minded on the matter, not limiting himself to the traditional litigation process and the arbitration mechanism. The papers in this monograph also touches on the ICSID and WTO dispute settlement mechanisms for international investment and trade disputes.

From the discussions in these papers, we can see that Prof. Chen adopted a pragmatic and flexible approach in dealing with different types of disputes. By examining the functioning of these mechanisms, Prof. Chen was able to put forward his insights on how to make use of these mechanisms to realize the best benefits of China. For instance, in the analysis of the WTO's law-enforcing body—the DSB, Prof. Chen mentioned that even though the WTO's dispute settlement system (DSS) has its distinctive status among all the available international economic dispute settlement mechanisms, it still owns "congenital deficiency and postnatal imbalance". [434] To be specific, Prof. Chen noted that the DSB system has "congenital deficiency" in the rules of agricultural products "three pillars" (i.e. market access, domestic support, and export subsidy) all contains "bad or evil" contents that run against the interests of the weak groups, which still unreasonably take effect in the WTO's DSB system. [435] And just being similar to other unfair treatment occurring in the accession process of developing countries to the WTO, the WTO/DSB did not take into account the "dual economic identity" of China, which represented the largest developing country in the world with a basic system of a market economy, thus not confirming the market economy status in China and forcing China to accept some "disadvantageous articles". [436] On the contrary, some developed countries in the WTO have benefited from the partial law-making and law-enforcing in the WTO/DSB. It is in the cases of Section 301 and Section 201 that Prof. Chen indicated that the superior status of the United States both in the global economy and the WTO, i.e. the "self-willed and hegemony-addicted" behaviour in the WTO law-abiding, has further hindered the WTO/DSB from becoming a more balanced and justice dispute settlement mechanism. The two cases further reflected that the WTO/DSB system is "postnatal imbalance". [437] However, Prof. Chen emphasized that since the WTO has been found and designed mainly by developed countries, developing countries including China should seek for a more flexible strategy to adapt to the rule system in the WTO. It is not that the developing countries should be afraid of assuming the burden of unfair commitment responsibility under current WTO rule system. It is just that the developing countries should make collective endeavour to nurture proficiency in various "rules of the games" as soon as possible, and stand together to make advocating sounds for the weak groups when confronting the unjustified law-making, law-abiding, law-enforcing and law-reforming circumstances in the WTO. [438] Prof. Chen mentioned this pivotal feature existing in the WTO membership, which is this "member-driven" characteristic functioning throughout the process of making, abiding, enforcing and reforming law. Therefore, the developing countries, acting as the weaker part in the "rules of the game" should combine their limited yet indispensable power in the international economic environment to pursue a level playing field in the context of a more balanced IEO and IEL background.

From the scholarly contributions reflected in this monograph, it is not difficult to find that Prof. Chen has unique insights and deep understanding of different judicial systems. For example, in chapter 24 of this monograph[439] —"Three aspects of inquiry into a judgment: Comments on the High Court Decision, 1993 No.A8176, in the Supreme Court of Hong Kong" , Prof. Chen critically commented on the specific High Court Decision case 1993 No. A8176, and compared different laws and judicial systems in Mainland China and Hong Kong, strictly following the principle of "taking facts as the basis, and taking laws as the criterion."[440] In this chapter, Prof. Chen analysed and queried this High Court Decision in three major aspects, i.e. the jurisdiction of the case, the so-called principle of autonomy in the Chinese Bills Law, and the defendant's right of defence during civil procedure.[441] The subject matter in dispute[442] is whether the Bills of Exchange "can stand independently" and owned "autonomy", i.e. whether the so-called "principle of autonomy of Bills of Exchange" has legal basis from the perspectives of international law, domestic law in China, and the Hong Kong judicial system in 1993. According to Prof. Chen, the judge in this case, Justice Kaplan, made the judgment according to the presumptuously fabricated rules made by Mr. Dicks.[443]

With regard to the jurisdiction of the case, Prof. Chen indicated that the question that needs to be answered is whether this case should be decided by the High Court of Hong Kong, or settled by the CIETAC through arbitration.[444] Prof. Chen noted that Judge Kaplan neglected the facts that both contracting parties in this case voluntarily chose the place of contracting, the place of performance, the entity for arbitration and the proper law (Contract A158[445]), and that the arbitration clause should be applied to the Bills of Exchange, thus violating the principles of Pacta Sunt Servanda and "Autonomy of Will".[446] Both the Hong Kong Arbitration Ordinance (Articles 2, 34A, and 34C[447]) and the New York Convention of 1958,[448] to which Hong Kong is legally bound, acknowledged the practice of party autonomy.[449] As such, the decision failed to pay due respect for Chinese Laws and Regulations that tally with international practice.[450] Prof. Chen summarized that "anyone who sincerely respects and complies with the major legal principles of 'autonomy of will' and 'the closest connection' will inevitably consider Chinese law as the only proper law to resolve all the relevant disputes arising from Sales Contract A, and anyone who shows due respect to Chinese law and honestly recognizes and confirms it as the proper law... will definitely not disregard the series of specific provisions under the Chinese legal system."[451] Hence, Prof. Chen concluded that the judgment was lack of legal basis.

Regarding the issue of the recognition in Chinese law of the "Autonomy" of the Bills of Exchange, Prof. Chen indicated that the argument raised by Mr. Dicks (Hong Kong Barrister representing the plaintiff) in terms of legal principles applicable in China to bills of exchange and other payment instruments were fabricated or misrepresented and not in conformity with the reality and the original meanings.[452] In order to elaborate on Mr. Dicks' fabrication and misrepresentation, Prof. Chen elaborated from the following five points: first, Chinese law did not have strange expressions of "the autonomy of bills of exchange" and absolute "independence" of bills of exchange, as worded by Mr Dicks; [453] second, Mr. Dicks' citation from the procedures for bank settlements were out of context; [454] third, Mr. Dicks had emasculated its prerequisite and garbled its original meaning when citing Mr. Guo Feng's article; [455] fourth, Mr Dick's opinion ran counter to the generally accepted viewpoints of Chinese academic works on bill laws, the stipulations of relevant international conventions, and the bills law in China [456]; and fifth, Mr Dicks had distorted the original text when quoting the Civil Procedure Law of PRC as evidence for the said "Autonomy of Bills of Exchange" [457]. Based upon these five points, it was thus safe to conclude that Mr. Dicks had submitted ill-grounded affidavit which misled Justice Kaplan in respect of China's legal principles on payment instruments. [458]

Prof. Chen then moved further to question on the defendant's right of defence in this case. Regarding Justice Kaplan's explanation in the judgment that "I refused an application by the Defendant to produce an additional report by Professor Chen An on the grounds that it was too late and in the special circumstances there was no opportunity for Mr. Dicks Q.C., the expert on the other side, to reply to it in sufficient time", Prof. Chen opined that it was hardly convincing. [459] Firstly, the reason "It was too late" was not tenable. The Judge permitted the extension of "the time within which Mr. Dicks had to submit his expert evidence for the plaintiff many times", [460] while the defendant's defence to Mr. Dicks' evidence was rejected for only 26 days after the presentation of Mr. Dicks' evidence. Justice Kaplan obviously had no persuasive explanation and concrete legal basis on this issue. Secondly, denial of the right to defence was contrary to the principle of equity and international practice on litigation procedures. [461] This principle had been reflected in many domestic and international laws, including "the rule of nature" in the Anglo-American procedural laws, the principle of "basing on facts and taking laws as criteria" in the Chinese Civil Procedure Law, "the right to defence" in the New York Convention of 1958 and the 1985 UNCITRAL Model Law on International Commercial Arbitration. [462] To sum up, the judgment based on the presumptuously fabricated rules made by Mr. Kaplan and Mr. Dicks had no legal basis.

In this chapter, Prof. Chen demonstrated the firm gesture of a leading international law scholar to argue strongly, reasonably, and pertinently against any unjust grounds, which deserves to be learnt by all legal scholars. As reflected in this chapter, Prof. Chen not only has a comprehensive understanding of domestic and international laws in the field, but also can proficiently and systematically apply relevant legal principles, substantial and procedural rules, academic works, and international practice to critically comment on the inappropriate and ill-grounded issues in the judgment.

The line of the above discussions exactly corresponds to the basic tone of this monograph and the essential subject for Prof. Chen, which is sovereignty. After the Second World War, international society reconstructed international economic order at the sacrifice of developing countries. China, as the largest developing country, should play an important role to change the unfair economic order. Taking dispute resolution as an example, Prof. Chen, having a deep understanding of the international dispute theory, was able to come up with realistic ideas on how to reconstruct a national dispute resolution framework while developing international economic and trade relationships with outside world. [463] With regard to the relationship among law-making, law-abiding, and law-reforming of the existing International Economic Law (IEL), Prof. Chen insisted that "a correct attitude" [464] should not break the balance of treating the weak groups fairly and justly in terms of making, abiding and reforming IEL. Hence, we should not treat demanding reform of the established International Economic Order(IEO) merely as a political slogan, but as a "legal" concept so that real legal reforming achievements can be expected in the IEO. Moreover, the weak groups in the international law environment should fight for themselves to contribute more advocacy and appeal for eliminating the unfair status quo of rules system in the IEL, because as current situation reflects, the developed countries are not willing to enforce their commitment to sacrifice their superior economic status for a level playground in law-reforming (e.g. in the process of Doha Agenda in the WTO, the developed country Members of the WTO refuse to comprise in Agriculture negotiation, thus making real progress in this field unpromising). It is in such severe IEL environment that Prof. Chen emphasized that "South-South Coalitions" are imperative considering the "collective power" is essential to promote solidified and fairly law-reforming progress. [465]

This underlying tone of Sovereignty is obvious from each and every paper collected in this monograph. While encouraging international transactions and exchanges, China should be able to protect its sovereignty and economic autonomy. I have deepest impression from my first meetup with Prof. Chen by end of 2015 when I was invited to give a series of seminar at Xiamen University. Prof. Chen wisely made his statement that it is important for the younger generation of international lawyers to actively participate in international academic exchanges and be familiar with international academic discussions; however, Chinese international lawyers should not blindly follow whatever other scholars proposed. One should have an independent mind and make suggestions by taking into account of the Chinese circumstance. This exactly demonstrate the unity of Prof. Chen as a well-respected scholar with his papers. Accordingly, the reading process of this monograph has been an extremely pleasant one. Readers will not only obtain knowledge on Chinese views on international economic law, but more importantly, has the opportunity to appreciate the charisma and patriotism of Prof. Chen, as a world-renowned international lawyer.

（翻譯：趙　雲）

二十一、駁「中國威脅」論——史學、政治學與法學的視角

——讀陳安教授《中國的吶喊》第四章

張祥熙*

《美國霸權版「中國威脅」讕言的前世與今生》是教育部立項遴選和定向約稿的哲學社會科學研究優秀成果普及讀物之一，由江蘇人民出版社二〇一五年出版。全書從史學、法學和政治學的三維角度，綜合地探討和剖析「中國威脅」論的古與今、點與面、表與裡。本書可視為陳安教授二〇一三年在德國Springer出版社出版的英文專論*The Voice of China: An CHEN on International Economic Law*第四章的最新詳細擴展。

該書的基本內容原是作者二〇一一至二〇一二年相繼發表於中外權威學刊的中英雙語長篇專題論文，題為《「黃禍」論的本源、本質及其最新霸權「變種」:「中國威脅」論》。發表以來，獲得中外學術界廣泛好評。該文的英文版本刊登於國際知名的日內瓦《世界投資與貿易學報》（*The Joural of World Ivestmett & Trade*），該刊主編Jacques Werner認為論文融合史學、政治學和法學，文章見解精闢，「讓我在審讀中享受到樂趣，因此樂於儘快採用此文」。隨即在該刊二〇一二年第一期作為首篇重點論文刊出，篇幅達五十八頁，占該期三分之一以上。數

十年來投身於「南南合作」事業的國際活動家、原「南方中心」秘書長Branislav Gosovic先生撰寫專文對論文給予高度評價，認為它「乃是一篇力排『眾議』、不可多得的佳作。這篇文章的確是一項研究與解讀當代世界政治的重大貢獻」，「分析透澈並且富有啟迪意義。我衷心期待：中國乃至其他發展中國家的領導人、決策者和智囊輿論人士們，都能閱讀並研究這篇文章，汲收其中的深刻見解和建議。對於那些想研究或理解當今中國與西方關係的人們來說，這也是一篇『必讀』文章」。

此書引起韓國出版界密切關注，一家出版機構已與江蘇人民出版社簽訂翻譯出版合同，預定二〇一七年推出韓文本。可以預期，其國際學術影響勢必逐漸擴大。

所謂的「中國威脅」讕言，喧囂迄今不止一百四十餘年，其直觀的表象即是以危言聳聽和蠱惑人心的話語，故意渲染、誇大、曲解中國各個方面的歷史和現狀，胡說中國會給西方帶來種種威脅。儘管這種罔顧事實的論調在實踐中一再被證偽，但是基於西方中心主義的視角的強權政治依舊存在和維護西方話語霸權的需要，「中國威脅」論並不會隨著時間的流逝而消失。學者們對於此種「真實的謊言」展開了各種研究與批判。廈門大學法學院陳安教授的《美國霸權版「中國威脅」讕言的前世與今生》一書無疑是這方面研究中的翹楚。

《美國霸權版「中國威脅」讕言的前世與今生》一書高屋建瓴，緊扣甚囂塵上的「中國威脅」論這一重大問題，嫻熟地運用跨學科的方法，探討了「中國威脅」論的來龍去脈，深刻理解其本源和本質，實現了由現實追溯歷史，又由歷史回歸現實的研究，提出了許多新觀點，為國家外交決策和對外交往提供了有益的參考。

誠如作者在書中所言，「以史為師，以史為鑑，方能保持清醒頭腦和銳利目光」[466]。正是基於其強烈歷史使命感，作者追根溯源，對「中國威脅」論的本源進行了由古及今、由點到面和由表及裡的全方位、多層次的系統考察和深入探討，釐清了「黃禍」論——「中國威脅」論的歷史演進進程，深刻指出當代「中國威脅」論就是十九世紀中後期一度甚囂塵上的俄國沙皇版的「黃禍」論和德國皇帝版「黃禍」論在新歷史條件下的「借屍還魂」。

在廓清了「中國威脅」論的前世與今生後，作者又進一步在歷史研究的基礎上，運用政治學研究的視角，對「中國威脅」論的實質進行了鞭辟入裡的分析論證。作者在查閱大量史料記載的基礎上正本澄源，指出西方人所認為的「蒙古人兩度西征對歐洲造成『黃禍』戰禍和威脅」的說法是於史無據之談。因為在中原大地建立元朝的蒙古統治者從未派兵入侵過歐洲，更遑論是講禮讓愛和平的中國漢人。緊接著，作者在分析了沙俄入侵中國、德國入侵中國和八國聯軍侵華，以及一九四九年中華人民共和國成立之後以美國為首的西方國家對中國推行的一系列敵視政策等歷史事實的基礎上，一針見血地指出，「黃禍」論——「中國威脅」論鼓吹者最慣用的伎倆是「賊喊捉賊」，威脅者自稱「被威脅」，加害人偽裝「受害人」，其實質乃是鼓吹「侵華有理」「排華有理」「反華有理」「遏華有理」，而鼓吹排華、反華和遏華，往往先導於和歸宿於軍事行動上的侵華。正因為如此，無論是「黃禍」論還是其後的「中國威脅」論，都只不過是西方國家在強權政治和霸權體系下自說自話的讕言。

作者運用法學研究的視角，分析其中蘊含的基本法理與和平內涵，有力地駁斥了「中國威脅」論這一「真實的謊言」。作者在考察了自漢唐至明朝中國對外經濟文化交流的大量史實後認為，中國人通過長期的獨立自主和平等互惠的對外經濟文化交往，既為自身經濟、社會和文化的進步起到了促進作用，也為全球經濟文化的不斷進步、共同繁榮和豐富多彩，做出了重大的貢獻。然而，鴉片戰爭之後，近代中國落後喪權、飽受欺淩。西方列強通過一系列條約的簽訂，迫使中國納入到由西方主導的資本主義殖民體系之中。中國的對外經濟交往，無論在國際貿易、國際投資、國際金融、國際稅收的哪一個方面，無論在國際生產、國際交換、國際分配的哪一個領域都須受制於列強，低人一等。弱肉強食的叢林法則顯露無遺。中華人民共和國成立之後，「中國開始在新的基礎上積極開展對外經濟交往，促使中國歷史傳統上自發的、樸素的獨立自主和平等互利的法理原則，開始進入自覺的、成熟的發展階段」。但「在這個歷史階段中，中國遭受兩個超級大國為首的封鎖、威脅和欺淩，中國依然是被威脅者、被侵害者，而包括美國在內的堅持殖民主義、帝國主義既得利益的列強，則仍然是無庸置疑的威脅者、加害者」。[467] 強權政治和叢林法則的影響也依然延續。正因為如此，冷戰結束之後，中國積極融入世界政治經濟體系，也迫切希望改變不公正、不合理的世界經濟體系。

中國要實現中華民族偉大復興的中國夢，需要努力營造一個長期和平穩定的國際環境，這就使得中國長期實行和平外交政策成了歷史的必然。但作者也不忘提醒我們，歷史發展之必然也猶如硬幣之兩面，既有順應歷史潮流的發展趨勢，也有悖逆歷史潮流的趨勢。美國長期推行侵華反華的政策也非歷史之偶然，這一點我們要有清醒的認識。例如，在美國支持下，菲律賓、越南等國在南海拋出的「中國南海威脅論」和日本拋出的「中國東海威脅論」，以及美國「亞太再平衡」戰略的推出就是最好的例證。這一歷史必然的總根源在於美國的帝國主義經濟體制。作者告誡善良的中國人切勿對「黃禍」論——「中國威脅」論的實踐後果掉以輕心，切勿「居安而不思危」或「居危而不知危」。

餘音尚未消散，我們的鄰國韓國某些當權人士就不顧中國的強烈反對，一意孤行要在韓國部署「薩德」系統。「薩德」探測距離最遠範圍遠遠超出防禦朝鮮導彈所需，不僅直接損害中國等國的戰略安全利益，也會破壞地區和全球的戰略穩定。不僅如此，韓國媒體也密集炒作「大國的報復」，認為中國對韓國施壓才剛開始。殊不知，韓國自身及其背後的美國才是這場風暴的肇事者，這不僅無助於東北亞局勢的緩和，而且極大地傷害了中韓關係，漁利的是美國。欣聞本書的韓文版將在韓國面世，希望韓國的領導人、決策者、智囊、輿論界人士，乃至普通學者、普通百姓都能好好閱讀此書，了解此書之富有洞見的觀點和建議，重新審視「薩德」部署一事，切勿利令智昏，做出搬起石頭砸自己的腳的事情。我想，這也正是此書重大現實意義的最好體現之一吧。

Rebutting "China's Threat" Slander from the Perspectives of History, Politics and Jurisprudence

—On Chapter 4 of Professor Chen's Monograph *The Voice from China*

"A Most Important Contributiontothis Kindof Researchat Present."

—Prof. B. Gosovic

Zhang Xiangxi*

The so-called "China Threat" slander has dinned in the Western world for more than one hundred and forty years. Its most commonly adopted form is by using of the scaremongering and demagogic words to intentionally pile up, exaggerate and distort various aspects of China's history and status quo, with an aim to create an illusion that China will bring threats for the West. Although this kind of facts-ignoring argument has been falsified repeatedly in practice, it will not disappear with the passage of time, as there is still need from the western center of power politics to maintain the western intellectual hegemony at the global level. Scholars have made a variety of research and criticism on this "living falsehood", and with its Chapter 4, this book is undoubtedly the top of such kind.

The basic contents of this Chapter is based on a previous Article published in the internationally renowned journal, i.e. *The Journal of World Investment & Trade*, entitled On the Source, Essence of "Yellow Peril" Doctrine and its Latest Hegemony "Variant"—the "China Threat" Doctrine: From the Perspective of Historical Mainstream of Sino-

Foreign Economic Interactions and their Inherent Jurisprudential Principles. For this 58-page article which accounted for more than a third of the whole issue's space, Jacques Werner, then Editor-in-Chief of that journal, noted its penetrating views, and "enjoyed reading it". Mr. Lorin S. Weisenfeld was happy to say that he found the work brilliant and fascinating, and it has pulled together a number of disparate areas for him and caused him to see things in a fresh light.

Mr. Branislav Gosovic, the former Secretary-General of the South Center, who has engaged in international activities for the cause of "South-South Cooperation" for decades, spoke highly of the article. He wrote in a review article that "it is stimulating to read such a rich and enlightening analysis coming from a developing country at a time when conformity, self-censorship or resignation vis-à-vis the reigning storyline is widespread in governments, the media, as well as the academia." And he "would like to see leaders, policy-and-opinion-makers, not only in China, but also in other developing countries, including those involved in Group of 77 and NAM activities, read and study Professor Chen's article and absorb the insights and conclusions presented by the author." Besides, "It is a 'must reading' for those who study or are trying to understand China-West relations of today. It helps one to appreciate China's sensitivities and reactions, as well as to grasp the Western, US-led, global, all-azimuth offensive against this country, of which the 'China Threat' intellectual construct, as a contemporary iteration of the earlier 'Yellow Peril' Doctrine, represents the overarching framework."

[468] So it can be expected that with the publication of this book, the academic influence of views the author put forward in the book will be bound to expand gradually at home and abroad.

This book holds tightly and makes a high level description of the rampant "China Threat", which is not only a historical issue, but also an important reality problem. The author sheds light on the roots, intellectual and policy antecedents, i.e. the "family tree", of the "China Threat" Doctrines by skillfully adopting the interdisciplinary approach from the perspectives of history, political theory and law. He also puts forward many new ideas and provides the beneficial reference for the national diplomatic decision-making and foreign communication. With great foresight and powerful writing, this book not only preserves the author's strong patriotic and sincere feelings, but also reflects his rigorous scholarly research attitude and profound knowledge.

As is stated in the book, it is only through taking the history as teachers and as mirrors can people keep sharp brain and incisive eyesight. Based on his strong historical sense of mission, the author is trying to carry out synthetic discussion and comprehensive dissection on the past and present, the points and facets, as well as the appearance and essence of "China Threat" Doctrine and clarifies the historical evolution process from "Yellow Peril" Doctrine to its new variant "China Threat" Doctrine. So in this book, the author profoundly points out that the contemporary"China Threat"Doctrine is nothing but a current"variant" under contemporary situations of the once clamorous "Yellow Peril"

Doctrine fabricated and preached by Russian Tsar and German Emperor in 19th century.

After making clear all the ins and outs of the "China Threat" Doctrine, the author further makes a thorough analysis on the essence of the "China Threat" Doctrine from both the historical and political perspectives. By consulting a large number of the original historical records, the author clarifies matters and points out that it is nonsense in the history that the twice Mongolian Westward March was the biggest "Yellow Peril" war and threat, because Yuan Dynasty of China had never sent a single soldier to invade Europe during its 98 years of existence. So the popular yet vague statements such as that "Yuan Dynasty of China sent a large army to invade Europe and caused Yellow Peril" did not accord to historical facts, let alone the Han Chinese people who are modest and courtesy and love peace. Then, based on the analysis of the Russian invasion of China, the German invasion of China, the aggression against China by the Eight-Power Allied Force and a series of hostile policies towards China implemented by the US-led western countries after the founding of the People's Republic of China, the author puts it succinctly that various versions of "Yellow Peril" Doctrine have been playing their customary trick of a thief crying "Stop thief", and its essence and core lie at the preaching and justification of invading into China, excluding Chinese, opposing against China and containing China; and such exclusion, opposition and containment always come before and lead to a final invasion. From these evidence it could be fairly put that both the "Yellow Peril" Doctrine and its new variant "China Threat" Doctrine are nothing more than a self-talking slander under the Western-system of power politics and hegemony.

Then the author utilizes the perspective of economic jurisprudence to analyze the basic and inherent jurisprudential principles and the real meaning of peace which is contained in the long standing mainstream of Sino-Foreign economic interactions, and refutes effectively that the "Yellow Peril" Doctrine and its new variant "China Threat" Doctrine are downright "living falsehood". Based on his thorough investigation into the development history of the long standing mainstream of Sino-Foreign economic interactions from the Han through Tang Dynasty and till to the Ming Dynasty, the author points out that just through their long-term external economic interactions of an equal and reciprocal nature, Chinese had made significant contributions towards the continuous improvement, common prosperity and colorful enrichment of global economics and culture.

However, after the Opium War, modern China had to surrender its sovereign rights under humiliating terms and suffered from bullying. And thus China was forced into the capitalist colonial system dominated by the West. In this case, because its political and economic sovereignty were severely damaged, China's external economic intercourse from whichever aspects such as international trade, international investment, international finance or international taxation, and within whichever domains such as international production, international exchange or international distribution were always in an involuntary and coerced condition, under others' control, at others'service. So China always suffered from humiliation of inequality, and it had to undergo unequal exchange and exploitation. The law of the jungle is exposed completely here.

After the founding of the People's Republic of China, China has begun to actively carry out foreign economic exchanges on the new base, and it would inevitably prompt the spontaneous and plain traditional principle of equality and reciprocity in its external economic intercourse shift to a conscientious and mature stage. But during this historical stage, new China had been blocked, threatened and bullied by various countries led by then two superpowers. China was still the country which was threatened and invaded, while the big powers including the U.S., who insisted on their colonial and imperial vested interests, were still the undoubted menacers and injurers. The influence of power politics and the law of jungle also continues till that time. As a result, after the end of the Cold War, China has been actively integrated into the world political and economic system, and is also eager to change the unfair and unreasonable world economic system.

In order to fulfill the Chinese Dream of achieving the great renewal of the Chinese nation, China needs to strive to create a peaceful and stable international environment for a long time, which makes it inevitable for China to unwaveringly follow the path of peaceful development and the win-win strategy of opening-up.

The author does not forget to remind us that the trees may prefer calm but the wind will not subside. The development of world history is just like a coin of two sides, with one complying with the tide of historical development, and another rebelling against the historical trend. The author told us that we should have a clear understanding that it is not the accident of history for U.S. to implement the long-term anti-China policy. Supported by the United States, for example, the Philippines, Vietnam and other countries have been vigorously preaching one after another the Doctrines of "China Threat in the South China Sea" and "China Threat in the East China Sea", and the United States having launched the strategy of "Asia Pacific Rebalancing" are all the best examples. The behaviors of the United States are rooted in its imperialist economic system. So the author has warned the kind and forgiving Chinese people must not treat the practice consequences of the "Yellow Peril" Doctrine and its new variant "China Threat" Doctrine lightly, and must prepare for danger in times of safety.

What the author warned has not been dissipated. Our neighbor, the Republic of Korea, disregarding the strong opposition from China, decided to deploy "THAAD" in South Korea. The furthest detecting distance range of "THAAD" is far beyond the needs of defense of North Korea's missile. Such decision not only directly harms the strategic security interests of the neighboring countries such as China, but also directly damages the regional and global strategic stability. Not only that, the medias in South Korea also densely hype the views of "revenge from the great power", and assume that the pressures putting on the South Kore from China has only just begun. However, South Korea and the United States behind him are just the troublemakers of the tense situation. The deployment of "THAAD" will not help to ease the tension as among northeast Asian region, while on the contrary, it would cause great damage to the Sino-South Korean relationship, with the United States being the only one profiting therefrom.

If the leaders, policy-makers, and also the common people in South Korea have a chance to read and study this book and absorb the insights and conclusions presented by the author, and reexamine closely the deployment of "THAAD", there is a reason to believe that South Korea will not be blinded by lust for "THAAD", and decides to lift a rock only to drop it on its own feet.

二十二、論國際經濟法的普遍性

——評《中國的吶喊：陳安論國際經濟法》

中川淳司*

國際經濟法是從什麼時候開始具有普遍性的？時至今日，世界貿易組織（WTO）的成員方業已超過一六〇個[469]，雙邊投資協定（bilateral investment treaties，以下簡稱「BIT」或「BITs」）的總數已接近三千個[470]，因此，現在還提出這個問題，多少會顯得有些奇怪。然而，如果把時鐘回撥到三十年前的一九八七年，這個問題的回答和今天的答案就迥然不同，而絕不僅僅是修辭上的差異。在一九八七年，WTO還不存在，其前身「關稅及貿易總協定」（GATT）所舉行的曠日持久的第八回合多邊貿易談判（即「烏拉圭回合」）也是一九八六年才正式開始。在一九八七年，GATT的締約方僅有九十一個。時值冷戰末期，包括蘇聯、中國在內的社會主義陣營國家大多數並沒有加入GATT[471]。BITs在一九八七年時的總數也只有約三百個[472]，而且大多是在西歐發達國家和發展中國家之間締結的。第二次世界大戰後，東西方國家之間的冷戰很快表面化，在此國際背景下，構成當代國際經濟法主體的各種國際組織和國際條約，其成員方／締約國幾乎全部都是西方的資本主義國家以及某些發展中國家，而絕大部分社會主義國家並沒有參加這些國際組織和國際條約。這意味著，國際經濟法獲得當今這種普遍性可以說是直到冷戰結束之後才開始形成的。

對於各個社會主義國家來說，冷戰結束意味著其國內的經濟體制需要引人與市場經濟相適應的新制度。與此同時，在對外戰略上，意味著需要正式加入之前由資本主義國家和某些發展中國家構成的國際組織和國際條約。對於社會主義各國來說，如何實行國內體制改革和承擔新的國際義務，是需要仔細研究的課題。然而，對於國際經濟法學來說，更重要的研究課題是，在冷戰結束後國際經濟法普遍化的過程中，國際經濟法發生了何種變化？

在思考這個問題時，以中國的經歷為視角進行研究具有以下重大意義：第一，中國經歷了國內體制改革以及承擔了新的國際義務，是體驗冷戰結束後國際經濟法普遍化的當事國之一。在鄧小平理論的指導下，一九七八年十二月，中國共產黨第十一屆三中全會提出「改革開放」的國策，決定由社會主義計劃經濟體制向市場經濟體制轉變。從此以後，與國內各項制度改革同時進行的，是對外開放政策的逐步推進。一九八六年，中國向GATT提出了「復關」申請，經過十五年多的談判，於二〇〇一年十一月正式加入WTO。在這個過程中，中國以一九八二年三月與瑞典締結BIT為開端，到二〇一七年二月為止，共締結了一三二件BITs。〔473〕第二，以加入WTO和締結BITs為象徵，意味著中國開始接受國際經濟法的制約，但並不是單單消極被動地接受原有的以資本主義各國和某些發展中國家為主體的國際組織和國際條約。正如Lim和Wag等人所指出的〔474〕，在與中國加入WTO同時開始的WTO多哈回合會議上，中國已逐漸代表發展中國家與歐美等發達國家形成對峙。相比於過去GATT時代的多邊貿易談判以主要發達國家的合意為主而推進，如今WTO多邊貿易談判的力量對比關係已經發生了變化。發生這種變化的決定因素之一，實際上就是因為中國的加入。這意味著，比起中國成為當今國際社會關注的焦點，以冷戰結束後國際經濟法的普遍化過程及由此帶來的變化為背景，中國更是思考和觀察國際經濟法未來發展前景的非常有益的基點。在這種歷史背景下，本篇書評鄭重推薦陳安教授於二〇一三年在德國Springer出版社出版的《中國的吶喊：陳安論國際經濟法》一書，這部專著收輯的多篇論文便是思考國際經濟法未來發展前景的最好素材。

陳安教授是中國國際經濟法學界的資深前輩、第一代國際經濟法學研究的代表人物。陳安教授一九二九年生於福建省福安市，一九五〇年從廈門大學法學院畢業後留校任教，一九五三年遵從當時中國的高等學校院系調整政策方針，研究方向改為馬克思列寧主義。中國實行改革開放國策後，陳安教授一九八〇年調回復辦的廈門大學法學院再次擔任法學教授，一九八一年至一九八三年應邀在哈佛大學法學院進行國際經濟法研究。一九九九年從廈門大學退休後，作為名譽教授接受返聘，繼續從事學術研究和博士生論文指導的工作。從一九九三年至二〇一一年，他被連續推舉擔任中國國際經濟法學會會長。二〇〇八年，陳安教授關於國際經濟法學的研究成果整理匯輯為五卷本系列專著，由複旦大學出版社出版發行。本篇書評所評析的《中國的吶喊：陳安論國際經濟法》這部英文專著，是陳安教授精選的關於國際經濟法學的代表作論文集，收集匯輯了從一九八四年至二〇一二年他撰寫的二十四篇論文，分列以下六部分：

第一部分當代國際經濟法的基本理論（論文一至論文三）

第二部分當代國家經濟主權的「攻防戰」（論文四至論文五）

第三部分中國在構建當代國際經濟新秩序中的戰略定位（論文六至論文八）

第四部分當代國際投資法的論爭（論文九至論文十二）

第五部分當代中國涉外經濟立法的爭議（論文十三至論文十九）

第六部分若干涉華、涉外經貿爭端典型案例剖析（論文二十至論文二十四）

限於篇幅，本篇書評無法對上述全部論文進行評析，而只能通過對各組成部分主要論文的介紹，以期讓陳安教授關於國際經濟法學的精華觀點浮現於世人眼前。

《中國的吶喊》第一部分收錄了三篇論文。（一）《論國際經濟法學科的邊緣性、綜合性和獨立性》（1991年第一次發表），論證國際經濟法的定義和調整物件；（二）《對中國國際經濟法學科發展現狀的幾種誤解》（1991年第一次發表），論證國際經濟法的獨立性；（三）《「黃禍」論的本源、本質及其最新霸權「變種」》（2012年第一次發表），尖銳批判當今甚囂塵上的「中國威脅」讕言。

論文一涉及的是國際經濟法的定義和調整物件，介紹了國際經濟法的「狹義說」，即認為國際經濟法只是用以調整國際經濟關係的國際公法的一個新分支；[475] 國際經濟法的「廣義說」，即認為國際經濟法乃是調整跨國經濟關係的國際公法、國際私法、國內經濟法以及國際慣例（軟法）的總和。[476] 接下來，陳安教授從跨國經濟關係多數由各種私人主體（非國家主體）承擔的現實出發，以求真務實致用（practicalities, starting from the reality, seeking truth from facts）哲學為基礎，對「廣義說」進行了論證和支持。雖然說「廣義說」是美國國際經濟法學界的主流學說，但陳安教授並沒有無條件地接受這一學說。例如，二〇〇二至二〇〇八年，美國Lowenfeld教授發表了新版的國際經濟法教科書，其中對《各國經濟權利和義務憲章》（1974年）的法律效力給予了極低評價，陳安教授對Lowenfeld教授的這種看法進行了批判，根據二三十年來的事實，指出《各國經濟權利和義務憲章》在二〇〇二至二〇〇八年當時在國際社會中已經獲得廣泛的承認，已經形成了共同的法律確信效力（opinio juris communis）。[477]

論文一的立場，係從求真務實致用的角度出發，深刻領悟國際經濟法的真諦，從中國的實際出發，站在發展中國家的立場，批判由發達國家所宣導的各種錯誤觀點。其實，論文一所持的這種立場，也是貫穿《中國的吶喊》一書始終的立場。

《中國的吶喊》第二部分中的論文四探討當代國家經濟主權的「攻防戰」（2003年第一次出版），剖析WTO成立前美國國內進行的「1994年主權大辯論」（The Great 1994 Sovereignty Debate）；剖析圍繞著美國貿易法「301條款」引起的WTO爭端案件；剖析圍繞美國的鋼鐵產業保護措施引起的WTO爭端案件。通過這些剖析，對美國為堅持自己的貿易主權而不惜損害WTO多邊貿易體制進行了批判。

「1994年主權大辯論」是指一九九四年WTO成立前夕美國國會對《烏拉圭回合協定》文本的採納與否而引發的「WTO爭端解決程式是否會損害美國主權」的爭論。[478] 依據烏拉圭回合所通過的《關於爭端解決規則與程式的諒解書》，WTO的爭端解決機構（DSB）有權設立爭端解決專家小組，而且專家小組報告和上訴機構報告的通過均採取「反向協商一致」（negative consensus）決策原則，幾乎就是賦予上述報告自動通過的法律效力。美國許多議員擔心這會因此損害美國的主權。對於這些擔心，美國John Jackson教授作了如下的解釋和「澄清」：依據美國法律，《WTO協定》在美國並不具有自動執行力，WTO專家小組報告和上訴機構報告同樣如此，如果要執行這些報告，需要美國國會的立法授權；當美國國會不希望執行WTO專家小組報告和上訴機構報告時，根據美國憲法，美國政府仍然有權貫徹執行自己的意志。最壞的情況下，美國還可以退出WTO（參見

《WTO協定》第15條第1款）從而不需要承擔《WTO協定》中的義務。

通過剖析Jackson教授的以上觀點，陳安教授敏銳地發現美國對於其主權（實為霸權）有著強烈的教義信條（creeds）。[479]因此，在美國已經批准加入《WTO協定》後，美國國會仍然維持和推行其貿易法301條款，以此經常單方面啟動貿易制裁措施（如1995年美日汽車摩擦案、1998年美歐香蕉案）。在美歐香蕉案中，歐共體針對美國的單邊措施申請設立的WTO專家小組發布報告認為，美國貿易法301條款雖然乍一看是違反了《WTO協定》，但美國政府在通過《烏拉圭回合協定》時作出的《政府行政聲明》（Statement of Administrative Action, SAA）中，表明了其承諾限制301條款實施從而確保《WTO協定》一致性的意願。陳安教授雖然對此表示了一定程度上的理解，但是對於該專家小組報告抑制美國單邊主義措施不力給予了尖銳的批評。[480]在這之後，在美國鋼鐵保障措施案中WTO專家小組裁定美國敗訴，被看作是多邊主義初步小勝。[481]

《中國的吶喊》第三部分（論文六至論文八）論述了中國在構建當代國際經濟新秩序（NIEO）中的戰略定位，這些論文為考察中國的參與給國際經濟法的組織與條約體制帶來怎樣的變化，提供了最為合適的素材。在此，我介紹一下概述中國在國際經濟新秩序中立場的論文六（2009年第一次出版）。在論文的開頭，陳安教授論證了從國際經濟舊秩序（OIEO）發展到國際經濟新秩序的「6C軌跡」或「6C律」，即矛盾（Contradiction）→衝突或交鋒（Conflict）→磋商（Consultation）→妥協（Compromise）

→合作（Cooperation）→協調（Coordination）→新的矛盾（Contradiction New）之「螺旋式上升」發展路徑[482]並且主張：中國作為和平崛起中的全球最大的發展中國家，應該致力於遵循以上路徑，為促進實現國際經濟新秩序而發揮重大的歷史作用，實現和平崛起的目標。從一九五五年不結盟各國首腦會議（「萬隆會議」）開始，經由一九七四年《建立國際經濟新秩序宣言》，直至現在確立的WTO體制，陳安教授強調在國際經濟法的上述發展進程中，中國應當強化發展中國家的地位，同時積極促進發展中國家之間的協作互助，成為「南南聯合自強」的驅動力量和中流砥柱。[483]

論文七（2006年第一次發表）論述了在WTO多哈回合談判過程中，以中國與印度、巴西為軸心的發展中國家所開展的團結合作，並闡明了陳安教授提倡的實現國際經濟新秩序的中國積極戰略。

《中國的吶喊》前面三個部分論文的探討焦點，集中於國際經濟法學一般理論和以WTO法為核心的國際貿易法。第四部分則主要探討國際投資法。論文九（2006年第一次發表）論述了中國簽訂的BITs中的爭端解決條款。該文發表時，中國已經締結了一一二部BITs，但是在投資爭端交付國際仲裁解決程式上仍然秉承嚴肅認真和慎之又慎的立場。經過多年的調查研究、政策諮詢和審慎考慮，中國直到一九九〇年二月才簽署了《華盛頓公約》，事後又經過三年的權衡利弊，才於一九九三年一月七日正式批准公約。在這之前，雖然中國簽訂的BITs中已有關於發生投資爭端可以提交國際仲裁的條款，但是並沒有規定具體的程式。

即使在之後中國簽訂的BITs中，依舊採取了限制提交ICSID仲裁的案件範圍，即僅限於東道國對投資者財產的徵用補償爭端才可以提交ICSID仲裁。論文九還剖析了美國二〇〇四年BIT範本和加拿大二〇〇四年BIT範本中關鍵性的投資爭端解決條款，並探討了中國是否應該採用同樣的規定。當時國際流行的大多數BITs都規定，對於外國投資者與東道國無法通過協商解決的所有投資爭端，都允許外國投資者將爭端提交國際仲裁。但是，陳安教授認為：這種條款反映的是作為資本輸出國的發達國家權益，中國是資本輸入國，採用此條款需要相當慎重。他建議，在談判締結BITs時，包括中國在內的發展中國家就投資爭端解決問題應當堅持設置四大「安全閥」即應該承認東道國享有（一）就是否提交國際仲裁的逐案審批同意權，（二）當地救濟優先權，（三）東道國法律優先適用權，（四）國家重大安全例外權。[484]

此論文公開發表於二〇〇六年，當時，中國已經不是單純的資本或者投資輸入國，因為第十一個五年規劃（2001-2005年）以來，中國開始採取積極的對外投資的戰略（即「走出去」政策），如果總是從淨資本輸入國立場考量條約規定似乎已不合時宜。但是，陳安教授根據二〇〇四年底的官方統計數字，指出中國對外直接投資的總量（潛在債權）對比外國在華投資的總量（潛在債務），幾乎「微不足道」其比率約為百分之四點五比百分之九十五點五，因此，改變上述保留四大「安全閥」方針，為時尚早。[485]同時，文章以阿根廷為前車之鑑，說明了其「不慎放權導致如潮官司」，再次主張對投資爭端交付國際仲裁應該繼續採取慎重之方針。在本篇論文中，陳安教授基於求真務實致用的理念，考量當時中國仍然主要作為投資輸入國的現實，其立論基調與前述第一至三部分多篇論文是一脈相承、一以貫之的。與此同時，鑒於將來中國的對外投資比重可能提高，本篇論文預期，日後中國對待投資爭端交付國際仲裁的方針，也可能隨之改變。從這個意義上說，陳教授的立場並不是教條主義，而是求真務實致用的。換言之，將求真務實致用在更長的時間維度上延伸，日後中國與接受中國投資的發展中國家簽訂的BITs，可以引人把投資爭端交付國際仲裁的條款；旦中國與作為資本輸出國的發達國家簽訂的BITs，則仍應繼續維持慎之又慎、保留四大「安全閥」的方針。論文十（2007年第一次發表）再次提倡採取這種「區別對待」的辦法。

《中國的吶喊》第五部分收錄了與中國制定的涉外經濟法相關的七篇論文。本篇書評介紹論文十六（1990年第一次發表）。這篇論文以經濟特區和沿海開放城市為例，論述當時的中國經濟發展和立法框架。需要注意的是，這篇論文發表於一九九〇年。中國在一九七八年實行改革開放政策後，一九八〇年開始依次設立了深圳、珠海、汕頭、廈門、海南（1988年）五個經濟特區（SEZs）。一九八四年進一步開放大連、天津、上海等十四個沿海城市（COPOCIs），一九八五年以後設立珠江三角區、長江三角洲等沿海經濟開放區（CEOAs），逐步推進經濟改革政策。但是，因為「1989年政治風波」中國遭受很多國家的嚴厲指責，改革開放政策被迫一時中斷。陳安教授於此時機執筆撰寫此文，顯然懷有向國內外宣告設立經濟特區、沿海開放城市等開放政策之正當性的意圖。當時中國國內有這樣一種聲音，即批判改革開放政策係戰前「租界」死灰復燃。面對這種質疑，陳安教授認為無論從其目的（實現社會主義現代化），還是中國政府對於外國在華投資的管轄權來看，這些開放政策與曾經的「租界」都迥然不同。[486] 此文對改革開放政策實施十年以來中國國內外投資的飛躍性增長給予了高度評價。對於階段性、漸進性開放進程中伴生的腐敗現象，陳教授也讚揚了中國當局所堅決採取的懲治措施。論文接著從法律角度對經濟特區這類開放政策進行詳細解讀，其目的是為了提升因政治風波而削弱的外國對華投資熱情。這與《中國的吶喊》第五部分收錄的從法律角度闡明中國對外經濟政策的其他各篇英文論文具有共通之處。例如，論文十八（1997年第一次發表）對中國《仲裁法》（1994年頒布1995年實施）的剖析，論文十九（2005年第一次發表）對中國承認、執行外國仲裁裁決的國內法令的剖析。

《中國的吶喊》第六部分收錄了對在華投資糾紛仲裁若干案件的評論和剖析。這是陳教授作為專家接受諮詢時撰寫的五份意見書和解說。本篇書評介紹的論文二十（2006年第一次發表），係應英國一家保險公司請求撰寫的、對被保險人的代位請求權的鑑定意見書。此案具體案情為，一家英國投資公司與中國公司合資設立電力公司，在中外合作經營投資合同中，約定向該英國投資公司保證付給投資額百分之十八的利潤。但是，根據中國國務院一九九八年第31號通知，禁止向外國投資者分配固定利率的利潤，導致該合同利潤分配條款無效，於是該英國投資公司認為這相當於英資被中國政府「徵收」，並依據中國的《仲裁法》提請仲裁，請求該英國承保的保險公司支付風險事故賠償金。陳安教授在鑑定意見書中認為，中國國務院通知的法律效力低於中國國內的制定法，《中外合作經營企業法》才是適用於本案的準據法。這就否定了變更《中外合作經營企業法》內容的國務院通知之法律效力。因此，在向英國保險公司請求代位求償前，應該慎重調查是否確因「徵收」產生相應損失。論文二十一（2006年第一次出版）是陳安教授對於英國保險公司再次諮詢問題的回答，他重申本案中採取的措施不是「徵收行為」，不應向該英國保險公司索賠。在這些鑑定意見書中，陳安教授對中國相關法律的解說清晰明快。此外，陳安教授在國際仲裁領域也發揮了相當大的作用。雖然在《中國的吶喊》這本書中沒有提及，但實際上陳安教授被中國政府指派為ICSID的仲裁員。二〇一一年陳安教授被辛巴威政府指定為兩件ICSID仲裁案的仲裁員，[487]這表明，在投資爭端仲裁實務中，中國政府非常信賴陳安教授。

以上介紹了《中國的吶喊》這部收錄陳安教授一九八四年以來撰寫的國際經濟法領域論文的英文著作的概要。如同本篇書評開頭提出的，冷戰結束後國際經濟法普遍化的過程中發生了什麼變化？解答這個問題，可以從陳安教授的這部著作中獲得啟發，這也正是我撰寫本篇書評的意圖所在。我認為：

第一，作為《中國的吶喊》這本書「一以貫之」的立論主張，中國加入國際經濟法的組織、條約體制，乃是中國推行改革開放政策的重要一環；同時，為進一步順利推進改革開放，中國必須對國際經濟法的內容有所權衡取捨，注意求真務實致用之基本取向。論文九最鮮明地表達了此種觀念。這篇論文中論證了引入投資爭端提交國際仲裁制度時，必須保持慎重態度。論文十則贊成在中國與吸收中國投資的發展中國家簽訂投資條約中，可以嘗試採用把投資仲裁提交國際仲裁的制度。論文七探討中國在WTO多哈回合談判中的戰略定位，論文一和論文二論證和肯定了國際經濟法之「廣義說」，也都同樣強調求真務實致用的取向。這是陳教授一以貫之的國際經濟法學理念。對中國來說，參與多邊貿易體制和締結BITs，一方面是向國內外表明中國堅持改革開放政策的承諾，同時也在促進外國投資和促進中國在國際貿易中的出口增長發揮了重要作用。但是，從計劃經濟體制向市場經濟體制轉變的過程，是一個伴隨著巨大的陣痛和各種摩擦的過程，因此在接納國際經濟法的過程中，也應力求確保這種漸進式的體制轉變得到應有的保障。本書中陳安教授貫徹始終的求真務實致用，是與中國的相關政策要求相吻合的。

第二，《中國的吶喊》清楚地表明，中國作為謀求和平崛起的最大發展中國家，堅決反對發達資本主義國家的專橫霸道。這一觀點在闡釋中國在建立國際經濟新秩序過程中的戰略定位的論文六中已有明確的表述。此外，在批判當今最大的霸權主義國家美國屢屢濫用單邊主義並將其淩駕於多邊主義之上的一系列論文中，也旗幟鮮明地表達了這一觀點。可見，陳安教授所提倡的國際經濟法的理念與美國的單邊主義是尖銳對立的。從這個意義上說，冷戰結束後的國際經濟法秩序的普遍化進程，實際上凸顯了自詡為「多邊主義代表」的美國，其實只是唯我獨尊的「自我中心主義者」。然而，不可否認，中國在多哈回合談判中的戰略導致了談判的長期化甚至停滯，造成多邊貿易體制有效性減損的後果。中國在加入WTO歷經十六年之後，現已成為全球最大的貿易大國。作為多邊貿易體制的最大受益者，中國難道不應該在謀求維持和發展該體制過程中發揮領導作用嗎？

現在，美國新任總統露骨地宣揚「美國第一」就任第一天就宣告退出TPP。與此相反，在二〇一七年的達沃斯會議上，中國的習近平主席宣導推進全球化。普遍化的國際經濟法今後將面臨兩個任務，一是抑制美國宣導的單邊主義，二是中國在全球化進程中如何發揮領導作用。與此同時，陳安教授在《中國的吶喊》這本書中一貫提倡的求真務實致用，也勢必會繼續引起全球學術界的廣泛關注和深入探討。

（翻譯：劉遠志，校對：李國安）

On the Universality of International Economic Law

—Comments on *The Voice from China: An CHEN on International Economic Law*

Ju j Nakagawa*

Since when has the international economic law (hereinafter "IEL") acquired universality? Nowadays, the World Trade Organization (hereinafter "the WTO") already has more than 160 members. [488] Meanwhile, the total number of bilateral investment treaties (hereinafter "BIT") has reached to around 3000. [489] So, it seems a little bit weird to raise such a question now. However, if we look back to 30 years ago in 1987, the answer to this question would be significantly different— and not only in the sense of rhetoric. In 1987, the WTO did not even exist, and its predecessor, the General Agreement on Tariffs and Trade (hereinafter "the GATT"), only began the time-consuming eighth round of multilateral trade negotiations (Uruguay Round) in 1986. Back then, the GATT had only 91 Contracting Parties. The Cold War was coming to its end, and most of the socialist countries, including the Soviet Union and China, did not join the GATT. [490] In 1987, the total number of BITs was about 300, [491] mostly concluded between developed countries in Western Europe and developing counties. The Cold War became worldwide immediately after World War II. In such an international context, the members/parties to international organizations and treaties, which constitute the majority of today's IEL, were almost always Western capitalist countries and some developing countries. Most of the socialist countries were not part of these international organizations and treaties. In other words, the universality of IEL as we see today was only established after the end of the Cold War.

For socialist countries, the end of the Cold War also implied the necessity to usher into their domestic economic systems a market economy model. In terms of international strategies, this means that the socialist countries needed to join the international organizations and treaties originally established by capitalist countries and several developing countries. How to conduct domestic institutional reforms and take new international obligations were two subjects that required careful research by these socialist countries. However, a more important subject for IEL is, what changes would be undergone by the IEL in its process of universality after the Cold War.

Taking this question into consideration, the study from the perspective of China's experience has the following significances: Firstly, China has undergone domestic institutional reforms and increasingly undertook new international obligations, and it is one of the many countries that experienced the universalization of IEL after the Cold War. Under the guidance of the "Deng Xiaoping Theory", in December 1978, the Third Plenary Session of the 11th Central Committee of the Communist Party of China put forward the national policy of "reform and opening up", and decided to change from the socialist planned economy system to the market economy system. Since then, the progressive opening up to the outside world was launched in parallel with its domestic institutional reform. In 1986, China applied to restore its identity as Contracting Party in the GATT. After more than 15 years' negotiations, China formally acceded to the WTO in November 2001. Since its conclusion of the BIT with Sweden in March 1982, China has entered into 132 BITs by February 2017. [492]

Secondly, the accession to the WTO and the conclusion of BITs means that China began to accept the binding force of the IEL, rather than to simply and passively accept the original international organizations and treaties dominated by capitalist countries and certain developing countries. In the WTO Doha Development Agenda, beginning in the same year as China's accession, China has gradually become the representative of developing countries and confronted the developed countries such as the United States and the EU. [493] Compared with the GATT era when the multilateral trade negotiations were promoted mainly by the intention of developed countries, the current WTO regime has seen a shift in negotiating powers. In fact, one of the decisive factors that has caused such shift was the accession of China. In other words, in the post-WWII context of the universality of the IEL and the accompanying changes, China serves as a very useful basis for observing and considering the future of the IEL. This should be more significant than simply regarding China as the focus of current international society. Under such circumstance, this Review strongly recommends the Chapters compiled within Prof. An Chen's book, *The Voice from China: An CHEN on International Economic Law*, published by Springer in Germany in 2013.These Chapters are the best materials and documents for considering the future of the IEL.

Prof. An Chen is the pioneer of Chinese scholars in the field of IEL in China and the representative figure of the first generation. Born in Fu' an City, Fujian Province in 1929, Prof. Chen graduated from the Law School of Xiamen University in 1950 and started his teaching career in that same University. Due to historical reasons, he shifted his research field from law to Marxism and Leninism in 1953. When the Law Department of Xiamen University was reestablished in 1980 as a result of China's reform and opening-up, he was appointed as professor of law. During 1981 to 1983, he was invited to conduct research on IEL at Harvard Law School. Although he retired from Xiamen University in 1999, he continued to teach as honorary professor and engaged in academic research and PhD student supervision. He was elected as President of the Chinese Society of International Economic Law during 1993-2011. In 2008, Prof. Chen's achievements on IEL were compiled into a five-volume collection, published by Fudan University Press. The current English monograph that this book review focuses on is actually a collection of Prof. Chen's English Chapters on IEL.24 selected and representative Chapters written during 1984 to 2012 are compiled in six parts:

Part I: Jurisprudence of contemporary international economic law (Chapters 1 to 3)

Part II: Great debates on contemporary economic sovereignty (Chapters 4 to 5)

Part III: China's strategic position on contemporary international economic order issues(Chapters 6 to 8)

Part IV: Divergences on contemporary bilateral investment treaty (Chapters 9 to 12)

Part V: Contemporary China's legislation on Sino-foreign economic issues (Chapters 13 to 19)

Part VI: Contemporary Chinese practices on international economic disputes (Case studies) (Chapters 20 to 24)

Due to length restriction, it is not possible to comment on all these Chapters. This review aims to show the essence of Prof. Chen's main viewpoints in IEL by introducing the major Chapters of each of the six Parts.

Part I contains three Chapters, including: Chapter 1"On the Marginality, Comprehensiveness, and Independence of International Economic Law Discipline"(first published in 1991) that discusses the exact connotation and denotation of the science of IEL, Chapter 2 "On the Misunderstandings Relating to China's Current Developments of International Economic Law Discipline"(first published in 1991), in which Prof. Chen agrees with the independence of IEL, and Chapter 3 (first published in 2012) that discusses the source, essence of "Yellow Peril"Doctrine and its latest hegemony"variant", and criticizes the"China Threat" Doctrine from a modern perspective.

Chapter 1 deals with the conception and the subject matter coverage of IEL. According to this Chapter, the "narrow interpretation" doctrine would consider IEL as a novel branch of public international law that only regulates international economic relations; [494] while the "broad interpretation" doctrine advocates that IEL refers to all legal norms regulating cross-border economic activities. [495] Then, starting from the reality that a variety of the cross-border economic intercourse with individuals, Prof. Chen advocates for the "broad interpretation" on the basis of the philosophy of practicalities. Therefore, he concludes that IEL generally refers to all legal norms that regulate international economic relations, comprising public international law, private international law, domestic economic law and soft rules that originate from international business practices. Even though the "broad interpretation" is the mainstream theory of American IEL scholars, Prof. Chen did not unconditionally accept this doctrine. For instance, in 2002-2008, Professor Andreas F. Lowenfeld published and reprinted a treatise titled International Economic Law, in which he gave a rather low evaluation of the legal force of the Charter of Economic Rights and Duties of States (1974), Prof. Chen criticized this opinion based on the fact that the Charter has won widespread recognition by international society and has already formed opinio juris communis. [496]

The position of Chapter 1 is based on pragmatic approach. It profoundly comprehends the connotation and denotation of IEL, supports the position of China as a developing country, and challenges the legitimacy of the viewpoints advocated from the standpoint of developed countries. In fact, the position of this Chapter is consistently adhered to this monograph. Chapter 4 (first published in 2003) of Part II relates to the Great 1994 Sovereignty Debate in the United States prior to the establishment of the WTO. It also discusses the disputes over Section 301 of the US Trade Act and US safeguard measures on imports of certain steel products under the WTO, and criticizes that the adherence of the United States to its own economic sovereignty had incurred damages to the multilateral trade system.

The Great 1994 Sovereignty Debate mainly refers to the nationwide discussion in 1994 prior to the establishment of WTO, when the US Congress was focusing on whether or not the United States should accept and implement the Uruguay Round results, and more specifically, "whether the acceptance of the WTO dispute settlement mechanisms was an inappropriate infringement on the United States'sovereignty." [497] According to the Understanding on Rules and Procedures Governing the Settlement of Disputes(hereinafter DSU) adopted at the Uruguay Round, the Dispute Settlement Body (DSB) shall have the authority to establish panels, adopt panel and appellate body reports under "reverse consensus", whereby reports are entrusted with the legal force of being adopted automatically. Many members of the Congress worried that the sovereignty of the United States would be impaired because of DSU. In addressing these viewpoints, Professor Jackson provided the following explanations and clarifications: WTO agreements will not be self-executing in US law, nor do the results of panel reports or appellate body reports automatically become part of U.S. law. Instead, the United States must implement the international obligations or the result of a panel report, often through legislation adopted by the Congress. In the case that the US Congress is not willing to execute panel reports or appellate body reports, the US Government still has the power to resist to adopt them under the US Constitution. In the worst case, the United States has the right to withdraw from the WTO, and thus need not bear its obligations under the WTO agreements.

By dissecting the viewpoints of Prof. Jackson, Prof. Chen keenly discovered that the United States had strong creeds on its own sovereignty. [498] Prof. Chen believes that is the reason for the US

Congress to still retain and enforce Section 301 of US Trade Act after its ratification of the WTO agreement. And the U.S. often unilaterally initiated trade sanctions (for example, the 1995 US-Japan Auto case, the 1998 US-EC Banana case). In the US-EC banana case, the WTO panel report concluded that although Section 301 seems to violate WTO agreements at the first glance, the US Government had demonstrated in its Statement of Administrative Action (SAA), which was made in the process of adopting Uruguay Round agreements, that it committed to limiting the implementation of Section 301 to ensure the consistency of WTO agreements. Prof. Chen expressed a certain degree of understanding of the panel report. Meanwhile, he criticizes sharply on its incapability of restraining the unilateral measures of the United States. [499] After that, in the US-Safeguard Measures on Steel Products case, the WTO panel ruled against the United States, which is regarded as the first minor victory of multilateralism. [500]

Part III discusses China's strategic position in the establishment of new international economic order (hereinafter "NIEO"). The book provides the most appropriate materials for examining changes brought by China's participation to the organizations and treaties of IEL. Here, I would like to introduce Chapter 6 (first published in 2009) on China's position in the NIEO. At the beginning of this Chapter, Prof. Chen demonstrates the "6C Trace" or "6C Rule" that leads the old international economic order (hereinafter "OIEO") to the NIEO. This path shows a spiral-up development, namely Contradiction→Conflict→Consultation

→Compromise→Cooperation→Coordination→Contradiction New.[501] Prof. Chen proposes that, as the largest developing country, China should be devoted to follow such development path, play an important role in the historical course of establishing the NIEO to realize the goal of peaceful rising. From the 1955 Summit of Non-Aligned Countries (Bandung Conference), through the 1974 Declaration on the Establishment of a New International Economic Order, to the final establishment of the WTO system, Professor Chen emphasizes that in the process of developing IEL, China should strengthen the position of developing countries and become one of the driving forces and mainstays for the establishment of the NIEO in joint effort with the South-South self-reliance through cooperation, that is cooperation between developing countries and mutual assistance.[502]

Chapter 7 (first published in 2006) demonstrates the coalition of developing countries, led by China, India and Brazil, in the process of the WTO Doha Development Round, and explains China's positive strategy on establishing NIEO as advocated by Professor Chen.

The first three parts of the book focus on the general theories of IEL and international trade law centering on WTO law. Part IV mainly concerns with international investment law. Chapter 9 (first published in 2006) discusses the dispute settlement provisions in Sino-foreign BITs (hereinafter referred to as the Chinese BITs). By 2006, China had concluded 112 BITs, and it still adhered to serious and cautious attitude on investment dispute settlement provisions. After many years' investigation, policy consultation and prudent thought, China signed the Convention on the Settlement of Investment Disputes Between States and Nationals of Other States (hereinafter referred as "ICSID Convention") on February 1990. After three years' of weighing the pros and cons carefully, China finally ratified it on January 7, 1993. Before that, although there were arbitration clauses that investment disputes can be submitted to the international arbitration in Sino-foreign BITs, no concrete procedures were set. Even in the BITs signed after 1993, China still restricted the scope of cases which may be submitted to ICSID, only to disputes concerning the amount of compensation for expropriation. Chapter 9 also devotes in examining some critical provisions concerning dispute settlement in the US and Canadian 2004 Model BITs, and discusses whether China should adopt the same rules. Most of the prevailing BITs provide that foreign investors are allowed to submit investment disputes between them and the host country for international arbitration if the disputes could not be resolved through settlement. Prof. Chen regards the above provisions as reflecting the rights and interests of developed countries or capital exporting countries. However, he argues that China, being a capital importer, needs to put special consideration on the adoption of such clause. Hence, he suggests that in the course of negotiating BITs, the host developing countries should stick to the following four "Great Safeguards", including (1) the right to consent to international arbitration on the case-by-case basis, (2) the right to require exhaustion of local remedies, (3) the right to apply the host country's laws as governing law, and (4) the right to invoke the exception for state's essential security. [503]

The above Chapter was published in 2006 when China could no longer be considered as merely a capital-importing country. Because since the eleventh five-year plan (2001-2005), China has begun to take active strategy promoting outward investment ("going-out" policy), it appeared to be no longer appropriate if China always concluded treaties from the position of a net capital importer. However, based on the official statistics by the end of 2004, Prof. Chen pointed that the ratio between China's outward investments (contingent credits) and its inward investments (contingent debts) is merely about 4.5% : 95.5%. Therefore, Prof. Chen thinks it is too early and too fast to change the policy. [504] Meanwhile, by taking lessons from the experience of Argentina, Prof. Chen explained that once a country loosens its jurisdiction imprudently, a tidal wave of litigations will follow. Therefore he asserted that China should take serious consideration again as to submitting investment disputes for international arbitration. In that Chapter, Prof. Chen still treated China as a major capital recipient, and continued to propose to make treaty based on practicalities. In this sense, the Chapter remains well connected with the foregoing Parts Ⅰ through Ⅲ. At the same time, in view that China's foreign investment proportion may increase in the future, he admits that the policy of investment disputes arbitration may also evolve. In this sense, Prof. Chen's position is not dogmatic, but practical. If we expand the philosophy of practicalities longer on the time dimension, investment arbitration clause may be prescribed in BITs between China and developing countries, but as to BITs between China and developed countries as capital exporter, we should remain prudent. Chapter 10 (first published in 2007) also advocates for this kind of a differential treatment.

Part V includes 7 relevant Chapters, relating to China's legislation on Sino-foreign economic issues. Chapter 16 (first published in 1990) is about the development and legal framework of China's Special Economic Zones and Coastal Port Cities. It is important to note that the Chapter was published in 1990.China adopted a basic state policy of reform and opening up in 1978. Since 1980, China has consecutively established the Special Economic Zones (SEZs) in Shenzhen, Zhuhai and Shantou in Guangdong Province, Xiamen in Fujian Province, and the entire province of Hainan (1988). In 1984, China further opened 14 Coastal Port Cities (COPOCIs) including Dalian, Tianjin, Shanghai. Since 1985, mainland China created the Zhujiang River Delta, the Yangtze River Delta etc., which were generally called as Coastal Economically Open Areas (CEOAs). The economic reform in China was progressively promoted, until it was temporarily interrupted, by the Tiananmen Event of 1989, to which China suffered from serious criticism from many countries. To write such an article as this Chapter at that specific historical background, Prof. Chen intended to declare the legitimacy of opening-up policy to set up Special Economic Zones and Open Coastal Port cities both at home and abroad. There was a voice in then China that criticized the reform and opening-up policy as "leased territories" or "concession". Faced with such challenge, Prof. Chen pointed out that the opening-up policy is completely different from the "concession" either from the policy's purpose (Socialist Modernization), or China's jurisdiction over foreign investment. [505] In addition, Prof. Chen praised highly to China's internal and external investment leap growth in the past ten years since the opening-up policy. With regard to corruptions occurred in the process of gradual opening-up, Prof. Chen also praised the anti-corruption measures taken by the Chinese authorities. Then the Chapter makes a detailed explanation on opening-up policy such as the Special Economic Zones from legal perspective, with a wish to promote the enthusiasm of the internal and external investments that had been weakened due to Tiananmen Event. This is in common with other Chapters in Part V that interpret China's foreign economic policy from a legal perspective. For example, Chapter 18 (first published in 1997) on China's Arbitration Law (issued in 1994, enforced in 1995), Chapter 19 (first published in 2005) on China's domestic law about acknowledgement and enforcement of foreign arbitral awards.

Part VI includes 5 comments and opinions, written by Prof. Chen as an expert when he offered consul service on investment arbitration cases in China. Chapter 20 (first published in 2006) is an "Expert's Legal Opinions" written upon the request by a British insurance company, regarding the subrogation right of the insured. The summary of the case is as follows: A British investment company and a Chinese enterprise established a power company, there were provisions of distribution of profit in the contractual joint venture (CJV) that constituted a guaranteed return in the ratio of 18% to the investment. But according to the State Council's Circular 〔1998〕 No. 31, a guaranteed fixed return to foreign investors in Sino-foreign joint ventures should be prohibited. Therefore, the provisions on distribution of profit in CJV were invalid and the British investment company claimed that the Circular constituted an act of expropriation. Then the British investment company initiated arbitration proceedings based on China's arbitration law, requested the British insurance company to pay insurance indemnity. Prof. Chen noted in the expert opinion that the legal effect of the State Council's Circular is lower than China's legislations. China's Contractual Joint Venture Law is the relevant governing legislation. Therefore, he denied the legal effects of the Circular that changed the contents of Contractual Joint Venture Law. Therefore, the British insurance company who insured the expropriation risk for British investment company should make careful investigation to check whether the covered risk has really happened and the assured has really suffered subsequent losses before relevant payment for subrogation claims.

Chapter 21 (first published in 2006) is the re-comments to the question raised by the British insurance company. Prof. Chen reiterated that the measures taken in this case are not "behaviors of expropriation", and the British investment company should not make subrogation claims toward the insurance company. In such expert's legal opinions, Prof. Chen explained Chinese law clearly as an expert on investment disputes in China. What's more, he has also played a considerable role in the international arena. Although it is not mentioned in this book, actually Prof. Chen is an arbitrator designated by the Chinese government in the panel list of ICSID, and was appointed as an arbitrator in two ICSID arbitration cases by the government of Zimbabwe in 2011. [506] It is indicated that in the investment arbitration practice, the Chinese government gives full trust to Prof. Chen.

Above offers a very concise introduction and summary of the Chapters written by Prof. Chen in the field of IEL since 1984. As the question raised at the beginning of this paper, what changes have taken place in the process of IEL's universality after the Cold War ended? It can be inspired by the Chapters of Prof. Chen. This is precisely also the intention of this review, which opines that:

Firstly, as the consistent stance of the book, China's accession to the organizations and treaty system of IEL is an important part for it to implement the policy of reform and opening-up. What's more, for the smooth progress of reform and opening-up, China has to weigh and balance different contents of IEL, and needs to pay attention to practicalities orientation. The most notable expression of this concept is included in Chapter 9, which recommends that China should maintain a cautious attitude when introducing the investment arbitration system.

Chapter 10 is in favor of the proposal of trying to introduce investment arbitration system into investment treaty between China and developing countries in which China has foreign direct investment. The same practicalities also appear in Chapter 7, which discusses China's strategic position in the WTO Doha Round negotiations, and in Chapters 1 and 2, which support "broad interpretation" concept of IEL. These are Prof. Chen's consistent views on IEL. For China, it means to show the promise of the reform and opening-up policy both at home and abroad when participates in the multilateral trading system and enters into BITs, in order to promote China's products export in the future. However, in the process of transition from the planned socialist system to the market economy system, accompanying by huge pains and frictions, China should try its best to seek safeguards in the gradual acceptance of IEL. Prof. Chen's practicalities throughout this book is in compliance with China's relevant policy requirements.

Secondly, as the largest developing country, China typically objects to the tyranny of developed capitalist countries on its road of "peaceful rise", a point clearly demonstrated in Chapter 6. Chapter 6 discusses China's strategic position in the establishment of NIEO, and criticizes today's biggest hegemonic power—the United States, who often takes unilateral measures over multilateralism. In other words, the ideas of IEL advocated by Prof. Chen are sharply opposite to the US unilateralism. After the Cold War, the process of universality of IEL highlights the fact that, the United States, although constantly praising itself as representative of multilateralism, is self-centered actually. On the other hand, it is undeniable that China's strategy has also drawn some criticisms, such as the cause of long-term or even stagnation of the WTO Doha Round, and the ineffectiveness of the multilateral trading system. After 16 years since its accession to the WTO, China has become the world's largest trading nation. As the biggest beneficiary of the multilateral trading system, shouldn't China play a leading role to maintain and develop the multilateral trading system?

The current President of the United States expressed a starkly view of "America First", and withdrew from the TPP on the first day he took office. On the contrary, in the Davos 2017 Conference, Chinese President Xi Jinping defended globalization once again. The universal IEL will face two tasks in the future: one is to curb the unilateralism advocated by the United States, and the other is how China should play a leading role in the process of globalization. Meanwhile, the practicalities advocated by Prof. Chen in the book *The Voice from China* will continue to attract wide concern and inspire deep discussion among the global academic circles.

（翻譯：劉遠志，校對：楊　帆）

国際経済法の普遍性について

— An Chen, *The Voice from China: An CHEN on International Economic Law*, Berlin/Heidelberg: Springer, 2013 を素材に

中　川　淳　司[1]

国際経済法（international economic law）が普遍性を獲得したのはいつのことだろうか？　WTO（世界貿易機関）の加盟国が160を超え，[2] 二国間投資条約（bilateral investment treaties, BITs）の総数が3000近くに達した今日，[3] この問いかけはいささか奇異に響くかもしれない．しかしながら，時計の針をわずか30年前の1987年に戻してみると，この問いかけは今日とは異なり，単なる修辞以上の意味があった．1987年にはWTOはまだ存在しなかった．WTOの前身であるGATT（関税と貿易に関する一般協定）の下で8回目に当たる多角的貿易交渉（ウルグアイラウンド）がその前年にスタートしていた．1987年時点でのGATTの締約国は91であった．東西冷戦の末期であり，ソ連，中国を初めとする社会主義諸国の大半はGATTには加わっていなかった．[4] 二国間投資条約の総数は1987年時点で約300であり，[5] その多くは欧州の先進国と開発途上国との間で締結されたものであった．第二次世界大戦後まもなく本格化した東西冷戦の下で，今日の国際経済法を構成する主要な国際組織や条約はもっぱら西側の資本主義諸国と一部の開発途上国を構成員としており，社会主義諸国の大半はこれらの国際組織や条約には参加していなかった．その意味で，国際経済法が今日の普遍性を獲得するのは冷戦終結後のことであるといえる．

社会主義諸国にとって冷戦の終結は，国内的にはそれまでの経済体制を改めて市場経済に親和的な諸制度を新たに導入することを意味した．それと同時に，対外的には，それまで資本主義諸国と開発途上国で構成されていた国際組織や条約に新たに加入することを意味した．国内の体制変革と新たな国際義務の受容を伴うこのプロセスを社会主義諸国がどのように通過したかは，それ自体として興味深い研究テーマである．しかし，国際経済法学にとってより重要な研究テーマは，冷戦終結後の国際経済法の普遍化の過程で国際経済法にいかなる変化がもたらされたかであろう．この問題を考える上で，中国の体験に焦点を当てることには以下の意義がある．第一に，中国は，国内の体制変革と新たな国際義務の受容を通じて，冷戦終結後の国際経済法の普遍化を当事者として体験した国である．中国は鄧小平の指導体制の下で，1978年12月の中国共産党第11期中央委員会第3回全体会議で改革開放政策を打ち出し，社会主義経済体制から市場経済体制への以降に踏み切った．それ以来，国内の諸制度の変革とともに対外開放政策を進め，1986年にはGATTへの加盟を申請，15年余りの交渉を経て2001年11月にWTOに加盟した．この間，1982

年3月にスウェーデンとの間でBITを締結したのを皮切りとして，2017年2月までの間に132のBITを締結している．[6] 第二に，WTO加盟とBITの締結に象徴される中国による国際経済法の受容は，資本主義諸国と一部の開発途上国で構成されていた国際組織や条約を単に受け入れるという消極的受容ではなかった．中国のWTO加盟と同時に開始されたWTOのドーハ開発アジェンダでの中国の交渉スタンスを克明にフォローしたLimらが指摘するように，[7] 中国はドーハ開発アジェンダで次第に開発途上国を代表して米欧などの先進国に対峙するようになる．GATTの時代の多角的貿易交渉が主要先進国の合意を軸として進められたのに対して，WTOの多角的貿易交渉の力学は変化しており，変化の一翼を中国が担ったといえる．その意味で，中国に焦点を当てることにより，冷戦終結後の国際経済法の普遍化の過程で国際経済法に生じた変化とその背景，さらには国際経済法の将来を考える上で有益な多くの知見が得られるだろう．そのための格好の素材となるのが，本稿で取り上げるAn Chen, *The Voice from China: An CHEN on International Economic Law*, Berlin/Heidelberg: Springer, 2013（lxiii+789pp.）である．

著者の陳安教授は中国の国際経済法研究の第一世代を代表する人物である．1929年福建省福安生まれ，1950年に廈門大学法学部を卒業して教職に就くも，1953年には当時の共産党政権の高等教育政策方針に従い専攻をマルクスレーニン主義に変えた．改革開放開始後の1980年に復活した廈門大学法学部で再び法学を教授するようになり，1981年から1983年にハーバード大学ロースクールで国際経済法の研究に従事した．1999年に廈門大学を定年退職するが，その後も名誉教授として教育，研究と論文指導を行っている．この間，1993年から2011年まで中国国際経済法学会の理事長を務めた．陳安教授の国際経済法に関する著作は2008年に著作集5巻にまとめられ，復旦大学出版社から出版されている．本書は陳安教授の国際経済法に関する代表的な著作を収録する論文集である．初出時期で1984年から2012年にまたがる以下の6部・24篇の論文が収められている．

第1部　国際経済法の理論（第1論文～第3論文）
第2部　国際経済法における主権論争（第4論文～第5論文）
第3部　現代国際経済秩序における中国の戦略的な位置（第6論文～第8論文）
第4部　二国間投資条約の多様性（第9論文～第12論文）
第5部　中国の対外経済法（第13論文～第19論文）
第6部　中国の国際経済紛争実践（事例分析）（第20論文～第24論文）

紙幅の関係で，全ての論文を取り上げて論評することはせず，各部の構成と主要な論文の紹介を通じて，陳安教授の国際経済法学のエッセンスを浮き彫りにすることとする．

第1部には3本の論文が収められている．国際経済法の定義と対象範囲を論じた第1論文「国際経済法学の周辺性，包括性と独立性について」（1991年初出），「中国の国際経済法学の発展に対する誤解について」論じ，その学問としての独立性を擁護する第2論文（1991 年初出），「黄禍論」の起源と本質を論じ，その現代的な表明として「中国脅威論」を批判的に論じる第 3 論文（2012 年初出）である．第 1 論文は，国際経済法の定義と対象範囲について，国際公法に限定する狭義説[8] と国境を超える経済関係を規制する国際法と国内法の総体と把握する広義説[9] を紹介する．そして，国境を超える経済関係の多くが私人によって担われている現実を的確に把握する必要があるというプラグマティックな理由から広義説を支持する．そして，国境を超える経済関係を規律する国際公法，国際私法，国内経済法，国際取引慣行から形成されたソフトなルールの総体で構成されるのが国際経済法であるとする．広義説は米国の国際経済法学における主流的見解といえようが，陳安教授はこれを無条件に受け入れるわけではない．例えば，Lowenfeld が 2002 年に刊行した国際経済法の教科書で諸国家の経済的権利義務憲章（1974 年）の法的効力について低い評価を下したことに対しては，同憲章は当時の諸国の共通の法的確信（*opinio juris communis*）を表明するものであったとして，これを批判する．[10]

第 1 論文のスタンス，すなわちプラグマティックな観点から国際経済法をとらえるとともに，開発途上国としての中国の立場を擁護し，先進国の立場から唱えられる見解の歪みを批判するというスタンスは，本書に通底するスタンスである．第 2 部の第 4 論文（2003 年初出）は，WTO 発足前の米国で戦わされた主権論争，米国通商法 301 条の発動をめぐる WTO 紛争，米国の鉄鋼セーフガード措置の発動をめぐる WTO 紛争という 3 つのトピックを取り上げて，通商問題に関する米国の主権と多角的貿易体制の関係を批判的に論じる．主権論争とは，WTO 発足直前の 1994 年に米国議会でウルグアイラウンド協定法の採択に際して戦わされた「WTO の紛争解決手続に服することで米国の主権が損なわれることになるか」をめぐる論議を言う．[11] ウルグアイラウンドで採択された紛争解決了解により，WTO の下では紛争解決小委員会の設置，小委員会報告・上級委員会報告の採択がネガティブ・コンセンサス方式により半ば自動化された．これにより米国の主権が損なわれるのではないかとの意見に対して，Jackson 教授は以下の通り反論した．WTO 協定は米国法上で自動執行力を持たない．小委員会報告・上級委員会報告も同様であり，これらを実施するためには議会の立法措置が必要である．議会が小委員会報告・上級委員会報告の実施を望まない場合，米国憲法上議会はその意思を貫徹する権限を有する．最悪の場合，米国は WTO から脱退することで WTO 協定上の義務から離脱することもできる．陳安教授は，Jackson 教授のこの説明に主権に対する米国の強い信念（creed）を見出す．[12] そして，米国議会が WTO 発足後も通商法 301 条を維持し，一方的な発動を行ったこと（1995 年の日米自動車摩擦に際しての発動，1998 年の EU バナナ紛争に際しての発動）をもって，その現われとする．後者の発動に対して EU が行った WTO 申立てを扱った小委員会報告は，301 条の文言は一見すると WTO 協定に違反するが，米国行政府がウルグアイラウンド協定法の採択に際して行った行政府行動宣言（SAA）で WTO 協定整合的な 301 条の実施を約束したことにより，WTO 協定との整合性が担保されたと判断した．陳安教授はこの小委員会報告の判断に一定の理解を示しながら，米国の一方主義を抑止する上では十分でないとして，詳細な批判を加える．[13] 他方で，その後の米国の鉄鋼セーフガード措置をめぐるWTO紛争で小委員会が米国敗訴の結論を導いたことに多国間主義の勝利を見出す．[14]

現代の国際経済秩序における中国の戦略的な位置を論じた第3部は，中国の参加で国際経済法の組織と条約体制にどのような変化が生じたかを考察する上で好個の材料を提供する．ここでは，現代国際経済秩序における中国の立場を総括的に解説した第6論文（2009年初出）を紹介する．論文の冒頭で，陳安教授は旧国際経済秩序（OIEO）から新国際経済秩序（NIEO）への以降が「6つのC」の螺旋的な発展という経路を辿るとの見方を示す．即ち，矛盾（contradiction）→対立（conflict）→協議（consultation）→妥協（compromise）→協力（cooperation）→新たな矛盾（contradiction new）という経路である．[15] そして，平和的台頭を目指す最大の開発途上国である中国は，以上の経路に沿って新国際経済秩序の実現に向けて尽力すべきであると主張する．1955年の非同盟諸国首脳会議（バンドン会議）から1974年の新国際経済秩序樹立宣言を経て今日のWTO体制に至る国際経済法の発展を踏まえて，開発途上国の地位の強化のために他の開発途上国とも協力しながら積極的な役割を果たすことを強調する．[16]

WTOドーハ開発アジェンダにおける中国，インド，ブラジルを軸とする途上国連携（coalition）の展開を論じた第7論文（2006年初出）は，陳安教授が提唱する新国際経済秩序の実現に向けた中国の積極的な戦略を解説したものである．

第3部までの論考が国際経済法学一般とWTO法を軸とする国際貿易法に焦点を当てたものであったのに対して，第4部は国際投資法を取り扱う．本稿では中国が締結した二国間投資条約における紛争解決条項について論じた第9論文（2006年初出）を紹介する．同論文の刊行時点で中国は既に112の二国間投資条約を締結していたが，投資紛争解決手続についてはきわめて慎重な立場を維持してきた．中国が投資紛争解決条約（ICSID条約に署名したのは1990年2月のことであり，条約の批准にはさらに3年を要した．それ以前に中国が締結した二国間投資条約では，投資紛争を国際仲裁に付託する可能性に言及する一方で，具体的な手続の定めは置かれなかった．その後に中国が締結した二国間投資条約においても，受入国による投資家財産の収用に対する補償をめぐる紛争についてのみICSID仲裁への付託を認めるという限定的な方針が採られてきた．第9論文は，米国の2004年モデル二国間投資条約とカナダの2004年モデル二国間投資条約の投資紛争解決手続に関する規定を検討し，中国が同様の規定を採用すべきか否かを論じる．いずれも，二国間投資条約が規定するあらゆる事項に関して生じた投資紛争が外国投資家と投資受入国の協議により解決されない場合，外国投資家が紛争を仲裁に付託することを認めている．陳安教授はこの規定を資本輸出国である先進国の利害を反映したものであると評価し，外国投資をもっぱら受け入れる立場にある中国が同様の規定を採用することには慎重であるべきと主張する．そして，投資紛争解決に当たっては，受入国に，（i）紛争の仲裁付託に当たっての同意権，（ii）国内救済原則，（iii）受入国国内法の準拠法としての適用，（iv）

核心的な安全保障に関わる紛争の適用除外という4つのセーフガードが認められるべきであると主張する．[17] この論文が公刊された2006年の時点で，中国は一方的な資本輸入国・投資受入国であったわけではない．中国は第11次5カ年計画（2001年～2005年）以来対外投資を積極的に展開する戦略（走出去）を採用するようになった．もっぱら資本輸入国としての立場から望ましい条約規定を提唱することには疑問なしとしない．これに対して，陳安教授は，2004年時点で中国の対内外国投資に比べて対外投資の比重はフロー，ストックともにきわめて小さいことから，上記の方針を転換することは尚早であると主張する．[18] それと同時に，国家債務の不履行をめぐり多数の投資紛争仲裁案件を提起されたアルゼンチンの事例を挙げて，投資紛争仲裁への慎重な方針を維持することを重ねて主張した．本論文における陳安教授の主張は，投資受入国としての中国の立場に配慮した現実的でプラグマティックなものであり，その姿勢は第1部～第3部を貫くプラグマティズムに通じる．それと同時に，中国の対内外国投資と対外投資の比重に言及したことを踏まえると，将来中国の対外投資の比重が高まれば，投資紛争仲裁に対する方針も変わりうることが想定されている．その意味でも，教授の姿勢は教条的でドグマティックなものではなくプラグマティックであるといえる．このプラグマティズムを延長すると，中国が対外投資を行う途上国と締結する二国間投資条約と中国が投資を受け入れる比重が大きい先進国と締結する二国間投資条約を区別し，後者では投資紛争仲裁への慎重な方針を維持しながら前者には投資紛争仲裁条項を採用するという方針が導かれるだろう．第10論文（2007年初出）はまさにこの意味での二重基準を提唱する．

第5部は，中国が策定した対外経済法に関する7本の論考を収める．本稿では，経済特区と沿海港湾都市に関する中国の制度の発展を解説した第16論文（1990年初出）を紹介する．この論文が刊行された1990年という時期には注意が必要である．中国は1978年の改革開放政策の開始後，1980年から順次，広東省の深圳，珠海，汕頭，福建省の廈門，海南島（1988年）に5箇所の経済特区（SEZs）を設置した．1984年にはさらに大連，天津，上海など14の沿海港湾都市（COPOCIs）を開放し，1985年以降は長江デルタなど沿海経済開放地帯（CEOAs）を設置し，開放政策を推進した．しかし，1989年の天安門事件で中国は諸外国から厳しい非難を浴び，改革開放政策は一時的に中断を余儀なくされた．このタイミングで執筆された本論文は，経済特区や沿海港湾都市などの開放政策の正当性を内外に示す意図があった．対内的には，開放政策が戦前の租界の復活につながるのではないかとの批判があった．本論文で陳安教授は，これらの開放政策が，その目的（近代化）から見ても，また外国投資に対する中国政府の管轄権の態様から見ても，かつての租界とは全く異なると主張する．[19] そして，開放政策開始以来の約10年間で中国の対内外国投資が飛躍的に増大したことを高く評価する．教授が特に評価するのは，段階的・漸進的に開放を進めるアプローチをとったこと，その過程で生じた腐敗に対して当局が断固たる対応をとったことである．論文は次いで，経済特区などの開放政策の法的側面を詳細に解説する．天安門事件で勢いがそがれた対内外国投資の再活性化を広く訴えることが狙いであった．中国の対外経済政策の法的側面を英文で解説するという狙いは第5部に収められた他の論文にも共通する．例えば，第18論文（1997年初出）は中国の仲裁法（1994年公布，1995年施行）の解説であり，第19論文（2005年初出）は外国仲裁判断の中国における承認・執行をめぐる国内法令の解説である．

第6部は対中投資に関わる仲裁等の紛争案件で専門家として意見を求められた著者が執筆した意見書や解説など5本を収める．本稿では，英国の保険会社の求めに応じて執筆された，被保険者の代位請求についての鑑定意見書として執筆された第20論文（2006年初出）を紹介する．事案は，中国会社との合弁で設立された電力会社に投資した英国企業が投資契約で投資額の18%の利益を保証されていたことに対して，外資合弁企業による固定利率での利益配分を禁じた国務院通知によりこの契約条項が取り消されたことが収用（expropriation）に当たるとして，同企業が中国仲裁法に基づく仲裁手続を提起し，英国の保険会社に保険金の支払を求めたものである．陳安教授は鑑定意見書で，国務院通知が中国国内法上制定法より低い効力しか認められていないとして，制定法である合弁法の内容を変更する趣旨の国務院通知の法的効力を否定した．そして，英国保険会社に対して，代位請求に先立って収用に当たる損失が生じているか否かを慎重に調査するよう勧告した．これを受けて英国の保険会社から追加の質問が陳安教授に出され，それに対して回答したのが第21論文（2006年初出）である．教授は本件措置が収用とみなされないことを重ねて説き，保険会社に代位請求を行うべきでないと説示した．これらの鑑定意見書における陳安教授の関連中国法の解説は明快であり，教授が中国の対内投資に関連する紛争処理において鑑定人として果たした役割の一端を伝える．本書には収録されていないが，陳安教授は中国政府により投資紛争処理条約の仲裁人候補者として指名されており，2011年にはジンバブエ政府により2件のICSID仲裁で仲裁人に任命されている．[20] 投資紛争仲裁の実務においても陳安教授に対する中国政府の信頼が厚いことを示している．

以上，陳安教授が1984年以降に執筆した国際経済法分野の論考を収録した著作の概要を紹介した．本稿の冒頭に掲げた，冷戦終結後の国際経済法の普遍化の過程で国際経済法にいかなる変化がもたらされたかという問いかけに対して，陳安教授の著作から得られる示唆を指摘して，本稿の結びとしたい．第一に，本書を通じて一貫する姿勢として，中国が国際経済法の組織と条約体制に参加することが改革開放政策の遂行にとって重要であり，かつ，改革開放政策の円滑な遂行に資する限りで国際経済法の内容を取捨選択するという，プラグマティックな姿勢が読み取れる．それが最も明瞭に現れたのは，投資紛争仲裁制度の導入に慎重な意見を述べた第9論文であり，中国が対外投資を行う途上国との二国間投資条約においては投資紛争仲裁制度の採用を考えても良いという二重基準を示唆した第10論文である．しかし，同様のプラグマティックな姿勢は，例えば，WTOのドーハ交渉における中国のスタンスを論じた第7論文，さらに，国際経済法の概念について国内経済法なども含めた広義説を支持した第1論文にも現れており，教授の国際経済法学を貫く一貫した姿勢といえる．中国にとって，多角的貿易機構への参加と二国間投資条約の締結は，改革開放政策へのコミットメントを内外に表明し，対内投資を盛んにして世界貿易における中国の輸出を伸ばしてゆく上で重要な役割を果たした．ただし，社会主義体制から市場経済への体制移行は大きな痛みと摩擦を伴うプロセスであり，国際経済法の受容に当たっても漸進的な体制移行を可能とするセーフガードを極力確保することが求められた．本書を貫く陳安教授のプラグマティズムは中国のこのような政策要求と整合的であった．

第二に，平和的台頭を目指す最大の開発途上国として中国をとらえ，先進資本主義諸国の専横には断固反対するという姿勢も明瞭である．この姿勢は現代国際経済秩序における中国の立場を総括的に解説した第6論文で表明されているが，最大の覇権国である米国がしばしば一方主義を多国間主義に優先させることを批判した一連の論考にも鮮明に現れている．陳安教授が唱える国際経済法の理念は米国の一方主義と鋭く対立する．その意味で，冷戦終結後の国際経済法秩序の普遍化は，多国間主義の担い手としての米国が抱える自国中心主義の矛盾を際立たせる意味を持った．他方で，WTOのドーハ交渉における中国の戦略が交渉の長期化と停滞を招き，多角的貿易体制の有効性を減じる結果をもたらしたことは否定できない．WTO加盟から16年を経て中国は世界最大の貿易国となった．多角的貿易体制の最大の受益者である中国には，この体制を維持し発展させる上での指導力を発揮することが求められるようになっているのではないか．

「米国第一」を露骨に唱える大統領が就任し，TPPからの離脱を通告した．ダボス会議では中国の習近平主席がグローバル化の推進を訴えた．普遍化した国際経済法の将来は米国の唱える一方主義の封じ込めと中国の指導力の発揮にかかっているように見える．本書で陳安教授が唱えたプラグマティズムの真骨頂が問われている．

（なかがわじゅんじ）

二十三、一部深邃厚重的普及讀物

——評陳安教授對「中國威脅」讕言的古今剖析*

徐 海**

大師寫小書以饗大眾

根據中央有關精神，二〇一三年起，教育部正式啟動規模宏大的「哲學社會科學研究普及讀物」的編寫與出版工程，動員全國高等院校一流的專家學者編寫通俗易懂、篇幅十至十五萬字左右的小書，內容涉及中國特色社會主義道路與中國夢、哲學、經濟學、政治學、法學、文學、史學、美學等人文和社會科學全方位領域。與一般意義的學術研究和科普讀物相比，教育部此項工程更側重對中國特色最新理論的宣傳闡釋，更強調學術創新成果的轉化普及，更凸顯「大師寫小書」的理念，努力產出一批弘揚中國道路、中國精神、中國力量的精品力作。所撰寫的作品必須具備相當的理論深度，同時又能深入淺出，推陳出新。這套叢書在強調理論普及的同時，特別注重對中國現實的高度關注。

誠然，歷代學富五車的鴻儒大師，不乏輝煌巨著，洋洋大觀。司馬遷的《史記》、司馬光的《資治通鑑》、馬克思的《資本論》……這些鴻篇巨製，即使多個世紀過去仍舊熠熠生輝。不過，縱觀歷史上的大量重要名篇，影響一個國家甚至世界多年的薄冊，也比比皆是，數量絕不亞於鴻篇。哥白尼的《天體運行論》、馬基雅維里的《君主論》、王國維的《人間詞話》、毛澤東的《論持久戰》……這些傳之久遠的著作，僅有不到十萬字左右的規模，有的甚至僅有四五萬字，《道德經》《金剛經》（鳩摩羅什譯本）只有五千字，儒家經典四書《大學》二千字，《中庸》三千字，《論語》一萬六千字，《孟子》只有三萬八千字。

媒體報導，鄧小平曾多次強調他反覆閱讀《共產黨宣言》，每每溫故而知新。一九四九年，百萬雄師突破長江天險，直搗國民黨南京「總統府」。在「總統府圖書室」，鄧小平與陳毅曾縱論旅歐經歷，都說是讀了《共產黨宣言》等啟蒙書的緣故，才走上革命道路。一九九二年，鄧小平在南方談話中又語重心長地對大家說：「我的入門老師是《共產黨宣言》。」有人計算過：這部迄今影響全球一七〇年的偉大經典著作，也只有一萬五千字左右。

借鑑中外歷史經驗，此項「大師寫小書」的出版工程，由教育部精心遴選，定向組稿，並授權委託江蘇人民出版社陸續推出。從目前已出版問世的四十餘本「小書」來看，基本體現了教育部的宗旨初心和嚴格要求。

題材獨特、思想深刻、旁徵博引、激情充盈

廈門大學陳安教授撰寫的《美國霸權版「中國威脅」讕言的前世與今生》，是這批已出版的「大師寫小書」中題材獨特、思想深刻、旁徵博引、激情充盈的作品，出版後深受廣大讀者歡迎，也引起了學術界的高度關注。該書不僅在一年內很快重印，而且引起了國際上的關注，海外出版公司即將翻譯出版。二〇一六年十月，在第十八屆全國社會科學普及讀物經驗交流會議上，這部小書被授予**「全國優秀社會科學普及作品」**榮譽稱號。

陳安先生係中國國際經濟法學界的泰斗，是享譽世界的學者。他鉤沉一四〇餘年的歷史，環顧世界發展進程的中外關係，窮本溯源，縱橫網羅，探究「黃禍」論的來源、表現形式、發生原因及本質特點。作者指出，今天「中國威脅」論其實是一百多年來「黃禍」論一以貫之的延續，是近代以來荒誕觀點的最新霸權變種。無論是歷史上的「黃禍」論，還是今日甚囂塵上的「中國威脅」論，本質上都反映了列強力圖殖民、侵略、污辱中國直至消滅中國的罪惡企圖，並通過編織和捏造這些讕言，欺騙世界，錯導後人，離間世上愛好和平的各國人民。

「黃禍」論肇始於近代史上中國最貧弱、中華民族災難最深重之時。當時的中國，內外交困、山河破碎、國門洞開。昏庸無能、專制腐敗的封建清朝政府對內為非作歹、窮奢極欲、盤剝百姓，對外卻卑躬屈節、軟弱無力，與列強簽訂無數喪權辱國的不平等條約，頻頻割地賠款，致使國家領土支離破碎，民不聊生。大量貧民被迫背井離鄉，近走南洋，遠逃北美，從事極端危險和困難的勞動，充當低賤「苦力」，築路開礦，寄人籬下，糊口謀生。他們備嘗艱辛，為所謂的「上帝選民」「高貴白人」做牛做馬，不但付出血汗，亦使家庭破碎，產生無數家破人亡悲劇。所謂的「高貴白人」不但不體恤遠走他鄉的華人的無奈與痛苦，更不深入探究他們這些「高貴白人」所在的列強侵略中國、掠奪中國財富也是導致中國貧民遠走他鄉糊口謀生的一個重要原因，反而時時恩將仇報，「卸磨殺驢」，誣衊黃皮膚的中國貧民為「黃禍」，欺騙和唆使白人勞工投入殘酷的排華、辱華、屠華活動。

陳安先生正是痛感昔日積貧積弱的舊中國同胞水深火熱的生

活，怒對列強當局及其御用智囊們肆意歪曲歷史、顛倒是非之無恥，遂在耄耋之年，進行深入專題研究，以深厚的學術功底，高屋建瓴，深入淺出，從史學、法學和政治學的三維角度，綜合地探討和剖析「中國威脅」論的古與今、點與面、表與裡，深刻揭露「黃禍論——中國威脅論」的來龍去脈。他指出：近十幾年來，美國某些政客、軍人和學者起勁地鼓吹的「中國威脅」讕言，日本右翼軍國主義者不遺餘力鼓噪應和的同類謬論，實則只不過是十九世紀中後期一度甚囂塵上、臭名遠揚的俄國沙皇版「黃禍」論和德國皇帝版「黃禍」論在新歷史條件下的最新霸權變種，它們之間的DNA，是一脈相承的。換言之，它們肆意歪曲和否定中國數千年來對外和平交往的歷史事實，賊喊捉賊，危言聳聽和蠱惑人心，只不過是為反華、侵華活動進行精神動員和輿論準備的「政治騙術」。

作者還依據大量歷史事實，揭示了美國立國前後四百年來向全球實行殖民擴張侵略的霸權行徑，提醒中國人民，切勿「居安而不思危」，「居危而不知危」；也提醒周邊鄰國，切勿忘恩負義，利令智昏，為美國霸權主義者火中取栗，以免自食其果。

本書的一大特色是，作者用心精選了極其生動鮮活的、與本書內容密切相關的一三七幀歷史圖片，穿插融入相關章節，並且不憚其煩，逐一作了大量腳註，說明所闡述的資料圖片的來源和出處，諄諄善誘地引導廣大青年讀者擴大閱讀面，增長知識，增強同仇敵愾之情。

作者運用大量事實，證明這樣一個重要結論：與「黃禍」論相反，自古以來黃皮膚的中國人從來不是「禍」，而是和平愛好者和對外交往的互惠者。新中國成立以來，特別是改革開放以來，中國結束了閉關自守的意識，努力做到與世界各國人民平等互利，一直是公正、合理的國際秩序的宣導者和執行者。

今天，經過改革開放三十餘年的拼搏發展，中國正在不斷崛起，已成為相對強大的國家。然而，我們極其遺憾地發現，伴隨著中國的崛起，當年西方列強刻意渲染「長辮醜惡」的中國人的形象雖然已一去不復回，但由「黃禍」論變種的「中國威脅」論，在二十世紀九〇年代卻又聒噪頻起，經過十來年的不斷大聲咆哮，近年來更是日益倡狂，並直接導致今日中國周圍「事件」不斷：美國霸權主義者與日本軍國主義者互相勾結，狼狽為奸，進行所謂「中國威脅」的反華大合唱，其險惡居心與侵華圖謀，猶如司馬昭之心，路人皆知！究竟誰是真正的威脅施加者？誰是真正的威脅受害人？太平洋何以如此不太平？何以時時濁浪排空，周邊雞犬不寧？「中國威脅」讕言後面的實質是什麼？細讀陳安先生的這部圖文並茂、雅俗共賞的優秀科普讀物著作，讀者自會找到最客觀、最科學的答案。

總之，我確信：《美國霸權版「中國威脅」讕言的前世與今生》既是一部歷史著作，又是一部現實作品；既是一部政治經濟著作，又是一部法律外交作品；既嚴肅深沉，又通曉暢達；既可作為培養和增強中國人民特別是青少年愛國主義情懷的讀本，又可向世界推廣，讓各國朋友認識一個歷史上和現實中的真實中國。謹此鄭重推薦，與廣大讀者共用。

A Profound but Popular Reading Material

—On the Anatomy of the "China Threat" Slander by Professor Chen

Xu Hai*

A Concise Book for the Public by a Great Master

In accordance with the relevant initiative by the Central Committee of the CPC, China's Ministry of Education has since 2013 launched a large-scale project for the redaction and publication of Popular Reading Materials on the Philosophy and Social Sciences. Top-ranking experts and scholars from institutions of higher learning across the country have been mobilized to write some concise books that are easy to understand, with a word count from 100 to 150 thousand. The contents cover almost all fields in humanities and social sciences, including the road of socialism with Chinese characteristics, the Chinese Dream, philosophy, economics, political science, law, literature, history and aesthetics, to name a few. In contrast with ordinary reading materials on academic research and science popularization, this project aims to produce a crop of excellent works advocating the Chinese road, the Chinese spirit and the Chinese power, by placing more stress on the publicity and elucidation of the latest theories with Chinese characteristics, on the transformation and popularization of innovative academic achievements, and on the idea of great master creating concise books. Not only with theoretical depth, but the works must also feature being explained in simple words and bringing forth the new through the old. This book series has prioritized China's reality while focusing on the popularization of theories.

Indeed, there were many great masters and learned scholars with spectacular works in the history of mankind, such as SIMA Qian's *Shih Chi* (Shi Ji), SIMA Guang's *History as a Mirror* (Zi Zhi Tong Jian), Marx's *Capital*, etc. These masterpieces have still been sparkling in the long process of human history after centuries of baptism. However, there were also a large number of famous articles or booklets that have over years been influencing a country and even the whole world at large. Like Copernicus's *On the Revolutions of the Celestial Orbiting*(De Revolutionibus Orbium Coelestium), Machinavelli's *The Prince*, WANG Guowei's *The Notes and Comments on Ci Poetry* (Ren Jian Ci Hua), and MAO Zedong's *On the Protracted War*, these long-lasting works are all below 100 thousand words, and some of them even with a word count of 40 or 50 thousand. Less still, *Tao Te Ching* (Dao De Jing) and *Diamond Sutra* (Kumarajiva version) has just around 5000 words for each. In addition, the Four Books on Confucianism, including *The Great Learning* (Da Xue), *The Doctrine of the Mean* (Zhong Yong), *The Analects of Confucius* (Lun Yu) and *Mencius* (Meng Zi), each has a word count of about 2000, 3000, 16000 and 38000 respectively.

It was reported that Mr. Deng Xiaoping on more than one occasion mentioned his experience of repeated reading of *The Communist Manifesto*, each time with a totally different new understanding. In 1949, millions of bold warriors of PLA strode over the Yangtze River and occupied the presidential palace of the Kuomintang (Chinese Nationalist Party) in Nanjing. In the library of the presidential palace, Deng Xiaoping and Chen Yi freely talked about their experiences in Europe and contributed their engagement in the revolution to such enlightenment book as *The Communist Manifesto.* In his south China tour in 1992, Deng Xiaoping addressed to the audience in sincere words and earnest wishes: "*The Communist Manifesto* is my first teacher in Marxism." This magnificent masterpiece which has been influencing the entire world for 170 years has, as calculated, only 15000 words.

Drawing lessons from historical experience both in China and abroad, this publication project of great master creating concise books has assigned the Ministry of Education to select qualified authors to write on designated topics and, has authorized the Jiangsu People's Publishing House to publish the works successively. Thus far, the already published more than 40 books have basically satisfied the original objectives and strict requirements of China's Ministry of Education.

Unique Theme, Profound Thoughts, Copious Arguments and Passionate Voice

The "China Threat" Slander's Ancestors & Its US Hegemony Variant, composed by Chen An, a professor of Xiamen University, was among the already published concise books. This book, with a unique theme, profound thoughts, copious arguments and passionate voice, has been highly popular and glued the attention of the academia. Reprinted within one year after its publication in China, this book has also aroused abroad interest and will soon be translated into English and published by an overseas publisher. In October 2016, this book was awarded as **"China's Excellent Popular Works on Social Sciences"** in China's 18th experience-exchanging meeting for popular reading materials on social sciences.

Mr. Chen An, a world-renowned scholar, is the leading authority in the Chinese academia of international economic law. In his book, Mr. Chen reviewed the Sino-foreign relations in the developmental process of the world history since 140 years ago and examined the origin, versions, causes and essential features of the "Yellow Peril" Doctrine by tracing its source and thorough search. He pointed out that the "China Threat" Doctrine today was actually the continuance of the "Yellow Peril" Doctrine some 100 years ago. It was nothing but a latest hegemony mutation inheriting the preposterous arguments in modern times. No matter the "Yellow Peril" Doctrine in history, or the rampant "China Threat" Doctrine today, they both in essence reflected the vicious intention of the imperialist powers to colonize, invade, ravage and even destroy China. They intended, by fabricating these slanders, to deceive the world, mislead the posterity and alienate the peace-loving people of all countries across the globe.

The "Yellow Peril" Doctrine started in a time when the disaster-ridden China was suffering the poorest and weakest downturn in the modern history. In that time, forced to open its doors, China became disintegrated and beset with troubles both internally and externally. Internally, the stupid, incompetent and highly corrupted Qing government implemented its autocratic ruling by doing evils to and exploiting the general public to satisfy the extreme luxury and extravagance of the aristocrats. Externally, the servile and spineless Qing government surrendered China's sovereignty and signed with the imperialist powers a series of unequal treaties by which China's territory was frequently ceded and substantial indemnities were paid, making China's territory fallen apart and the life of the Chinese people miserable. A large number of Chinese refugees were forced to leave their native land for as near as Southeast Asia and as far as North America to make a living under aliens' roof. They undertook the most dangerous and difficult jobs and served as cheap manual labor in road construction and mining. In the process of serving the so-called "God's chosen people" and "noble white people", they worked hard like horses, only to end up with tragedy where their family members were either dispersed or dead. Under this context, the so-called "noble white people" had never shown any solicitude for the helpless and painful Chinese refugees, as they hardly imagined that it was the imperialist powers in which they were domiciled that drove the Chinese refugees away from home by invading China and rapaciously plundering China's wealth. How dare the "noble white people" bite the hand that feeds them, defame the Chinese refugees with yellow skin as "Yellow Peril" and even instigate the white workers to oust, humiliate and exterminate the Chinese refugees working there! How dare they!

It was out of the sympathy for the miserable life suffered by the Chinese compatriots in the then poor and weak China and the anger at the distortion of history and turning the facts upside down by the imperialist powers as well as their think tanks that Mr. Chen as an octogenarian delved into the monographic study on this theme. In a strategically advantageous position, with profound academic foundation and from the perspectives of history, law and political science, he in simple terms explored the past and today, the individual and general, the exterior and interior of the "China Threat" Doctrine, and deeply disclosed the origin and development as well as the cause and effect of the "Yellow Peril-China Threat" Doctrine. Mr. Chen pointed out in his book that the "China Threat" slander preached by some of the U.S. politicians, militants and scholars and the similar absurd defame clamored by the right-wing militarists in Japan are nothing but the latest hegemony mutations of the notorious "Yellow Peril" Doctrine fabricated by the Russian Tsar and the German emperor—each with a different version—in the middle and late 19th century. The "Yellow Peril" Doctrine and the "China Threat" slander shared the same DNA and came down in one continuous line. In other words, by recklessly distorting and denying the historical facts of China's peaceful external exchanges, they were just weaving sensational "political frauds" confusing people's minds in preparation for their invasion into China. They were the thieves crying “stop thief ” !

In the book, the author also revealed, based on quantities of historical facts, the U.S. hegemonic actions that invade and colonize across the world in a span of 400 years before and after the founding of the United States. He reminded the Chinese people to be prepared in times of safety and sober in times of danger; he also alerted China’s neighboring countries not to cut down the tree that gave them shade or pull chestnuts out of the fire for the U.S. hegemonists for the fear that they may reap what they had sown.

One of the features of the book is the careful selection of 137 vivid pictures that are relevant to the contents of the book. The pictures are properly inserted into the related chapters and sections, with many footnotes illustrating the sources of the pictures in an attempt to guide the young readers to enlarge their knowledge through extensive reading and to share a bitter hatred against the enemy.

Through volume facts, the author has drawn an important conclusion: contrary to the “Yellow Peril” Doctrine, since ancient times, the yellow-skin Chinese people has never been a peril, but a peace-loving benefactor in its external exchanges. Since the founding of the People’s Republic of China, and since the Reform and Opening-up Policy in particular, China has ended its self-seclusion policy and has been an advocate and performer of a fair and justified international order by observing the principle of equality and mutual benefit in its international exchanges with people of all countries in the world.

Today, China has become a relatively big power after over 30 years of development since the Reform and Opening-up Policy, and it is still on the peaceful rise. The image of the Chinese people with a "long ugly braid" intentionally depicted by the western imperialist powers has already been a thing of the past. However, we feel regrettable to find that the "China Threat" slander as a mutation of the "Yellow Peril" Doctrine has again emerged since the 1990s. After 10 years of clamor, it has become increasingly rampant and caused many "incidents" surrounding China. The U.S. hegemonists and the Japanese militarists orchestrated in collusion an anti-China chorus of "China Threat". Their vicious intention of invading China was as obvious as a louse on the head of a monk. Who is the true inflicter of threat? Who is the true sufferer of threat? Why are there so many undercurrents and turbid waves in the Pacific Ocean? What is the essence behind the "China Threat" slander? To find the most objective and scientific answer to these questions, the captioned book authored by Mr. Chen An, which is excellent in both its texts and accompanying pictures and which suits both the refined and the popular tastes, provides an access.

In conclusion, I firmly believe that the book entitled *The "China Threat" Slander's Ancestors & Its US Hegemony Variant* is a historical work, but more of a reality book; it is not only a book on political economy, but also a book on law and diplomacy; it has a serious and grave theme, but also a familiar and smooth style of literature; it can not only serve as a reading book that cultivates patriotism of the Chinese people and the young generation in particular, but also as a medium via which peace-loving friends from all over the world can better understand a true Chine both in history and in reality. I hereby sincerely recommend this book to the reading public and would like to share it with you.

（翻譯：張川方）

二十四、揭露「中國威脅」論的本質：三把利匕剖示美霸讕言真相

蔣 圍*

陳安教授的《美國霸權版「中國威脅」讕言的前世與今生》一書，是教育部遴選立項、定向約稿、統一由江蘇人民出版社出版的優秀科研成果普及讀物之一。在「大師寫小書」系列已經問世的幾十種書中，這本書題材獨特、有的放矢、切中時弊、思想深刻、激情充盈、圖文並茂、雅俗共賞，出版後深受廣大讀者歡迎，也引起了學術界的高度關注。

此書以史為鑑，以史為師，探討了「中國威脅」論的本源、本質及其最新霸權「變種」——美國霸權版「中國威脅」論。針對國際上東海版、南海版「中國威脅」論，陳安教授擺事實、講道理，廓清形形色色「中國威脅」論的迷霧，批判國際強權政治和霸權主義，弘揚中華正氣，弘揚中華民族愛國主義。

五年前，筆者有幸參與此書的資料收集工作，事後又經反覆精讀本書，領悟到其中史論結合、夾敘夾議、有理有據、言簡意

賅、辛辣犀利的層層論證，旗幟鮮明，猶如三把鋒利匕首，戳中錯誤言論的要害：

第一把鋒利匕首：戳中和剖開「中國威脅」論的「層層畫皮」，揪出其臭名昭著的列祖列宗，擺明其族譜世系，把一四〇多年來形形色色「中國威脅」論的原始杜撰者以及花樣翻新的後繼者們分門別類，條分縷析，把他們的錯誤言論及危害本質公之於眾。

第二把鋒利匕首：戳中和剖開錯誤言論持有者的「軀體動脈」，從嚴複檢，揭示美國立國前後四百多年來的殖民擴張歷史，劣跡斑斑，罪行纍纍，指出美國霸權主義者當今強化在全球的侵略擴張行徑，絕非歷史的偶然，而是其祖祖輩輩基因的必然傳承和惡性發展。

第三把鋒利匕首：戳中和剖開錯誤言論持有者的「大腦和心臟」，即在唯物史觀的指引下，剖析美國四百多年來藉以立國的經濟基礎及其上層建築，揭示當今美國極力推行的侵略擴張國策，乃是深深植根於美國的壟斷資本主義——帝國主義的經濟體制，也深深植根於美國主流社會意識和價值體系。

綜上，可以說，陳安教授正是通過回顧歷史，擺出事實，講明道理，創造性地運用上述三把鋒利的理論匕首，戳穿層層偽善畫皮，全面深入解剖「美利堅帝國」的軀幹、動脈、大腦、心臟，令人信服地揭示了美國長期推行侵華反華政策絕非歷史的偶然，而是「美利堅帝國」建國前後四百多年來的惡性殖民擴張的歷史延伸和必然結果，乃是國際反華勢力逆時代潮流而動的最新表現。

基於此，陳安教授特別強調，世人應當以史為師，以史為鑑，方能保持清醒頭腦和銳利目光，避免遭受「黃禍」論二十一世紀最新變種美國霸權版「中國威脅」論的欺蒙和利用。同時，也鄭重提醒中國周邊國家善良的人們，切勿見利忘義，利令智昏，為霸權主義者及其盟友火中取栗。

當前，面對某些國家邊「笑容可掬，握手言歡」，邊「調兵遣將，巨艦軍機，頻頻入侵」的兩面派手法，人們不能不認真學習和師承前輩革命家對付帝國主義和一切反動派的豐富鬥爭經驗，牢記和踐行其一系列的諄諄教導，諸如：必須「丟掉幻想，準備鬥爭」，「以鬥爭求和平則和平存，以退讓求和平則和平亡」；必須針鋒相對，必須「人不犯我，我不犯人；人若犯我，我必犯人」，必須發揮高度的政治智慧，善於做到策略的靈活與原則的堅定結合。

近兩年來，面對複雜多變的國際形勢和中國周邊東海南海的風雲變幻，我們作出了一系列重要的判斷，諸如：「要善於運用底線思維的方法，凡事從壞處準備，努力爭取最好的結果，做到有備無患、遇事不慌，牢牢把握主動權」；中國人「決不拿國家主權和核心利益做交易」，中國人「不惹事，但也不怕事」；中國人民解放軍必須加強戰備，隨時「能打仗，能打勝仗」等，顯然都是既學習、師承和發揚前輩革命家的鬥爭經驗和諄諄教導，又在新的歷史條件下「與時俱進」，加以發展、豐富和創新。

中國人今後也勢必更加自覺地繼承和發揚中華民族數千年來的「鐵骨錚錚，巋然屹立，不畏強權，抗暴自強」的優良傳統，為保衛國家領土主權的獨立和完整，開展更有力更頑強的鬥爭。

"China Threat" Slander's Ancestors & Its US Hegemony Variant: Disecting with Sharp Daggers

Jiang Wei*

The book, *The "China Threat" Slander's Ancestors & Its US Hegemony Variant*, written by Senior Professor of Law Mr. Chen An and published by the Jiangsu People's Publishing House, is one of the popular books selected from excellent social science research achievements. This publishing program is approved and sponsored by the Ministry of Education of the People's Republic of China. Among these published popular books, this one is objectives-oriented, with unique subjects, full of passion and sharp insights. The author has utilized both text and graphics to address the international community problems of the times, well suiting both refined and popular tastes. It has caused the high attention of the academic community, and is popular among the readers.

This book explores the origin, essence of "China Threat" theories and its newest US hegemony variant through taking history as teachers and as mirrors. In terms of "China Threat" theories on the South China Sea and East China Sea situations, the author, by means of presenting facts and reasoning, tries to clarify the origin and essence of the problem, to rebut international power politics and hegemony behind them, as well as to carry forward China's national righteousness and promote Chinese patriotism.

Five years ago, I had the opportunity to take part in collecting materials for this book. I have also repeatedly read its finalized and published version. From the way I understand, there are three well-grounded and sharp systematical arguments expressed in the book. Through concise and comprehensive language, and by integrating narrative and comments, these three arguments stick at the heart of "China Threat" theories as three sharp daggers.

The first argument serves as a sharp dagger that stabs and rips off the masks of "China Threat" theories layer upon layer. It discloses their absurd opinions and harm essence by pointing out their notorious ancestors, their developing venation, the lineage of consanguinity, as well as originators and successors of various versions for over 140 years.

The second argument serves as a sharp dagger that stabs and splits the advocates' body and artery. It points out that the global aggression and expansion behaviors taken and strengthened by American hegemonists are not a historic accident, but an inevitable lineage and malignant development from its ancestral gene, by recalling and revealing the sleaze and criminality of American notorious colonial expansion history for over 400 years before and after it has been founded.

The third argument serves as a sharp dagger that stabs and splits the advocates' heart and brain. It discloses that American aggressive national policy is deep rooted in its monopoly capitalism, an imperialistic economic system, and in American leading social consciousness and value system, by analyzing its economic foundation and super structure which are the foundation of the United States for over 400 years from the perspective of the historical materialism.

In a word, it may be said that through looking back into the history, laying out the facts on the originators and successors of "China Threat" theories, clarifying their harm essence, Professor Chen creatively utilizes above-mentioned three systematic arguments. Just like three sharp daggers pierce through the American hypocritical masks layer upon layer and dissect its truncus, artery, brain, as well as heart, they have disclosed that American aggression against China and its anti-China policy in a long time are no accident, but a continuation and an inevitable result of the malignant colonial expansion for over 400 years before and after the American Empire has been founded. The American hegemonic version of "China Threat" is the newest manifestation of the international anti-China forces against the trends of the time.

Thus, Professor Chen particularly calls upon that common people should keep a clear mind and sharp-sight through taking the history as mirrors and teachers, to avoid being blinded and utilized by the American hegemonic version of "China Threat", the newest variant of "Yellow Peril" doctrine in the twenty-first century. Through careful reflection on the past, he reminds kind-hearted people in our neighboring countries not to forget moral principles on the sight of profits, and nor be blinded by lust for money, acting as cat's paw for American hegemonists and its allies.

At present, some countries play a double game. While they are smiling and shaking hands with our country, they also deploy forces, warships and military aircrafts to intrude our territory in the South China Sea. People in China must learn and inherit abundant fighting experiences against imperialists and all reactionaries from their revolutionary predecessors, bearing in mind the good instructions from revolutionary predecessors. We should "discard illusion and prepare to fight"; and know "fighting for peace, peace existing; concession for peace, peace perishing", as well as "tit for tat is fair play". We should give play to high politic wisdom to be good at combining tactical flexibility with a firmness in principle.

In recent two years, facing with a complex and changeable international situation and a rapidly ever-changing situation in the East China Sea and South China Sea, our country has made a series of important judgments. Among them are, for example, that "making good use of the bottom-line thinking, preparing for the worst, striving for the best, so as to make well preparation and keep unflappable facing difficult affairs, as well as firm grasp the initiative"; that Chinese people "never take the national sovereignty and core interests to make a deal"; that Chinese People's Liberation Army must strengthen war preparedness, so as to have the ability to fight and win a fight at any time etc. These judgments obviously not only are learned, inherited and promoted from, but also are a development, enrichment and innovation in the new historical circumstances of the revolutionary predecessors' fighting experiences and earnest instructions.

Chinese people certainly will inherit and develop good Chinese traditions for thousands of years of "firm and unyielding character corpse, no afraid of power, opposing violence", strongly struggling for protecting their country's territorial integrity and independence.

（翻譯：蔣圍）

注釋

〔135〕其中，日本東京大學中川淳司教授所撰書評原為日文，現譯為中英雙語，同時保留日文，便於讀者參考。

〔136〕陳欣，廈門大學法學院國際經濟法研究所副教授；楊帆，廈門大學法學院國際經濟法研究所助理教授。

〔137〕《習近平在聯合國教科文組織總部的演講》，http://news. xinluanet. com/politics/2014-03/28/c_119982831. htm.

〔138〕《習近平接受拉美四國媒體聯合採訪》http://news. xinluanet. com/world/2014-07/15/c_ 126752272. htm

〔139〕Xi Jinping's Speech at UNESCO Headquarts, http: //news. xinhuanet. coni/politics/2014-03/28/c_ 119982831.htm.

〔140〕Xi Jinping Was Interviewed by the Media from Four Countries in latin America, http://news. xinhuanet. com/world/2014-07/15/ c_126752272. htm.

* 郭壽康，時任中國人民大學資深教授、博士生導師，中國國際法學界的前輩權威學者，2012年獲得「全國傑出資深法學家」榮譽稱號。

* Senior Professor of International Law, Renmin University of China; widely recognized predecessor within jurisprudential circle, awarded with the honorable title "National Eminent & Senior Jurist" in 2012.

* 曹建明，國際經濟法教授，時任最高人民檢察院檢察長，原華東政法學院院長。

* Current Procurator-General of the Supreme People's Procuratorate, PRC; Professor.

* 號子，指集體勞動協同用力時，為統一步調、減輕疲勞等階唱的歌，通常由一人領唱，大家應和。參見《現代漢語詞典》（第7版），商務印書

館2016年版，第521頁。

**曾令良，時任武漢大學資深教授、「長江學者」特聘教授、國際法研究所所長。

〔141〕See An Chen, On the Marginality, Comprehensiveness, and Independence of International Economic Law Discipline, in An Chen, *The Voice from China: An CHEN on International Economic Law*, Springer, 2013, pp. 3-29.

〔142〕See An Chen, A Reflection of the South-South Coalition in the Last Half Century from the Perspective of International Economic Lawmaking: From Bandung, Doha, and Cancún to Hong Kong, in An Chen, *The Voice from China: An CHEN on International Economic Law*, Springer, 2013, pp. 207-239.

〔143〕See An Chen, On the Source, Essence of "Yellow Peril" Doctrine and Its Latest Hegemony "Variant"—the "China Threat" Doctrine: From the Perspective of Historical Mainstream of Sino-foreign Economic Interactions and Their Inherent Jurisprudential Principles, in An Chen, *The Voice from China: An CHENon International Economic Law*, Springer, 2013, pp. 45-99.

〔144〕An Chen, What Should Be China's Strategic Position in the Establishment of New International Economic Order? With Comments on Neoliberalistic Economic Order, Constitutional Order of the WTO, and Economic Nationalism's Disturbance of Globalization, in An Chen, *The Voice from China: An CHEN on International Economic Law*, Springer, 2013, pp.167-206.

〔145〕Ibid.

〔146〕Ibid.

〔147〕See An Chen, A Reflection of the South-South Coalition in the Last Half Century from the Perspective of International Economic Lawmaking: From Bandung, Doha, and Cancún to Hong Kong, in An Chen, *The Voice from China: An CHEN on International Economic Law*, Springer, 2013, pp. 207-239.

〔148〕See Branislav Gosovic, WTO Citadel Needs to Be Challenged by the South; An Important and Creative Contribution from China to the

Ideology of Third World, both compiled in An Chen, *The Voice from China*: *An CHEN on International Economic Law*, Springer, 2013, pp. 754-765.

* Yangtse River Scholar Professor; Senior Professor of International Law, Wuhan University, China.

〔149〕 See An Chen, On the Marginality, Comprehensiveness, and Independence of International Economic Law Discipline, in An Chen, *The Voice from China: An CHEN on International Economic Law*, Springer, 2013, pp. 329.

〔150〕 See An Chen, A Reflection of the South-South Coalition in the Last Half Century from the Perspective of International Economic Lawmaking: From Bandung, Doha, and Cancún to Hong Kong, in An Chen, *The Voice from China: An CHEN on International Economic Law,* Springer, 2013, pp. 207-239.

〔151〕 See An Chen, On the Source, Essence of "Yellow Peril" Doctrine and Its Latest Hegemony "Variant" —the "China Threat" Doctrine: From the Perspective of Historical Mainstream of Sino-foreign Economic Interactions and Their Inherent Jurisprudential Principles, in An Chen, *The Voice from China*: *An CHEN on International Economic Law*, Springer, 2013, pp. 45-99.

〔152〕 See An Chen, What Should Be China's Strategic Position in the Establishment of New International Economic Order? With Comments on Neoliberalistic Economic Order, Constitutional Order of the WTO, and Economic Nationalism's Disturbance of Globalization, in An Chen, *The Voice from China*: *An CHEN on International Economic Law*, Springer, 2013, pp.167-206.

〔153〕 Ibid.

〔154〕 See An Chen, What Should Be China's Strategic Position in the Establishment of New International Economic Order? With Commentson Neoliberalistic Economic Order, Constitutional Order of the WTO, and Economic Nationalisms Disturbance of Globalization, in An Chien, *The Voice from China: An CHEN on International Economic Law*, Springer, 2013, pp.167-206.

〔155〕 See An Chen, A Reflection of the South-South Coalition in the Last Half

Century from the Perspective of International Economic Lawmaking: From Bandung, Doha, and Cancún to Hong Kong, in An Chen, *The Voice from China: An CHEN on International Economic Law*, Springer, 2013, pp. 207-239.

〔156〕See Branislav Gosovic, WTO Citadel Needs to Be Challenged by the South; An Important and Creative Contribution from China to the Ideology of Third World. The above papers are both compiled in An Chen, *The Voice from China: An CHEN on International Economic Law*, Springer, 2013, pp. 754-765.

* 車丕照，清華大學法學院前院長，教授。

〔157〕參見高鴻鈞：《美國法全球化：典型例證與法理反思》，載《中國法學》2011年第1期，第5頁。

〔158〕張文顯：《法哲學範疇研究》（修訂版）中國政法大學出版社2001年版，第195頁。

〔159〕See An Chen, On the Marginality, Comprehensiveness, and Independence of International Economic Law Discipline, in An Chen, *The Voice from China: An CHEN on International Economic Law*, Springer, 2013, p. 27.

〔160〕An Chen, What Should Be China's Strategic Position in the Establishment of New International Economic Order? With Comments on Neoliberalistic Economic Order, Constitutional Order ofthe WTO, and Economic Nationalism's Disturbance of Globalization, in An Chen, *The Voice from China: An CHENon International Economic Law*, Springer, 2013, p.203.

〔161〕An Chen, What Should Be China's Strategic Position in the Establishment of New International Economic Order? With Comments on Neoliberalistic Economic Order, Constitutional Order of the WTO, and Economic Nationalism's Disturbance of Globalization, in An Chen, *The Voice from China: An CHENon International Economic Law*, Springer, 2013, p. 204.

〔162〕四大「安全閥」是指在處理東道國與外國投資者的關係時，有利於東道國的「逐案審批同意」權、「當地救濟優先」權、「東道國法律適用」權和「重大安全例外」權。

〔163〕See An Chen, Should the Four "Great Safeguards" in Sino-foreign BITs Be Hastily Dismantled? Comments on Critical Provisions Concerning Dispute Setlement in Model US and Canadian BITs, in An Chen, *The*

Voice from China: *An CHEN on Intrnatinal Economic Law*, Springer, 2013, p. 273.

〔164〕An Chen, On the Marginality, Comprehensiveness, and Independence of International Economic Law Discipline, in An Chen, *The Voice from China*: *An CHEN on Intrnatinal Economic Law*, Springer, 2013, p. 5.

〔165〕See An Chen, A Reflection of the South-South Coalition in the Last Half Century from the Perspective of International Economic Lawmaking: From Bandung, Doha, and Cancún to Hong Kong, in An Chen, *The Voice from China*: *An CHEN on International Economic Law*, Springer, 2013, p. 234.

〔166〕An Chen, Some Jurisprudential Thoughts upon WTO's Law-Governing, Law-Making, Law-Enforcing, Law-Abiding, and Law-Reforming, in An Chen, *The Voice from China*: *An CHEN on International Economic Law*, Springer, 2013, p. 246.

〔167〕An Chen, A Reflection of the South-South Coalition in the Last Half Century from the Perspective of International Economic Lawmaking: From Bandung, Doha, and Cancún to Hong Kong, in An Chen, *The Voice from China*: *An CHENon International Economic Law*, Springer, 2013, p.212.

〔168〕An Chen, *The Voice from China*: *An CHEN on International Economic Law*, Springer, 2013, p. v.

〔169〕See An Chen, On the Marginality, Comprehensiveness, and Independence of International Economic Law Discipline, in An Chen, *The Voice from China*: *An CHEN on International Economic Law*, Springer, 2013, p.3.

〔170〕Ibid., pp. 32-43.

* Professor of Law, former Dean of law School, Tsinghua University, China.

〔171〕See Gao Hongjun, The Globalization of American Law, *China Legal Science*, Vol.1, 2011, p. 5.

〔172〕Zhang Wenxian, *Studies on Basic Categories of Legal Philosophy (revised edition)*, China University of Political Science and Law Press, 2001, p.195.

〔173〕See An Chen, On the Marginality, Comprehensiveness, and Independence of International Economic Law Discipline, in An Chen, *The Voice from*

China: An CHEN on International Economic Law, Springer, 2013, p. 27.

〔174〕An Chen, What Should Be China's Strategic Position in the Establishment of New International Economic Order? With Comments on Neoliberalistic Economic Order, Constitutional Order of the WTO, and Economic Nationalism's Disturbance of Globalization, in An Chen, *The Voice from China: An CHEN on International Economic Law*, Springer, 2013, p. 203.

〔175〕Ibid., p. 204.

〔176〕The four Great Safeguards include the four rights of the host country in its relations with foreign investors, namely, the right to "consent case by case", the right to require "exhausting local remedies", the right to"apply host country's laws"and the right to invoke the"exception for state essential security."

〔177〕See An Chen, Should the Four "Great Safeguards" in Sino-foreign BITs Be Hastily Dismantled? Comments on Critical Provisions Concerning Dispute Settlement in Model US and Canadian BITs, in An Chen, *The Voice from China: An CHEN on International Economic Law*, Springer, 2013, p.273.

〔178〕An Chen, On the Marginality, Comprehensiveness, and Independence of International Economic Law Discipline, in An Chen, *The Voice from China: An CHEN on International Economic Law*, Springer, 2013, p. 5.

〔179〕See An Chen, A Reflection of the South-South Coalition in the Last Half Century from the Perspective of International Economic Lawmaking: From Bandung, Doha, and Cancún o Hong Kong, in An Chen, *The Voice from China: An CHEN on International Economic Law*, Springer, 2013, p. 234.

〔180〕An Chen, Some Jurisprudential Thoughts upon WTO's Law-Governing, Law-Making. Law-Enforcing, Law-Abiding, and Law-Reforming, in An Chen, *The Voice from China: An CHEN on International Economic Law*, Springer, 2013, p. 246.

〔181〕An Chen, A Reflectionofthe South-South Coalition in the Last Half Century from the Perspective of International Economic Lawmaking: From Bandung, Doha, and Cancún to Hong Kong, in An Chen, *The*

Voice from China: *An CHEN on International Economic Law*, Springer, 2013, p.212.

〔182〕An Chen, *The Voice from China: An CHEN on International Economic Law*, Springer, 2013, p. v.

〔183〕An Chen, On the Marginality, Comprehensiveness, and Independence of International Economic Law Discipline, in An Chen, *The Voice from China*: *An CHEN on International Economic Law*, Springer, 2013, p. 3.

〔184〕Ibid., pp. 32-43.

〔185〕習近平主席在接受拉美四國媒體的聯合採訪時表示，中國「將更多提出中國方案、貢獻中國智慧，為國際社會提供更多公共產品」，詳見《習近平接受拉美四國媒體聯合採訪》。http://news. xinhuanet. com/world/2014-07/ 15/c_126752272. htm.

* 趙龍躍，時任南開大學教授、美國喬治城大學客座教授、世界銀行諮詢專家。

〔186〕參見《習近平在金磚國家領導人第五次會晤時的主旨講話（全文）》，http://politics. people. com. cn/n/ 2013/0328/c1001-20941062.html。

〔187〕參見《習近平接受拉美四國媒體聯合採訪》http://news. xinhuanet. com/world/2014-07/15/c_126752272. htm。

〔188〕參見《加快實施自由貿易區戰略　加快構建開放型經濟新體制》，http://politics. people. com. cn/n/2014/ 1207/c1024-26161390. html。

〔189〕參見趙龍躍：《中國參與國際規則制定的問題與對策》，載《人民論壇·學術前沿》2012年第16期，第84-94頁。

〔190〕See An Chen, Some Jurisprudential Thoughts upon WTO's Law-Governing, Law-Making, Law- Enfrcing, Law-Abiding, and Law-Reforming, in An Chen, *The Voice from China*: *An CHEN on International Economic Law*, Springer, 2013, pp. 241-269.

〔191〕See An Chen, What Should Be China's Strategic Position in the Establishment of New International Economic Order? With Comments on Neoliberalistic Economic Order, Constitutional Order of the WTO, and Economic Nationalism's Disturbance of Globalization, in An Chien, *The Voice from China: An CHEN on International Economic Law*, Springer, 2013, pp.167-206.

〔192〕參見〔美〕約翰·傑克遜：《國家主權與WTO變化中的國際法基

礎》，趙龍躍、左海聰、盛建明譯，社會科學文獻出版社2009年版，第65-93頁。

〔193〕See An Chen, On the Implications for Developing Countries of "the Great 1994 Sovereignty Debate" and the EC-US Economic Sovereignty Disputes, in An Chen, *The Voice from China: An CHEN on International Economic Law*, Springer, 2013, pp.159-153.

〔194〕See An Chen, The Three Big Rounds of US Unilateralism Versus WTO Multilateralism During the Last Decade: A Combined Analysis of the Great 1994 Sovereignty Debate Section 301 Disputes (1998-2000) and Section 201 Disputes (2002-2003), in An Chen, *The Voice from China: An CHEN on International Economic Law*, Springer, 2013, pp. 103-158.

* Xi Jinping Was Interviewed by the Media from Four Countries in Latin America, http://news. xinhuanet. com/world/2014-07/15/ c_126752272. htm.

**Professor of Nankai University, Adjunct Professor of Georgetown University and the World Bank Consultant.

〔195〕See Xi Jinpings Speech in the Fifth Summit of BRICS Leaders, http:// politics. people. com. cn/n/2013/0328/c1001-20941062. html.

〔196〕See Xi Jinping Was Interviewed by the Media from Four Countries from Latin America, http://news. xinhuanet. com/world/2014-07/15/ c_126752272. htm.

〔197〕See Accelerate Implementing Strategy of Free Trade Zone and Buliding New Open Economy System, http://politics. people. com. cn/ n/2014/1207/c1024-26161390. htm.

〔198〕See Zhao Longyue, Problems and Countermeasures of china's Partecipation in Making International Rules, *People's Tribune. Academic Frontiers*, No. 16, 2012, pp. 84-94.

〔199〕See An Chen, Some Jurisprudential Thoughts upon WTO's Law-Governing, Law-Making, Law-Enfrcing, Law-Abiding, and Law-Reformiing, in An Chen, *The Voice from China: An CHEN on International Economic Law*, Springer, 2013, pp. 241-269.

〔200〕See An Chen, What Should Be China's Strategic Position in the Establishment of New International Economic Order? With Comments on Neoliberalistic Economic Order, Constitutional Order of the WTO, and Economic Nationalism's Disturbance of Globalization, in An Chen, *The Voice from China: An CHEN on Intenatiml Economic Law*, Springer, 2013, pp. 167-206.

〔201〕See John H. Jackson, *Sovereignty, te WTO, and Changing Fundamental's of Intenatinal Law*, Cambridge University Press, 2006. Chinese version of this book is translated by Zhao Longyue, Zuo Haicong and Sheng Jianming, Social Sciences Academic Press, November, 2009, pp. 65-93.

〔202〕See An Chen, On the Implications for Developing Countries of "the Great 1994 Sovereignty Debate" and the EC-US Economic Sovereignty Disputes, in An Chen, *The Voice from China: An CHEN on International Economic Law*, Springer, 2013, pp.159-163.

〔203〕See An Chen, The Three Big Rounds of US Unilateralism Versus WTO Multilateralism During the Last Decade: A Combined Analysis of the Great 1994 Sovereignty Debate Section 301 Disputes (1998-2000) and Section 201 Disputes (2002-2003), in An Chen, *The Voice from China: An CHEN on International Economic Law*, Springer, 2013, pp. 103-158.

* 本篇書評對本書作者個人的學術理念、獨到觀點和學術創新加以全面概括，寫得比較簡明扼要和重點突出，故特同時移置於本書第一卷，作為「導言I」冀能便於許多青年讀者對照閱讀中英雙語文本，從中受益：也便於日後出版書評單行本時加以剪裁。請參看本書末「後記」第三點和第四點的説明。

**李庸中（Eric Yong Joong Lee），韓國東國大學法學院教授，李儁（YIYUN）國際法研究院院長，《東亞與國際法學刊》（*Journal of East Asia and International Law*）主編。

〔204〕See A Dialogue wih Judicial Wisdom, Prof. An CHEN: A Flag-Holder Chinese Scholar Advocating Reform of International Economic Law, *Journal of East Asia and Intenainal Law*, Vol. 4, No. 2, pp. 477-502; An Chen, *The Voice from China: An CHENon International Economic Law*, Springer, 2014, pp xxxi-lvii.

〔205〕Dong Chen, Who Threatens Whom? The "Chinese Treat" and the Bush Doctrine, *Jounal of East Asia and International Law*, Vol. 7, 2014, p. 32.

〔206〕Ibid.

〔207〕Dong Chen, Who Threatens Whom? The "Chinese Treat" and the Bush Doctrine, *Jounal of East Asia and International Law*, Vol. 7, 2014, pp. 39-40.

〔208〕G. Ikenbery, America's Imperial Ambitions, *Foreign Affairs*, Vol. 81, 2002, p. 44.

〔209〕Dong Chen, Who Threatens Whom? The "Chinese Treat" and the Bush Doctrine, *Journal of East Asia and International Law*, Vol.7, 2014, pp.42-43.

〔210〕An Chen, *The Voice from China: An CHEN on International Economic Law*, Springer, 2014, pp. 64- 65.另參見陳安：《評「黃禍」論的本源、本質及其最新霸權「變種」「中國威脅」論》，載《現代法學》2011年第6期，第20-21頁。

〔211〕See An Chen, *The Voice from Chin: An CHEN on International Economic Law*, Springer, 2014, pp. 67-68。另參見陳安：《評「黃禍」論的本源、本質及其最新霸權「變種」「中國威脅」論》，載《現代法學》2011年第6期，第22頁。

* Professor of Dongguk University College of Law, President of YIJUN Institute of International Law, Editor-in-Chief of the *Journal of East Asia and International Law.*

〔212〕See A Dialogue wih Judicial Wisdom, Prof. An CHEN: A Flag-Holder Chinese Scholar Advocating Reform of International Economic Law, *Journal of East Asia and Intenainal Law*, Vol. 4, No. 2, pp. 477-502; An Chen, *The Voice from China: An CHEN on International Economic Law*, Springer, 2014, pp xxxi-lviii.

〔213〕Dong Chen, Who Threatens Whom? The "Chinese Treat" and the Bush Doctrine, Journal of East Asia and International Law, Vol. 7, Iss. 1, 2014, p. 32.

〔214〕Ibid.

〔215〕Dong Chen, Who Threatens Whom? The "Chinese Treat" and he Bush Doctrine, *Journal of East Asia and International Law*, Vol. 7, Iss. 1, 2014, pp. 39-40.

〔216〕G. Ikenberry, America's Imperial Ambitions, *Foreign Affairs,* Vol. 81, 2002 , p. 44.

〔217〕See Dong Chen, Who Threatens Whom? The "Chinese Treat" and the Bush Doctrine, *Jounal of East Asia and International Law*, Vol. 7, Iss.1, 2014 , pp. 42-43.

〔218〕An Chen, *The Voice from China: An CHEN on International Economic Law*, Springer, 2013, pp. 64- 65. See also An Chen, Onthe Source, Essence of "Yellow Peril" Doctrine and Its Latest Hegemony "Variant"—the "China Threat", *Modem Law Science*, No. 6, 2011, pp. 20-21。

〔219〕An Chen, *The Voice from China: An CHEN on International Economic Law*, Springer, 2013, pp. 67- 68. See also An Chen, On the Source, Essence of "Yellow Peril" Doctrine and Its Latest Hegemony "Variant"—the "China Threat", Modern Law Science, No. 6, 2011, p. 22.

* 帕特麗莎・沃特斯（Patrica Wouters），廈門大學法學院國際法教授、中國國際水法項目主任、英國蘇格蘭鄧迪大學教授、UNESCO水法科學中心前主任。

* Professor of International Law, School of Law, Xiaman University; Director, China International Water Law Programme; former Director, University of Dundee UNESCO Centre for Water Law, Policy and Science, Scotland.

* 黃雁明，中國國際經濟法學會理事，SCIA、CIETAC以及上海國際仲裁中心仲裁員。

〔220〕See An Chen, The Truth Among the Fogbound "Expropriation" Claim: Comments on British X Investment Co. Versus British Y Insurance Co. Case; The Approach of "Winning from Both Sides" Used in the "Expropriation" Claim: Re-comimients on British X Investment Co. Versus British Y Insurance Co. Case; On the Serious Violationof Chinese Jus Cogens: Comments on the Case of Importing Toxic Brazilian Soybeans into China (Expert's Legal Opinion on Zhonghe Versus Bunge Case) ; Isn't the Strict Prohibition on Importing Toxic Brazilian Soybeans into China "Illegal"?—A Rebuttal to Lawyer Song's Allegation, in An Chen, *The Voice from China: An CHEN on International Economic Law*, Springer, 2013, pp. 635-716.

〔221〕See Michael Hwang and Amy Lai, Do Egregious Errors Amount to a Breach of Public Policy? *Arbitration*, Vol. 71, No.1, 2005, pp.1-24; Michael Huang, Do Egregious Errors Amount to a Breach of Public

Policy? *Arbitration*, Vol. 71, No.4, 2005, pp. 364-371.

〔222〕Michael Hwang and Amy Lai, Do Egregious Errors Amount to a Breach of Public Policy? *Arbitration*, Vol71, No.1, 2005, p.24．

〔223〕Michael Hwang and Amy L.ai, Do Egregious Errors Amount to a Breach of Public Policy? *Arbitration*, Vol. 71, No.1, 2005, p. 24. And note 21 on the same page: The errors considered miaterial were that the arbitrator (1) failed to apply his miind properly to certain questions he had to decide;... (4) failed to decide another miaterial question, which effectively resulted in a ruling favoring one party (emphasis added). Ibid., paras. 10. 8-10. 84.

〔224〕參見陳安：《國際經濟法學芻言》，北京大學出版社2005年版，自序。

* Council member of the Chinese Society of International Economic Law; arbitrators with SCIA, CIETAC and Shamghai International Arbitration Centre.

〔225〕See An Chen, The Truth Among the Fogbound "Expropriation" Claim: Comments on British X Investment Co. Versus British Y Insurance Co. Case; The Approach of "Winning from Both Sides" Used in the "Expropriation" Claim: Re-comimients on British X Investment Co. Versus British Y Insurance Co. Case; On the Serious Violationof Chinese Jus Cogens: Commentsonthe Case of Importing Toxic Brazilian Soybeans into China (Expert's legal Opinion on Zhonghe Versus Bunge Case) ; Isn't the Strict Prohibition on Importing Toxic Brazilian Soybeans into China "Illegal"?—A Rebuttal to Lawyer Song's Allegation, in An Chen, *The Voice from China*: *An CHEN on International Economic Law*, Springer, 2013, pp. 635-716.

〔226〕An Chen, The Truth Among the Fogbound "Expropriation" Claim: Comments on British X Investment Co. Versus British Y Insurance Co. Case, in An Chen, *The Voice from China*: *An CHEN on International Economic Law*, Springer, 2013, p. 643.

〔227〕Ibid., pp. 643-646.

〔228〕See An Chen, On the Serious Violation of Chinese Jus Cogens: Comments on the Case of Importing Toxic Brazilian Soybeans into China (Expert's

Legal Opinionon Zhonghe Versus Bunge Case), in An Chen, *The Voice from China: An CHEN on International Economic Law*, Springer, 2013, pp. 687-688.

〔229〕See Art. 6 of the CISG.

〔230〕An Chen, On the Serious Violation of Chinese Jus Cogens: Comments on the Case of Importing Toxic Brazilian Soybeans into China (Expert's Legal Opinion on Zhonghe Versus Bunge Case), in An Chen, *The Voice from China: An CHEN on International Economic Law*, Springer, 2013, pp. 687-689.

〔231〕Quoted from the English Edition of the Contract Act of PRC by Harmony Consultants Ltd.

〔232〕Michael Hwang and Amy Lai, Do Egregious Errors Amount to a Breach of Public Policy? *Arbitration,* Vol. 71, No. 1, 2005, p. 24. And note 21 on the same page: The errors considered material were that the arbitrator (1) failed to apply his mind properly to certain questions he had to decide;... (4) failed to decide another material question, which effectively resulted in a ruling favoring one party (emphasis added). Ibid., paras. 10. 8-10. 84.

〔233〕Ibid., pp. 1-24.

〔234〕See Michael Hwang and Amy Lai, Do Egregious Errors Amount to a Breach of Public Policy? *Arbitration*, Vol.71, No.1, 2005, p.24.And note 21 on the same page: The errors considered material were that the arbitrator (1) failed to apply his mind properly to certain questions he had to decide;... (4) failed to decide another material question, which effectively resulted in a ruling favoring one party (emphasis added). Ibid., p. 24.

〔235〕An Chen, *The Voice from China: An CHEN on International Economic Law*, Springer, 2014, pp.li-lii.

* 石靜霞，對外經濟貿易大學法學院教授、博士生導師，對外經濟貿易大學法學院院長；孫英哲，對外經濟貿易大學法學院2014級博士研究生。

〔236〕See An Chen, *The Voice from Chin: An CHEN on International Economic Law*, Springer, 2013, pp. 337-372.

〔237〕See Ping An Life Insurance Company of China, Limited and Ping An

Insurance (Group) Company of China, Limited v. Kingdom of Belgium, ICSID Case No. ARB/12/29; China Heilongjiang International Economic& Technical Cooperative Corp., Beijing Shougang Mining Investment Company Ltd., and Qinhuangdaoshi Qinlong International Industrial Co. Ltd. v. Mongolia, PCA; Beijing Urban Construction Group Co. Ltd. v. Republic of Yemen, ICS ID Case No. ARB/14/30

〔238〕該法第153條規定：「中華人民共和國締結的國際協定，中央人民政府可根據香港特別行政區的情況和需要，在徵詢香港特別行政區政府的意見後，決定是否適用於香港特別行政區。」

〔239〕See Lao Holdings N. V. v. Lao People's Democratic Republic, ICSID Case No. A(AF)/12/6.

〔240〕Ibid., pp. 232-269.

〔241〕謝業深案的裁定僅援引了VCLT，並未引用VCST進行論證。

〔242〕VCST第15條「對領土一部分的繼承」規定：「一國領土的一部分，或雖非一國領土的一部分但其國際關係由該國負責的任何領土，成為另一國領土的一部分時：(a)被繼承國的條約，自國家繼承日期起，停止對國家繼承所涉領土生效，(b)繼承國的條約，自國家繼承日期起，對國家繼承所涉領土生效，但從條約可知或另經確定該條約對該領土的適用不合條約的目的和宗旨或者根本改變實施條約的條件時，不在此限。」

〔243〕See Tza Yap Shum v. Republic of Peru, ICSID Case No. ARB/07/6, p. 76.

〔244〕See Lao Holdings N. V. v. Lao People's Democratic Republic, ICSID Case No. A(AF)/12/6, p.295.

〔245〕Ibid., p. 329.

〔246〕該法第31條第1款規定：「條約應依其用語按其上下文並參照條約之目的及宗旨所具有之通常意義，善意解釋之。」

〔247〕中國—秘魯BIT第8條第3款規定：「如涉及徵收補償款額的爭議，在訴諸本條第一款的程式後六個月內仍未能解決，可應任何一方的要求，將爭議提交根據一九六五年三月十八日在華盛頓簽署的《關於解決國家和他國國 民之間投資爭端公約》設立的『解決投資爭端國際中心』進行仲裁。締約一方的投資者和締約另一方之間有關其他事項的爭議，經雙方同意，可提交該中心。如有關投資者訴諸了本條第二款所規定的程式，本款規定不應適用。」

〔248〕See Tza Yap Shum v. Republic of Peru, ICSID Case No. ARB/07/6, pp . 163-165.

〔249〕Ibid., p. 77

〔250〕中國—秘魯BIT第1條第2款第1項。

〔251〕該法第3條規定：「中華人民共和國不承認中國公民具有雙重國籍。」第4條規定：「父母雙方或一方為中國公民，本人出生在中國，具有中國國籍。」

〔252〕歸後的香港在國際法意義上成為中國領土的一部分，香港公民獲得中國國籍。

〔253〕在英國與秘魯簽訂BIT時，香港在國際法意義上仍然是英國的領土。

〔254〕See An Chen, *The Voice from China: An CHEN on International Economic Law*, Springer, 2013, pp.341-348. 同時參見《〈中國—秘魯1994年雙邊投資協定〉可否適用於「一國兩制」下的中國香港特別行政區》，載陳安：《陳安論國際經濟法學》（第五卷），復旦大學出版社2008年版，第1155-1162頁。

〔255〕An Chen, *The Voice from China: An CHEN on International Economic Law*, Springer, 2013, pp.344.

〔256〕Ibid., p.343.

〔257〕例如，由於《中英聯合聲明》並不對香港政府自動生效，因此香港政府的措施並不受《中英聯合聲明》的拘束，而只受到《香港特區基本法》及其項下法律法規的規制。因此，英國下議院於2014年12月16日對占中分子進行聽證，並決定對香港政局作出調查的行為是於法無據的。See Evidence Session Announced with Protesters from Hong Kong, http://www.parliament.uk/business /committees / committees-a-z /commons-select/foreign - affairs-committee /news / hong-kong-evidence -wprotesters /.

〔258〕參見《香港大學生赴英「聽證」聲稱英國應重啟〈南京條約〉》，http: //news.ifeng. com/a/20141219/42757765_0.shtml.

〔259〕參見《英質詢聯合聲明在港實施　中國強烈不滿》，http: //www. zaobao. com.sg/wencui /politic/story20140727-370611.

〔260〕參見《 2014年12月3日外交部發言人華春瑩主持例行記者會》，http://www.fmprc.gov.cn/ce/cgct/chn/fyrth/t12162342.htm.

〔261〕全國哲學社會科學規劃辦公室下達「關於《中國的 喊》書稿的專

家評審意見」，2013年11月22日。

〔262〕參見汪洋：《加強涉外法律工作》，載《人民日報》。

〔263〕An Chen, *The Voice from China: An CHEN on International Economic Law*, Springer, 2013, pp.273.

* Shi Jingxia, PhD Tutor, Professor of Law, Dean of Law School, University of International Business and Economics; Sun Yingzhe, 2014 Class Doctoral student of Law School, University of International Business and Economics.

* 孔慶江，中國政法大學國際法學院院長、教授。

* Professor of Law, Dean of International Law School, China University of Political Science and Law.

* 李萬強，西安交通大學法學院「騰飛人才計畫」特聘教授，原西北政法大學國際法學院院長。

〔264〕See An Chen, On the Marginality, Comprehensiveness, and Independence of International Economic Law Discipline, in An Chen, *The Voice from China: An CHEN on International Economic Law*, Springer, 2013, pp. 8-12.

〔265〕See An Chen, On the Misunderstanding Relating to China's Current Developments of International Economic Law Discipline, in An Chen, *The Voice from China: An CHEN on International Economic Law*, Springer, 2013, p. 34.

〔266〕See An Chen, What Should Be China's Strategic Position in the Establishment of New International Economic Order? With Comments on Neoliberalistic Economic Order, Constitutional Order of the WTO, and Economic Nationalism's Disturbance of Globalization, in An Chen, *The Voice from China: An CHEN on Internatinal Economic Law*, Springer, 2013, p. 204.

〔267〕See An Chen, What Should Be China's Strategic Position in the Establishment of New International Economic Order? With Comments on Neoliberalistic Economic Order, Constitutional Orderofthe WTO, and Economic Nationalism's Disturbance of Globalization, in An Chen, *The Voice from China: An CHEN on International Economic Law*, Springer, 2013, pp.174-175.

〔268〕See An Chen, Some Jurisprudential Thoughts upon WTO's law-

Governing, Law-Making, Law-Enforcing, Law-Abiding, and Law-Reforming, in An Chen, *The Voice from China: An CHEN on International Economcc Law*, Springer, 2013, pp. 245-248.

〔269〕See An Chen, What Should Be China's Strategic Position in the Establishment of New International Economic Order? With Comments on Neoliberalistic Economic Order, Constitutional Order of the WTO, and Economic Nationalism's Disturbance of Globalization, in An Chen, *The Voice from China: An CHEN on International Economic Law*, Springer, 2013, pp.190-204.

〔270〕See An Chen, A Reflection of the South-South Coalton in the last Half Century from the Perspective of International Economic Lawmaking: From Bandung, Doha, and Cancún to Hong Kong, in An Chen, *The Voice from China: An CHEN on International Economic Law*, Springer, 2013, p. 207.

〔271〕Ibid., pp. 233-238.

〔272〕See An Chen, To Open Wider or to Close Again: China's Foreign Investment Policies and Laws; To Close Again or to Open Wider: The Sino-US Economic Interdependence and the Legal Environment for Foreign Investment in China After Tiananmen, in An Chen, *The Voice from China: An CHEN on International Economic Law*, Springer, 2013, pp. 407, 453.

〔273〕See An Chen, Should the Four "Great Safeguards" in Sino-foreign BITs Be Hastily Dismantled? Commentson Critical Provisions Concerning Dispute Setlementin Model US and Canadian BITs; Distinguishing Two Types of Countries and Properly Granting Differential Reciprocity Treatment: Re-comments on the Four Safeguards in Sino-Foreign BITs Not to Be Hastily and Completely Dismantled; Should"The Perspective of South-North Contradictions" Be Abandoned?Focusing on 2012 Sino-Canada BIT, in An Chen, *The Voice from China: An CHEN on International Economic Law*, Springer, 2013, pp.273, 309, 373.

〔274〕See An Chen, On the Supervision Mechanism of Chinese Foreign-Related Arbitration and Its Tally with International Practices, in An Chen, *The Voice from China: An CHEN on International Economic Law*,

Springer, 2013, p. 581.

〔275〕 See An Chen, The Three Big Rounds of US Unilateralism Versus WTO Multilateralism During the Last Decade: A Combined Analysis of the Great1994 Sovereignty Debate Section 301Disputes (1998-2000) and Section 201 Disputes (2002-2003); On the Implications for Developing Countries of "the Great 1994 Sovereignty Debate" and the EC-US Economic Sovereignty Disputes, in An Chen, *The Voice from China: An CHEN on International Economic Law*, Springer, 2013, pp.103, 159.

* Professor of Law, Xi'an Jiaotong University, China; former Dean of International Law School, North-Western University of Political Science and Law, China.

〔276〕 See An Chen, On the Marginality, Comprehensiveness, and Independence of International Economic Law Discipline, in An Chen, *The Voice from China: An CHEN on International Economic Law*, Springer, 2013, pp. 8-12.

〔277〕 See An Chen, On the Misunderstanding Relating to China's Current Developments of International Economic Law Discipline, in An Chen, *The Voice from China: An CHEN on International Economic Law*, Springer, 2013, p. 34.

〔278〕 See An Chen, What Should Be China's Strategic Position in the Establishment of New International Economic Order? With Commentson Neoliberalistic Economic Order, Constitutional Order of the WTO, and Economic Nationalism's Disturbance of Globalization, in An Chien, *The Voice from China: An CHEN on International Economic Law*, Springer, 2013, p. 204.

〔279〕 See An Chen, Some Jurisprudential Thoughts upon WTO's Law-Governing, Law-Making, Law-Enforcing, Law-Abiding, and Law-Reforming, in An Chen, *The Voice from China: An CHEN on International Economic Law*, Springer, 2013, pp. 245-248.

〔280〕 See An Chen, What Should Be China's Strategic Position in the Establishment of New International Economic Order? With Comments on Neoliberalistic Economic Order, Constitutional Order of the WTO, and Economic Nationalism's Disturbance of Globalization, in An Chen,

The Voice from China: An CHEN on International Economic Law, Springer, 2013, pp.190-204.

〔281〕See An Chen, What Should Be China's Strategic Position in the Establishment of New International Economic Order? With Commentson Neoliberalistic Economic Order, Constitutional Order of the WTO, and Economic Nationalism's Disturbance of Globalization, in An Chen, *The Voice from China: An CHEN on International Economic Law*, Springer, 2013, pp.174-175.

〔282〕See An Chen, A Reflection of the South-South Coalition in the Last Half Century from the Perspective of International Economic Lawmaking: From Bandung, Doha, and Cancún to Hong Kong, in An Chen, *The Voice from China: An CHEN on International Economic Law*, Springer, 2013, p. 207.

〔283〕Ibid., pp. 233-238.

〔284〕See An Chen, To Open Wider or to Close Again: China's Foreign Investment Policies and Laws; To Close Again or to Open Wider: The Sino-US Economic Interdependence and the Legal Environment for Foreign Investment in China After Tiananmen, in An Chen, *The Voice from China: An CHEN on International Economic Law*, Springer, 2013, pp. 407, 453.

〔285〕See An Chen, Should the Four "Great Safeguards" in Sino-foreign BITs Be Hastily Dismantled? Commentson Critical Provisions Concerning Dispute Setlementin Model US and Canadian BITs; Distinguishing Two Types of Countries and Properly Granting Differential Reciprocity Treatment: Re-comments on the Four Safeguards in Sino-Foreign BITs Not to Be Hastily and Completely Dismantled; Should"The Perspective of South-North Contradictions" Be Abandoned? Focusing on 2012 Sino-Canada BIT, in An Chen, *The Voice from China: An CHEN on International Economic Law*, Springer, 2013, pp.273, 309, 373.

〔286〕See An Chen, On he Supervision Mechanism of Chinese Foreign-Related Arbitration and Its Tally with International Practices, in An Chen, *The Voice from China: An CHEN on International Economic Law*, Springer, 2013, p.581.

〔287〕See An Chen, The Three Big Rounds of US Unilateralism Versus WTO Multilateralism During he Last Decade: A Combined Analysis of the Great 1994 Sovereignty Debate Section 301 Disputes (1998-2000)and Section 201 Disputes (2002-2003); On the Implications for Developing Countries of "the Great 1994 Sovereignty Debate" and the EC-US Economic Sovereignty Disputes, in An Chen, *The Voice from China*: *An CHEN on International Economic Law*, Springer, 2013, pp.103, 159.

* 韓立余，中國人民大學法學院教授，WTO爭端解決專家組指示性名單成員。

* Professor of Law, Renmin Universiy of China; Panelist of WTO/DSB.

* 何志鵬，2011計畫．司法文明協同創新中心成員，吉林大學法學院、公共外交學院教授。

〔288〕See Peter Malanczuk, *Akehurst 's Modern Introduction to International Law*, 7th ed., Rou tledge, 1997, pp .15-18.

〔289〕E. g., Andreas F. Lowenfeld, *International Economic Law*, 2nd.ed., Oxford University Press, 2011.

〔290〕E. g., Andrew Land, *World Trade Law After Neoliberalism : Re-imagining the Global Economic Order,* Oxford University Press, 2011.

〔291〕See John Finnis, *Natural Law and Natural Rights*, 2nd ed., Oxford University Press, 2011, pp .27-29, 281-285; Robert George, In Defens eof Natural Law, Oxford University Press, 1999, pp .108-109.

〔292〕參見陳安主編：《國際經濟法學專論》，高等教育出版社2002年版，第31-32、38-39頁。

〔293〕See Philippe Sands, *Lawless World : Making and Breaking Global Rules,* Penguin Books, 2005, p .95.

〔294〕See An Chen, Some Jurisprudential Thoughts upon WTO' s Law-Governing, Law-Making, Law-Enforcing, Law-Abiding, and Law-Reforming, in An Chen, *The Voice from China: An CHEN on International Economic Law*, Springer, 2013, pp .243-244.

〔295〕「第二次世界大戰結束以來，眾多發展中國家強烈要求徹底改變數百年殖民統治所造成的本民族的積貧積弱，要求徹底改變世界財富國際分配的嚴重不公，要求更新國際經濟立法，建立起公平合理的國際經濟新秩序。但是，這些正當訴求，卻不斷地遭到了在國際社

會中為數不多的發達強國即原先殖民主義強國的阻撓和破壞。它們憑借其長期殖民統治和殖民掠奪積累起來的強大經濟實力，千方百計地維持和擴大既得利益，維護既定的國際經濟立法和國際經濟舊秩序。由於南北實力對比的懸殊，發展中國家共同實現上述正當訴求的進程，可謂步履維艱，進展緩慢。」參見陳安：《中國加入WTO十年的法理斷想：簡論WTO的法治、立法、執法、守法與變法》，載《現代法學》 2010 年第6期。

〔296〕See John W. Yound and John Kent, *International Relations Since1945*, 2nd ed., Oxford University Press, 2013, pp.274, 303.

〔297〕參見陳安:《論中國在建立國際經濟新秩序中的戰略定位——兼評「新自由主義經濟秩序」論、「WTO憲政秩序」論、「經濟民族主義擾亂全球化秩序」論》，載《現代法學》2009年第2期，第4頁。

〔298〕陳安：《論中國在建立國際經濟新秩序中的戰略定位——兼評「新自由主義經濟秩序」論、「WTO憲政秩序」論、「經濟民族主義擾亂全球化秩序」論》，載《現代法學》2009年第2期，第7-8頁；《再論旗幟鮮明地確立中國在構建NIEO中的戰略定位——兼論與時俱進，完整、準確地理解鄧小平「對外二十八字方針」》，載《國際經濟法學刊》2009年第16卷第3期；陳安：《三論中國在構建NIEO中的戰略定位：「匹茲堡發軔之路」走向何方——G20南北合作新平臺的待解之謎以及「守法」與「變法」等理念碰撞》，載《國際經濟法學刊》2009年第16卷第4期。See also An Chen, What Should Be China's Strategic Position in the Establishment of New International Economic Order? With Comments on Neoliberalist Economic Order, Constitutional Order of the WTO, and Economic Nationalism's Disturbance of Globalization, in An Chen, *The Voice from China: An CHEN on International Economic Law*, Springer, 2013, pp .169, 174-175

〔299〕See M. Matsushita, T. J. Schoenmaum, and P. C. Mavoidis, *The World Trade Organization: Law, Practice, and Policy*, 2nd ed., Oxford University Press, 2006, pp.912-913

〔300〕See E.-U. Petermann, ed., *Reforming the World Trade Organization: Legitimacy, Efficiency, and Democratic Governance*, Oxford University Press, 2005, pp.233-2743

* Professor of Law, Collaborative Innovation Center of Judicial Civilization,

Jilin University, China.

〔301〕See Peter Malamczuk, *Akehurst's Modern Introduction to International Law*, 7th ed., Routledge, 1997, pp.15-18

〔302〕E. g., Andreas F. Lowenfeld, *International Economic Law*, 2nd.ed., Oxford University Press, 2011.

〔303〕E. g., Andrew Land, *World Trade Law After Neoliberalism : Re-imagining the Global Economic Order*, Oxford University Press, 2011.

〔304〕See John Finnis, *Natural Law and Natural Rights*, 2nd ed., Oxford University Press, 2011, pp.27-29, 281-285; Robert George, *In Defense of Natural Law*, Oxford University Press, 1999, pp .108-109

〔305〕See An Chen(ed.), *Problems of International Economic Law*(in Chinese), Higher Education Press, 2002, pp.31-32, 38-39

〔306〕See Philippe Sands, *Lawless World: Making and Breaking Global Rules*, Penguin Books, 2005, p.95.

〔307〕See An Chen, Some Jurisprudential Thoughts, upon WTO's Law-Governing, Law-Making, Law-Enforcing, Law-Abiding, and Law-Reforming, in An Chen, *The Voice from China: An CHEN on International Economic Law*, Springer, 2013, pp .243-244.

〔308〕See Peter Malamczuk, *Akehurst's Modern Introduction to International Law*, 7th ed., Routledge, 1997, pp327, 233-235

〔309〕See John W. Yound and John Kent, *International Relations Since1945*, 2nd ed., Oxford University Press, 2013, pp.274, 303.

〔310〕See An Chen, What Should Be China's Strategic Position in the Establishment of New International Economic Order? With Commentson Neoliberalist Economic Order, Constitutional Order of the WTO, and Economic Nationalism's Disturbance of Globalization, in An Chen, *The Voice from China*: *An CHEN on International Economic Law*, Springer, 2013, p.169.

〔311〕Ibid. pp.169, 174-175.

〔312〕See M. Matsushita, T. J. Schoenniaum, and P. C. Mavroidis, *The Wor Ld Trade Organization: Law, Practice, and Poicy*, 2nd ed. , Oxford University Press, 2006, pp. 912-913.

〔313〕See E.-U.Petersmann ed. *Reforming the World Trade Organization*:

Legitimacy Efficiency and Democratic Governance, Oxford University Press, 2005, pp.233-274.

* 王江雨，新加坡國立大學法學院教授、亞洲法律研究中心副主任。

〔314〕參見《國家社科基金中華學術外譯專案申報問答》，http: //www. npopss-cn. gov. cn/n/2013/0228/ c234664-20635114. html.

〔315〕全國哲學社會科學規劃辦公室下達「關於《中國的吶喊》書稿的專家評審意見」，2013年11月22日。

〔316〕The scientific and detailed analysis on nationalism by Prof. Chen, see An Chen, *The Voice from China*: *An CHEN on International Economic Law*, Springer, 2013, pp. 200-203. 對「民族主義」一詞的科學解速和具體剖析，參見陳安：《陳安論國際經濟法學》（第一卷），復旦大學出版社2008年版，第130-134頁。

〔317〕See Eric Yong Joong Lee, A Dialogue with Judicial Wisdom, Prof. An CHEN: A Flag-Holder Chinese Scholar Advocating Reform of International Economic Law, *The Journal of East Asia and International Law*, Vol. 4, No.2, 2011, pp.477-514. Korean Prof. Eric Lee is now the Editor-in-Chief of the said Journal.This long Dialogue with 28 pages is now compiled in the Introdction of the English monograph *The Voice from China* (Springer, 2013, pp.xxxi-lviii).

* Professor of Law, Deputy Director, Centre for Asian Legal Studies, Faculty of Law, National University of Singapore.

〔318〕See Q&A upon the Application for the Chinese Academic Foreign Translation Project Under the National Social Science Fund of China, http://www. npopss-cn. gov. cn/n/2013/0228/c234664-20635114. html.

〔319〕See Expert Review Report on the monograph manuscript of *The Voice from China*, issued by CAFTP under NSSFC, Nov. 22, 2013.

〔320〕The scientific and detailed analysis on nationalism by Prof. Chen, see An Chien, *The Voice from China: An CHEN on International Economic Law*, Springer, 2013, pp.200-203.

〔321〕See Eric Yong Joong Lee, A Dialogue with Judicial Wisdom, Prof. An CHEN: A Flag-Holder Chinese Scholar Advocating Reform of International Economic Law, *The Journal of East Asia and International Law*, Vol. 4, No.2, 2011, pp. 477-514. Korean Prof. Eric Lee is now the Editor-in-

Chief of the said Journal. This long Dialogue with 28 pages is now compiled in the Introdction of the English monograph *The Voice from China* (Springer, 2013, pp.xxxi-lviii).

* 斯蒂芬・坎特（Stephen Kanter），美國俄勒岡州波特蘭市路易士與克拉克西北法學院法學教授（1986-1994年任該院院長）。

〔322〕See An Chen, *The Voice from China: An CHEN on International Economic Law*, Springer, 2013.

〔323〕Ibid., pp. 453-466.

〔324〕See An Chen, *The Voice from China: An CHEN on International Economic Law*. Springer, 2013, pp. 459-465.

* Professor of Law (Dean 1986-1994), Lewis & Clark Law School, Portland, Oregon.

〔325〕See An Chen, *The Voice from China: An CHEN on International Economic Law*, Springer, 2013.

〔326〕See An Chen, *The Voice from China: An CHEN on International Economic Law*, Springer, 2013, pp. 453-466.

〔327〕Ibid., pp. 459-465.

* 格斯・范・哈滕（Gus Van Harten），加拿大約克大學奧斯古德堂（Osgoode Hall）法學院副教授，法學博士。此前，他曾任職於倫敦大學政經學院法律系，著有《投資條約仲裁與公法》（牛津大學出版社2007年版）、《主權選擇與主權約束：投資協定仲裁中的司法限制》（牛津大學出版社2013年版）、《一邊倒的交易：加拿大與中國投資協定評述》（國際投資仲裁與公共政策資助，作者自行出版，2015年），並在投資法與仲裁領域發表諸多專論。作者的相關著述可通過社會科學研究網路（Social Science Research Network）獲得。

〔328〕See Treaty Between the United States of America and the Republic of Ecuador Concerning the Encouragement and Reciprocal Protection of Investment, Protocol Articles 2, 4.美國對國民待遇事項作出的保留有17項之多，厄瓜多爾僅有2項。

〔329〕參見2012年中加BIT第16條的規定。「拒絕授益」條款又譯為「不予授益」條款或「不予施惠」條款。

* Gus Van Harten is an Associate Professor at York University's Osgoode Hall law School in Toronto, Canada. He was previously a member of faculty at

the London School of Economics. He has written three books on investment treaties: *Investment Treaty Arbitration and Pubic Law* (OUP, 2007), *Sovereign Choices and Sovereign Constraints: Judicial. Restraint in Investment Treaty Arbitration* (OUP, 2013) and *Sold Down, the Yangtze: Canada's Lopsided Investment Deal with China* (IAPP, Self-published, 2015). Open access to his publications can befound at the Social Science Research Network and his research data base on international investment arbitration and public policy can be found at IIAPP.

〔330〕See Treaty Between the United States of America and the Republic of Ecuador Concerning the Encouragement and Reciprocal Protection of Investment, Protocol Articles 2, 4.

〔331〕See 2012 Canada-China Treaty, Article 16.

* 陳輝萍，廈門大學法學院教授。1994-1999年師從陳安教授，攻讀國際經濟法專業博士學位。

〔332〕該書評發表在2011年秋季出版的《東亞與國際法學刊》第4卷第2期，第533-536頁。《中國的吶喊》第lix—lxiii頁再次刊登了該書評。

〔333〕引自加利致陳教授函。

〔334〕See ECPD International Round Table "Global Souths: At 50 and Beyond", http://ecpd. org. rs/index2. php? option= com_content&do_pdf= 1 & id = 185.

〔335〕這篇英文論文發表在2015年春季出版的《東亞與國際法學刊》第8卷第1期第75-105頁。該刊總主編Eric Lee評論道：「您對即將來臨的國際經濟秩序和全球性的南南聯合自強的洞見和科學分析，給我留下了深刻印象。……您的論文從國際法的視角揭示了中國對二十一世紀全球社會的偉大願景和中國對全球共用繁榮昌盛的胸懷。在國際法論壇上表達如此真誠的亞洲立場，極為鮮見和難能可貴。」參見Eric Lee 2015年3月4日致陳安教授函。

* Dr. Huiping Chen is now Professor of International Law at the School of Law, Xiamen University. She was a Ph. D. candidate of international economic law under the supervision of Prof. An Chen during 1994-1999.

〔336〕This book review was published in *The Journal of East Asia and International Law (JEAIL)*, Vol.4, No.2, Autumn 2011, pp.533-539. It is reprinted in this new book *The Voice from China* at lix-lxiii.

〔337〕Quoted from a letter by H. E. Boutros Boutros-Ghali to Prof. An Chen.

〔338〕ECPD International Round Table "Global South: At 50 and Beyond", http://ecpd. org. rs/index2. php? option= com_content&do_pdf=1 & id =185.

〔339〕This long Article has been published in *The Journal of East Asia and International Law (JEAIL)*, Vol. 8, No.1, Spring 2015, pp. 75-105. As *JEAIL's* Editor-in-Clief Eric Lee commented: "It has totally impressed me with your insightful and scientific analysis on the newly coming international economic order, the global south-south coalition... Your paper is showing the great vision as well as Chinese mind for the common prosperity in the 21st century's global community through the angle of international law. We have rare seen such a genuine position of Asia in international law forum." See letter from JEAIL's Editor-in-Clief Eric Lee to Prof. An Chen, 2015/03/04.

* 洛林・威森費爾德（Lorin S. Weisefeld），美國法學界資深入士，曾長期擔任國際組織「多邊投資擔保機構」法律總顧問，現為Felsberg & Associates律師事務所華盛頓辦公室主任。

* 趙雲，香港大學法律學院教授，法律系系主任。感謝香港大學法律系博士研究生陳暉和陳志傑協助作者就本文寫作進行的研究工作。

* Mr. Weisenfeld, an American senior attorney, had been the General Counsel of the Multilateral Investment Guarantee Agency(MIGA) for a long period during last 1980s-2000s. He is the current head of the Washington office of Felsberg& Associates, a corporate law firm based in Sao, Paulo, Brazil.

〔340〕See An Chen, *The Voice from China: An CHEN on International Economic Law*, Springer, 2013, pp. 593-594.

〔341〕See Eric Yong Joong Lee, A Dialogue with Judicial Wisdom, Prof. An CHEN: A Flag-Holder Chinese Scholar Advocating Reform of International Economic Law, *The Journalof East Asiaand International Law*, Vol 4, No.2, 2011, pp.477-514.

〔342〕See An Chen, *The Voice from China: An CHEN on International Economic Law*, Springer, 2013, pp.xiv-xxvii.

〔343〕See An Chen, *The Voice from China: An CHEN on International Economic Law*, Springer, 2013, p.vi.

〔344〕Ibid., pp.xiv-xxvii.

〔345〕Ibid. pp. 593-594.

〔346〕Ibid. pp. 594-595.

〔347〕Ibid. pp. 581, 590, 595-596, 617-618.

〔348〕Ibid. pp. 592-596.

〔349〕Ibid. pp. 596-600.

〔350〕Ibid. pp. 600-608.

〔351〕Ibid. pp. 608-618.

〔352〕Ibid. p. 590.

〔353〕Ibid., p.581.

〔354〕See An Chen, *The Voice from Chin*: *An CHEN on International Economic Law*, Springer, 2013, p. 594.

〔355〕Ibid., pp. 595-596.

〔356〕Ibid., p. 596.

〔357〕Ibid., p. 597.

〔358〕《紐約公約》第5條第2款規定，倘聲請承認及執行地所在國之主管機關認定有下列情形之一，亦得拒不承認及執行仲裁裁決：（一）依該國法律，爭議事項係不能以仲裁解決者；（二）承認或執行裁決有違該國公共政策者。

〔359〕See An Chen, *The Voice from China: An CHEN on Intrnatinal Economic Law*, Springer, 2013, pp. 597-598. 根據陳安教授的觀點，一九五八年《紐約公約》上述條文中使用了英美法系所慣用的「公共政策」一詞，其含義相當於大陸法系中的「公共秩序」（public order），或中國法律用語中的「社會公共利益」（social public interests）。這些同義語的共同內涵，通常指的是一個國家的重大國家利益、重大社會利益、基本法律原則和基本道德原則。

〔360〕《華盛頓公約》第52條規定，任何一方可以根據下列一個或幾個理由，向秘書長提出書面申請，要求撤銷裁決：（一）仲裁庭的組成不適當；（二）仲裁庭顯然超越其權力；（三）仲裁庭的成員有受賄行為；（四）有嚴重的背離基本程式規則的情況；（五）裁決未陳述其所依據的理由。

〔361〕See An Chen, *The Voice from Chin*: *An CHEN on International Economic Law*, Springer, 2013, p. 599.

〔362〕Ibid., p. 600.

〔363〕See An Chen, *The Voice from Chin*: *An CHEN on International Economic Law*, Springer, 2013, p.605.

〔364〕Ibid., pp. 606-607.

〔365〕See S. Zamora & R. A. Brand, eds., *Basic Documents of International Economic Law*, Vol.2, CCH International, 1990 , pp. 975-984. 作者在文中提到：「聯合國大會於1985年12月11日通過專門決議，向整個國際社會鄭重推介這部《國際商事仲裁示範法》，建議『全體會員國對這部示範法給予應有的考慮』，以作為各國國內仲裁立法的重要參考和借鑑。這種鄭重推介，客觀上無異於承認了和進一步加強了示範法各有關條款作為國際通行做法（通例）的應有地位。」

〔366〕See An Chen, *The Voice from China*: *An CHEN on International Economic Law*, Springer, 2013, p.610.

〔367〕Ibid., pp. 619-611.

〔368〕這些不法仲裁行為包括：仲裁員在仲裁中憑偽證作出裁決或收受賄賂、舞弊，或者枉法裁決等。

〔369〕See An Chen, *The Voice from Chin*: *An CHEN on International Economic Law*, Springer, 2013, p.612.

〔370〕See An Chen, *The Voice from Chin*: *An CHEN on International Economic Law*, Springer, pp.608-618.

〔371〕Ibid., pp. 249-252.

〔372〕Ibid., p. 249.

〔373〕Ibid., pp.249-250.

〔374〕See An Chen, *The Voice from China*: *An CHEN on International Economic Law*, Springer, pp.252-253.

〔375〕Ibid. pp 254-258.

〔376〕Ibid. pp 717-752.

〔377〕Ibid. p 717.

〔378〕Ibid. p. 718.

〔379〕Ibid. pp 718-723.

〔380〕Ibid., p.717.

〔381〕Ibid., p.723.

〔382〕See An Chen, *The Voice from China*: *An CHEN on International Economic*

Law, Springer, p. 726. 在A158號買賣合同第7條中，雙方明確約定：「與合同有關的分歧通過友好協商解決。如不能達成協議，將提交中國國際〔經濟〕貿易仲裁委員會仲裁。」

〔383〕Ibid., pp. 724-729.

〔384〕Ibid.根據香港地區《仲裁條例》第2條、第34A條和第34C條的規定，涉及香港地區當事人的國際仲裁協定以及按國際協定進行的仲裁，應當適用聯合國貿易法委員會於一九八五年六月二十一日頒行的《國際商事仲裁示範法》第一至七章。《國際商事仲裁示範法》第8條明文規定：（一）法院受理涉及仲裁協議事項的訴訟，為當事人一方在不遲於就爭議實質提出第一次申述之際，即要求提交仲裁，法院應指令當事人各方提交仲裁。但法院認定仲裁協議無效、失效或不能履行者，不在此限。（二）已經提起本條第1款規定的訴訟，儘管有關爭端在法院中懸而未決，仲裁程式仍可開始或繼續進行，並可作出裁決。

〔385〕Ibid., p. 731. 一九五八年《紐約公約》第2條第3款明文規定：當事人就有關訴訟事項訂有本條所稱之（書面仲裁）協議者，各締約國的法院在受理訴訟時，應依當事人一方的請求，指令各方當事人將該事項提交仲裁。但前述協議經法院認定無效、失效或不能實行者，不在此限。

〔386〕Ibid., pp. 729-730.澳大利亞著名學者賽克斯（E.I. Sykes）和普賴爾斯（M. C. Pryles）在《澳大利亞國際私法》一書中也引證典型判例，對當事入選擇仲裁地的法律意義作了更加明確的闡述：〔在合同中〕設立條款規定在某特定國家裡提交仲裁，這就仍然是一種強有力的推定：實行仲裁的所在地國家的法律就是合同的準據法。這種推定，只有另設明文規定的法律選擇條款，或者另有其他具有絕對優勢的綜合因素表明應當適用其他法制，才能加以改變。因此，訂有仲裁條款的合同的準據法，往往就是仲裁舉行地當地的法律。

〔387〕Ibid., pp. 734-736. 陳安教授指出，該案判決缺乏對於「《中華人民共和國民法通則》第8章第145條的規定」「《中華人民共和國涉外經濟合同法》第5條的規定」「中國司法解釋對『涉外合同爭議』準據法的規定」，以及「中國大學教科書對『涉外合同爭議』準據法的基本主張」的應有尊重。

〔388〕Ibid., p.739.

〔389〕Ibid., p. 740.

〔390〕See An Chen, *The Voice from Chin: An CHEN on International Economic Law*, Springer, 2013, p.740.

〔391〕Ibid, p. 741. 狄克斯先生任意閹割了適用第22條規定的法定前提：票據經過「背書轉讓」並且以移花接木和張冠李戴手法，把它強加於談案10732C號這份未經背書轉讓的匯票頭上：同時忽略或「回避」了《結算辦法》第14條第2款和第3款的規定，即對商業匯票使用範圍及其票據權利加以重大限制。

〔392〕Ibid., pp. 743-744. 郭文探討的主題乃是：票據經背書轉讓之後，票據債務人對於持票的善意第三人的票據債權，應當承擔什麼責任。換言之，全文的論述主題，特別在論述普通債權與票據債權的區別時，其大前提乃是：第一，票據已經背書轉讓：第二，已經出現持票的善意第三人……狄克斯先生在援引郭文這些論點用以論證他自己所極力強調的票據權利的autonomy時，卻有意無意地忽略或刪除了郭文立論的這兩個大前提。談案涉訟的10732C號匯票，其票據雙方當事人始終就是買賣合同原來的雙方當事人，從未發生過「背書轉讓」情事，因此，這場票據糾紛的當事人也百分之百的就是原來買賣合同糾紛的當事人，絲毫不涉及任何持票的善意第三人問題。

〔393〕Ibid., p. 745. 在中國內地，一九九四年二月出版的《票據法全書》（全書1950頁，約315萬字）中就闢有一章專門論述「票據抗辯」。書中多處論證、肯定和支援票據債務人依法行使抗辯權，從而很不利於或否定了狄克斯先生論證票據的絕對autonomy。中國內地學者的上述一貫觀點和聯合國上述公約所規定的票據法基本原則，不但已經體現在一九八八年《銀行結算辦法》的前引條文之中，而且尤其鮮明地體現在一九九五年五月十日通過的《中華人民共和國票據法》之中。它強調：票據的簽發、取得和轉讓，都必須「具有真實的交易關係和債權債務關係」。

〔394〕Ibid., p. 748，根據陳安教授的分析與對比解釋，狄克斯先生轉述了《民事訴訟法》第189-192條所規定的「督促程式」，但狄克斯先生在轉述這些條文的時候，將自己不正確的理解強加給中國內地的有關法律。

〔395〕Ibid., p. 740.

〔396〕Ibid., p. 750.

〔397〕Ibid.

〔398〕Ibid., p. 751.

〔399〕See An Chen, *The Voice from China: An CHEN on International Economic Law*, Springer, 2013, pp. 751-752.

〔400〕Ibid., p. 167.

〔401〕Ibid., p. 111.

〔402〕Ibid., p. 207.

* Professor of Law, The University of Hong Kong. The author is grateful to two PhD candidates from the Universityof Hong Kong, Hui Chen and Zhijie Chen, for their research assistance.

〔403〕See An Chen, *The Voice from China: An CHEN on International Economic Law*, Springer, 2013, pp. 593-594.

〔404〕See Eric Yong Joong Lee, A Dialogue with Judicial Wisdom, Prof. An CHEN: A Flag-Holder Chinese Scholar Advocating Reform of International Economic Law, *The Journal of East Asia and International Law*, Vol 4 , No.2, 2011, pp. 477-514.

〔405〕An Chen, *The Voice from China: An CHEN on International Economic Law*, Springer, 2013, pp.xiv-xxvii.

〔406〕An Chen, *The Voice from China: An CHEN on International Economic Law*, Springer, 2013, P. vi.

〔407〕Ibid.pp.xiv-xxvii.

〔408〕Ibid.pp.593-594.

〔409〕Ibid.pp.594-595.

〔410〕Ibid.pp.581, 590, 595-596, 617-618.

〔411〕Ibid.pp.592-596.

〔412〕Ibid.pp.596-600.

〔413〕See An Chen, *The Voice from China: An CHEN on International Economic Law*, Springer, 2013, pp. 600-608.

〔414〕Ibid. pp.608-618.

〔415〕Ibid., p.590.

〔416〕Ibid., p.581.

〔417〕Ibid. p.594.

〔418〕Ibid. pp.595-596.

〔419〕Ibid., p.596.

〔420〕See An Chen, *The Voice from Chin*: *An CHEN on International Economic Law*, Springer, 2013, p. 597.

〔421〕According to Section 2, Article 5 of New York Convention of 1958, if the competent authority in the country where enforcement is sought (the host country) finds that (a) the subject matter of the difference is not capable of settlement by arbitration under the law of that country or, (b) the recognition or enforcement of the award would be contrary to the public policy of that host country, recognition and enforcement of an arbitral award may be refused.

〔422〕See An Chen, *The Voice from China: An CHEN on International Economic Law*, Springer, 2013, pp. 597-598. According to Prof. Chen, the term "public policy" which is commonly used by common law systems is employed in the above stipulation of the New York Convention of 1958. Its meaning is equivalent to the term "public order" in a civil law system or to the term "social public interests" in Chinese law. The common implication of these synonyms usually refers to the fundamental interest of a state and society and the basic legal rules and basic moral rules of the country.

〔423〕According to Article 52 of the Washington Convention of 1965, either party can request annulment of the award by an application to the ICSID, on one or more of the following grounds: (a) that the tribunal was not properly consulted; (b) that the tribunal had manifestly exceeded it powers; (c) that there was corruption on the part of a member of the tribunal; (d) that there had been a serious departure from a fundamental rule of procedure; or (e) that the award had failed to state its reasons on which it was based.

〔424〕See An Chen, *The Voice from China*: *An CHEN on International Economic Law*, Springer, 2013, p.599.

〔425〕Ibid., p. 600.

〔426〕See An Chen, *The Voice from Chin*: *An CHEN on International Economic Law*, Springer, 2013, p. 605.

〔427〕Ibid., pp. 606-607.

〔428〕According to Basic documents of international economic law, by S.Zamora & R.A.Brand, eds, *Basic Documents of International Economic Law*, Vol.2, CCH International, 1990, pp.975-984, the United Nations General Assembly adopted a special resolution on 11 December 1985, seriously recommending this Model Law on International Commercial Arbitration to the whole international society and suggesting that "all States give due consideration to the Model Law" as a main reference for national enactments on arbitration.

〔429〕See An Chen, *The Voice from Chin*: *An CHEN on International Economic Law*, Springer, 2013, p.610.

〔430〕Ibid., pp. 619-611.

〔431〕Including awards made on the basis of perjury or an arbitrator's corruption, malpractice, distorting the text of law in the arbitration, etc.

〔432〕See An Chen, *The Voice from China*: *An CHENon International Economic Law*, Springer, 2013, p.612,

〔433〕See An Chen, *The Voice from China*: *An CHEN on International Economic Law*, Springer, 2013, pp. 608-618.

〔434〕See An Chen, *The Voice from China*: *An CHEN on International Economic Law*, Springer, 2013, pp. 249-252.

〔435〕Ibid., p. 249.

〔436〕Ibid., pp. 249-250.

〔437〕Ibid., pp. 252-253.

〔438〕See An Chen, *The Voice from China*: *An CHEN on International Economic Law*, Springer, 2013, pp. 254-258.

〔439〕Ibid., pp.717-752.

〔440〕Ibid., p.717.

〔441〕Ibid. p.718.

〔442〕Ibid., pp.718-723.

〔443〕Ibid. p. .717.

〔444〕See An Chen, *The Voice from Chin*: *An CHEN on International Economic Law*, Springer, 2013, p. 723.

〔445〕Ibid., p. 726. According to Clause 7 in Contract A, they agreed that: "

Any difference relating to the contract will be resolved by compromise. If compromise cannot be reached, it will be submited to the China International (Economic and) Trade Arbitration Commission for arbitration,"

〔446〕Ibid., pp. 724-729.

〔447〕Ibid., pp.729-730. Under the provisions of Articles 2, 34A, and 34C of the Hong Kong Arbitration Ordinance (Cap.341), an international arbitration agreement and an arbitration pursuant to an international arbitration agreement are governed by Chapters I to VII of the Model Law on International Commercial Arbitration adopted by the United Nations Commission on International Trade Law on 21 June 1985 (hereinafter "UNCITRAL Model Law"). Article 8 of the UNCITRAL Model Law explicitly provides: A court before which an action is brought in a manner which is the subject of an arbitration agreement shall, if a party so requests not later than when submitting his first statement on the substance of the dispute, refer the parties to arbitration unless it finds that the agreement is null and void, inoperative, or incapable of being performed; Where such an action has been brought, arbitral proceedings may nevertheless commenced or continued, and an award may be made, while the issue is pending before the court.

〔448〕Ibid., p.731. Section 3 of Article II of the New York Convention of 1958 provides: The court of a Contracting State, when seized of an action in a matter in request of which the parties have made an (written arbitration) agreement within the meaning of this Article, at the request of one of the parties, refers the parties to arbitration unless it finds that the said agreement is null and void, inoperative or incapable of being performed.

〔449〕Ibid., pp.729-730. Famous Australian scholars E.I. Sykes and M.C. Pryles also cited typical precedents in their work, Australian Private International Law, and made the precise statement that: Nevertheless, a clause specifying arbitration in a particular country remains a strong inference that the proper law is that of the country where arbitration is to be held. The inference can be displaced only by an express choice-of-law clause or by a fairly overwhelming combination of factors pointing to another legal system. Thus, often the proper law of a contract (including the arbitration clause) will be the law of the place where the arbitration is to be held.

〔450〕Ibid., pp.734-736. Prof. Chen indicates that the Judgment is a lack of due respect for Article 145 of Chapter VII, General Principles of Civil Law of the People's Republic of China, Article 5 of the Law of the People's Republic of China on Economics Contracts Involving Foreign Interests, a judicial interpretation by the People's Supreme Court of the PRC, and also the Chinese collegiate textbook's basic position on the proper law of disputes arising from the economic contracts involving foreign interests.

〔451〕See An Chen, *The Voice from Chin*: *An CHEN on International Economic Law*, Springer, 2013, p. 739.

〔452〕Ibid., p. 740.

〔453〕Ibid., p. 740.

〔454〕Ibid., p.741. He (Mr. Dicks) emasculates the prerequisite of Article 22 that the Bill of Exchange should have been"transferred by endorsement" and forcibly applies the garbled stipulation to the case of Bill of Exchange 10732C. Meanwhile, he neglects or, in another word, evades the provisions of paragraphs 2 and 3 of Article 14 which apply major limitations to the sphere of application of the rights to a bill of exchange.

〔455〕Ibid., pp.743-744. The subject of Mr. Guo's article is the liability of the debtor on a payment instrument transferred by endorsement to the holder of the instrument who is a bona fide third party. In other words, the prerequisites of the argument of the whole article, inter alia those arguments on the differences between an ordinary debt and a debt upon a payment instrument, are that, firstly, the instrument has been transferred by endorsement; and secondly, it has been held by a bona fide third party... However, Mr. Dicks ignored or intentionally garbled the two prerequisites of Mr. Guo's article when citing it as evidence for his so-called autonomy of payment instruments. The Bill of Exchange has nothing to do with any third party because it has never been transferred by endorsement and the payee and the payer are consistently the original two parties of Sales Contract A.

〔456〕Ibid., p.745. *In China, the 1984 Complete Compilation of and Comments on Bill Laws* (with 1950 pages and about 3.15 million words) contains a chapter devoted to "The Defence Against Payment Instrument". In this book, there are many arguments for defence by the obligors of payment instruments; these are unfavourable to the absolute "autonomy" of payment instruments insisted on by Mr. Dicks... the above viewpoints and principles are embodies not only in the 1988 Settlement Procedures of Banks but also more explicitly in the Law of Bills of the People's Republic of China, promulgated on 10 May 1995, which stressed that the issue, obtainment, and transfer of a payment instrument (bill) shall all "be based on a real transaction and credit-debt relation".

〔457〕See An Chen, *The Voice from China: An CHEN on International Economic Law*, Springer, 2013, p.748. According to Prof. Chen's analysis and comparison interpretation, Mr. Dicks restated his so-called supervisory procedure (procedure for hastening debt recovery) provided by Articles 189 to 192 of the Civil Procedure Law, but Mr. Dicks rewrite the original text of the aforementioned provisions in the Civil Procedure Law, in which he forced his incorrect understandings upon the law.

〔458〕Ibid., p.740.

〔459〕Ibid., p.750.

〔460〕Ibid.

〔461〕Ibid., p.751.

〔462〕Ibid.pp.751-752

〔463〕See An Chen, *The Voice from Chin: An CHEN on International Economic Law*, Springer, 2013, p.167.

〔464〕Ibid., p.111.

〔465〕See An Chen, *The Voice from China: An CHEN on International Economic Law*, Springer, 2013, p. 207.

* 張祥熙，廈門大學南洋研究院博士生。本書評原發表於《中華讀書報》

2016年8月31日第10版。

〔466〕陳安：《美國霸權版「中國威脅」讕言的前世與今生》，江蘇人民出版社2015年版，第3頁。

〔467〕參見陳安：《美國霸權版「中國威脅」讕言的前世與今生》，江蘇人民出版社2015年版，第132頁。

* PhD Candidate, Research School for Southeast Asian Studies, Xiamen University.

〔468〕Branislav Gosovic, China—"Threat" or "Opportunity"? Professor An Chen's Article on "Yellow Peril"/"China Threat" Doctrines—An Important Contribution to the Study and Understanding of Contemporary World Politics, *Journal of International Economic Law*, Vol.20, No.2, 2013.

* 中川淳司，東京大學社會科學研究所教授。

〔469〕到二〇一七年二月為止，WTO的成員國為一六四個，另有二十一個國家正在進行加入WTO的談判。See WTO, Membersand Observers, htps://www. wto. org/english/thewto_e/whatis_e/tif_e/org6_e. htm.

〔470〕截至二〇一五年末，BITs的總數為二九四六個，除此之外，還有三五八個自由貿易協定（FTAs）。合計起來的國際投資協定（international investment agreements, IIAs）總數達到了三三〇四件。See UNCTAD, World Investment Report 2016 Investor Nationality: Policy Challenges, Geneva: UNCTAD, 2016, p.101.

〔471〕有若干例外。除GATT原締約國、一九五九年革命後繼續保留GATT締約國身份的古巴以外，同樣為原締約國的捷克斯洛伐克、波蘭（1967年加盟）、羅馬尼亞（1971年加盟）、匈牙利（1973年加盟）仍為GATT加盟國。

〔472〕See UNCTAD, Trends in International Investment Agreements: An Overview, Geneva: UNCTAD, 1999, p.22, Figure2 ·

〔473〕See UNCTAD, International Investment Agreements Navigator, China, http://investmentpolicyhab. unctad. org/IIA/CountryBits/42#iiaInnerMenu.

〔474〕See C. L. Lim and J. Y. Wang, China and the Doha Development Agenda, *Journal of World Trade*, Vol. 44, Iss.6, 2010.

〔475〕陳安教授對其代表學說，列舉了G. Schwazenberger、金沢良雄、D. Carreau作 為 例 子。See An Chen, *The Voice from China: An CHEN on*

Internatinal Economic Law, Springer, 2013, p. 5.

〔476〕陳安教授對其代表學說，列舉了P. C. Jessup、H. J. Steiner & D. F. Vagts、J. H. Jackson、A. Lowenfeld、櫻井雅夫作為例子。See An Chen, *The Voice from China: An CHEN on International Economic Law*, Springer, 2013, p.6.

〔477〕See An Chen, *The Voice from China: An CHEN on International Economic Law*, Springer, 2013, pp. 15-17.

〔478〕See John H. Jackson, The Great 1994 Sovereignty Debate: United States Acceptance and Implementation of the Uruguay Round Results, *Columbia Journal of Transnational Law*, Vol. 36, 1997, pp. 157-188.

〔479〕See An Chen, *The Voice from China: An CHEN on International Economic Law*, Springer, 2013, pp.119-120.

〔480〕See An Chen, *The Voice from China: An CHEN on International Economic Law*, Springer, 2013, pp. 148-156.

〔481〕Ibid., p. 157.

〔482〕Ibid., p. 168.

〔483〕陳安教授曾提到為南南聯合之目的協調金磚國家的立場。

〔484〕See An Chen, *The Voice from China: An CHEN on International Economic Law*, Springer, 2013, pp. 282-287.

〔485〕Ibid., p. 289.

〔486〕See An Chen, *The Voice from China: An CHEN on International Economic Law*, Springer, 2013, pp. 484-486.

〔487〕這兩個案件是：Bernhard von Pezold and Others v. Republic of Zimbabwe (CSID Case No. ARB/10/15); Border Timbers Limited, Border Timers International (Private) Limited, and Hangani Development Co. (Private) Limitedv. Republic of Zimbabwe (ICSID Case No. ARB/10/25).

* Professor of International Economic Law, Institute of Social Science, University of Tokyo.

〔488〕As of February 2017, WTO has 164 members. In addition, 21 countries are in the process of negotiations to join the WTO. See WTO, Members and Observers, https://www.wto.org/english/thewto_e/whatis_e/tif_e/org6_e.htm.

〔489〕By the end of 2015, the total number of BIT is 2946. Besides, there are

358 Free Trade Agreement (FTA) with investment chapters. Accordingly, the total number of international investment agreements (IIAs) reaches 3304. See UNCTAD, World Investment Report 2016 Investor Nationality: Policy Challenges, Geneva: UNCTAD, 2016, p.101.

〔490〕There are certain exceptions. In addition to Cuba, which remained as the GATT member after its revolution in 1959, Czechoslovakia, Poland (joined in 1967), Romania (joined in 1971) and Hungry (joined in 1977) are already contracting parties to the GATT.

〔491〕See UNCTAD, Trends in International Investment Agreements: An Overview, Geneva: UNCTAD, 1999, p.22, Figure 2.

〔492〕See UNCTAD, International Investment Agreements Navigator, China, http:// investmentpolicyhub.unctad.org/IIA/CountryBits/42#iiaInnerMenu.

〔493〕See C. L. Lim and J. Y. Wang, China and the Doha Development Agenda, *Journal of World Trade*, Vol.44, Iss.6, 2010.

〔494〕For the "narrow interpretation", Professor Chen takes the opinions of GG Schwarzenberger, Kanazawa Yoshioand D. Carreau as example. See An Chen, *The Voice from China*: *An CHEN on International Economic Law*, Springer, 2013, p. 5.

〔495〕For the "broad interpretation", Professor Chen takes the opinions of P. C. Jessup, H. J. Steiner and D. F. Vagts, J. H. Jackson, A. Lowenfeld and Sakurai Masao as example. See An Chen, *The Voice from China*: *An CHEN on International Economic Law*, Springer, 2013, p. 6.

〔496〕Ibid., pp. 15-17.

〔497〕See John H. Jackson, The Great 1994 Sovereignty Debate: United States Acceptance and Implementation of the Uruguay Round Results, *Columbia Journal of Transatinal Law*, Vol. 36 , 1997, pp. 157-188.

〔498〕See An Chen, *The Voice from China*: *An CHEN on International Economic Law*, Springer, 2013, pp. 119-120.

〔499〕See An Chen, *The Voice from China*: *An CHEN on International Economic Law*, Springer, 2013, pp. 148-156.

〔500〕Ibid., p. 157.

〔501〕Ibid., p. 168.

〔502〕Prof. Chen once mentioned that for the purpose of promoting South-

South coalition, BRIC countries should coordinate their positions.

〔503〕See An Chen, *The Voice from China: An CHEN on International Economic Law*, Springer, 2013, pp.282-287.

〔504〕Ibid., p.289.

〔505〕See An Chen, *The Voice from China: An CHEN on International Economic Law*, Springer, 2013, pp.484-486.

〔506〕Bernhard von Pezold and Others v. Republic of Zimbabwe(ICSID Case No. ARB/10/15); Border Timbers Limited, Border Timers International (Private) Limited, and Hangani Development Co. (Private) Limited v. Republic of Zimbabwe(ICSID Case No. ARB/10/25).

1) 東京大学社会科学研究所教授

2) 2017年2月現在のWTOの加盟国数は164である．この他に21の国が加盟交渉中である．参照，WTO, Members and Observers. Available at [https://www.wto.org/english/thewto_e/whatis_e/tif_e/org6_e.htm]

3) 2015年末時点で，BITの総数は2946である．この他に，自由貿易協定（FTA）で投資章を設けているものが358あり，これらを合計した国際投資協定（international investment agreements, IIAs）の総数は3304件に上る．参照，UNCTAD, *World Investment Report 2016 Investor Nationality: Policy Challenges*, Geneva: UNCTAD, 2016, p.101.

4) 若干の例外はあった．GATTの原締約国であり，1959年の革命後も引き続いてGATT締約国であったキューバの他，同じく原締約国であったチェコスロバキア，ポーランド（1967年加盟），ルーマニア（1971年加盟），ハンガリー（1973年加盟）は既にGATTに加盟していた．

5) 参照，UNCTAD, *Trends in International Investment Agreements: An Overview*, Geneva: UNCTAD, 1999, p.22, Figure 2.

6) 参照，UNCTAD. International Investment Agreements Navigator, China. Available at [http://investmentpolicyhub.unctad.org/IIA/CountryBits/42#iiaInnerMenu]

7) C. L. Lim and J. Y. Wang, "China and the Doha Development Agenda", 44 *Journal of World Trade* 1309 (2010).

8) 陳安教授は代表的な学説としてG. Schwarzenberger, 金沢良雄，D. Carreauを挙げる．参照，An Chen, *The Voice from China: An CHEN on International Economic Law*, Berlin/Heidelberg: Springer, 2013, p.5.

9) 陳安教授は代表的な学説として，P. C. Jessup, H. J. Steiner & D. F. Vagts, J. H. Jackson, A. Lowenfeld, 櫻井雅夫を挙げる．参照，*ibid.*, p.6.

10) *ibid.*, pp.15-17.

11) 參照，John H. Jackson, "The Great 1994 Sovereignty Debate: United States Acceptance and Implementation of the Uruguay Round Results", 36 *Columbia Journal of Transnational Law* 157(1997.)

12) 參照，An Chen, *supra* n.6, pp.119-120.

13) 參照，*ibid.*, pp.148-156.

14) 參照，*ibid.*, p.157.

15) 參照，*ibid.*, p.168.

16) 陳安教授は，そのための方策としてBRICSの協調に言及する．参照，*ibid.*, p.204.

17) 參照，*ibid.*, pp.282-287.

18) 參照，*ibid.*, p.289.

19) 參照，*ibid.*, pp.484-486.

20) 以下の２件である．*Bernhard von Pezold and Others v. Republic of Zimbabwe* (ICSID Case No. ARB/10/15); *Border Timbers Limited, Border Timbers International (Private) Limited, and Hangani Development Co. (Private) Limited v. Republic of Zimbabwe* (ICSID Case No. ARB/10/25).

* 陳安教授撰寫的《美國霸權版「中國威脅」讕言的前世與今生》是中國教育部特約立項的優秀科研成果普及讀物。其原始藍本是中英雙語長篇學術論文《評「黃禍」論的本源、本質及其最新霸權「變種」、「中國威脅」論》（On the Source, Essence of "Yellow Peril" Doctrine and Its Latest Hegemony "Variant"—the "China Threat" Doctrine），分別發表於中國《現代法學》2011年第6期和日內瓦*The Journal of World Investment and Trade*, Vol.13, No.1, 2012。其英文本經改寫收輯為英文專著《中國的吶喊：陳安論國際經濟法》（*The Voice from China: An CHEN on International Economic Law*）第三章，由德國Springer出版社於二〇一三年推出。

**徐海，江蘇人民出版社資深編審、總經理。

* *The "China Threat" Slander's Ancestors & Its US Hegemony Variant* written by Professor Chen An is an outstanding popular reading material on scientific achievements sponsored by a special project of China's Ministry of Education. Its original version is the academic paper entitled "On the Source, Essence of 'Yellow Peril' Doctrine and Its Latest Hegemony 'Variant' —the 'China Threat' Doctrine" in both Chinese and English which was published in *Modern Law Science* (No.6, 2011) in China and *The Journal of World Investment and Trade* (No.1,Vol.13, 2012) in Geneva, Switzerland respectively. The English version has been included after adaption as the third chapter of *The Voice from China: An CHEN on International Economic Law* published by Springer, a German publisher, in 2013.

**Xu Hai is a Senior Editor and General Manager of Jiangsu People's Publishing House.

* 蔣圍，時任西北政法大學國際法研究中心講師。

* Dr. Jiang Wei is a lecturer at International Law Research Center, Northwest University of Political Science and Law.

陳安早期論著書評薈萃（1981-2008）

一、立意新穎務實　分析縝密深入　理論實踐交融

——對陳安主編《國際投資法的新發展與中國雙邊投資條約的新實踐》一書的評價*

中華人民共和國商務部條法司

廈門大學法學院：

收到你院寄來《國際投資法的新發展與中國雙邊投資條約的新實踐》一書後，我司組織相關業務處室進行了認真的研讀。同志們普遍感到該書立意新穎務實、資料翔實充分、分析縝密深入，是一本國內目前少有的研究雙邊投資條約理論與實踐問題的專業書籍，對於我司的商簽投資保護協定工作能夠起到良好的參考作用。特別是在第三編「中國雙邊投資條約新實踐」中，對我國雙邊投資保護協定談判遇到的新問題的性質認定、應對技巧以及發展方向進行的深入分析，更具有現實意義。

特以此函表示謝意，並望你院教師一如既往地以更多的學術創作支持我國國際經濟法理論與實踐的發展。

商務部條約法律司

二〇〇八年四月二十八日

二、內容豐富　系統完整　洵是佳作

——《美國對海外投資的法律保護及典型案例分析》評介*

遊　斌

一九八五年一月，在武漢召開的「中、美、加三國學者關於國際投資與貿易法律討論會」上，一篇題為《美國對海外投資的法律保護及典型案例分析》的長篇論文，得到與會者的交口稱譽。法學界權威韓德培教授指出，這篇論文「以中國人的眼光來談美國對海外投資的法律保護問題，確可謂獨具新意，不落窠臼」。已故《中國國際法年刊》主編、北京大學陳體強教授曾稱之為「內容豐富，系統完整，洵是佳作」。

這部專著的作者、廈門大學陳安教授治學嚴謹，在完成書稿後並不急於付梓，而是先將文稿的主要部分分兩次在《中國國際法年刊》上登載，廣泛聽取意見，經過認真修改，再三潤色，然後才交鷺江出版社出版。

作為世界上最大的發達國家和最大的海外投資國家，美國對其遍及全球的海外投資，歷來是不遺餘力地實行法律保護的，並精心設計了一整套法律保護體制。這一體制的核心內容就是設置了一個特殊的政府機構——官辦的「海外私人投資公司」，充分發揮了它的特殊職能，對於保護海外美資來說，是切實有效的。美國的上述體制已被聯邦德國、日本、英國、加拿大等十多個發達國家所師法和仿效，因此，它具有相當廣泛的典型意義。

該書的一大特點，是以大量的篇幅，對於有關海外美資風險事故的典型索賠案例，從法令與事實、理論與實踐的結合上加以剖析。另一特點，是以更大的篇幅，編譯和附錄了相當豐富和珍貴的英文原始文檔。

這部書有理有據地揭示了美國怎樣通過法律手段在對外投資方面為資產階級利益服務。對我們來說，這部書的最大價值就在於對今後我國的吸引外資的談判、簽約以及研究涉外投資糾紛案件的處斷，能起到殷鑒作用。

一九八六年五月

三、評陳安主編的國際經濟法系列專著（1987年版）*

余勁松

我國實行對外開放政策以來，對外經濟交往事業蓬勃發展。為研究和解決在對外經濟交往中出現的一系列新的法律問題，國際經濟法學作為一門新興的、綜合性的邊緣學科，在我國應運而生，並逐步發展。數年來，我國法學界已陸續發表了一些研究國際經濟法的文章、單科教材和專著，做出了開拓性貢獻。一九八七年十一月，由廈門大學陳安教授主編，並由他和安徽大學朱學山教授，南開大學高爾森教授、潘同瓏副教授，以及復旦大學董世忠教授分別審訂的我國第一套國際經濟法系列專著成套出版，在我國國際經濟法學術研究領域中做出了新的貢獻。

這套國際經濟法系列專著分為五卷，即《國際投資法》《國際貿易法》《國際稅法》《國際貨幣金融法》以及《國際海事法》，共約一五〇萬字。《國際投資法》對保護、管制和鼓勵國際投資的法律制度，中外合營企業的法律問題，中國境內外資企業的法律制度，中外合作開採海洋石油資源的法律制度，以及國際投資爭端的解決等七個專題分別加以論述。該書聯繫我國實際，概括了國際投資法的主要內容。《國際貿易法》論及國際貨物買賣法以及與之有關的國際貨物運輸、保險、國際結算和產品責任方面的法律，國際技術貿易方面的法律以及各國政府管制對外貿易的法律。《國際稅法》共有九章，前六章介紹國際稅法的基本理論和一般制度，其中論述了國際稅法的概念、對象及淵源、國際稅收管轄權、國際雙重徵稅及其解決、國際雙層徵稅及其解決、防止國際逃稅避稅、國際雙重稅收協定等內容；後三章介紹中國的涉外所得稅法律制度，包括中國對外國投資人的徵稅、中國對外國個人的徵稅以及中國對外國投資人徵稅的稅收優惠和徵收管理制度。《國際貨幣金融法》包括外匯交易的法律問題、國際證券交易的法律問題、國際貸款協定、國際信貸實務的其他法律問題、國際貨幣的法律制度等五章。《國際海事法》分為十六章，分別介紹和闡述了中國的海事立法與海事制度、船舶、船員及水域、提單運輸、租船運輸、海上旅客運輸、船舶碰撞、海上救助、共同海損、海上人員傷亡及賠償、海上留置權與船舶抵押權、責任限制、海洋環境保護與油污事故處理、海上保險合同、海事爭議的解決、國際海事法的發展趨勢、國際海事組織等內容。

這套系列專著，內容豐富、涉及面廣。通觀全書，具有如下特點和優點：

一是密切聯繫中國實際，注意從中國的立場來研究和評析國際經濟交往中的有關法律問題。美國紐約大學法學院教授洛文費爾德編寫的一套以「國際經濟法」命名的六卷本叢書，是近年來在世界國際經濟法學術界具有一定影響的著作。其基本特點之一，是立足於美國的實際，以美國的利益為核心，來分析美國涉外經濟法以及國際經濟法的各種問題，闡述和論證了西方發達國家對這些問題的基本觀點。陳安教授主編的這套國際經濟法系列專著，則從中國的實際出發，把對中國涉外經濟交往法律問題的研究放在重要地位；同時，注意闡述和論證第三世界發展中國家對有關法律問題的立場。

作者在這套專著中除系統介紹國際投資、貿易、貨幣金融、稅收、海事等方面的法律制度外，還用相當篇幅結合論述我國這些領域中的涉外法律規範。例如，在《國際投資法》中，以三章的篇幅專門論述了中外合營企業的法律問題、中國境內外資企業的法律制度以及中外合作開採海洋石油資源的法律制度；在「國際稅法》中，將中國對外國投資人的徵稅、對外國個人的徵稅以及對外國投資人徵稅的稅收優惠和徵收管理制度，分別列為專章加以闡述；《國際海事法》則在開頭第一章就介紹中國的海事立法與海事制度。

與此同時，作者還注意從中國的角度和第三世界的立場來研究和評析國際經濟交往中的法律問題。例如，在《國際投資法》中，對國有化及補償爭議問題的評介，對中外合營企業管理權分享的具體安排、技術轉讓、產品銷售安排等問題的剖析，都注意從中國立場出發，論證和維護中國權益。又如，在《國際稅法》關於國家稅收管轄權問題的論述中，強調利潤所得來源國稅收管轄權優先原則；在論及國際雙重稅收協定內容時，否定了西方某些學者要求給予外國人以所謂「國際最低標準」的稅收優惠待遇的觀點，認為為了促進國際經濟交往，可採取「無差別待遇」原則，但是，對「無差別待遇」原則不能作絕對的理解，等等。這些觀點是符合中國立場和利益的。

二是本套系列專著中的《國際貨幣金融法》一書，在我國第一次系統地論述了國際貨幣與金融法律制度，填補了我國在這方面的空白。我國以前在這方面的著作，有的是專門論述國際貨幣制度的，如盛愉的《國際貨幣法》；有的是論述國際融資的法律問題的，如沈達明、馮大同編的《國際資金融通的法律與實務》。而《國際貨幣金融法》一書則從國際貨幣買賣法、國際信貸法以及國際貨幣合作法三個方面來安排體系，從而把國際貨幣法與國際金融諸法律問題結合起來，既符合歷史與邏輯相一致的原則，又能使讀者對國際貨幣金融法律制度有系統的了解。

三是本套系列專著在我國現有其他教材、專著的基礎上，增添了許多新的內容。例如，以前的有關國際稅法方面的著作，對於國際雙重徵稅問題，主要論及兩個以上主權國家就同一徵稅物件對同一納稅人行使稅收管轄權而造成的雙重徵稅，即所謂「法律上的雙重徵稅」，而對國際上有些學者提出的所謂「經濟上的國際雙重徵稅」，即兩個國家對在經濟上具有同一性或聯繫性的不同納稅人，就相同的徵稅對象徵稅，則論述不多。而本套系列專著中的《國際稅法》一書，除介紹了前一種國際雙重徵稅外，還在第四章專門對後者進行了介紹，並闡述了解決的措施和方法。同時，還專闢第五章論述了防止國際逃稅和避稅問題，這是國際經濟交易中一個引人注目的問題，因為跨國納稅人總是尋找各種機會通過濫用轉移定價以及利用避稅港逃避稅收。我國實行對外開放和吸收外資中也會遇到這些問題，而我國以前的著作對此也論述不夠。此外，在本套系列專著的《國際貿易法》一書中增加了產品責任法的內容，《國際海事法》中還專門敘述了關於海洋環境保護與油污事故處理、國際海事組織等新內容。

四是材料豐富、新穎。這套系列專著在論述取材上，力求其新，廣泛吸收國內外的最新學術成果。許多資料直接來源於近來的國外最新出版物，並綜合了國內的最新研究成果，從而反映了目前國際投資、貿易、貨幣金融、稅收及海事等法律領域中的最新動態和學術觀點。此外，這套專著各書在正文外，還分別翻譯和輯集了一些重要的原始文檔，作為附錄，這給讀者學習、研究和查證原文提供了方便。

五是理論與實務相融通，介紹與分析相結合。這套系列專著既涉及國際投資、貿易、貨幣金融、稅收、海事等領域中的法律理論問題，也涉及大量的法律實務問題。作者在介紹基本理論的基礎上，又輔之以許多事例加以說明，並盡可能援引和評析國際經濟法律訟爭的具體案例，深入淺出，有助於讀者掌握基本理論知識和提高解決實際問題的能力。

當然，這套國際經濟法系列專著在某些方面還可以進一步加以考慮和完善，表現為以下幾方面：

一是作為國際經濟法系列專著，有關各書對國際經濟法的概念、範圍、體系等都沒有予以論述和說明。在國內外學者中，對國際經濟法的概念、性質、範圍、解釋不一，尚無定論。主要有兩種觀點：一種觀點認為國際經濟法屬於國際公法的範疇，是經濟領域的國際公法，屬於國際公法的一個分支，各國國內的涉外經濟法規範應排除在國際經濟法之外；另一種觀點認為，國際經濟法不限於、不等於經濟領域的國際公法，而應綜合調整國際經濟關係的國內法規範和調整國際經濟關係的國際法規範，成為一門新的獨立的法學部門。從這套系列專著的內容和體系安排來看，作者顯然是贊成後一種觀點，並據此來安排整套專著的體系。因此，似應在本系列專著開頭對此闡明自己的觀點和看法。

二是作為國際經濟法系列專著，有關各書在內容安排上尚需作某些協調，以避免重複。作者在這方面注意到了這個問題，例如，關於國際支付、國際結算等法律問題，本應屬於國際貨幣金融法的範圍，但考慮到《國際貿易法》一書中對這些問題已有詳盡的論述，因而在《國際貨幣金融法》一書中就從略了。但對於其他某些問題似乎還有疏忽，例如，關於國際海上貨物運輸和海上貨物運輸保險問題，在本系列專著中的《國際貿易法》和《國際海事法》兩書中幾乎都以相當的篇幅談到了這一問題（盡管內容詳略有所不同），造成某些重複。這部分內容似可考慮在《國際貿易法》一書中從略，而由《國際海事法》一書來詳細敘述。

三是有些問題還可以進一步考慮和探討。例如，《國際投資法》一書依國際投資法律制度的不同作用（保護、管制、鼓勵）來分章論述，體系安排新穎。但是，一項法律制度有時同時具有幾種作用，既是保護性的、鼓勵性的，也是管制性的。例如，關於貨幣自由匯兌問題，許多國家在管制的前提下，又規定在某種條件下允許自由匯出，這既是一種管制措施，又是對外資實行的鼓勵和保護。我國與某些外國政府簽訂的關於鼓勵和相互保護投資協定中，也規定了這一內容。因此，似以綜合論述為好。此外，對於我國涉外經濟交往實踐中尚待解決的問題，例如，關於中外合作經營企業的稅收問題、債務責任問題以及某些其他有關的法律問題，還可從理論上進一步深入探討。

總的來說，這套國際經濟法系列專著是具有中國特色的、開拓性的好書，結構合理，條理分明，內容充實，材料新穎，理論與實際相結合，法律與實務相融通，既可作為高等學校學生的教材，也是從事國際經濟法教學和研究的人員以及涉外法律實務工作者有價值的參考書。

四、新視角：從南北矛盾看國際經濟法

——評陳安主編的《國際經濟法總論》*

徐崇利

近年來，我國學術界對國際經濟法這門新興邊緣學科的研究逐步深入，有關國際經濟法各分支學科以及專門問題的著述陸續出版。然而，在此期間，還沒有一本對國際經濟法最基本的理論和實踐原則加以概括和綜合論述的專著。一九九一年五月法律出

版社出版、廈門大學法律系陳安教授主編的《國際經濟法總論》（朱學山教授、曾華群教授、劉智中講師參加撰稿，以下簡稱《總論》）一書，填補了我國在這方面研究的空白。

《總論》作為高等學校法學試用教材出版，具有體系完整、結構合理、內容全面、材料翔實、文筆流暢等特點。通觀全書，人們不難發現，本書同時不失為一部頗有研究深度的學術專著。

當前，在西方學術界，用以維護發達國家利益的國際經濟法學說層出不窮，而由於歷史的原因，廣大發展中國家長期以來缺乏自己的國際經濟法理論體系，難以適應建立國際經濟新秩序鬥爭的現實需要。《總論》一書作者在對國內外國際經濟法兩大基本學派的觀點作了深入細緻的分析之後，在方法論上肯定了「廣義說」，但又不囿於純理念上的探討，而是進一步論證了這一學派某些代表學者的根本立場，以美國的傑塞普和洛文費爾德為例，說明他們在許多理論問題上貌似持平公正，不偏不倚，實則主要是以本國資產者利益為最終依歸的本質；其中許多觀點和論據，滲透著、散發出濃烈的霸權主義和強權政治的氣息。析微而知著，作者提出，對待現有的國際經濟法知識和體系，應當兼采「拿來主義」和「消化主義」兩種方法，即在「拿來」之後，認真咀嚼消化，吸收其營養，剔除其糟粕，逐步創立起以馬克思主義為指導的、體現發展中國家共同立場的、具有中國特色的國際經濟法學科新體系。《總論》作者正是以此作為主線和導向，力求建立自己的理論體系。

這種努力首先體現在本書對當代國際經濟法發展歷史的論述上。作者就我國一些學者對二十世紀四〇年代以來建立的布雷頓森林體制多加溢美的傾向悉心論證，當時廣大發展中國家在政治上尚未完全獨立，在經濟上仍處於不合理的國際分工體系之中，它們的利益和願望在該體制中不可能得到應有的反映和尊重。以《關稅及貿易總協定》為例，由於發展中國家和發達國家經濟發展水準懸殊，無條件實行「互惠」，完全「對等」地大幅度削減關稅，只能導致發展中國家國內市場的丟失、民族工業的受害和對外貿易的萎縮。因此，作者認為，對這一時期建立起來的國際經濟秩序不宜估價過高，更不能認為它「具有劃時代的意義」。隨後，作者又詳加論述，從一九五五年萬隆會議發端，到二十世紀七〇年代聯合國大會通過《建立國際經濟新秩序宣言》和《各國經濟權利和義務憲章》（以下簡稱《宣言》和《憲章》），廣大發展中國家在創立國際經濟法新規範的幾個回合鬥爭中，逐步取得勝利，昭示了當代國際經濟立法發展的歷史新趨勢。

作者的上述努力又在本書對國際經濟法基本原則的闡述中得到進一步體現。國際經濟法基本原則是國際經濟法各種法律規範的核心。作者牢牢抓住這個核心，潑墨論述了國際經濟法中的四大基本原則，即經濟主權原則、公平互利原則、全球合作原則以及有約必守原則。其中對於《宣言》和《憲章》，作者在關於國際經濟法發展史的闡述中，已經論證和確認它們是國際經濟法新舊更替、破舊立新過程中的一項重大飛躍和明顯轉折。在這一章中，進一步從歷史到現實，詳盡論述了這兩個綱領性文件中所包含的國際經濟法基本原則，從而大大深化了人們對《宣言》和《憲章》歷史意義的認識。由於整章論述緊扣維護發展中國家利益這一主題，給人以渾然一體的感覺：為了維護得來不易的政治主權，發展中國家勢必要爭取經濟上的主權；在有了經濟主權之後，由於各國在經濟上的相互依存關係，發展中國家勢必也要謀求全球間的「南北合作」和「南南合作」；在合作過程中，由於經濟實力對比懸殊，發展中國家勢必要求在公平互利的基礎上與發達國家進行經濟交往；為了保證這種經濟交往得以正常進行，又勢必要求雙方做到有約必守。

此外，《總論》的主旨在全書的其他各大章節均有體現。篇幅所限，茲不贅述。

由於國際經濟法是一門新興的邊緣性學科，有許多理論問題需要加以深入的研究和探討，而國內外學者對其中的一些問題又存有不同程度的爭議。由此，《總論》一書作者在建立自己理論體系的過程中，就諸多理論問題，特別是重大的基本理論問題，提出並論證了自己的觀點。

有關國際經濟法的含義問題。國內外學術界歷來有「狹義說」與「廣義說」之分，前者主張國際經濟法是調整國際經濟關係的國際法規範的總和，是國際公法的一個新分支；後者主張國際經濟法是調整國際經濟關係的各種法律規範的總和，是綜合有關國內法和國際法規範的邊緣性的獨立法律部門。作者認為，由於對國際經濟法調整對象——「國際經濟關係」一詞理解不同，也由於觀察角度和研究方法上的差異，以致形成上述兩大學派。這種提法綜合了國內外學者的觀點。值得注意的是，作者的研究並不僅僅停留於此，在詳細評述兩種學說之後，作者提出在方法論上「廣義說」可取的觀點，最後把支援該說的根據提高到劃分法律部門和法學部門分類標準的高度去認識，闡明從「狹義說」

到「廣義說」的發展，正是國際經濟法分類辦法和分科標準從「以傳統的法律類別為中心」到「以現實法律問題為中心」的轉變。同時，這種轉變頗有助於解決國際經濟法與國際法、國際私法等相鄰學科之間長期以來因劃分標準混亂而造成的界限不清、分野不明的問題。

有關國際經濟法的範圍問題。不同於其他著述，作者不但把國際商務慣例作為國際經濟法的淵源之一，而且把它列為與國際經濟法相鄰的法律部門，認為這種由各種國際性民間團體制定的用以調整國際私人經貿關係的商務規則，是國際經濟法這一邊緣性綜合體的有機組成部分。但是，就其特點來看，又大大有別於國際經濟法整體中的其他組成部分（諸如國際法、國際私法以及各國涉外經濟法等範疇），而自成一類；作者還專題探討了國際經濟法與國內經濟法的關係問題。從「廣義說」的方法論出發，作者認為各國涉外經濟法也是國際經濟法的有機組成部分，批判了來自某些強權發達國家的一種有害傾向，即藐視弱小民族東道國涉外經濟立法的權威性，削弱這些法律規範對境內涉外經濟關係實行管轄的「域內效力」；與此同時，作者又提醒人們，要注意防止和抵制發達國家強化和擴大本國涉外經濟立法「域外管轄」或「域外效力」的另一種有害傾向。作者密切注視當代全球性「南北矛盾」的普遍存在以及強權政治傾向仍在頑固地表現自己的客觀現實，從涉外經濟法和國際經濟關係的角度，即從「涉外」到「國際」應有的科學內涵及其合理的外延界限來論述這一問題，其研究的角度可謂「慧眼獨具」。

有關國際經濟法的發展階段問題。國內外有關著述一般都以二戰以後布雷頓森林體制建立作為劃界標準。作者始終認為對該體制不宜評價過高，相應地也沒有採用這一通例，而是沿著「南北矛盾」的歷史淵源及其現實發展這一客觀軌跡，詳細回顧國際經濟關係發展史，提出在此基礎上劃分國際經濟法歷史發展階段的主張。作者認為，從宏觀上分析，迄今為止國際經濟法經歷了萌芽、發展、轉折更新三大階段。從西元前一直到十五世紀，國際經濟交往的發展節奏比較緩慢，形式比較簡單，規模也比較有限，國際經濟法由於規範種類不全，數量不多，只是處在「萌芽」的階段；十六世紀以後，資本主義世界市場逐步形成，國際經濟交往空前頻繁，用以調整國際經濟關係的國際條約、國際習慣大量出現，日益完備，延續到二十世紀四〇年代，國際經濟法一直處於不斷「發展」的階段；二戰結束以後，發展中國家紛紛獨立，構成第三世界，作為一支獨立的力量登上國際政治經濟舞臺，它和第一、第二世界既相互依存，又相互爭鬥，國際經濟法發展進入「轉折更新」的階段。需要指出的是，作者在這裡雖然也把二戰結束作為劃界的時間，但在劃界標準上卻與其他人不同：一是以「布雷頓森林體制建立」為準，一是以「發展中國家興起」為準，二者的基本著眼點及其歷史意義截然不同。

有關國際經濟法的基本原則問題。國內有關著述一般都限於簡單援用國際公法一般概念的提法，把「平等互利原則」作為國際經濟法的基本原則之一，而缺少深入具體的科學論證。作者則以聯合國大會通過的《宣言》和《憲章》這兩大綱領性國際文獻作為根據，以馬克思在《哥達綱領批判》一書中關於「平等」觀的著名論斷作為指導，提出創見，闡發了「公平互利原則」，認為國際經濟法中的「公平互利原則」與國際法中傳統意義上的「平等互利原則」，既有密切聯繫，又有重要區別。「公平」和「平等」有時是近義的，但在某些場合，表面上的「平等」實際上是不公平的，而表面上的「不平等」卻是公平的。例如，《國際貨幣基金協定》依據各國繳金份額多少決定投票權大小的做法，貌似「平等」，實際上往往導致「以富欺貧」現象的發生；反之，貌似對發達國家「不平等」的普惠制，實際上卻是十分公平合理的。可見，「公平互利原則」是對「平等互利原則」的重大發展。另外，作者把「有約必守原則」納入國際經濟法基本原則之列，這也是其他著述所沒有的。該原則之所以成為國際經濟法基本原則之一，是由國際經濟關係本身的基本要求所決定的。國家間、不同國籍的當事人之間簽訂的各種經濟條約、經濟合同，只有在締約國各方或合同各方誠信遵守和切實履行的條件下，才能產生預期的效果，才能維持和發展正常的國際經貿交往和國際經濟關係，從這個意義上說，「有約必守原則」，乃是國際經濟法必不可少的主要基石之一。另外，作者又強調：「有約必守原則」須受「所約合法」以及「情勢變遷」兩項條件的制約，這就加深了對「有約必守原則」的全面理解。

《總論》一書理論體系的建立以及許多觀點的提出，都是建立在對國際經濟關係歷史回顧基礎之上的。本書開篇設置了「國際經濟關係的歷史發展與南北矛盾」一節，就當代國際經濟關係中的主要矛盾——南北矛盾，從歷史到現實，闡明其癥結淵源和發展進程，進而剖析當前國際經濟秩序除舊布新、破舊立新的時代趨向。這樣的安排頗具匠心，它是經濟與法律關係的唯物史觀在國際經濟法研究中的具體運用，也是由國際經濟法總論的特點所決定的。評斷現行國際經濟法的基本規範和實踐原則，一則需要回溯歷史，從中尋找其存在的根據，例如，如果不懂得近代殖民主義者對弱小民族興兵索「債」的歷史，就無法理解拉美國家長期以來堅持「卡爾沃主義」，要求西方國家在特定條件下放棄「外交保護權」的堅定立場。二則需要回溯歷史，從中尋找其現實意義，例如，如果不懂得近代殖民主義者對弱小民族瘋狂掠奪的歷史，就無法理解廣大發展中國家要求對境內一切自然資源享有「永久主權」的重大意義。三則需要回溯歷史，從中尋找判別是非的標準，例如，如果不懂得殖民主義者對弱小民族盤剝的歷史，就無法理解發展中國家為恢復和維護經濟主權，在必要時，對外資實行國有化並給予適當補償的合理性。從研究方法來看，由於現行的國際經濟法律新規範是發展中國家和發達國家長期鬥爭和妥協的結果，不採用歷史的研究方法不足以反映其來龍去脈和發展軌跡。這一點尤其突出地表現在對歷屆聯合國大會關於建立國際經濟新秩序的一系列決議精神的前後對比上。

在所難免，本書也有某些不足之處。例如，有關國際經濟法的構成體系問題，國內外學者的觀點不盡相同，作者根據「以現實法律問題為中心」的分類標準，把國際經濟法劃分為國際貿易法、國際投資法、國際貨幣金融法、國際稅法以及國際經濟組織法等若干大類，並且認為，每一大類還可以進一步劃分為若干較小的專門分支和再分支。由於缺少進一步的理論探討，給人以意猶未盡的感覺。又如，本書在個別用詞上前後不一，如「國際商務慣例」和「國際經濟慣例」交叉使用，容易引起誤解。對於此類不足之處，如在本書再版時能予補正，則可使其臻於完善。

五、獨樹中華一幟　躋身國際前驅

——評陳安主編的《MIGA與中國》*

吳煥寧

廈門大學陳安教授牽頭撰寫的《MIGA與中國：多邊投資擔保機構述評》一書由福建人民出版社出版後，引起了國內外有關各界矚目。

本書是「國家社會科學基金專案」和國家教委「國際問題專項科研基金專案」的主要研究成果。

眾所周知，政治風險，如戰爭、內亂、國有化和徵收、禁兌等，一向是跨國投資者最為擔憂的問題之一。而二十世紀六七〇年代發展中國家國有化風潮的興起，更使得政治風險成為跨國投資，尤其是對發展中國家投資的嚴重阻礙。至八〇年代初期，發展中國家的直接投資流入量直線下降。建立一個世界性的專門承保跨國投資政治風險的保險機構，以消除跨國投資中的非商業性障礙，已成為時代之亟需。在這種背景下，經世界銀行籌畫，多邊投資擔保機構（MIGA）於一九八八年成立了。該機構包含了一套精心設計的國際投資政治風險保險機制，對於消除跨國投資的非商業性障礙、促進國際資本向發展中國家流動，能夠起到重大的促進作用，因而受到了全球南、北兩大類國家的普遍歡迎。可以說，該機構的成功設立，是近年來國際投資法領域最為重要的成就。

在MIGA醞釀組建期間，中國就對它採取積極支援的態度，並於一九八八年成為該機構的首批成員國之一。在短短幾年內，MIGA在我國的業務量不斷攀升，這對於改善我國的整體投資環境，促進外資源源流入，產生了不可忽視的積極影響。

但是，國內對這樣一個重要的國際經濟組織的研究，除了已經發表的數篇論文之外，幾乎是一片空白。廈門大學陳安教授所牽頭的科研群體，經過數年鑽研，撰寫了《MIGA與中國：多邊投資擔保機構述評》一書，立足於中國國情，緊緊扣住「南北矛盾」這一主線，從發展中國家的共同利益出發，對MIGA的淵源、機制、運作狀況及其與我國的諸般關係，多角度、多層面地進行了周全的介紹和精闢的剖析，從而使我國對MIGA的研究由幾近空白一躍而躋身於世界先進水準。可以說，在國際上研究MIGA的眾多論著中，本書能「發他人之所未能發」獨樹一幟，頗具中國特色。

從該書的內容可以看出，這部專著的資料豐富翔實，並且十分新穎。其中許多係採用有關國際組織專門提供的第一手材料，反映了相關領域中的最新資訊和學術動態。同時，MIGA法律部首席顧問Lorin Weisenfeld先生直接參與該書的創作，世界銀行資深副行長、MIGA締造者之一Shihata先生撥冗作序，更為該書添色不少。

同時，由於該書對MIGA經營機制的闡述相當全面和透徹，並對中國加入MIGA的利弊得失作了深入而獨到的探討和論證，因而具有很高的科學性和可靠性，使得該書對於我國有關部門的外資決策和外資立法，具有重大的、不可替代的參考價值。

總而言之，這部專著堪稱我國國際經濟法學界的一部力作，是廈門大學國際經濟法專業諸多學人對我國法學事業做出的新的重要貢獻。

六、深入研究　科學判斷

——《「解決投資爭端國際中心」述評》簡介*

單文華

《「解決投資爭端國際中心」述評》一書是中國國際經濟法學會會長、廈門大學政法學院院長、博士生導師陳安教授等接受我國對外經貿部的國策諮詢，參與有關論證和研究的一項科研成果，也是國家教委博士點專項基金選定的重點科研專案的成果。一九九四年該書榮獲福建省第二次哲學社會科學優秀科研成果一等獎。

「解決投資爭端國際中心」（ICSID）是根據一九六五年《關於解決國家與他國國民之間投資爭端公約》（以下簡稱《華盛頓公約》）設立的一個國際機構，總部設在美國華盛頓。截至一九九四年六月底，全球已有一三〇個國家簽署（其中113國已批准）《華盛頓公約》。中國應否參加《華盛頓公約》、接受ICSID體制，事關既要貫徹對外開放國策，與國際慣例接軌，又要維護中國國家主權的問題，這是一對「矛盾」。因此，國內法學專家約於一九八五年開始展開國策諮詢討論，見仁見智，歧議甚多，但可大體歸納為兩種主張：（一）促進開放，從速參加。（二）珍惜主權，不宜參加。陳安教授在對外經貿部條法局主持的專家討論會上，提出了第三種主張，即（三）積極研究，慎重參加。他認為，在參加《華盛頓公約》、接受ICSID體制問題上，既不能過於保守，舉棋不定，又不可掉以輕心，盲目從事。要作出正確和科學的判斷，就必須在對外開放基本國策和獨立自主的一貫立場的綜合指導下，抓緊對《華盛頓公約》和ICSID體制的歷史、現狀以及它們在實踐中的具體運作情況開展全面、深入的研究，並且在充分了解有關實況和全貌的基礎上，慎重地決定應否參加、如何參加。這第三種主張，獲得許多學者的贊同。

該書就是針對上述問題進行「積極研究」的初步成果。全書的主要特點是：立足於理論與實際的緊密結合，在研究大量原始資料和典型案例的基礎上，對ICSID體制的實際運作情況進行評介，並密切聯繫中國的具體國情，就中國加入《華盛頓公約》、接受ICSID體制所可能遇到的若干主要問題進行預測，初步探討了基本對策和防範措施，向中國的有關決策部門提出了一些有價值的、可供參考的建議。具體說來，本書論證了對《華盛頓公約》和ICSID加以深入、全面研究的現實必要性，提出了待決的諸多問題；平論了ICSID的管轄權問題；剖析了ICSID仲裁的法律適用問題； 闡述了中國加入《華盛頓公約》、接受ICSID體制的可行性以及應當採取的主要對策；提出了對《華盛頓公約》及其體制應作的保留、限制以及應當採取的其他相應措施等。

《「解決投資爭端國際中心」述平》一書是我國第一部也是目前唯一一部比較系統、深入地研究ICSID體制的著作，不僅其實踐價值得到充分肯定，其學術價值在國內和國際學術界也備受推崇。一九九〇年二月，國家經過對該國策諮詢成果的審議，採納了其建議，正式加入了《華盛頓公約》；國家有關部門還多次來函稱讚該成果「對我們立法工作有莫大幫助」一九九三年八月，我國政府正式委派陳安教授出任中國向ICSID選派的四名國際仲裁員中的首席仲裁員，再一次肯定了這一學術成果在理論與實踐上的重要價值。

七、國際投資爭端仲裁研究的力作

——評《國際投資爭端仲裁

——「解決投資爭端國際中心」機制研究》*

張乃根

自一九七九年七月一日第五屆全國人民代表大會第二次會議通過《中外合資企業法》以來，中國以吸收外國（外商）直接投資（FDI）為突破口，實施對外開放、對內改革的基本國策，已取得了舉世矚目的偉大成就。中國早已成為全球吸收外資的一片「熱土」。為了切實保障外商在華投資的合法權益，中國政府於一九九三年二月六日正式成為世界銀行集團管轄的《關於解決國家與他國國民間投資爭端公約》（又稱《華盛頓公約》）締約國，並莊嚴聲明中國將把由徵收和國有化而引起的有關補償的爭端提交解決投資爭端國際中心（ICSID）仲裁解決。

儘管迄今尚未發生一起在ICSID仲裁解決的中國政府與外商投資者的爭端，但是，作為《華盛頓公約》的重要締約國，中國如何在該公約機制內發揮一個負責任的大國應有的作用，非常值得全面、深入的研究。由我國著名國際經濟法學者、中國國際經濟法學會會長、廈門大學法學教授、博士生導師陳安先生主編，復旦大學出版社於二〇〇一年九月出版的《國際投資爭端仲裁——「解決投資爭端國際中心」機制研究》（以下簡稱《仲裁》）一書，堪稱國際投資爭端仲裁領域的一部力作。該書與同時出版的《國際投資爭端案例精選》相輔相成，填補了該領域研究的一項空白。

該書包括緒論和三編。由陳安教授撰寫的緒論以獨特的筆觸，提出了一個鮮明的問題：在中國境內的涉外投資爭端中，外國的「民」可否控告中國的「官」，這使讀者頓感似乎是深奧莫測的國際投資爭端解決，其實就是我們身邊經常發生的尋常事。根據《中華人民共和國行政訴訟法》和《中華人民共和國行政複議法》，外商投資者在華對於各級政府及其主管部門違反有關法律、法規或不當的具體行政行為，均可通過行政訴訟或行政複議程式提起爭端解決。既然如此，允許外商投資者到國際上去訴告中國政府，豈不多此一舉？對於讀者可能產生的這一疑問，陳安教授以其親身經歷的當年圍繞中國是否加入《華盛頓公約》的爭論，澄清了問題的實質，即首先要了解ICSID的體制，「對於中國應否加入上述《華盛頓公約》以及在何種保留條件下方可參加這個《華盛頓公約》的問題，中國人應當儘早做到情況明瞭，胸有成竹，慎重決策，果斷行事」（《仲裁》第41頁）。這是非常務實的立場。正是基於這樣的立場，陳安教授及其研究團隊，通過三年緊張的研究，發表了《「解決投資爭端國際中心」述評》一書，為中國政府決策加入《華盛頓公約》提供了不可多得的國際法學理依據。事實證明，中國政府僅將徵收與國有化而產生的有關補償的爭端提交ICSID管轄，是完全正確的。這既通過中國加入《華盛頓公約》表明其對外開放、保障外商在華投資利益的堅定立場，又最大限度地避免了外商投資者在ICSID訴告中國政府的可能性，因為中國實行開放政策、吸收外資以來，從未發生過任何徵收在華外資與國有化事件。陳安教授在緒論中審時度勢，提出中國在面臨新的國內外形勢下是否應對一九九三年所作的保留再作適當的調整。根據《華盛頓公約》第二十五條第四款，任何締約國可以在正式加入該公約之後的任何時候，決定本國增加或減少接受ICSID管轄的爭端。在跨入二十一世紀的今天，這一提示，如同在二十世紀八〇年代中期提出是否加入該公約的問題一樣，促使中國人，尤其是中國的國際法學人開展腳踏實地的研究。

該書第一編分「管轄權」「法律適用」「臨時措施」「裁決撤銷」（英文「annulment」可譯為「取消」「使無效」）、「裁決的承認與執行」「比較研究」六部分詳細分析了ICSID的法律制度，構成了全書的核心內容。管轄權是ICSID受理國際投資爭端的前提，法律適用是解決爭端的關鍵，臨時措施是保障爭端當事方合法權益的必要手段，裁決撤銷是作為國際仲裁機構的該中心內部特有的審查機制，裁決的承認與執行是維係仲裁成效的最終環節。

任何國家加入《華盛頓公約》，意味著將或多或少地接受該中心的仲裁管轄權。從國際法的角度看，主權國家接受國際司法或仲裁機構的管轄，屬於讓渡主權的行為。任何一個國家都不能迫使另一個國家接受國際司法或仲裁機構的管轄。是否讓渡其部分主權，本身是國家行使其主權的表現。《華盛頓公約》第二十五條第四款規定，任何締約國可以在加入時聲明，或加入後的任何時候增減同意接受ICSID的管轄權範圍。這與國家主權原則是一致的。關鍵在於ICSID解決的主權國家與他國國民之間的投資爭端。在傳統國際法上，個人不是國際法的主體。但是，在國際投資領域，由於《華盛頓公約》的存在，個人根據國際公約的規定，有權訴告主權國家，因而成為國際法上的主體。這是國際法的重大變化。如何從國際法的一般原理上，對這一法律現象作深入分析，是推進《華盛頓公約》研究的理論意義之一。

基於國際仲裁的特點，ICSID在決定法律的適用問題上，首先尊重爭端當事方的協議選擇準據法，然後在沒有這種協定選擇的情況下，由仲裁庭決定可適用的法律（包括爭端當事方的實體法與衝突法，或國際法規則）。無論在哪種情況下，作為主權國家的一方和爭端當事方，都會面臨適用他國法律或國際法的可能性。《仲裁》一書花費一定筆墨分析了與之相關的國內法與國際法問題，認為「從理論上講，國內法與國際法應是協調一致的。不應存在衝突的情況，自然也不存在效力高低之分。一些國家規定國內法與其所訂立的條約抵觸時，優先適用條約規定，是國家協調整個法律體系的主動意願的表現，並非國際法自然優先於國內法」（第159頁）。這是中國國際法學界的一般觀點。不過，正如該書所指出的，在ICSID的實踐中，當適用國內法不能給投資者充分補償時，國際法往往處於優先地位。這與《華盛頓公約》第一條規定的「根據本公約」解決各締約國與其他締約國國民之間投資爭端這一宗旨是相吻合的，因為任何締約國加入《華盛頓公約》就意味著在其接受管轄的投資爭端領域，將讓渡其部分主權，這本身就是國際法優先。可見，研究《華盛頓公約》的法律文本及其實踐，對於我們進一步理解國內法與國際法的關係，不無裨益。

臨時措施是《華盛頓公約》第四十七條所規定的一項授予仲裁庭在必要時採取的程序性措施。《仲裁》一書根據ICSID的實踐，並結合ICSID《仲裁程式規則》新增第三十九條第五款認為，除非雙方當事人另有特別約定，ICSID仲裁庭對臨時措施申請享有排他的管轄權。這說明，該項程式性措施如同爭端當事方接受ICSID的管轄，都取決於雙方的約定。尤其是新增的第三十九條第五款表明先前仲裁庭在行使自由裁量權時存在偏差，因而需要法律本身的調整，以完善ICSID體制。這也證明該體制處在動態的完善過程中，需要我們跟蹤研究，而不能只停留在原先的了解水準。

ICSID的撤銷程式是指對仲裁庭不當構成、裁決明顯越權、仲裁員受賄等嚴重違法情況，任何一爭端當事方可以申請撤銷仲裁，由ICSID行政理事會主席從該中心仲裁員名單中指定成立的三人「專門委員會」（an ad hoc committee）審理，決定是否撤銷。顯然，這是ICSID內部獨特的監督機制。《仲裁》一書對該機制作了很深入的剖析，並提出國際上已有通過研究來自ICSID的仲裁實踐，反過來對其實踐又起著重要影響的案例。這種影響會越來越重要，我們必須對這一問題予以足夠的關注，以便應對今後中國在ICSID的可能爭端裁決。

與一般的國際仲裁裁決承認與執行（如《承認及執行外國仲裁裁決公約》）不同，ICSID的裁決等同於締約國國內法院的最終判決，每一締約國都應予以承認和執行，不得以任何理由（包括公共秩序保留）拒絕承認和執行裁決。這使得整個ICSID的機制具有了暢通的實施管道，即只要是締約國接受管轄，爭端當事方願意提交ICSID解決的國際投資爭端，最後由仲裁庭裁決，且沒有被撤銷的，都可在當事國內得到執行。由此可見，《華盛頓公約》是一個具有強約束力的國際法體系。

相比上述各部分的研究，「比較研究」顯得有些內容上的重複，如果在體系上將其比較有機地納入各部分，可能更好一點。

《仲裁》的第二編對ICSID解決的阿德里昂諾·加德拉公司訴象牙海岸共和國政府案、班弗努蒂和邦芬特公司訴剛果人民共和國政府案、阿姆科（亞洲）公司等訴印尼共和國、克勞科納公司訴喀麥隆政府案、大西洋特里頓公司訴幾內亞人民革命共和國案、南太平洋房地產（中東）有限公司等訴阿拉伯埃及共和國案、國際海運代理公司訴幾內亞人民革命共和國案七個成案的評述，可使讀者具體了解ICSID的運作機制。該書第三篇彙編了ICSID的基本法律文獻，可供讀者查閱。

八、俯視規則的迷宮

——讀陳安教授主編的《國際經濟法學專論》*

車丕照

國際經濟法學在法學各分支當中屬新興學科，其邊緣性和綜合性決定了所覆蓋內容的廣博和複雜，也成為接觸和研究本學科的難點和障礙。初識者往往畏其艱巨，感到難以入手；而研究者中則少有能夠縱橫各領域，融會精通諸多問題的全才。學習國際經濟法學只有先大體掌握有關的基礎知識，再進一步擴大學術視野和專業知識面，由淺入深，循序漸進。這就有賴於高水準的教材的引導。

《國際經濟法學專論》是廈門大學陳安教授等編寫的一部專門針對研究生的教材，單看其參編人員名單和目錄就能感覺到陣容之強大，內容之專深。本書所意圖面向的讀者，「主要是為法學、經濟學以及管理學這三個一級學科的碩士研究生」，「他們既有進一步學習國際經濟法學的共同需要，而其原有的知識結構和理論基礎又各有不同」。這樣的設計定位，在目前的教材中即使不是絕無僅有，也當屬少見，因為讀者對這一專業的知識既有可能是初次接觸，也有可能已經具備了相當的基礎，要兼顧兩者，則是對編撰提出了頗有難度的考驗，正如作者們自己所說，「是一種新的任務和新的嘗試」。

從我們做學生、做教師的體驗來看，一部好的法學教材至少應具有體系化的結構設計、啟迪性的理論闡述和與時俱進的實踐追蹤。也就是說，作為教材，它必須肩負著引領入門的功能，保證將學科內容完整地呈現於前，使讀者對該學科基本知識形成系統化認識。《國際經濟法學專論》一書承繼了諸多優良教材的傳統，同時基於其特殊的定位，該書又強調基礎理論的分析，並有意在各章節的篇幅安排上，「側重於對當代國際經濟法學科領域中重大的理論爭議問題、前沿性的熱點難點問題以及具有重大意義的實務問題，做出比較深入的剖析和評介」。從這些方面來看，本書又不囿於教材的框架束縛，而力圖以新穎的視角「激發讀者進一步學習的興趣和熱情，自行加深鑽研當代新鮮有益的知識和追蹤國際前沿的學術發展」，因此，這套書也可看作對深入研究本學科具有啟迪作用的專門著作。

筆者對這部教材只是通讀了一遍，但也為其鮮明的個性特色所吸引。通觀下來，其內容和結構上的獨特之處至少有以下幾個方面：

一是這部教材對國際經濟法學的知識覆蓋達到了相當的廣度和深度，在借鑑和吸收國內外現有的理論研究成果的基礎上，系統地闡明了本學科的基本原理。作為教育部研究生工作辦公室推薦的第一批研究生教學用書之一，這套書首先應具有教材的功用，須具有教材嚴密清晰的邏輯體系結構。法學是一門特別講求邏輯嚴謹的學科，體系思維作為法學的方法由來已久。借助體系，不但有助於保證一門學科內容的完整性，形成對該學科基本知識的全面認識，而且可以通過體系本身的邏輯推理獲取新知。這套教材體例結構上共分十章，上下兩編各含五章。上編為「國際經濟法學總論」，系統闡述了國際經濟法的基本理論，包括國際經濟法的含義、主體、淵源和基本原則等；下編為「國際經濟法學分論」，包括國際貿易法、國際投資法、國際貨幣金融法、國際稅法和國際海事法，概述了國際經濟法各分支學科的基本知識，分別探討了各分支的重要理論問題，並有重點地介紹一些主要的難點和熱點問題。全書的安排，對有關知識板塊是全面完整的，使讀者能夠從宏觀上對國際經濟法整個學科有概括的了解，即使是初學者也不會有片面和偏頗的理解，可對專業全貌了然於胸，不至於有以管窺豹之虞。

二是書中所引用的背景資料翔實新穎，跟蹤和反映了國際經濟法學科的最新發展。強調這一點是因為，國際經濟法學相對其他法學科目而言是一門新興的學科，緊跟和關注國際學術前沿顯得尤為重要。本書的各位作者長期關注國內外的學術研究狀況，從而可以在這套教材當中自如地援引和評判國外的研究成果。例如，本書在國際經濟法的基本原則「經濟主權」一節中所簡介的由世界貿易組織體制而引發的美國「1994年主權大辯論」大量引用了漢金教授和傑克遜教授著作中的內容，盡可能地貼近事實原貌和第一手材料，將辯論過程的來龍去脈娓娓道來，使讀者能夠比較客觀詳盡地了解事情的始末。而後，作者又對這次主權大辯論和美國的「301條款」加以評論並且對其後續影響進行概括性的分析，所有這些都是基於二〇〇〇年前後事態的最新局勢作出的論述。在該小節末了，作者又深刻剖析了這場激烈論戰的實質和核心，筆鋒回轉到經濟主權對於發展中國家的重要性主題上來，這樣在充分鮮活的證據上得出的結論確鑿可信，一反這種純理論問題空洞口號式的面目，讀之使人頓感耳目一新、視野大開。如此行文布置，正是本書面對特定讀者的匠心所在，冀以提供新的視角，引發深層思考。

三是這套教材十分重視國際經濟法的總論部分，獨立成編，有五章之多，在篇幅上占全書的百分之四十強。當下的國際經濟法教材大多不很重視總論部分的論述，究其原因，大概是由於國際經濟法學本身還是一門新興的邊緣性學科，其內容範圍、法律規範的源起和發展、與相鄰法律部門的關係等基本問題都仍然存在諸多歧義，學術界眾說不一。僅以「國際經濟法」的含義和範圍為例，就有認定其為國際公法新分支的狹義說和認為是調整國際經濟關係的國際國內法綜合體的廣義說兩種學術觀點，前者以英國的施瓦曾伯格、日本的金澤良雄以及法國的卡羅為代表，後者則為美國的傑塞普、斯泰納、瓦格茨、傑克遜、洛文費爾德以及日本的櫻井雅夫所主張。雖然以往的國際經濟法學教材也都會在總論部分力求給讀者一個學理上的說明，但是像這套書這樣對總論施以濃墨重彩的尚不多見。比如上面的例子，書中不僅介紹了兩種學說的分歧，歸納了每位代表學者各自的觀點，還對兩大學派觀點進行了整體分析。整個上編都以這種細緻的態度將國際經濟法學的概念、淵源、主體、基本原則以及國際經濟爭端的解決梳理透澈。這對於讀者深入了解國際經濟法學科無疑是大有裨益的。

四是本書在分論中將國際海事法以專章納入，擴大了學科的研究範圍，體現了本學科體系的廣博複雜。如前所述，國際經濟法的綜合性代表著它必然與諸多相鄰門類有多方面的相互交叉、相互滲透和相互融合的關係，這些複雜的關係也是學界歷來關注的重點之一。本書沒有拘泥於國際經濟法傳統意義上的分支歸類，轉而採取「以現實法律問題為中心」，以某種國際經濟法律關係或某類經濟法律問題為中心的研討途徑或剖析方法，將國際海事法歸為國際經濟法的一個組成部分。海事法通常被認為屬於商法範疇，但是，本書認為「航海貿易活動和海事行為由於其國際性或者涉外性極強而成為一種國際經濟現象，應該屬於國際經濟法學的研究範疇」。因此，本書從研究實際問題的角度出發，探討了有關國際航運的法律法規的現狀及其理論研究狀況，涉及國際海事關係包括航海貿易的國際公約和國際慣例。對於這樣的劃歸各家當然可以見仁見智，但實際上，很多國際經濟法領域是離不開海事法的相關內容的，尤其是海上運輸、海上保險、共同海損以及海事賠償責任限制等，幾乎是與國際貿易如影隨形的問題。既然如此，將國際海事法寫進國際經濟法的教科書中，也是順理成章的事情。

五是這套書在內容上密切聯繫中國實際，結合中國國情，剖析了南北矛盾的發展和國際經濟新秩序的進程，反映出中國國際經濟法學的特色。任何法學學科研究最終的目的還是要服務於社會實踐，國際經濟法這樣一個實踐性很強的學科尤應如此。各國的國際經濟法學者通常也都是從本國實際出發，研究本國政府和私人在對外經濟交往活動中所涉及的國際法和國內法問題。本書在總論中對中國對外經濟交往及其與學習國際經濟法學的關係，乃至中國目前國際經濟法學的研究概況都有介紹，在分論中所有重要的法律問題後面都對中國目前的相關情況加以概括和評析，並對中國未來應採取的立場和對策提出了建議，這些已經在書中奠定為基本的研究方法和思維方式，貫徹全書始終。

當然，一部教材要做到「雅俗共賞」，令不同讀者各有收益、各取所需實非易事。儘管編著時可能已經竭盡所能在內容編排和知識材料上精益求精，但是仍然有值得商榷和探討的地方存在。從書本身的定位來說，其創意堪稱上佳，然而書名既為「專論」，無妨專業性再加強一些，在教材的普及性和專著的深入性之間向後者再稍作傾斜，突顯研究生教育術業專攻的特色。加強專業理論的同時，一些史料性的常識作適當的指導即可，引導讀者以本書為綱，展開延伸性的閱讀，充分發揮研究生的自主學習研究特性，有選擇和有重點地傳道授業。另外，書中某些具體的說法似乎還可推敲。例如，在分析中國《關於外商投資舉辦投資性公司的暫行規定》第十條時，本書認為，由於投資性公司儘管為外國投資者設立，但仍然是中國法人，不符合《中外合資經營企業法》第一條有關「外國合營者」的定義，因此，允許投資性公司或投資性公司與其他外國投資者在中國投資的外匯投資比例占註冊資本百分之二十五以上的企業享受外商投資企業待遇，是與《中外合資經營企業法》的有關規定相抵觸的。其實，此處「享受外商投資企業待遇」並不意味著就將其劃歸為中外合資企業，只是在待遇上給予相同的優惠。準用類似規定，並無定性的意圖，應該不存在相互抵觸的問題。

總體說來，這是一套高水準的教材。作學科啟蒙之用，她可以給讀者以準確而全面的引導；作專業研討之用，她又可以不時地激發學術爭鳴。綜觀目前國內的本學科教材，就品質而言能達此高度進而出其之右者可謂鮮矣。

九、「問題與主義」中的「問題」

——讀《國際經濟法學專論》*

車丕照

自二十世紀五四運動以降，中國理論界呈現為「問題與主義」之間的巨大分野，個中分殊使得所持論者成家、成言、成派。這種先決研究導向的對峙始終伴隨著理論界的發展，或可與我們文化傳統中在乎的名分、大統攸攸相關。然而，在「百家爭鳴」「百花齊放」中恢復活力的中國法學界，「問題」與「主義」間的「杯葛」的確為復興的法學研究貢獻了氛圍、繁榮乃至前進的動力。究竟什麼是我們的研究範圍？我們的研究範圍是先於問題而設定呢，還是通過問題來圈定我們的研究邊界？我們研究的意義在何處？這些「問題與主義」的設問現在看來已經頗具歷史氣息，卻曾經纏繞著許多學科，國際經濟法學作為法域中的後起之秀在此間的搖擺尤為激烈。在這個論域中，如果將堅守國際法傳統學科劃分的學人們比作「主義」的倡言人，那麼號召國際經濟法以問題導向而應自成體系的則是「問題」一派。無疑，陳安教授是「問題」一派的領軍人物和傑出代表，先生多年來孜孜以求，著述等身，為「問題」下了一個個有力的注腳。而《國際經濟法學專論》，正是先生為「問題」所下注腳的鮮活教案。

（一）

對「主義」論者而言，範圍設定的優先性先於問題，在他們看來，是範圍制約了問題的尋找和解決。與之相對應，「問題」論者眼中的範圍卻因問題而設，是問題廓清了研究範圍的邊界。於是，學科的劃定及其任務的紛爭就在「問題與主義」的屋簷下展開。透過「問題與主義」的對話與對峙，我們見到的是方法論之間的交鋒。如果只是純粹從價值角度出發，殊難判別兩種方法間的優劣高下。然而，結合國際經濟法生成歷史來看，卻別有一番韻味。如書中開篇所示，國際經濟法所調整法律關係的外延因不同的歷史時期而呈現擴大的趨勢。從羅得的商人習慣法、羅馬法、中世紀《康索拉多海商法典》，經歷了近現代的雙邊、多邊的商務規約和習慣，乃至現今的轉折、更新階段的專題公約和慣例，有兩條重要線索的延伸方向值得我們關注，一是量的累積，即法律關係所涉範圍的不斷擴大；二是質的遞進，即從習慣到條約所帶來的約束力和確定性增加。兩條線索鋪陳了國際經濟法所調整法律關係由簡到繁的成長路徑，這個歷程也是國際經濟法律關係所涉問題不斷產生的過程。顯然，如書中對這個學科發展的描述，這是一條「轉折尚在更新」中的道路，要先決式地確立自己的研究範圍，進而又能通過設定成熟的方法普適地解決其中問題仍顯過早。

由此看來，我們甚至可以說，國際經濟法學是一個在問題產生和問題解決鏈條上不斷延伸中形成的學科。或許在這根鏈條能夠延伸到足夠遠時，我們才能確定它的邊界。

（二）

究竟什麼是國際經濟法學所關注的「問題」呢？作者從歷史的視角，比較、總結前人的研究之後認為，國際經濟法「是一個涉及國際法與國內法、公法與私法、國際私法以及各國涉外經濟法、民商法等多種法律規範的邊緣性綜合體」。這一定義對國際經濟法學中「問題」的特點進行了抽象和概括，是在實證層面進行了充分論證之後得出的結論。為此，書中以一家跨國公司為例證，從六個方面對國際經濟活動中可能衍生問題的方向進行了具體闡釋，其中的法律關係從效力層面來看有條約法律關係、合同法律關係；從經濟活動範圍層面來看，有投資法律關係、買賣法律關係、稅收法律關係以及爭端解決等等。所涉法律關係阡陌縱橫，既包含平權的國家與國家、私人與私人、國家與私人之間的法律關係，也包含非平權的國家與私人間的法律關係。這些「問題」構成要素的交錯和邊緣化，使得人們無法從傳統國際法的單一視角出發找到問題的解決方法。此時，一個開放、全方位的審視就顯得突出而必要。因此，如作者所言，「國際經濟法是根據迫切的現實需要『應運而生』的綜合性法律部門，從而，國際經濟法學乃是一門獨立的邊緣性法學學科。這門新興學科的邊緣性和綜合性，並非出於人為的任意湊合，而是國際經濟法律關係本身極其錯綜複雜這一客觀存在的真實反映，也就是科學地調整這種複雜關係，對其中複雜的法律癥結加以綜合診斷和辨證施治的現實需要」。這是全書「問題」意識最為直接的表達。

全書的上下兩編分別為總論與分論，互有分工，互為映襯。兩編有著相同的「問題」觀，從體例安排上徹底將「問題」體系化。從內容上看，上編對「問題」進行了全面的統攝，囊括的所有內容由一條主線統領，這條主線牽扯了針對「問題」全部共有屬性的總結。從國際經濟法內涵的界定、規範的淵源澄清、主體範圍的歸納，到所有「問題」共戴原則的分析以及與「問題」相關的爭端解決機制，作者在對理論上的存疑、爭論梳理的過程中破立相承，逐漸闡明了對待「問題」的開放態度，從而固守了「國際經濟法學這一新興學科具有邊緣性、綜合性和獨立性」的立場。而下編的內容則是對「問題」的具體化，將問題落實在幾個實在的分支中，包括國際貿易法、國際投資法、國際貨幣金融法、國際稅法和國際海事法，這種橫向的布局使得所涉領域幾乎涵蓋了全部的國際經濟活動。可以看出，在「問題」的引導中形成的國際經濟法學，並非一個自足自閉的體系，然而上述「開放式」的體例安排卻為新「問題」的產生和舊「問題」的延展提供了足夠的空間。

（三）

在解決「問題」的過程中，我們應該持有怎樣的態度和立場呢？這關涉到學科研究的效用和命運。對此，筆者認為有兩個方面值得關注，其一是「問題」的定位，這實際上是對「問題」進行「識別」；其二是解決「問題」的立場，到底我們應該為誰服務？毫無疑問，立場關係到我們看待「問題」的價值評判並制約著解決方案的產生。

該書在對國際經濟法進行了「邊緣性、綜合性」的學科定位之後，通篇以實際的議論對「問題」解決方法賦予了多學科、多部門的大視野。這意味著，當一個具體的問題擺在我們面前時，我們面臨的首要任務就是「識別」。只有將其歸入某類法律部門範疇，才有可能從權利義務的角度對這個問題進行剖析。同時，還要關注這一問題是否還兼具其他部門或學科的特點。這是因為國際法與國內法、私法與公法對待權利義務的看法並不一致，對待權利衝突的方式也各不相同。例如，涉及國家在國際經濟法中的地位問題時，如果將國家放在國與國之間的關係的背景下加以研究的話，那麼我們所面臨的其實是國際公法的問題，應用於問題解決的方法自然要從國際公法的立場出發。如果把國家放在與國際交往的當事人法律關係的背景下加以考察，此時所面臨的問題則主要是內國法的非平權主體間的法律問題。由此可以看出多視角對於一個邊緣學科發展的重要意義，而書中所論的最大特點就是很好地貫徹了這一基點。

在國際經濟法學中，如果說明晰「問題」中的多元化因素是從客觀上澄清「問題」的癥結，無疑，對待「問題」的立場表達則是從主觀上尋找「問題」解決的努力。顯然，立場將決定我們到底維護著怎樣的利益。二戰後，所有的發展中國家面臨著一個秩序難題，即如何推倒一個舊有經濟秩序和重塑一個新經濟秩序，這是戰後國際政治經濟格局巨變給民族國家造成的影響。對這一歷史潮流，書中通過對「經濟主權原則」「公平互利原則」「全球合作原則」的描述，著重強調發展中國家的身份對國際經濟新秩序的貢獻和塑造，一再重申了發展中國家的立場。對此，筆者認為，儘管發展中國家身份是開展國際經濟法研究時不可忽略的一種身份，然而作為民族國家的身份才是我們參與經濟活動最原始、最根本、最核心的身份，而民族國家的立場則是我們開展研究的基礎和出發點。這是因為，雖然發展中國家有改造經濟秩序的初衷和動力，但是秩序的改變終究依靠的是實力的對比。隨著時間的推移，秩序中所謂南北力量的博弈並沒有出現發展中國家所期待的那般消長。此外，隨著全球化進程的加快，國家之間的利益連接較之過往更加密切，也使得發展中國家共同的利益越來越模糊。當發展中國家的身份無助於我們對現行秩序的改變時，就只有以民族國家的身份加強對現行秩序的參與。況且，這種強調民族國家立場的地方性共識越來越成為全球化過程中的主流話語了。

（四）

為「問題」構築一個體系是本書作者們的治學觀。對國際經濟法學而言，這是一個開放的「問題」體系，「問題」的發展和更新對體系的完善不可或缺，而本書在這方面的作為令人稱道。「問題」的歸納、演繹、銜接被作者把握得非常流暢，例如，議論經濟主權時談及由WTO體制引發的美國「1994年主權大辯論」就大量引用了漢金（Henkin）教授和傑克遜（Jackson）教授著作中的內容，盡可能地利用第一手材料，將辯論過程準確地描述出來，使讀者能客觀詳盡地了解事情的始末。而後，作者針對主權大辯論和美國的「301條款」進行評論以及對其後續影響進行概括性的分析時，都是基於二〇〇〇年前後的最新態勢作出的論述。

面對問題叢生的國際經濟法律實踐，多談些「問題」，少談些「主義」，讓我們在尋找「問題」答案的過程中，且行且珍惜。相信水到渠成，這個過程本身就寄寓了尋找「問題」邊界的意義。這份務實態度和成熟的「問題」觀不僅是我對作者欣賞的理由，而且為我們的貢獻指明了方向。

十、高屋建瓴　視角獨到

——推薦《晚近十年來美國單邊主義與WTO多邊主義交鋒的三大回合》*

戚燕方

陳安教授撰寫的《晚近十年來美國單邊主義與WTO多邊主

義交鋒的三大回合》（The Three Big Rounds of U. S. Unilateralism Versus WTO Multilateralism During the Last Decade）原以英文發表於美國天普大學《國際法與比較法學報》二〇〇三年第十七卷第二期（*Temple International & Comparative Law Journal*, Vol. 17, No. 2, 2003），全文約六萬五千字。其後，應本刊約稿，陳安教授摘取其中部分內容約二萬字，並增補最新資訊，題為《美國單邊主義對抗WTO多邊主義的第三回合——「201條款」爭端之法理探源和展望》，發表於《中國法學》二〇〇四年第二期。

文章從此次「201條款」爭端說起，首先簡要回顧了晚近十年來美國單邊主義與WTO多邊主義交鋒的三大回合，然後從宏觀上綜合探討了其中蘊含的原則碰撞和法理衝突，並對今後可能的發展進行了預測。作為本文中文版的責任編輯，我認為，該文高屋建瓴、視角獨到，具有極強的現實針對性和學術理論性，其資料翔實全面，邏輯嚴謹，說理透澈，是這一學術領域中研究相關問題不可多得的佳作。

據我們獲得的資訊，陳安教授撰寫的上述論文相繼發表後，引起了較大反響，獲得了國內外的廣泛好評。在國內，中國國際法學會二〇〇四年四月的研討會和中國法學會世界貿易組織研究會二〇〇四年五月的研討會，均將上述中文版論文收人專輯文集，引起廣泛重視。

在國際上，美國上述學報的責編Laura Kolb指出，該刊選擇發表的論文，是他們認為「當前最受關注的、最引人人勝和最有創見的」文章。陳教授的這篇文章「論證有理有據，主題緊扣時局，資料豐富翔實」，「雄辯犀利，發人深思」，「會使國際法理論界和實務界都大感興趣」。總部設在美國華盛頓的「多邊投資擔保機構（MIGA）」首席法律顧問Lorin Weisenfeld認為這篇文章「確實是具有頭等水準的佳作」，「論據充分，雄辯有力」，促使他全面反思近年來布希政府在國際舞臺上的所作所為和霸道行徑。特別值得注意的是：總部設在日內瓦的政府間國際組織「南方中心」是由六十一個發展中國家（含中國）簽署國際協定共同組建的「思想庫」和「智囊機構」。最近，其秘書長Branislav Gosovic來函告知：擬將這篇文章作為「南方中心」的專題出版物，即「貿易發展與公平」專題議程（T. R. A. D. E.）的系列工作檔之一，重印和擴大發行，使廣大讀者均能看到，特別是提供給眾多發展中國家政府，作為議事決策參考。同時擬將本文列人「南方中心」的專門電子網站，供讀者自由免費下載。據我們所知，中國法學家的長篇學術論文能有如此國際影響並引起國際政府間組織如此重視者，並不多見。

綜上情況，我們鄭重推薦陳安教授的上述中、英文版論文，參加申報學術評獎。

二〇〇四年六月六日

十一、以史為師　力排「眾議」　說理透闢

——推薦《南南聯合自強五十年的國際經濟立法反思》*

戚燕方

WTO第六屆部長級會議二〇〇五年十二月在中國香港地區

召開，重啟「多哈發展回合」多邊談判。對此次香港會議的結局及其發展前景，國際輿論見仁見智，褒貶不一：或「樂觀」認為WTO多邊體制從此步人坦途；或「悲觀」認為WTO多邊體制瀕臨瓦解；或畏難，或失望，或茫然。

陳安教授多年來跟蹤研究南北矛盾和南北合作問題，積累豐厚，他全面地收集、整理香港會議後國際上出現的各種看法和見解，有的放矢地加以綜合剖析，撰寫了英、中兩種文本的長篇論文。英文本題為「Reflections on the South-South Coalition in the Last Half Century from the Perspective of International Economic Law-making」中文本題為《南南聯合自強五十年的國際經濟立法反思》，先後投寄國外學術期刊和《中國法學》本刊。

作者主張：應當認真回顧五十年來發展中國家在南北矛盾中實行「南南聯合自強」、力爭更新國際經濟立法的主要史實和曲折進程，以史為師，從宏觀上總結經驗，學會運用歷史的慧眼，正視當代「南弱北強」和「南多北寡」的客觀現實，自覺地認識和運用五十年來南北矛盾和南北合作中反覆出現的螺旋式「6C律」，排除「速勝」論、「坦途」論和「瓦解」論的影響，多一份冷靜、耐心和韌性，少一些脫離實際的盲目「樂觀」或無端「悲觀」。即使香港會議之後，多哈回合各項重大難題的談判再次出現「拉鋸」或僵局，甚至再次不歡而散，也早在意料之中，國際社會弱勢群體即眾多發展中國家應早作思想準備，繼續以南南聯合自強的韌性奮鬥精神和靈活多樣的策略，從容應對，力求「多哈發展回合」的新一輪多邊談判在其後續的二〇〇六年底，或更遲一些，得以在公平互利、南北合作的基礎上全面完成。總之，要逐步更新國際經濟立法、建立起國際經濟新秩序，舍韌性的南南聯合自強，別無他途可循！

我作為本文中文本的責任編輯，在審閱過程中，深感此文旗幟鮮明，站在國際弱勢群體的共同立場，以史為據，以史為師，史論結合，視角獨到，「力排眾議」，頗多創新，具有極強的現實針對性和學術理論性。其資料翔實全面，邏輯嚴謹，說理透徹，論證雄辯，是這一學術領域中不可多得的力作和佳作。

有關資訊資料顯示此文在本刊發表後，獲得讀者廣泛好評。其英文本在日內瓦引起廣泛重視，先由國際組織「南方中心」機關報發表了其中的核心部分，並公布於ICSID網站，擴大宣傳；另有兩家國際性學刊相繼全文刊載。據我們所知，中國法學家撰寫的長篇學術論文，能引起國際組織和國際性學刊如此重視、具有如此國際影響者，尚不多見。

綜上，我們鄭重推薦陳安教授的上述中、英文版論文，參加申報學術評獎。

二〇〇六年五月三十一日

十二、緊扣學科前沿　力求與時俱進

——推薦《國際經濟法學》（第三版）*

楊立範

廈門大學陳安先生主編的《國際經濟法學》一書，綜合反映了國際經濟法學這一新興邊緣學科的基本理論和基本知識，是對國際經濟法主要內容的精心濃縮和精闢論述。全書內容科學、立論獨到、取材新穎、涵蓋全面、重點突出，在國內同類出版物中達到領先水準，深受讀者喜愛。本書第一版自一九九四年十二月由北京大學出版社出版以來，迄二〇〇一年三月，先後重印七次，累計五一五二〇冊。由於本書具有以上特點和優點，又被全國高等教育自學考試指導委員會指定為全國高等教育自學考試統編教材，並於一九九四年十二月至二〇〇一年三月，先後重印十二次，印數達二三一一〇〇冊。以上兩項合計，迄二〇〇一年三月為止，印數共達二八二六二〇冊。

二〇〇一年四月，本社推出《國際經濟法學》（第二版），由作者們依據本書第一版推出後七年來的形勢發展，對原書加以認真修訂、增補，添加了大量新鮮知識和前沿信息，進一步提高了學術水準，並繼續作為高等學校法學教材以及全國高等教育自學考試指定教材被廣泛採用。第二版問世以來短短三年半，經過三十一次印刷，兩種印數共二三〇二〇〇冊。與第一版總印數合計，兩版總印數五一二八二〇冊，足見本書很受廣大讀者歡迎。

二〇〇四年一至八月，本書作者們又根據經濟全球化加速發展和中國加入世界貿易組織後出現的國際經濟政治秩序的最新格局，並結合近十年來本書在全國高等教育教學實踐中被廣泛採用的效果和經驗，對本書內容再次作了全面的修訂、增補和更新。

本書第三版於二〇〇四年十一月底以嶄新面貌問世，全書共七十三點三萬字，首印八千冊，在兩個多月內迅即售罄，隨即在二〇〇五年二月第二次印刷一萬二千冊，市場需求繼續看旺；經作者們再稍加修訂，近期內即將進行第三次印刷。十年來本書前後三種版本的累計印數，已達五三二八二〇冊。這種情況表明：十年來本書內容的不斷更新和提高，確實做到了「緊扣學科前沿，力求與時俱進」，因而切合當代中國高校讀者學習新知的需要，具有旺盛的學術生命力。

基於以上情況，茲特鄭重推薦上述著作參加省部級、國家級優秀科研成果及優秀教材評獎活動。

二〇〇五年三月十五日

注釋

* 這原是中華人民共和國商務部條法司致廈門大學法學院的一份公函「感謝信」，文號為「商法投資函〔2008〕40號」。標題為本書作者所加。
* 本篇書評原發表於《福建日報》1986年5月10日。作者是當時鷺江出版社社長兼總編輯。
* 本篇書評原發表於《中國國際法年刊》，法律出版社1988年版，第407-502頁。作者余勁松當時在武漢大學法學院執教，現為中國人民大學法學院教授、博士生導師。
* 本篇書評原發表於《廈門大學學報（哲學社會科學版）1992年第3期，第132-134頁。作者徐崇利現為廈門大學法學院教授、博士生導師。
* 本篇書評原發表於《文匯讀書週報》1996年3月23日。作者吳煥寧現為中國政法大學國際法學院教授、博士生導師。
* 本篇書評原發表於《福建日報》1995年3月31日。作者單文華當時在廈門大學法學院攻讀博士學位，現為英國牛津布魯克斯大學法學院和西安交通大學法學院教授、博士生導師。
* 本篇書評原發表於《中國圖書評論》2002年第5期，第43-45頁。作者張乃根現為復旦大學法學院教授、博士生導師。
* 作者車丕照現為清華大學法學院教授、博士生導師。
* 本篇書評原發表於《政法論壇》2005年第1期，第189-191頁。作者車丕

照現為清華大學法學院教授、博士生導師。

* 本篇評論是《中國法學》雜誌社戚燕方副編審撰寫的參評推薦意見。現徵得作者同意，輯入本書

* 本篇評論是《中國法學》雜誌社戚燕方副編審撰寫的參評推薦意見。現徵得作者同意，輯入本書。

* 本篇評論是《國際經濟法學》一書的責編、北京大學出版社楊立范副總編撰寫的參評推薦意見。現徵得作者同意，輯入本書。

第四章

群賢畢至，少長咸集，坐而論道，暢敘舊情

二〇〇九年五月，陳安教授八十誕辰之際，廈門大學法學院國際經濟法專業歷屆博士生學友，從全國各地風塵僕僕趕來母校，濟濟一堂，舉行「中國國際經濟法的研究方法暨陳安教授學術思想」研討會，猶如王羲之《蘭亭序》所說「群賢畢至，少長咸集」，坐而論道，暢敘友情。會後廈大《校友通訊》整理了九篇發言稿，集中刊發。作為歷史資料，輯錄於本書第六編，以饗同道，並祈惠正。

一、在「中國國際經濟法的研究方法暨陳安教授學術思想」研討會上的致辭

辜芳昭*

尊敬的陳安教授、尊敬的各位來賓、老師們、同學們：

上午好！

今天，我們歡聚一堂，共同慶賀陳安教授八十華誕暨從教五十八週年，隆重召開「中國國際經濟法的研究方法暨陳安教授學術思想」研討會。這是廈門大學的一件喜事，也是一件盛事。在

這裡，請允許我代表廈門大學向陳安教授表示熱烈的祝賀和崇高的敬意！向前來參加大會的社會各界朋友、校友表示熱烈的歡迎！同時祝賀「中國國際經濟法的研究方法暨陳安教授學術思想」研討會隆重召開！作為陳安教授多年的同事和晚輩，還想借此機會向陳安教授表示我良好的祝願！

陳安教授是我國法學界知名的學者，也是德才雙馨的名師。陳安教授一九五〇年七月畢業於廈門大學法律系，隨後從事過短暫的司法審判工作，於一九五一年一月調回母校廈門大學法律系任教，從此與廈門大學的教學事業結下了不解之緣。

陳安教授是廈門大學國際經濟法學科的創建人和學術帶頭人。早在我校法律系復辦伊始，陳安教授與法律系的其他同仁為適應改革開放之急需，確立了創建國際經濟法專業的學科發展戰略，並先後於一九八二年、一九八五年和一九八六年獲准招收國際經濟法專業的碩士生、本科生和博士生。一九八七年，陳安教授主編出版的國內第一套國際經濟法系列著作，為我校國際經濟法學科的發展奠定了基礎。陳安教授是中國特色國際經濟法的奠基人之一，也是這個學科永不知疲倦的開拓者。一九九三年起，陳安教授連選連任中國國際經濟法學會的會長。陳安教授還是中國國際經濟法實踐的先行者之一。他承擔、承辦了許多重要的國策諮詢和典型的國際經貿仲裁司法案件，是我國政府根據《華盛頓公約》遴選向「解決投資爭端國際中心」（ICSID）指派的國際仲裁員。我們都知道，陳安教授是改革開放之初，我國較早走出國門在國際舞臺同外國同行同臺競技、同臺抗辯的一位出色學者，他的作為為廈門大學贏得了榮譽，為國家爭得了尊嚴。

今天，我們在這裡慶賀陳安教授八十華誕暨從教五十八週年，就是要學習他為人師表的典範和追求科學的精神。陳安教授孜孜不倦地追求著學術，而科學的高峰是無止境的，攀登這座高峰，不僅需要堅韌的毅力，也需要一種不畏勞苦的勇氣。古人常說「學海無涯苦作舟」，陳安教授就是一位在學海中不畏艱險、乘風破浪的掌舵手。陳安教授著作等身，他的鴻篇巨著《國際經濟法學芻言》和《陳安論國際經濟法學》，以及發表於海內外權威學術期刊上的中英文學術論文，忠實地記錄了他對學術的執著和對中國特色國際經濟法學的傑出貢獻。陳安教授現雖已八十高壽，但仍然以老驥伏櫪、志在千里的精神從不懈怠，從事著他鍾愛的學術活動。這種堅持、這份追求永遠是我們學習的榜樣。

陳安教授學為人師、行為示範。他對大學講壇的敬重，對教學的認真，同樣令我們敬佩。陳安教授熱愛教師職業，喜愛他的學生。記得我在法學院工作的多年時間裡，陳安教授已經是一名很有名望的教授，也已經不是一位很年輕的教授。但他不僅帶好他的研究生，還經常騰出時間給本科生開設講座。這也正是我們廈門大學現在一直提倡和要求的，即教授要給本科生開課。凡是有緣於陳安教授授課的學生，對他講課的嚴謹和講課的精彩，以及從課堂上所獲取的知識與能力，都會留下終生難忘的印象。我知道在這個精彩的背後，付出的是十倍的艱辛。願意這樣付出的老師源於他對教育事業的忠誠，對學生的責任，這種精神是我們應該提倡和學習的。陳安教授既教書又育人，對他的學生既言傳又身教，誨人不倦，以提攜後人為己任。他真誠地關心每一位學生的成長，指導了眾多的青年教師。我相信在座的很多人，都曾經得益過、受惠過陳安教授的教誨與關心。從教五十八年來，陳安教授和他的團隊已經為國家和社會培養了一大批優秀的、出類拔萃的人才。這批人，大多在教學、科研、政府機關、企事業單位成為中堅力量，為國家做出了突出的貢獻。

借此機會，我要再次恭祝陳安教授健康長壽、學術之樹常青；預祝「中國國際經濟法的研究方法暨陳安教授學術思想」研討會取得圓滿成功！謝謝！

二、我與陳安教授

趙龍躍*

我認識陳安教授的時間並不長，那是在四年前的一次國際學術會議上。

二〇〇五年二月，在美國國際法學會舉辦的國際年會上，我非常榮幸地認識了陳安教授。陳教授在大會上的精彩演講，觀點鮮明、論據翔實，直接抨擊了美國實行單邊貿易保護主義的危害。再加上他那純正的美國英語發音、層次分明的演示框架，給包括我在內的所有與會的各國專家學者留下了深刻的印象；陳教授的機智反應，以及與世界著名國際經濟法學專家、被譽為「WTO之父」的約翰·傑克遜教授的一番精彩辯論，更是讓我們深深地折服。那次陳教授在華盛頓訪問不到一個星期，日程安排得很緊張，每天晚上我都要開車到陳教授下榻的飯店，開懷暢談，一談就談到深夜，大有如遇知音、相見恨晚之感。但是，無論從陳教授的身體狀況，還是從他充滿追求的精神狀態，我都沒有想到他已經是一位快到八十歲的人了。

這次我非常榮幸能應邀參加「中國國際經濟法的研究方法暨陳安教授學術思想」研討會，我覺得活動舉辦得十分成功，具有重要意義。我相信每一位校友和在校的師生都和我一樣，受到了極大的鼓舞和鞭策。我十分羡慕陳教授為我國國際經濟法學的創立和發展，為廈門大學法學院學科建設和人才培養所做出的巨大貢獻；羨慕陳教授學富五車、著作等身、桃李滿天下的豐碩成果。從事教育工作，成就是可以疊加和倍增的，這種成就帶來的欣慰和滿足，是從事其他工作所難以得到的。

出席今天會議的嘉賓，從各個方位給陳教授作了一個全面的總結，如知識淵博、學貫中西、治學嚴謹、疾惡如仇、知識報國、兼濟天下等，對這些我深有同感。另外，我覺得陳教授還有幾個很獨特的方面，非常值得我們學習。一是老驥伏櫪、志在千里；二是思想活躍、開拓創新；三是立足中國、放眼全球。陳教授雖然已經是八十高齡，但是他的思想依然非常活躍，很容易接受新鮮事物；面對困難不畏縮，解決問題不機械。陳教授年過半百後才到哈佛大學學習，回國後就著手國際經濟法學的教學與研究工作。當時在沒有師資、沒有教材、沒有學生的情況下，他先從培養師資入手，招收了四名研究生，然後才招本科生；先翻譯引進美國的原著，然後又編寫了我國自己的國際經濟法學教科書；學生從無到有，現在廈門大學法學院培養的學生已經都成為我國法學界的骨幹，有的是兄弟院校的校長或法學院的院長，有的是活躍於我國各地律師事務所的法律工作者，以及世界各地法學界的教授和學者。這是陳教授策劃和推進的一項多麼偉大的工程。我們今天慶祝陳教授八十壽辰，就是要學習他的這種精神，要有理想要有追求，爭取多為社會做一些有意義的工作。同時，陳教授的成功對我們今天的年輕人來說也是一個巨大的鼓舞，我們生活在這麼好的年代，有這麼好的條件，所以應該也相信你們會做得更好。

三、誨人不倦　師道悠悠

鍾興國*

陳安教授從事教學科研六十年，六十年在人類歷史的長河中是非常短暫的一剎那，但是陳安教授教學科研的六十年卻向人們展示了一幅「學而不厭，誨人不倦，格物致知，修身成德」的精彩畫卷，真可謂：道德文章，堪稱楷模；釋疑解惑，獨具一流。

陳安教授的教學科研，首先致力於傳道。他以自己從善如流、疾惡如仇的做人品格，格物致知、鍥而不捨的做學問的風格直接影響著他的同事、學生。我是一名公務員，每當談到黨內、社會上的一些腐敗現象和個別幹部庸俗的行為時，陳安教授總是聲色俱厲、鞭辟入裡地提醒我一定要勤政、廉政，恪守從政之道；我是一名從外文專業轉攻法學的博士，每當談到個別學生不求甚解、巧言令色、只圖文憑、不求學問的習氣，陳安教授總是諄諄教導我要囊螢映雪，寒窗苦讀，恪守求學之道。真可謂：師道尊嚴。

陳安教授的教學科研，特別精攻於授業。他學識淵博、學富五車、邏輯縝密、辯才無礙，讀他的著作常常感到如飲甘泉，唇齒留芳；聽他的講課常常覺得醍醐灌頂，茅塞頓開；與他的交談常常使人豁然開朗，疑團頓消。真可謂：師道睿智。

陳安教授的教學科研，尤其擅長於解惑。他有教無類、因材施教；他妙語連珠、妙音解惑；他教會學生知識，更交給學生打開知識寶庫的鑰匙；他教會學生知識之其然，更教會學生知識之所以然。課堂上，他是個良師；課堂外，他是個益友。他待人處事既嚴肅認真，又不失詼諧幽默。真可謂：師道可親。

尊敬的陳老、親愛的老陳、敬愛的陳安教授，我們衷心地祝福您：幸福、快樂、健康、長壽！

四、陳安老師與中國國際經濟法事業

徐崇利*

在中國，國際經濟法可以說是法學中最年輕的學科，應改革開放之運而生。陳安老師是中國國際經濟法事業的先行者和奠基者之一，他與北京大學的芮沐、中國人民大學的劉丁、武漢大學的姚梅鎮、復旦大學的董世忠、南開大學的高爾森和上海社科院的周子亞等老先生一道，開創了中國國際經濟法的科學研究和人才培養事業。

二十世紀八〇年代初，在中國國際經濟法學科始創之時，人才匱乏。包括陳安老師在內的一批老先生於一九八四年在江西盧山開辦了中國國際經濟法講習班，培養了中國最早的一批國際經濟法人才。現在，他們中的許多人已成為名享中國法學界的學者，包括廈門大學國際經濟法學科的學術帶頭人曾華群教授和廖益新教授。這次講習班被後人譽為是推動中國國際經濟法事業起步和發展的「黃埔軍校」。

早在一九八一至一九八三年，陳安老師就赴美國哈佛大學研究、講學，為系統地將國際經濟法學科引入中國做了充分的準備。回國後，陳安老師組織學術團隊，結合中國實際，精研國外最新成果，經過數年的努力，於一九八七年在國內首次推出了國際經濟法系列專著——《國際投資法》《國際貿易法》《國際貨幣金融法》《國際稅法》和《國際海事法》。這套專著以及後來出版的《國際經濟法總論》為學界提供了系統化的國際經濟法知識，對構建中國國際經濟法學科體系做出了歷史性的貢獻。通過這套專著的撰寫，廈門大學國際經濟法學科也初步搭建了一個比較完整的學術團隊。至今，學術梯隊的完整性仍然是廈門大學國際經濟法學科的優勢所在。

一九九二年起，中國國際經濟法學界公推陳安老師擔任中國國際經濟法學會常務副會長、會長，這是學界同仁對陳安老師學術地位的高度承認。自此，在陳安老師的精心組織下，中國國際經濟法學會的工作更上層樓，成為推動中國國際經濟法事業發展的一個重要的全國性學術平臺，並經中國民政部註冊登記成為國家一級學術團體，其法人住所和秘書處設在廈門大學。十七年來，一年一度的中國國際經濟法學會年會成了彙聚海內外學科精英進行學術研討的盛會。

一九九八年以來，陳安老師又親自擔任主編，主持出版了《國際經濟法學刊》（原《國際經濟法論叢》），連續十一年未有中斷。現在，學刊已成為匯輯國際經濟法領域優秀學術著述的另一重要的全國性學術平臺，也是目前國內唯一一個國際經濟法綜合性學術集刊。二〇〇六年，學刊首批入選CSSCI學術資料來源集刊。在國際上，學刊也已逐步成為一個反映中國國際經濟法研究動向和水準的學術品牌。

三十年來，陳安老師為中國國際經濟法事業的發展筆耕不輟，始終立基於中國國情和發展中國家的共同立場，開科立派，致力於開拓具有中國特色的國際經濟法學科。此次八十華誕彙集出版的《陳安論國際經濟法學》共五卷三百餘萬字，記載了陳安老師對中國國際經濟法事業的巨大學術貢獻，也展示了一個老知識份子畢生以知識報國為己任的輝煌學術歷程。

對於我們來說，最寶貴的學術基業是陳安老師開創的廈門大學國際經濟法學科。在京城之外的諸多綜合性大學的法學院中，能夠白手起家，將一個學科發展成全國領先的法學學科，迄今恐怕也只有廈門大學的國際經濟法學科。

學科要發展，人才是關鍵。二十世紀八九〇年代，全國高校難以吸引優秀人才，國際經濟法又是一個應用性很強的法學學科，出國、從商、為官者眾多，甘於在高校「坐冷板凳」者寥寥。因此，在全國的絕大多數高校中，都沒能建立一個比較穩定的國際經濟法學術團隊。同期，廈門大學的國際經濟法學科雖然也經歷了大量的人才流動，但在陳安老師的苦心經營下，始終保持著一個比較完整的學術團隊，這是廈門大學國際經濟法學科起步和發展的根基。本人就是在陳安老師的感召下，一九九〇年從上海社科院碩士研究生畢業後回母校任教，加入這個學術團隊的。

從某個角度上講，創業維艱，守業更加困難。當下，全國法學學科競爭激烈，學科建設不進則退。如何守護和提升廈門大學國際經濟法學科的學術地位，已成為交到年輕一代團隊成員手中一份沉甸甸的責任。只有凝練隊伍，居安思危，潛心學問，團結協作，奮力進取，才能使廈門大學國際經濟法學科成為一個富有生機和活力、長久不衰的中國國際經濟法學術重鎮。

陈安教授与曾华群、徐崇利、廖益新、李国安教授合影

五、知識報國　後學師範

曾華群*

在祝賀陳安老師八十華誕和從教五十八週年的時刻，撫今憶昔，令人感慨。從陳老師的奮鬥歷程和奉獻，我們深切感受到老一輩知識份子的愛國情懷、責任意識和價值取向。

八十年歲月崢嶸。在民不聊生、戰亂頻仍的舊中國，陳老師少年立振興中華之志，勤奮用功。第二次世界大戰後考入廈門大學，修習法學之餘，開始接觸和接受馬克思列寧主義的啟蒙和陶治。一九五一年以來，陳老師任教於廈門大學，法律系停辦期間，由法學轉為馬克思列寧主義領域。改革開放三十年，是陳老師學術生涯的黃金時期。一九八一年，陳老師以「知天命」之年，遠赴重洋，進修和講學於哈佛大學，開始了專攻國際經濟法的漫漫征程。

陳老師是廈門大學國際經濟法學科的創建人和學術帶頭人，一九七九年我校法律系復辦伊始，與陳朝璧教授、盛新民教授、胡大展教授等同仁，為適應改革開放形勢之急需，及時確立了以國際經濟法專業為重點的學科發展戰略。先後於一九八二年、一九八五年和一九八六年獲教育部批准招收國際經濟法專業碩士生、本科生和博士生，並於一九八七年主編出版了國內第一套國際經濟法系列著作，為我校國際經濟法學科的發展奠定基石。

陳老師是中國國際經濟法學會的創建人之一。在一九八四年廬山國際經濟法講習班講學期間，與上海市社會科學院周子亞教授、武漢大學姚梅鎮教授、復旦大學董世忠教授、南開大學高爾森教授和中國社會科學院盛愉教授等發起創立了國際經濟法研究會（即中國國際經濟法學會的前身）一九九三年起，陳老師連選連任中國國際經濟法學會會長。二十六年來，作為國際經濟法領域的全國性民間學術團體，學會發展之路關山重重。陳老師身先士卒，篳路藍縷，團結全國學界和實務界同仁，積極開展國際經濟法領域的國內外學術交流，逐漸形成和確立了「以文會友，以友輔仁，知識報國，兼濟天下」的學會宗旨和共識。

陳老師是中國特色國際經濟法學的奠基人之一。在潛心治學中，一向堅持馬克思列寧主義，追求公平正義的法治精神，積極倡導「知識報國，兼濟天下」的治學理念。一介書生，位卑未敢忘憂國，為振興中華竭盡心力。一介書生，時刻關注天下大勢，始終不渝地堅持改革國際經濟舊秩序、建立國際經濟新秩序的目標和立場，奮力為飽受欺淩壓迫的廣大發展中國家弱勢群體的正義要求吶喊和鼓呼。天道酬勤。陳老師創辦和主編的《國際經濟法學刊》、撰寫的鴻篇巨製《國際經濟法學芻言》和《陳安論國際經濟法學》以及發表於海內外權威學術刊物的中英文學術論文，忠實記錄了其「板凳甘坐卅年冷」的執著和對中國特色國際經濟法學的傑出奉獻。

陳老師還是中國國際經濟法律實踐的先行者之一。在教學研究百忙之中，承擔和承辦了一系列重要的國策諮詢和典型國際經貿仲裁、司法案件，是中國政府根據《華盛頓公約》遴選向「解決投資爭端國際中心」（ICSID）指派的國際仲裁員。

艱難困苦，玉汝於成。陳老師在長達五十八年的執教生涯中，以其堅韌不拔的精神和持之以恆的努力，成就了利國利民的不平凡業績，實現了其報效國家人民之志，亦成為後學之師範。

得益於陳老師的言傳身教，經過近三十年的發展，廈門大學國際經濟法學科及學術團隊逐漸形成其傳統和特色。主要表現在：

第一，立足中國國情，理論緊密聯繫實際。與商務部等政府部門和涉外經貿實務界長期保持密切的合作關係，結合改革開放實際，力圖較全面、深入研究我國在國際投資、國際貿易、國際貨幣金融和國際稅務等方面的法律問題，為我國法治建設和改革開放事業做出應有貢獻。

第二，關注南北問題，堅持第三世界立場。在全球化背景下，銘記作為中國學者的歷史責任和使命，堅持改革國際經濟舊秩序、建立國際經濟新秩序的目標和立場，重視研究國際經濟法基本理論，特別是經濟主權、公平互利和合作發展等國際經濟法基本原則的理論和實踐問題，努力維護發展中國家的權益。

第三，追求嚴謹學風，重視學術道德修養。深知為人師表，道德文章須經得起歷史的檢驗。潛心鑽研學問，崇尚淡泊明志，寧靜致遠。提倡學術民主，博采眾長，百家爭鳴。注重學術規範，嚴格自律，以身作則。

第四，勇於開拓創新，促進國際學術交流。創建廈門國際法高等研究院並連年舉辦「國際法前沿問題研修班」連續參加「Willem C. Vis國際商事模擬仲裁庭辯論賽」（維也納）和「Jessup國際法模擬法庭辯論賽」（華盛頓特區）並屢獲佳績，持續在國際性專業刊物和出版社發表學術論著等，均反映了本學科師生走向國際的初步努力。

第五，強化團隊意識，凝聚學科建設合力。在本學科建設的各項工作中，如《國際經濟法學刊》的編輯、中國國際經濟法學會秘書處事務、國際專業大賽辯論隊的指導，以及廈門國際法高等研究院行政事務等，本學科師生基於共同的世界觀和價值觀，甘當「義工」，勇挑重擔，體現了強烈的事業心、責任感和團隊意識。

光陰荏苒，時不我待。祈望本學科廣大師生志存高遠，繼往開來，為學科和廈門大學的進一步發展，為中國的民主法治事業而不懈努力。

六、春分化雨育新人

林 忠*

光陰似箭，博士畢業已經將近十三年了。回想在陳安教授指導下攻讀學位的日子，印象最深或說受益最大莫過於陳老師的正直為人以及他的認真嚴謹的學術態度。

在跟隨陳老師的六年中，我見過不少「達官富豪」慕名前來要求做他的博士生，但他從來不因為對方是何權貴而作任何妥協或「通融」。在對待學術問題上，他對於他的學生，不論是何種背景，一律嚴格要求，不作任何妥協。對於應考者，也是同樣要求按統一的錄取標準。但是，陳老師的「苛刻」並不是刻板。對於付出努力的學生，他總是予以充分認可，並給予各種支持和培養。陳老師的確是疾惡如仇。他不能容忍的是請托求情和為非作歹。對於任何違規違法的事情，他總是堅決抵制並毫不留情地予以嚴厲批評。在市場經濟時代，這樣做似乎不太迎合潮流，甚至得罪了某些人。但是，陳老師首先自己行得正，坐得直，他的強烈的正義感染了很多人，也讓我們做學生的學到了為人做事的真諦。如果中國像這樣的知識份子多一些，我們的社會風氣應當會有很大的不同。

陳老師讓人印象深刻之處，還在於他的平易近人。身為學術界的權威，陳老師對於同道乃至晚輩學生都是十分客氣，從來沒有擺出一副權威的架子。他總是以理服人，諄諄教誨。對於不同的觀點，他總是認真傾聽，兼收並蓄。

陳老師的治學態度非常嚴謹。他撰寫或主編的書稿不計其數。但他數十年如一日，每一部學術著作、每一篇文章都是認認真真校對，每一處引用、注解都按規範嚴格要求。對學生如此要求，自己也是這樣做的。出版社的編輯感歎，陳老師經手的文章著作，他們這些編輯都不用複校了。

陳老師讓人感動之處還在於他對國家、對學校和對學術的熱愛。對於國際經濟活動中涉及維護國家主權的事宜，他總是挺身而出，大聲疾呼。對於經濟霸權主義等各種損害我國國家或企業利益的事情，他總是如秋風掃落葉一般進行嚴厲抨擊。對於廈門大學，他可以說是傾注畢生精力，去為她添磚加瓦。對於學科建設，他是鞠躬盡瘁，嘔心瀝血。可以說，陳老師堪稱「中國的脊梁骨」的知識份子的典範。

七、八十感懷*

陳安

回首近八十年磋跎歲月，不無點滴感悟。概而言之，就是以勤補拙、羨魚結網、薄技立身、赤子情懷、知識報國。

若論天賦，我自幼雖非愚魯不堪，也絕非穎聰過人，平平庸庸而已。五歲隨同兄姐入學，一次考試遇若干填空選擇題，一頭霧水，但硬著頭皮「填上」空格，居然僥幸全數正確，得了「滿分」。慈母聞訊攬入懷中，愛撫、期許有加。嚴父得悉僥倖實情，則表揚期許之餘，又有批評教誨：「為人、做事、治學，來不得半點僥倖取巧。天賦平庸，可以以勤補拙。事事如此，日日如此，方能真正成長。」

日常見同儕中突出優秀者，讀史中慕博學廣識者，常有豔羨之言。又獲嚴父耳提面命：「臨淵羨魚，不如退而結網。」家境清貧拮据，但父親仍勉力送諸子女入學，諄諄相告：「我家無恆產，日後不可能留下什麼遺產。現在送你們入學，便是我日後贈給你們的唯一遺產。積財千萬，不如薄技在身，學得薄技，方能立身不敗。學必恃勤，技必求精。」

時值日寇侵華，國難當頭。師長、家長反覆喻以至理：愛我中華，不畏強暴；多難興邦，眾志成城。身為稚童，弱腕無力握大刀殺敵，唯有勤奮掌握知識，日後方能參與振興中華，報效祖國。服膺儒學的父親，對歷史上毀家紓難、忠貞殉國、視死如歸的文文山，更是推崇備至，且對其《正氣歌》作獨到解讀：「天地有正氣，雜然賦流形。下則為河嶽，上則為日星；於人曰浩然，沛乎塞蒼冥。」——這是千古不朽的座右銘。文天祥那般光照日月的浩然正氣，雖非人人可及，卻是人人可學、應學、應養。個人的剛正，赤子的情懷，民族的氣節，都要從大處著眼，從小處著手，長期自律自養，才能逐步走向孟軻所宣導的『富貴不能淫，貧賤不能移，威武不能屈』之境界。」家長和師長的此類教誨，點點滴滴，沁入稚嫩心田，此後數十年來未嘗或忘，成為做人和治學南針。

抗日戰爭勝利前夕，父親病逝。翌年，我考入廈門大學。此後三年，大學圖書館豐富的圖書以及地下黨領導的多次反美反蔣愛國學生運動，使我開始接觸和接受馬克思列寧主義的啟蒙和陶冶。一九四九年十月新中國成立，鴉片戰爭以來百餘年中國罹受的民族災難和喪權辱國慘痛，終於結束。那時那種「四海歡騰，普天同慶」的情景，至今記憶猶新。

正是在這樣的歷史環境下，我逐步形成了個人基本的理念定位、價值座標和觀察視角，並在大學畢業後迄今五十八年的粉筆生涯和偷閒爬格過程中，歷經寒暑風雨，始終未變，又有所發展。平生著述不敢侈言豐碩，唯幸能以「知識報國，兼濟天下」自勉不懈，尤其在蹉跎半生而重返法學殿堂之後，三十年來更是廢寢忘餐，焚膏繼晷，不息筆耕，博采、消化和吸收中外新知，力求開拓創新，其主要特色可略舉數例如下：

・闡明特定的學術理念和學術追求。當代發達國家國際經濟法諸多論著的共同基本特點，是重點研究發達國家對外經濟交往中產生的法律問題，作出符合發達國家權益的分析和論證。反觀中國，作為積貧積弱的發展中國家之一員，這樣的研究工作還處在幼弱階段，遠未能適應中國對外交往的迫切需要和對外開放的嶄新格局。因此，我們必須實行「拿來主義」和「消化主義」，在積極引進和學習西方有關國際經濟法學新鮮知識的基礎上，密切聯繫中國國情，站在中國和當代國際弱勢群體即第三世界的共同立場，從第三世界的視角，認真加以咀嚼消化，取其精華，棄其糟粕，逐步創立起以馬克思主義為指導的，具有中國特色的國際經濟法學這一新興邊緣性、綜合性學科的體系和理論體系，努力為國際社會弱勢群體提供維護應有平等權益的法學理論武器。當然，完成此等大業，需要幾代中國學人的共同刻苦鑽研和齊心奮力開拓。

・探索建立國際經濟新秩序的規律和路徑。當今國際經濟秩序和國際經濟法律規範的破舊立新，勢必循著螺旋式上升的「6C

軌跡」即Contradiction（矛盾）→ Conflict（衝突或交鋒）→ Consultation（磋商）→ Compromise（妥協）→ Cooperation（合作）→ Coordination（協調）→ Contradiction New（新的矛盾），依靠群體力量，聯合奮鬥，步履維艱，迂回曲折地逐步實現。既不能盲目「樂觀」，期待「畢其功於一役」；也不能盲目「悲觀」，遇到挫折就灰心喪志；更不能奢望只憑孤軍奮鬥，即可克敵制勝。總結歷史，以史為師，國際弱勢群體爭取和維護平權地位和公平權益，舍韌性的「南南聯合自強」，別無他途可循。

・論證當代國際經濟法的首要基本原則。當代國際經濟法貫穿著四大基本原則，其中經濟主權原則是首要的基本規範，全球弱勢群體務必增強憂患意識，珍惜和善用經濟主權以確保和維護民族正當權益，警惕當代霸權主義的「雙重標準」和偽善本質，切忌懵懵然地附和、接受當今頗為「時髦」的、來自西方霸權主義國家的經濟主權「淡化」論、「弱化」論和「過時」論，切忌墜入理論陷阱。作為中國人，同時還應當加深認識當代中國實行對外開放基本國策的歷史淵源和深厚積澱，從而更加自覺推動其優良歷史傳統及其獨立自主、平等互惠的法理原則「與時俱進」。

・研究國際投資條約及其相關體制。筆者長期重點研究有關國際投資的雙邊協定、多邊公約以及相關的OPIC、MIGA、ICSID等基本體制及其實際運行，探討中國和其他發展中國家如何在這些體制中趨利避害；並依據研究成果，努力踐行知識報國素志，多次應邀積極向國家主管部門提供決策諮詢建議和立法建言。

・澄清和批駁外國媒體等對中國的誤解和非難。多年來，筆者有的放矢，針對外國媒體、政壇和法學界對中國的各種誤解和非難，撰寫多篇雙語專論，予以澄清和批駁；通過學術論證，努力維護中國的國家尊嚴、國際信譽和民族自尊，弘揚中華愛國主義。

較之海內外同行先進，筆者學術途程起步甚晚，實為「後學」，積澱殊薄。承學界同行專家厚愛，評議認為筆者近三十年來所論，堪稱「躋身國際前驅，獨樹中華一幟」，乃是創建具有鮮明中國特色的國際經濟法學理論的奠基之作，為創立具有中國特色的國際經濟法學理論體系開了先河；其特點是運用當代國際法理論，致力為包括中國在內的發展中國家弱勢群體「依法仗義執言」，力爭成為當代第三世界爭取國際經濟平權地位的法學理論武器，可謂「一劍淬礪三十年」。筆者理解：學界同仁的上述溢美之詞，是對本人「薄技立身、赤子情懷、知識報國」感悟的認同、鼓勵和最新鞭策。如今已屆耄耋之年，滿目青山，夕霞天際，益感「老牛最解韶光貴，不待揚鞭自奮蹄」。

八、高山仰止

——寫於陳安老師八十壽誕之際

單文華*

光陰似箭。初次接觸陳安老師的場景如同昨日，卻已經是十六年以前的事情了。這十六年裡，雖然大多數時間有重洋阻隔，我與先生的聯繫卻從未中斷過。可以說，大洋之外，我知道先生之冷暖，先生也知道我的憂樂。

再過幾天，就是先生的八十壽誕。廈大師友來信囑我就當年師從先生求學之經曆心得略寫一二，以為紀念。我驚喜之餘，頗覺惶恐。去國十餘年，外文或有些許長進，國文功夫卻日見荒疏。開口提筆，時感詞不達意，深恐寫壞了，寫偏了。然時間所迫，義不容辭，且記三事（求學、在讀、畢業）以為紀念。不確不妥之處，還請先生及諸師友惠正。

海上仙山

我求學先生之路，並不平坦。一九九一年初，我在暨南大學經濟學院讀研究生，導師是經濟法系的系主任張增強教授。張老師特別強調國際經濟法學的學習，並很推崇陳安老師的著作。當時同學院有一位會計學的碩士生學業優異，提前一年畢業考取了廈大會計學的博士，令在讀碩士生同學們十分豔羨。我當時便想，能不能也效法一下，爭取兩年畢業，提前攻博。於是便嘗試著與廈大研招辦聯繫。研招辦的老師（我記得是關筱燕主任）很熱情，告訴我雖然正式的報考期限已過，但我如能得到陳安老師的同意，他們還可以接受我的報名。關老師並建議我最好能前往廈門拜訪一下陳先生。於是，一九九三年五月一日，我登上了廣州去廈門的海輪。這是我生平第一次坐輪船。在海鷗翔集、波濤洶湧之際，憑欄望遠，想著很快就要登上廈門這座海上仙山，見到令人景仰的陳安老師，心情十分激動。

然而，我那次並沒有見到陳老師。五月二日抵達廈門之後，我直接人住廈大的淩雲招待所。或許是因為過於興奮，一夜未眠，又或許是因為不習海風，我竟然感冒了。儘管如此，我一住下便給陳老師家打電話，告知我到了廈門，想去拜見他。誰知陳老師卻並不讓我去見他，只讓我在下午三點鐘時給他去電話詳談。三點整，我在淩雲招待所樓下公用電話室裡撥通了陳老師家的電話。電話那頭傳來了陳老師親切中透著威嚴的聲音。通話持續了一個多小時。陳老師不僅詢問了我的經歷、學習的課程，還問了許多專業上的問題，我都一一認真作答。當時廈門天氣很熱，我感冒在身，衣著甚厚，加之那次與先生通話十分緊張，打電話時渾身熱汗直流。臨了，先生說了一句：「你可以報考了。」我心中一塊石頭落了地，感冒好像也立時好了。事後得知，原來先生極不喜歡那些可能送「見面禮」的考生，故特設此嚴格的「預防措施」，以杜絕此類陋習。接下來是緊張的複習、考試，所幸最後考上了——我終於成了廈門大學陳安教授的一名學生！

後來我才知道，陳老師的嚴格是出了名的。這種嚴格，在招生環節就表現得十分明顯，比方說他主張「逢進必考」，不喜歡招收保送生之類的免試生，更不喜歡與政府官員或大款、大腕們拉「關係」「走後門」，在博士入學方面開綠燈。我記得他後來還專門寫了篇短文《「博士」新解》，諷刺這種種不正常的現象。

「板凳願坐十年冷」

現在回想起來，廈大三年博士生期間，是我這輩子最快樂的時光之一。我們住在高高的淩雲樓上（淩雲三608）每天看著海闊天空、雲卷雲舒，時感壯懷激烈。幾乎每天下午，樓上會有人吼一聲「打球囉」，我們便離巢出動，奔赴籃球場。打完球回來，有時球友們還會在芙蓉湖邊小坐，談天說地。大多數時間則直接奔回宿舍，很快沖涼房便響起此起彼伏的歌聲。

生活而外，更大的收穫是學業上的。陳老師平時給我們說得最多的一句話是「板凳願坐十年冷」，要求我們守得住清貧，耐得住寂寞，因為學術之路、博士之路注定是清貧而寂寞的。在具體的教學方法上，令我印象深刻的是，陳老師從不拘泥於那種刻板的上課模式，而是強調人才培養與科研專案的結合、言傳與身教結合，做到出「人才」的同時出「成果」。這種方法很能發揮研究生的主動性與積極性，取得了很好的效果。記得我的第一門專業課叫作「國際經濟法文獻精讀選擇」，課程主要是練習翻譯一部關於多邊投資擔保機構（MIGA）的英文專著的若干章節。第一次翻譯外文專業文獻，感覺難度很大，初時幾乎是寸步難行。譯稿先經同學校勘，修改後再由陳老師批閱，多次反覆修改後方能交卷。一開始我並不理解這種訓練的意義，認為它有點費而不惠，因為翻譯是天大難事，譯出來的東西卻又不算是原創性的成果，費時費力，卻又成效不彰。直到我過後再次嘗試去閱讀和翻譯其他英文著作，才發現其中妙處。這種訓練貴在讓你認真揣摩原文中每一句話的句法結構，對加強英文專業文獻的閱讀能力，提高閱讀速度大有裨益。難怪先生對此十分看重，並告訴我們這也是北大王鐵崖等國際法先生們最常用的學術訓練方法之一。後來我在譯稿的基礎上作了進一步的研究、更新和修正，寫成一篇文章，收入陳老師主編的一部專著。專著的出版令我深受鼓舞，我研讀原始國際經濟法文獻的興趣也由此大有增強。

這三年裡令我同樣記憶深刻的是我有幸給先生做了一些他自

己文稿的校對工作。先生學貫中西，識見宏深，每有心得，往往寫成一篇傳世佳作；加之課題不斷，著作等身，時有新著出版，或舊著更新。我作為他為數不多的弟子之一，時時往返於先生白城的家裡與經濟學院列印室之間，傳送文稿，並對列印稿作初步校對。記得先生每次對文稿的品質都精益求精，幾近苛刻。當時經濟學院經常為我們列印文稿的是一位叫作「小翁」的姑娘，在打字員中當屬極為細心和有耐心的一位。有一次她偷偷地跟我說，她其實「最怕」打先生的文稿，不僅因為過於專業、難以理解，所以打字較慢，更因為先生在每次校對稿上都會有許多處新的添加或修改，這些又都需要經過一而再再而三的校訂。我後來意識到，這種校對工作其實是一種很好的學術訓練，它使我不僅有機會接觸一流的學問與作品，更重要的是知道這樣的學問與作品是怎樣做出來的。我體會到全面廣泛的資料，深入的研析，創新的思維和精益求精、一絲不苟的治學態度，是所有好作品的不二法門。

另外，十分難得的是，先生雖然學高於世，對我們這些學生等所秉持的是一種完全平等的態度。例如，有時我會斗膽對他文中的個別字句作點修改，他不但不怪我冒犯威嚴，反而時時褒獎有加，稱我為「一字之師」。這種大家風範至今令我感動。

後來，我有一次去威爾士旅遊，在一家紀念品商店看到一張父親節節日賀卡，上面寫著：「謝謝您，父親。因為您不僅指明了星星的所在，還告訴我怎樣去找到它們。」一日為師，終身為父。我常常想，陳老師就像我學業上的「嚴父」，不僅讓我知道什麼是大學問和大學問家，還讓我體會到怎樣才能成就大學問和大學問家。這些年來，我雖然談不上取得了什麼成就，但陳老師的這種種言傳身教，卻一直是鼓勵我進取向上的一種強大的精神力量。

鳳凰花開

鳳凰花是廈大的校花，年開二度，一度迎新，一度送舊。迎新的花季洋溢著喜悅，但送舊的鳳凰花卻總讓離校的廈大學子無限惆悵。

一九九六年七月，又是鳳凰花開的時節，眾生惜別依依之際，我也面臨著生命中一次不大不小的抉擇。當時我曾聯繫過去北大法學院做博士後，或去清華法學院做講師。兩個地方都已表示接受。同時，蒙先生抬愛，母校表示希望我能留校任教。一方是京畿法學重地，另一方是恩師與母校，這個選擇不可謂不艱難。然而，我沒多少猶豫便選擇了後者，且始終不後悔自己的這一選擇。根本原因，是出於對恩師與母校的一種深深感恩與無限眷戀。

許多人不理解先生早年執行的「博士生留校」政策，認為有「近親繁殖」之嫌。對此，先生作了有力的反駁。我記得先生常常跟我說，廈大法學學科屬於後發後進學科，研究人才嚴重缺乏，而每年招研究生的名額又極其有限，他如果不這麼做，就形不成「生產力」，產不出「產品」。廈大法學不僅不能發展繁衍，甚至會有「斷子絕孫」的危險。事實證明，先生的做法是明智和卓有成效的。廈大國際法學科二十世紀八〇年代建立博士點，九〇年代以來獲得飛速發展，先後取得了博士後流動站和國家重點學科等重大突破，其中一個最重要的因素，便是先生當年下大力氣打造的一支強有力的國際法學術梯隊。現在，當我在思考如何在欠發達的西北地方建設一個後發的法學院時，我更能深刻體會到先生當年的苦衷。是一份對廈大國際法學事業的堅強信念與執著追求支撐了先生這些不尋常的舉措，而正是這些不尋常的舉措為廈大國際法學科近年來在全國脫穎而出，並在國際上嶄露頭角奠定了基礎。

「高山仰止，景行行止。」每年五月的這個日子，都是我特別感懷的一個日子。而今年這個日子更有特別重要的意義。令我遺憾的是，由於與倫敦一個國際會議的時間相衝突，我將不能趕赴盛會，當面表達我的感念和祝福。但願這篇小文能於此有所彌補。

謹此敬祝先生生日快樂，龍馬精神！

謹祝母校事業蒸蒸日上，迭創輝煌！

九、五「嚴」源自一「愛」

李萬強*

今天我們齊聚一堂共祝陳安老師八十華誕，並對中國國際經濟法研究方法暨陳安老師的學術思想進行深入研討。在此場合，由於時間所限，我無法描述陳老師在學生心目中的全貌，由於能力所限，我也不敢嘗試綜述陳老師的成就與影響。思之再三，還是摘取片段的印象和感受與大家分享。

陳老師為人很嚴，「嚴格」「嚴厲」「嚴謹」「嚴肅」，都可以用來形容陳老師，甚至不乏一點點「嚴酷」。與陳老師相處的日子裡，他即使是臥病在床也不肯收受學生聊表心意的一點薄禮。對學生論文當中的一點文字差錯他都會「上綱上線」加以批評。還有在我們博士生當中傳聞頗廣的陳老師的「魔鬼訓練法」，那時候我們常常覺得陳老師「不近人情」。

二〇〇一年由於一些個人的原因，我不顧學科建設的需要離開了廈大，在最初的一段時間裡，即使是在逢年過節的時候，我也不敢和陳老師聯繫。然而，這些年來，陳老師通過各種方式為我提供非常難得的機會，在學術上給予我很大的支援，包括發表論文、參加學術會議等等。我漸漸體會到了陳老師「五嚴」的另一層意蘊。的確，這種對青年學生和同行在學術上與事業上的關心與提攜，難道不是一種超越凡俗、至純至真的大大人情？！

陳老師愛好獨立思考和學術爭鳴。一直以來，都會或耳聞或眼見他與國內外同行大家學術論辯的事例。他甚至放下「身段」，平等地、認真地與年輕學者「交手過招」。幾年前，他與一位年輕學者平等、認真的學術爭鳴催生了他洋洋幾萬言的學術成果——系列論文，並且獲得了國家人文社科最高獎。前幾日，又看到陳老師發表在《現代法學》上的一篇論文，儘管在這篇文章當中沒有指名道姓，但其筆鋒所指一目了然。該文對學界當前對於WTO的盲目推崇進行了嚴肅的學術批評，足夠令人或幡然醒悟，或由衷嘆服。仔細想來，陳老師在學術上的「不依不饒」不正是對學術高度負責的體現，不正是對青年學者另一種真摯的關愛嗎？

著作等身的陳老師、行事低調的陳老師、辯才出眾的陳老師、文才橫溢的陳老師、愛恨分明的陳老師、信念堅定的陳老師、宣導學術道德的陳老師、極具現實關懷的陳老師，在學生心中有一位說不盡的陳老師，陳老師不僅是引領中國國際經濟法學界的學術旗幟，更是散發著無窮魅力的人生燈塔。

一九九六年，我剛來廈大讀書的時候聽到一個故事：廈大法學院有一位學生對陳老師無比崇拜，常常以朗讀陳老師的文章為樂事；同時，每當別人提起陳老師的時候，如果他當時正躺著或坐著，一定會立即起身肅立以示敬仰。這個故事是真是假我沒有考證。但是，我想，即使這個故事是杜撰的，那麼杜撰在陳老師身上，又有誰會懷疑它的合理性呢？

祝陳老師健康長壽，學術青春永駐！

注釋

* 辜芳昭，時任廈門大學黨委副書記、副校長。
* 趙龍躍，國際貿易政策專家、世界銀行國際貿易問題諮詢專家、美國喬治城大學特聘教授。
* 鐘興國，廈門大學1999屆國際經濟法專業博士畢業生，時任中共廈門市委常委、海滄區委書記。
* 徐崇利，廈門大學1996屆國際經濟法專業博士畢業生，時任廈門大學法學院院長，教授、博士生導師。
* 曾華群，廈門大學1990屆國際經濟法專業博士畢業生，現任中國國際經濟法學會會長、廈門大學國際經濟法研究所所長，教授、博士生導師。
* 林忠，廈門大學1996屆國際經濟法專業博士畢業生，畢業後曾留校任教，現為上海瑛明律師事務所合夥人、律師。
* 本文原是復旦大學出版社2008年12月出版的《陳安論國際經濟法學》（五卷本）的作者自序。限於篇幅，編入時有較多刪節和適當改動。
* 單文華，廈門大學1996屆國際經濟法專業博士畢業生，畢業後曾留校任

教。1998年赴英國劍橋大學留學，獲法學博士學位。現任英國牛津布魯克斯大學法學院國際法教授，西安交通大學法學院院長、「騰飛人才計畫」特聘教授、博士生導師。

* 李萬強，廈門大學1999屆國際經濟法專業博士畢業生，畢業後曾留校任教。時任西北政法大學國際法學院院長、教授。

第七編——有關陳安學術活動的報導、函件等

媒體報導

一、在哈佛的講壇上

——訪廈門大學政法學院副院長陳安*

陳福郎

哈佛，美國這所國際性的名牌大學，雲集著來自全球各地的訪問學者。哈佛一個豪華而又雅致的會議廳裡，正在舉行午餐會。一位中國法學學者正用流利的英語演講。四十多位聽眾中，主要是美國、日本的教授和學者，還有西歐、澳洲、東南亞諸國以及臺灣地區的留美研究生。他們來自地球的不同角落，對中國的對外開放和吸收外資政策，內心都隱伏著程度不同的疑慮以及形形色色的惶惑。

……由於中國政府近來對經濟犯罪採取必要的打擊措施，一些外國人就猜疑中國的風向正在變：似乎是天剛放晴不久又要下雨了。美國一家報紙的社論甚至推斷說：「中國現在正在返回到教條主義」。有些外國朋友擔心中國現行的對外開放和吸收外資政策不久就會變，他們告誡其他人，向中國投資要謹慎小心，看看再說，免得遇上麻煩，甚至發生風險……

演講者陳安，是廈門大學法律系的副教授。他於一九八一年底以訪問學者身份，前來哈佛大學法學研究院，研究國際經濟法。

今天演講的題目是：《是進一步開放？還是重新關門？——評有關中國吸收外資政策法令的幾種議論》。

當時是一九八二年秋，國內正開展打擊經濟領域重大犯罪的鬥爭。一些外國人對於這場鬥爭議論頗多，嘖有煩言，間夾非難。我國的對外開放政策正受到一些人的誤解和曲解。有的贊成重新關門，有的擔心重新關門，有的希望繼續開放。作為來自社會主義中國的法學副教授，陳安的辦公室經常有人來叩門，種種發問，把他攪得心神不寧。

祖國的對外開放政策正在堅定貫徹，方興未艾，絕不能為外人所誤解，甚至歪曲。陳安強烈的責任感油然而生，他想，是時候挺身而出，作一番公開的澄清、解答甚至駁斥了。他明白，以一個中國法學學者的身份，在這個國際學術講壇上發言，論述涉及中國的法律問題，是外國法學家們所無法替代的。我們在國際論壇上必須占得自己應有的席位。

中國法學學者那瀟灑的風度、雄辯的說理、精闢的闡析，緊緊地攫住了聽眾的心。

……對所有正派、誠實和守法的外商來說，打擊行賄、受賄、索賄，打擊走私活動，僅僅意味著：中國對他們打開了一扇更寬敞的大門，開闢了一條更平坦的道路。因為，橫在正路和正門上的路障和垃圾被清除了，非法的「競爭」手段和勒索行徑被禁止了……

這場將近兩小時的專題學術演說，系統闡述了我國有關政策法令的歷史根據、立法精神和條款內容。講演以事實為根據，從法學理論上說明我國今後既要繼續堅持對外開放政策，進一步積極吸收外資，保護合法外資、外商；又要繼續嚴肅認真地打擊同吸收與外資有關的一切經濟犯罪行為，從而為建設中國特色社會主義服務。

午餐會上的氣氛漸漸活躍起來。有的快速記錄，有的會心微笑，有的頻頻頷首。

在聽眾中，有一位日本訪美研究員、金融經濟專家杉原啟示，他所服務的日本國家石油公司係日本政府國營機構，已向中國投資參加中日合作開發渤海灣及鄂爾多斯地區石油。他原來疑團滿腹，可現在臉上卻露出愉悅的神情。演講一結束，他就索要了一份英文講演細綱。事後，他送來一封短簡，並附一份日文摘譯，說已將「先生日前發表的高見……迅即摘譯要旨，並已速送日本國家石油公司參考」。

演講結束了，大廳裡響起熱烈的掌聲。這掌聲，是屬於中國的。這天恰是一九八二年十月一日，祖國人民正在歡度國慶，而陳安則在地球的另一面，通過自己的聲音，讓世界了解中國，一種欣慰之情漲滿了他的心懷。有位臺灣地區留美研究生擠到他身旁說：「佩服！佩服！外國人給你鼓掌，掌聲這麼響，作為中國人，我們也有份，覺得很體面！」在哈佛修習「中美商務法律問題」課程的許多研究生，因為有課未能參加，紛紛要求為他們補講。他想，要調動國外各種積極因素，支援我國「四化」建設，就必須增進外國人對我國的了解和信任。重講誠然辛苦，卻是當仁不讓。

在此之前，他還在哈佛課堂上，對近百名哈佛法學研究院研究生及旁聽的外國訪問學者，做過另一場演講。那次演講的題目是《是棒打鴛鴦嗎？——就「李爽案件」評〈紐約時報〉報導兼答美國法學界同行問》。這篇英文演講稿經整理，在紐約法學院《國際法與比較法學刊》雜誌上發表。雜誌主編艾姆林・希加（Emlyn H. Higa）對此文的評價是：「您的文章提出了人們所殷切期待的答案」，「您對於美國和中國的刑事法制所作的比較分析，是特別有教益和富有啟發性的」。

二十世紀五〇年代之初，陳安畢業於廈大法律系，當過一段審判員，隨後回校任教。一九五三年院系調整時，廈大法律系撤銷了，他奉命轉行，一晃就是二十七年。一九八〇年廈大複辦法律系，他才重新回到自己的本行。隨著我國對外開放政策的實行，國際經濟法這一新興邊緣學科中的許多嶄新課題深深地吸引了他。他的英語學習已中斷三十年。為了探索新知，以應祖國「四化」急需，他日夜兼程，訓練口語，並以「半百」之年參加出國考試。好心的朋友說：你已是副教授了，何必如此自苦！他說：職稱只是探索新知的新鞭，不是故步自封的包袱。在哈佛，為了準備這兩場演講，陳安副教授付出了多少勞動！他面對的是美國聽眾，對美國的歷史背景和社會制度、法令規章和類似的案例處斷，不能不預先作一番認真的研究和查索，他沒日沒夜地查找和研究資料，眼窩更加深陷，身形愈益瘦削，但是他換來的是祖國的榮譽，他感到生活的充實。陳安副教授在哈佛的二十個月中，還寫成了學術論文《論美國對海外美資的法律保護》，全文五萬餘字，寄回國內。這篇論文對於今後我國吸收外資的談判、簽約以及研究涉外投資糾紛案件的處斷有重要的現實意義。有關出版社已建議擴大篇幅，作為專著出版。他還為瑞士日內瓦國際研究所教授哈裡什・卡普爾（Harish Kapur）選編的一本書《中國閉關自守的終結》（*The End of Isolation*）撰寫專章，論述中國吸收外資的基本政策和法律體制。此書即將在海牙問世，發行歐美。

去年，他參加了由教育部和司法部聯合選派的「中國國際法教育考察團」。在近兩個月的時間裡，這個三人代表團曆訪了西歐、北美五個國家三十多個學術單位。回國後，同事們問他有什麼新的收穫和體會，他說：「國際法學新知，可謂琳琅滿目。但願常如乾海綿，涓涓滴滴，能吸即吸，俾為我國所用。我贊成這樣的『螺旋式』循環：學而後知不足，知不足而後學。」

二、他把法的目光投向世界與未來

——訪廈門大學法律系陳安教授*

甘景山

開拓法律科學新領域

「鐺，鐺，鐺……」清晨，廈門大學校園的鐘聲響了。我走進海濱新村六樓四〇二號房間，這是法律系陳安教授的家。房間裡到處都是書，他在書的海洋裡生活。

窗外的大海在強烈的陽光照耀下，閃射著刺眼的光芒。我提出看看有關資料，他抱來兩三包他撰寫的著作、論文。

我打開紙包，一本又一本翻過。當我翻到一本封面為天藍底色襯著白色世界地圖圖案的《國際經濟立法的歷史和現狀》時，立即被吸引住了。這是由陳教授編譯、法律出版社出版的國際經濟法新書。

國際經濟法是法學中新興的學科，是邊緣性學科，是國際法學科中一個新的重要分支，國內外學者還在探索中。我問陳教授：

「您怎麼會想起去開闢這個新領域呢？靈感從何而來？」

「說來話長。『國際經濟法』這個名詞，是美國的一個法學專家洛文費爾德一九七六年才提出的。一九七九年，武漢大學七十多歲的法學老教授姚梅鎮也開始了研究。」

「那您是哪年開始的？」

「也是七九年。」

「您的步子真快。」

「研究國際經濟法是形勢的需要。現在，舊的世界經濟秩序開始打破，新的經濟秩序開始建立，國際經濟交往日益頻繁，打國際官司也在增加，為了在簽訂協定、合同，違約索賠，以及處理投資、貿易、關稅、金融等法律糾紛時，不受外商愚弄或欺騙，為保護國家權益不受損失，一定要加強國際經濟法的研究。今後，需要大量通曉國際經濟法的專業人才。」

我聽了以後明白了，他想的是世界，是祖國的未來。廈大法律系一九八一年就開始招收國際經濟法研究生，到現在這個學科的研究生已有幾十名，其中已畢業的幾名在答辯中名列前茅，寫出了高品質的學術論文。

在全國國際經濟法學科中，廈大法律系已遙遙領先。經國家教委批准，廈大法律系率先正式設置國際經濟法專業，從一九八五年開始每年招收一個本科生班。

為了創立國際經濟法新的法學科學領域，陳教授嘔心瀝血；現在，為了發展和服務於這個領域，更是廢寢忘食，四處奔忙。他除了自己搞科研、講授「國際經濟法概論」等數門課程外，還有許許多多的社會活動和行政工作，請看他的纍纍頭銜：廈門大學政法學院院長、廈大法律系國際經濟法教研室主任、中國國際經濟法研究會副會長、中國經濟法研究會理事、全國高等教育自學考試委員會委員、廈門經濟特區法律顧問、福建省華僑律師事務所法律顧問、福建省保險公司法律顧問、美國國際法學會會員、福建省人大常委，等等。這些頭銜，是社會對他的評價。在短短的數年裡，他脫穎而出，走向全國，走向世界。

一九八二年十月一日，他在美國做了題為《是進一步開放？還是重新關門？評有關中國吸收外資政策法令的幾種議論》的講演，闡述了我國有關政策法令的歷史根據、立法精神，解釋我國參加簽訂的保護外國投資的國際協定；從法理上說明我國今後既要繼續堅持對外開放，進一步積極吸收外資，保護合法外資和守法外商，又要繼續嚴厲地打擊一切經濟犯罪行為，從而消除了外國友人的顧慮和駁斥了個別人的攻擊。不久，此篇論文被收進了海牙馬爾丁出版社出版的《中國閉關自守的終結》一書。

此外，他還在《中國國際法年刊》上撰文，讓世界人民了解中國的法律。

當鋪路的石子

我翻閱著陳教授案頭上的《訪美小結》，其中有一段語重心長的話：「建議今後在國內加緊培養年輕的專業人員（他在『年輕的』下面打了三個著重號），從中擇優送往國外深造。」

在另一份考察歐美的報告裡疾呼：「關於國際法專業人才的培養，感到數量少、品質低，與西方國家相比，與十億人口泱泱大國舉足輕重的國際地位相比，差距極大，培養這方面的人才是當務之急，急中之急！」

這時，陸續來了幾位國際經濟法專業的研究生，有的拿論文給陳教授修改，有的打報告要陳教授批准出外調查等等。陳教授指了指其中一位戴眼鏡的瘦個子說：「我們要給年輕人壓擔子，他剛剛畢業，因為他學得好，系裡已經研究確定，國際經濟法教研室準備讓他負責。我們這些老頭子已經不行了，因此要把希望寄託在年輕人身上。我還不夠格當人梯，可是我可以當鋪路的石子，儘快填補人才斷層。」

他無私的心深深地感動了我。

為了提高教學品質，加速培養高品質的法學人才，陳教授提倡加強國際交流，力避「近親繁衍」，見聞受囿，他提倡「拿來主義」，吸收外國的好經驗，教學、科研要不斷創新。他根據美國哈佛大學的教學經驗，逐步糾正「純理論」的偏向，引導學生研究分析典型案例，活躍課堂對話。廈大法律系還組織學生辦刊物，刊名是《法學與現代化》。他把這種學生辦的刊物稱作「拔尖人才的搖籃」。

陳教授還告訴我，廈大法律系招收國際經濟法本科生，採取高分定向招生法，即向開放城市和特區定向招生，吸引那裡的優秀生報考廈大法律系。在學期間，到香港、特區實習，同外商、港商打交道，「真刀真槍」打官司。對於優秀生，將分期分批送往外國深造。

我在陳教授的一本書裡看到一張收據，原來是陳教授在出國期間將節省下來的兩千多美元都買了法律書籍，分別贈送給學校圖書館和法律系資料室，為師生提供研究資料。我還看到一份報告，是陳教授聯繫了外國的幾個圖書館贈送給廈大大批法律書籍，要求上級解決運輸問題的。總之，他一切想著法律系，想著學生，想著人才，想著「四化」建設。最後，我問陳教授有什麼打算，他謙虛地說：「我也是剛剛起步，盛名之下，其實難副，主要靠大家……」

當採訪將要結束的時候，我望著窗外的大海，不免心潮起伏。我想，還是引用陳安教授寫的「小結」末段來結束本文：「今後，我定將更加謙虛謹慎，繼續努力，為社會主義法學繁榮和祖國四化事業盡綿薄之力。」

三、適應對外開放和發展外向型經濟需要，國際經濟法系列專著問世*

林鴻禧　陳有仁

本報訊　由廈門大學政法學院院長陳安教授主編的我國第一套國際經濟法系列專著《國際投資法》《國際貿易法》《國際貨幣金融法》《國際稅法》《國際海事法》已由鷺江出版社出版。這是我國涉外經濟法律的重要學術論著。它為我國高等院校提供了涉外經濟法律的新教材。

陳安教授早年畢業於廈門大學法律系和復旦大學政治學研究生班，一九八一至一九八三年應邀在美國哈佛大學從事國際經濟法研究。

這套一百五十五萬字的涉外經濟法律學術專著收集了當今世界主要國家有關經濟立法的最新資料，並在引進新鮮知識的基礎上，結合我國涉外經濟交往的實際，對改造國際經濟舊秩序、建立國際經濟新秩序所面臨的各種法律問題進行分析論證，觀點新穎，條理分明。目前已有多所大學的法律系準備將這套書作為教材。

四、為對外開放鋪路

——記廈門大學法學教授陳安*

楊亞南

「陳安教授：感謝你贈送的五本巨作。當前全省上下議外向、想外向、幹外向的形勢下，外向知識何等重要又何等貧乏。這五本書可算及時雨，大大有助於人們提高外向型知識，推動沿海開放事業發展……」

福建省副省長游德馨在這封親筆謝函中提到的五本書是：《國際投資法》《國際貿易法》《國際貨幣金融法》《國際稅法》《國際海事法》。這五本由廈門大學法學教授陳安主編的書，是我國第一套國際經濟法系列專著。

陳安一九五〇年畢業於廈大法律系。三年後，中斷法學生涯，開始了長達二十七年的馬克思主義政治理論、歷史等方面的研究與教學。一九八〇年，半百之年的他重返法學領域。

在應衝刺的年齡才起跑，他帶著閩北山區人的執拗與狠勁，硬是在法學界占了一席之地。重返法學界六年之後，他成為國務院學位委員會評定的國際經濟法專業全國最年輕的博士生導師。他現在是廈大法學院院長、國際法比較學會國際委員會委員、中國國際經濟法研究會副會長、中國國際法學會理事、中國經濟法研究會理事、全國高等教育自學考試指導委員會法律專業委員、中國國際經濟貿易仲裁委員會仲裁員。

陳安於改革開放之始重返法學界，他的學術生命從此與改革開放緊密相連。

「……由於中國政府近來對經濟犯罪採取必要的打擊措施，一些外國人就猜疑中國的風向正在變：似乎是天剛放晴不久又要下雨了。」一九八二年秋，陳安以高級訪問學者的身份站在哈佛大學的講壇上，面對美、日等國的學者及西歐、澳洲的研究生慷慨陳詞：「對所有正派、誠實和守法的外商來說，打擊行賄、受賄，打擊走私活動，僅僅意味著中國對他們打開了一扇更寬敞的大門，開闢了一條更平坦的道路。因為，橫在正路和正門上的路障和垃圾被清除了……」演講後的熱烈掌聲證明，陳安為中國的開放事業又贏得了一些國際上的信任和理解。

一九九一年，美國俄勒岡州路易士與克拉克西北法學院《律師》雜誌上刊載了一篇論文《是重新閉關自守？還是擴大對外開放？》。論文原是陳安教授的演講稿。演講後他收到了中國駐美領事館官員的來信：「很欣賞你的智慧、才幹和勇氣。此舉很有意義。由此，使我聯想到，如果我們的學者和學生中能有一批像你這樣的民間大使，對反駁美政壇對我國的非難，以及消除一些美國友人的疑慮和誤解，無疑將起到非同一般的影響和作用……」

這些年，陳安教授時刻注視著中國開放實踐中的法律問題，寫出了一篇篇論文，為開放事業提供了有效的法律武器。

「法律領域是四十年來最枯萎的一朵花，而對外經貿中的法律則更是萎縮……」陳安教授對我國法學研究的現狀充滿焦慮。「應當建立具有中國特色、體現第三世界共同立場的國際經濟法學科體系和理論體系」，這不僅成為他的主要學術主張之一，也成為他的奮鬥目標。

他指出，在許多發達國家中，已經出版了有關國際經濟法的大量著作，相繼建立了相應的學科體系和理論體系。其基本特色之一，是立足於本國的實際，以本國利益為核心，重點研究本國對外經濟交往中產生的法律問題，作出符合其本國立場和本國權益的全面分析和系統論證。反觀發展中國家，由於歷史的和現實的原因，尚未形成比較成熟的、能夠充分反映第三世界共同立場的國際經濟法學科體系和理論體系。因此，應當在積極研究當代國際經濟法新知識、新成果的基礎上，從第三世界的共同立場出發，逐步創立起具有中國特色的、維護第三世界眾多弱小民族利益的國際經濟法學科體系和理論體系，藉以加速國際經濟法律秩序新舊更替的進程。

「對於中國法學界來說，這是責無旁貸的歷史職責！」陳安教授十年來出版了十餘部系列專著。為了博采他山之石，十年來，他十一次出國，足跡遍布五大洲十多個國家。新思想、新成果，每次他都滿載而歸。去年他回國時，自費運回三十餘箱共七八八本書，全部捐給了學校，價值近十萬元。

國際經濟法是廈門大學的重點專業，作為學科帶頭人，陳安教授和他的同事及學生們日夜兼程。他的胃切除了三分之二，他卻樂觀地說：我要幹到八十歲。目前，他有一個強烈的願望，就是他們的國際經濟法專業爭取早日進入全國重點學科的行列，以求得對外交流、科研經費等方面更大的支持。「一個學科體系的建立需要幾代人的不懈努力」，他說，「我願意做鋪路石。」

五、就閩臺兩省結拜「姊妹」一事，廈門大學法學教授發表看法*

記者　張　莉

中新社福州電　據臺灣《經濟日報》報導：臺灣地區「立委」沈世雄於四月十六日提出一項書面質詢，呼籲臺灣地區「行政院」在「海峽兩岸人民關係法」（即「臺灣地區與大陸地區人民關係暫行條例」，下同）尚未制定實施以前，先行與福建省結為「姊妹省」，簽訂「自由貿易協定」。此事引起福建各界關注。

為此，記者走訪了廈門大學法學教授、福建省人大常委會委員陳安。

記者：臺灣地區的沈先生建議閩臺兩省結為「姊妹省」，您有何看法？

陳：據考證，臺灣省居民百分之七十以上祖籍為福建，臺灣地區政要李登輝等人的先輩都是福建人，閩南話至今仍是通行臺灣的主要方言。因此，閩臺兩省間的兄弟姊妹關係無須「結拜」，早就是「天生」形成的了。

記者：您對關於閩臺兩省簽訂「自由貿易協定」的動議持何評價？

陳：「自由貿易協定」主要內容為貨物、人力、資金的自由流通以及稅捐平等互惠等四方面。其基本著眼點是從切實保障臺商合法權益出發，要求率先在閩臺間建立平等互利的經濟關係。這個建議具有前瞻性和開拓性，有利於促進兩岸經濟共同繁榮，符合孫中山先生提倡的「人盡其才、地盡其利、物盡其用、貨暢其流」精神，體現了「孫文學說」中的一項基本原則，即行事應當「適於世界之潮流」，「合乎人群之需要」。

記者：閩臺兩省間的「自由貿易協定」在法律上屬什麼性質？

陳：中國只有一個。福建和臺灣兩個省級地方立法機構都有依照法定程式制定本省地方法規的立法權。閩臺簽訂「自由貿易協定」，實質是兩省地方立法機構共同立法，即適用於兩省全部地區的單行性地方經濟法規。這種省際地方立法一旦正式生效，就成為用以調整兩省經濟交往和貿易投資活動的行為規範和行動守則，對於兩省的有關經貿活動都具有法律上的約束力。

記者：從報端消息看，沈先生建議的兩省「自由貿易協定」的簽訂和實施，是在「海峽兩岸人民關係法」正式制定和實施之前。若上述協定簽訂之後，「關係法」亦出臺，兩者之間如何協調一致？

陳：這就看臺灣當局的決心和「立委」們的立法技巧了。若臺灣地方當局不同意擴大推行，則不妨仍保留上述兩省協定，作為與「關係法」這一普通法並存的特別法。

六、理性務實的學術交流盛會

——一九九三年兩岸法學學術研討會綜述*

記者　姚小敏

海峽兩岸法學專家、學者日前聚首北京，交流學術，探討兩岸交往、交流中衍生的有關法律問題。此次研討會薈萃了海峽兩岸一百六十餘位頗具名望的法學教授、律師，規模之大，前所未有，可說是兩岸關係發展中的一件盛事。

兩岸法學學術交流始於一九八八年，當時僅是單向的，只有臺灣地區學者來大陸。到去年十一月，大陸十一位法學家應臺灣東吳大學之邀，首次赴臺參加兩岸法學學術研討會，邁出了兩岸法學雙向交流的第一步。

此次研討會是上次會議的繼續和發展。在這次會議上，兩岸學者針對近年來兩岸交往中出現的一些法律問題展開務實而理性的探討，提出了一些富有建設性的建議。

保障臺商權益大陸有法規

臺商投資大陸，近年來可謂高潮迭起。到今年四月底，臺商在大陸投資達一萬多項，累計協定金額逾九十億美元。由此，臺商權益的保障問題，成為兩岸經貿關係中的一個「焦點」，亦成為此次研討會的議題之一。

臺灣當局一九八七年十一月開放民眾赴大陸探親。在此之後半年多，我國及時制定並頒布了《國務院關於鼓勵臺灣同胞投資的規定》，即「二十二條」迄今施行五年有餘，績效顯著。但臺灣地區某些人士認為，此項法規不過是行政規定，「很容易說變就變」，「不足以保障臺商的權益」，因而希望將「以行政命令方式」保障臺商權益的「二十二條」「提升至雙方簽署協議的位元階」。

對此，廈門大學法學教授陳安、講師彭莉指出，中國的成文法按其地位的高低依次分為憲法、法律、行政法規和地方法規。根據現行《憲法》，「行政法規」是指最高國家行政機關國務院制定的一種規範性檔，它是成文法的重要淵源之一，是具有普遍約束力和相當穩定性的行為規範和行動準則，並非某些臺灣人士所想像的，是什麼「說變就變」的行政命令。

至於兩岸簽署有關保障臺商權益的協議需要何種條件或說障礙何在？陳安、彭莉認為，一個重要的障礙在於，臺灣當局至今依然堅持「間接、單向」的交流原則，不准臺商直接以自身的名義赴大陸直接投資。因此，現有在大陸投資的一般臺商從法律「身份」上來說都是「外商」或「港商」。這種「名實不盡一致」的微妙身份，使得一般臺商在實踐中不但可以享受「二十二條」的優待，而且可以獲得大陸有關外商投資的一系列法律、法規的全面保護；此外，還可以獲得大陸和該臺商投資經由的第三地區所屬國家簽署的投資保護協定的保護。可見，在臺灣地區現行的大陸經貿政策下，兩岸簽署共同保障臺商權益的法律檔並沒有名正言順的適用物件，也不具有實質性的意義。他們認為，解開這一癥結的途徑顯然在於：臺灣當局儘早拋棄「國統綱領」中所設的人為局限，實現兩岸經貿的「直接、雙向」交流。

保護智慧財產權需兩岸努力

近年來，海峽兩岸人民智慧財產權時有受到對方單位和個入侵犯的現象發生。因此，保護智慧財產權的問題日漸引起人們的關注。

研討會上，兩岸學者均肯定兩岸在智慧財產權制度的建立和改進方面所作的努力。

臺灣學者劉紹梁認為，大陸這幾年來有關智慧財產權體制的發展可說是突飛猛進，相當值得臺灣學界深思、學習。但他也指出，兩岸智慧財產權的發展似乎都在急速地建立制度，以因應經濟發展的需求，然而在執行方面，或許都還不算完備。

大陸學者種明釗、李昌麒比較了兩岸專利法律制度的異同後認為，兩岸專利法律制度各有特色，就臺灣地區專利制度而言，規定得比較詳盡具體，更早地接近了國際保護標準。大陸地區的專利法律雖然起步較晚，但起點較高，立法技術比較先進，特別是修改後的《專利法》，正如國外所評論的，是「一部在各方面堪稱典範的專利法」。種、李二位先生指出，無論從立法技術和立法內容上講，還是從進一步完善兩岸專利法律制度來講，兩岸彼此都有互相借鑑之處。

這兩位學者認為，現在擺在兩岸法學家面前的一個重要任務，就是要進一步研究擴大兩岸經濟技術交流和合作的法律問題，其中包括建立兩岸技術專利資訊系統以及互相提供專利保護等問題，以使兩岸的經濟技術合作得到進一步發展。

兩岸律師攜手合作此其時

隨著兩岸人民交往的增進，引發和衍生了許多法律問題，其中不少問題兩岸互涉性強，因之，兩岸律師的協作日益突出和重要。

臺灣學者李念祖分析比較了兩岸不同法律制度下的律師從事業務合作的諸種方式，認為目前兩岸律師以個案合作方式較具可能性，即相互介紹辦案、委託辦案或共同辦案。

大陸學者張斌生在研究兩岸律師具體合作方式時，所得結論與臺灣學者大體相同。張斌生設想的協作方式有：互相提供諮詢意見、相互介紹業務、相互委託、轉委托業務、共同協辦案件或法律事務、簽訂業務合作協定、成立聯名的兩岸法律服務機構等等。

張斌生認為，在目前兩岸關係現狀下，以律師的管道辦理兩岸互涉的有關法律事務，不僅可以增進雙方當事人的信賴程度，而且可解決目前官方管道所暫時無法通融的問題。

綜觀此次研討會，自始至終充盈著一種理性、務實的學術氣氛。研討會的時間雖短，但成果頗豐。兩岸學者在討論中所提出的一些富有建設性的意見將可供有關方面參考。這對於進一步加強兩岸法學交流，促進兩岸關係發展大有裨益。

七、春風吹拂紫梅　白鷺振翅騰飛

——陳安教授談廈門獲得立法權*

記者　翁黛暉　黃文啟

八屆全國人大二次會議通過了授予廈門立法權的決定。當前，我市首先要做的是什麼呢？中國國際經濟法學會會長、廈門市人民政府法律顧問陳安教授在接受記者採訪時強調：廈門目前最急需做的，應是「為貫徹自由港某些政策立法」，使人們談論已久的「自由港某些政策」具體化、明朗化、規章化和法規化，從而依法治市，依法治港。

陳安教授說，中央授予立法權，這當然是廈門市的一大殊榮，但這也意味著廈門要擔當起更大的責任。中央允許廈門實施自由港某些政策，這在全國是「僅此一家」。廈門應當沿著中央指示的這個大方向，「敢為天下先」，充分發揮最新開闢的「立法試驗區」的作用，「膽大心細」地為貫徹自由港某些政策進行立法，加大改革開放力度，為建設現代化港口城市提供法律依據、法律保證和法律規範，要擔當起既為改革開放服務，又為全國探索新路子的雙重任務。

中央說的「自由港某些政策」，其中的「某些」兩字，據陳安教授理解，就是要求我們根據中國的國情和本市的市情，對世界各地的自由港政策，有所抉擇，有所取捨，既要博采眾長，又忌盲目照搬。給了立法權，我們就要去研究，去探索，摸著石頭過河，立足於國情、市情，參照世界各地自由港的有關法規和章程，取其精華，棄其糟粕，制定出具有中國特色的自由港法規和規章。在立法中，既要遵循我國憲法和其他基本法律原則，又要體現出「中國式自由港」的某些特色，具有較大的前瞻性和開拓性，在廈門地區率先試行。按照法律上的說辭，「特別法優先於普通法」，在廈門特區內實行某些特別法，將更有助於特區經濟建設的長足發展。實行自由港的某些政策，就應當認真考慮在國際經貿往來、商品流通、金融流通、資金流轉、人才流通、人員進出境和旅遊方便等方面，通過法規和規章的保證，具有更大的「自由」度和規範性。

黨的十四大明確提出建立社會主義市場經濟體制的改革目標，全方位對外開放。陳教授認為，建設社會主義市場經濟，需要有一系列相應的體制改革、政策更新、法律調整與完善，才能在更大的廣度與深度上參與和拓展國際經貿往來，充分利用國際市場經濟所提供的各種資源和機遇，更卓有成效地促進我國社會主義經濟建設。這就要求我們在對外經貿交往實踐及其行為規範方面更多、更好、更快地與國際經貿慣例接軌。因此，應當「適時修改和廢止與建立社會主義市場經濟體制不相適應的法律和法規，加強黨對立法工作的領導，完善立法體制，改進立法程式，加快立法步伐，為社會主義市場經濟提供法律規範」。陳安教授熟練地引用了黨的十四屆三中全會決定中的這段話。

陳安教授是廈門大學政法學院院長，著名的國際經濟法教授。由於他有很深的學術造詣，他已被列入英、美等五種版本的國際名人錄。據說，他的講座總是座無虛席，甚至其他專業的師生也常被吸引。在接受記者採訪時，他就顯示了其深厚的知識功底和灼見。在談到「與國際慣例接軌」這一問題時，陳安教授特別強調了「適用國際慣例與有法必依」的辯證關係，他說，廈門特區對外開放以來，「按國際慣例辦事」和「與國際慣例接軌」的觀念，日益為人們所接受。它開闊了人們的視野，更新了人們的觀念，使人們勇於和善於吸收外國的先進經驗和有效的舉措。但是，在參照和吸收適合我國需要的國際慣例，進一步改善、完善我國涉外經濟法律體系過程中，對於法定的立法程式，務必嚴格遵守，做到依法「變法」，依法「改法」或依法立法。有法必依，決不能以言代法或亂闖法律禁區。

隨後，陳安教授對「適用國際慣例」與「有法必依」作了如下闡述：中國具有獨特的綜合性國情，它既是發展中國家，又是社會主義國家，既是全球人口最多的國家，又是當前全世界經濟發展最快的國家之一。面對形形色色的國際慣例，在深入研究和認真鑑別的基礎上，只要它確實有利於促進中國社會主義市場體制的建立，就應當大膽地「拿來」。拿來之前要鑑別，拿來之後要消化。原則是：立足國情，以我為主；博采眾長，為我所用，趨利避害，取精華而棄糟粕。某些在西方國家盛行的國際慣例，如出版發行淫穢書刊和視聽作品、賣淫嫖娼、開設賭場等，在當地是合法的，在我國則是違法或犯罪的行為。因為它們毒化社會風氣，敗壞公序良俗，危害民族健康，刺激作奸犯科。對於此類國際慣例，自應依據我們的現行法律，予以抵制和排斥。對於那些以「適用國際慣例」為藉口，為謀私利或逞私欲「以身試法」的當事人，則應予以制裁和懲罰，這就是「有法必依」的體現。

陳安教授還強調：廈門在爭取特區立法權方面雖然曾經失去了一點時機，但是，「後來者居上」，事在人為。在春風吹拂之下，三角梅（廈門市市花）定將綻放得更加姹紫嫣紅，白鷺（廈門市市鳥）也勢必憑藉這股風力，扶搖直上，飛向新的、更新的高度。

八、第十二屆「安子介國際貿易研究獎」頒獎大會圓滿結束*（摘要）

記者　蓉　一

【對外經濟貿易大學】**宣傳部訊**　注重學術含量與社會價值的「安子介國際貿易研究獎」以下簡稱「安獎」）第十二屆頒獎大會，十二月十六日在誠信樓三層國際會議廳隆重舉行。本屆有七部著作、十二篇論文分獲優秀著作、優秀論文獎，十七人獲學術鼓勵獎。

商務部副部長廖曉淇、外貿司司長魯建華，教育部社政司副司長袁振國、北京大學校長助理海聞，我校校長、「安獎」評委會主任陳准民教授出席大會。校辦主任劉園主持大會。

第十二屆「安獎」共收到參評著作二十八部、參評論文六十七篇，共有三十三名學生參評學術鼓勵獎。經過嚴格評選，七部著作獲優秀著作獎，其中一等獎空缺，二等獎二部，三等獎五部；二篇論文獲優秀論文獎，其中一等獎一篇，二等獎三篇，三等獎八篇；十七人獲學術鼓勵獎。

陳准民校長在致辭中特別強調，「安獎」作為我國經貿研究領域的最高學術獎，在國內外享有很高聲譽。為繼續提高「安獎」評選的科學性、公平性和嚴肅性，本屆評委會對「安獎」評獎的指標體系作了系統調整和完善，注重從選題、內容、創新和成果等方面綜合評價研究成果，從而進一步優化評獎機制。本屆「安獎」評選繼續遵循公正、公開、回避、擇優的原則，確保了「安獎」評選結果的學術性和權威性。

據悉，本屆獲獎作品的特點是，選題範圍廣泛，涉及大經貿領域的許多重大前沿問題、熱點和難點問題；內容新穎，創新程度較高，作品的學術性和社會價值十分突出。廈門大學陳安教授撰寫的論文「The Three Big Rounds of U. S Unilateralism Versus WTO Multilateralism During the Last Decade」以其高度的理論與實踐意義獲得優秀論文一等獎。

頒獎在十分熱烈的氣氛中進行。「安獎」評委王林生教授宣讀本屆「安獎」獲獎名單，廖副部長、魯司長、袁副司長、陳校長先後為獲獎者頒獎。

九、第十二屆「安子介國際貿易研究獎」頒獎*

記者　劉　菲

本報訊　近日，第十二屆「安子介國際貿易研究獎」頒獎大會暨學術報告會在對外經濟貿易大學舉行。「安子介國際貿易研究獎」是由已故全國政協副主席，香港著名實業家、社會活動家、學者，對外經濟貿易大學名譽教授安子介先生於一九九一年出資設立的，該獎自一九九二年第一屆評選以來，已成功舉辦了十二屆。

經多年努力，「安子介國際貿易研究獎」已有了較高的學術含量，在國際經貿研究領域聲譽卓著，被視為中國經貿領域中的最高學術獎。

本屆「安子介國際貿易研究獎」共收到參評著作二十八部、參評論文六十七篇，另有三十三名學生參評學術鼓勵獎。其中評出優秀著作獎七部，優秀論文獎十二篇，學術鼓勵獎十七人。本屆參評作品和獲獎成果的品質較以往明顯提高。獲獎作品的共同特點是選題與時俱進，涉及經貿領域的許多前沿問題、重大問題、熱點問題和難點問題，內容新穎，創新程度較高，成果的學術價值含量和社會價值突出。獲得本屆優秀論文一等獎的廈門大學陳安教授的論文《晚近十年來美國單邊主義與WTO多邊主義交鋒的三大回合》，被總部設在日內瓦的發展中國家政府間組織「南方中心」列為出版物之一，並在該機構網站上全文公布。

十、中國特色國際經濟法學的探索者和開拓者

——陳安教授*

記者　陳　浪

廈門大學最高榮譽獎項「南強獎」每兩年評選一次。二〇〇八年「南強獎」特等獎獲得者陳安是法學院教授、國際經濟法專業博士生導師。一九二九年五月出生，一九五〇年從廈門大學法律系畢業，一九五一年初應聘返回廈大工作，五十七年來，陳安堅持「以知識報國，為廈大增光」的理念，為廈大的法學教育辛勤耕耘，特別是近三十年來，始終立足中國國情，致力於對國際經濟法這一新興邊緣學科進行探索和開拓，為我國的國際經濟法學科做出了影響深遠的貢獻。

在教學方面，陳安牽頭組織撰寫並及時修訂國際經濟法各版教科書，被全國高校廣泛採用，據此開設的我校「國際經濟法學」課程入選為「本科國家級精品課程」；創辦《國際經濟法學刊》並長期擔任主編，成績顯著，使該刊成為全國性專業同行交流和爭鳴的重要學術平臺，並於二〇〇六年入選為「中國社會科學引文索引」（CSSCI）學術資料來源集刊。陳安還參與創建「中國國際經濟法學會」並長期擔任會長，成績顯著。二〇〇六年七月，該學會獲得民政部登記發給社團法人證書，成為全國性一級學術社團，法人住所設在廈門大學。迄今，陳安連續主持召開了該學會一九九三至二〇〇七每年年會。

在科研方面，陳安著作等身，撰寫和主編的主要著作有：《中國大百科全書——法學卷（修訂版）》中「國際經濟法」分

支學科詞條、《國際經濟法學（第1-4版）》《國際經濟法總論》《國際經濟法學新論》《國際經濟法學專論（第1-2版）》（教育部主管司推薦的研究生教材）、「國際經濟法系列專著」（含《國際貿易法》《國際投資法》《國際貨幣金融法》《國際稅法》《國際海事法》全套五卷）、《美國對海外投資的法律保護及典型案例分析》《「解決投資爭端國際中心」述評》《國際投資爭端仲裁：ICSID機制研究》《MIGA與中國：多邊投資擔保機構述評》《國際投資法的新發展與中國雙邊投資條約的新實踐》等等。陳安教授經常自謙：這些論著都是他所牽頭帶動和積極參與的學術團隊多年來通力協作，集體攻關，與時俱進所取得的成果。

二〇〇七年十月，陳安根據自己三十年來研究國際經濟法這一新興邊緣學科取得的主要成果獨立撰寫的《國際經濟法學芻言》（北京大學出版社出版，分上、下卷，二百一十二萬字）獲第五屆「吳玉章人文社會科學獎」一等獎。該獎面向全國，每五年評獎一次，是全國性高檔次文科獎項之一，自該獎項設立二十年來，廈大教授首次獲得該獎項一等獎。專家評議認為，本書是創建中國特色國際經濟法學這一新興邊緣學科理論體系的奠基之作，是第三世界國家爭取國際經濟平權地位的理論武器。

除了專著，近兩年來，陳安的論文《南南聯合自強五十年的國際經濟立法反思：從萬隆、多哈、坎昆到香港》（載於《中國法學》2006年第2期）獲得「福建省第七屆社會科學優秀成果獎」一等獎。另外，近兩年來他撰寫的五篇英文論文，均發表於《世界投資與貿易學報》《日內瓦天下大事論壇》《南方公報》等權威性國際學術刊物，在海外具有一定的學術影響。

近兩年，陳安承擔了兩項科研課題。其中，以陳安、曾華群為課題組組長承擔了商務部條法司關於《中華人民共和國雙邊投資保護協定範本》的委託專案，該課題為國策諮詢項目，將於今年底完成；以陳安為課題組組長承擔並完成了全國「法學精品教材建設規劃」委託研究開發專案《國際經濟法學新論》系列。

陳安旗幟鮮明地站在全球發展中國家和弱小民族的共同立場，把握當代南北矛盾的實質，遵循建立國際經濟新秩序的發展方向，來探討當代國際經濟法學所面臨的各種理論和實踐問題，從而為構築具有中國特色的國際經濟法學理論框架和學科體系做出了重要的開拓性貢獻。改革開放以來，他先後作為中國各類法學代表團成員或法學界知名教授，多次出國訪問，前往美國、加拿大、德國、英國、瑞士、比利時、澳大利亞、韓國、法國等國家和地區參加國際法學術會議或講學，積極開展國際交流。

近三十年來，陳安的各項工作成果，均取得了較大的全國性影響和一定的海外影響，基本達到了國內先進水準，取得了較顯著的社會效益，為我校贏得了榮譽，陳安先後獲得國家級、省部級科研成果一等獎十一項，國家級、省部級科研成果二等獎七項，合計十八項。二〇〇七年，陳安教授被我國媒體「大學評價課題組」評選為「2007中國傑出社會科學家」。

十一、十位廈大學者入選中國傑出社會科學家 *

記者　王瑛慧

十二月二十四日，由中國校友會網「大學評價課題組」編制的《2007中國傑出社會科學家研究報告》正式發布。報告公布了五〇五名入選「2007（首屆）中國傑出社會科學家」名單的學者。我校十人入選，入選數名列第十二。從傑出社會科學家的畢業院校分布來看（僅統計1952年以後），我校和中山大學各八人並列第十。

我校入選的十位學者是：陳安（法學）、陳詩啟（歷史學）、陳振明（公共管理）、葛家澍（應用經濟學）、胡培兆（理論經濟學）、錢伯海（應用經濟學）、曲曉輝（工商管理）、鄔大光（教育學）、吳世農（工商管理）、莊國土（政治學）。

據介紹，此次遴選依照的指標有六項：一是國家社會科學基金專案優秀成果獎二等獎以上第一完成人；二是中國高校人文社會科學研究優秀成果獎一等獎以上第一完成人；三是國務院學位委員會委員；四是教育部社會科學委員會委員；五是中國社會科學院學部委員；六是「長江學者獎勵計畫」特聘教授。

課題組負責人指出，此次遴選採用成果評價僅有國家社科基金獎和高校社科優秀獎的重大獎勵成果，一些在某學科領域內較有影響力的基金獎因為評獎數量過多、獎勵沒分等級等原因暫未被採納，從而使一些學者未被納人最終名單。這也從側面反映出，我國人文社會科學成果評價機制存在缺陷，亟待改進。

「2007中國傑出社會科學家研究報告》由中國校友會網、《大學》雜誌和《21世紀人才報》等聯合完成，是我國首個針對人文社會科學領域的傑出學者展開的調查研究報告。報告呼籲國家及社會各界應儘早遏制普遍存在的「重理輕文」現象，儘快設立「文科院士」和「國家級社會科學獎勵」制度，以真正體現國家和社會對於人文社會科學價值的肯定和重視。

注釋

* 本篇報導原發表於《生活・創造》1985年第12期，第6-8頁。作者陳福郎時任廈門大學出版社總編輯。
* 本篇報導原發表於《福建司法》1988年第5期。作者甘景山當時是《福建日報》資深記者。
* 本篇報導原載於《光明日報》1988年4月26日。作者林鴻禧當時是廈門大學校長辦公室主任、《光明日報》通訊記者，陳友仁當時是《光明日報》資深記者。在此之前，中國新聞出版總署主辦的《新聞出版報》1988年1月9日在《人以少勝多，書以優取勝》一文中率先報導了鷺江出版社推出陳安教授一系列專著的資訊，並作了評論，指出：該社「出版了《美國對海外投資的法律保護及典型案例分析》及其姊妹篇《舌劍唇槍——國際投資糾紛五大著名案例》，在學術界和社會上引起很大反響。法學界權威韓德培教授贊曰：『以中國人眼光來談美國對海外投資的法律問題，確可謂獨具新意。』已故北大教授陳體強生前稱讚該書：『內容豐富，系統完整，洵是佳作。』最後，鷺江出版社又出版了一套國際經濟法的系列專著，即《國際金融法》《國際貿易法》《國際海事法》《國際投資法》，為創立具有中國特色的國際經濟法學科體系開了先河。這套專著被國家教委擬作推薦教材，並獲得了廈門大學頒發的『南強獎』。」接著，《中國青年報》1988年5月11日在「法制與社會」專欄的一則短訊中向全國讀者推薦說：這套系列專著在論述取材上，力求其新，許多資料直接來源於近年的國外最新出版物。在吸收國外有關研究成果和介紹有關基本理論的基礎上，力求從中國的實踐出發，從中國人的角度和第三世界的立場來研究和評析當代的國際經濟法，同時，每一分冊都用相當篇幅結合論述我國在相應領域中的涉外法律規範，注意及時反映我國涉外經濟立法的最新進展和總結有關的實踐經驗。」隨後，上述報導引起了《人民日報》（海外版）記者張安南和陳樹榮的注意，並相繼在該報1988年10月26日和1991年12月31日的兩篇專訪中一再地向讀者推薦陳安教授撰寫和主編的上述一系列專著。前一篇專訪仍題為《人以少勝多，書以優取勝》，指出：「《美國對海外投資的法律保護及

典型案例分析》和《舌劍唇槍——國際投資糾紛五大著名案例》姐妹篇，還有包括《國際投資法》《國際貿易法》《國際貨幣金融法》《國際稅法》《國際海事法》五冊一套的國際經濟法系列專著，是國家教育委員會博士點專項基金選定科學研究專案的初步成果。鷺江出版這套系列專著，為創立具有中國特色的國際經濟法學科體系開了先河。而且，在短時間內集中出版同一研究領域的多部學術專著，這在地方出版社中也是罕見的。」後一篇專訪題為《廈門大學發揮師資的優勢，為特區建設積極培養人才》，其中指出：「上述系列專著是我國第一套涉外經濟法律的最新專著，對我國發展外向型經濟具有理論研究和實用價值。」

* 本篇報導原載於《人民日報》（海外版）1992年7月7日。作者是當時國家教委幹部、《人民日報》（海外版）專欄撰稿人。

* 本篇報導原載於《人民日報》（海外版）1989年5月8日。

* 本篇報導原載於《人民日報》（海外版）1993年8月27日。

* 本篇報導原載於《廈門日報》1994年3月27日。

* 本篇報導原發表於對外經濟貿易大學網站（http://www. uibe. edu. cn/）2004年12月18日。

* 本篇報導原發表於《人民日報》（海外版）2004年12月21日。

* 本篇報導原載於《廈門大學報》2008年5月3日第1版。記者陳浪根據相關材料整理。

* 本篇報導由廈門大學黨委宣傳部於2007年12月27日編發，宣傳部王瑛慧綜合報導。

學界來函

一、來函概述

中國實行改革開放基本國策以來，陳安教授開始立足中國國情和國際弱勢群體的共同立場，致力於中國特色國際經濟法學的學習、探索和研究。陳安教授於一九八一至一九八三年應邀在美國哈佛大學從事國際經濟法研究，兼部分講學工作。一九九〇至一九九一年以「亞洲傑出學者」名義應聘在美國俄勒岡州路易士與克拉克西北法學院擔任客座教授，兼任該學院國際法研究專案顧問。

自一九八一年至二〇〇七年，除在美國上述兩所大學從事三年多的研究、講學外，陳安教授先後十幾次應邀和奉派出國，參加國際性法學學術活動，前往比利時（歐共體總部）、瑞士（聯合國歐洲總部）、聯邦德國、加拿大、美國、澳大利亞、荷蘭、英國、法國、韓國等國家和地區，參加國際學術會議，為東道國和當地多所大學法學院和律師事務所講學，宣講中國改革和開放的政策、法律和法規，積極開展國際學術交流。在此期間，先後在外國學術刊物上或法學合著中發表了多篇論文或論著專章。與此同時，又接受中國政府有關部門的委託，有的放矢地從事專項科學研究，並以研究成果提供決策參考。以下選輯近三十封信件[1]，從一個小側面，具體而微地反映了陳安教授的上述學術活動以及國內外人士對這些學術活動所作的評價。大體上可歸納為以下八項事例：

（一）對《國際經濟法學芻言》[2]一書的評價

中國法學界老前輩韓德培先生、朱學山先生以及郭壽康先生於二〇〇五至二〇〇七年先後來函對本書惠予良好評價，並對本書作者鼓勵、鞭策有加。韓老先生認為：「短短二十餘年，竟有如此豐碩研究成果，實屬少見」；朱老先生函稱：「我已將其常置案頭，以供不時研讀，我一向以為您的文章是耐得百回讀的，何況這些文章全是中國國際經濟法學理論的奠基之作，應該反覆研讀。」郭老先生認為本書作者「是中國國際經濟法的奠基人之一，也是中國國際經濟法這門前沿學科的領軍人物」。改革開放以來，作者「積極宣導建立中國國際經濟法這門課程與學科，逐步形成了中國國際經濟法的體系」，《國際經濟法學芻言》一書，是作者「二十餘年來其著作的精華與代表，也是本學科發展中又一里程碑」。該書「為當代國際社會弱勢群體爭取經濟平權地位提供有力的理論武器。尤其是用英語發表的作品，在國際上影響很大，既體現出發展中國家的主張與立場，也擴大了我國的國際影響，為我國的國際經濟法學贏得了國際聲譽」。（見本章後附「來函選輯」A部分之（一）（二）（三））

（二）對《南南聯合自強五十年的國際經濟立法反思》[3]一文的評價

本文全文約六萬四千字。發展中國家的政府間組織「南方中心」秘書長Branislav Gosovic教授收閱本文的英文版後，於二〇〇六年二月來函稱：「我認為它能給人以清晰鮮明的方針政策性的啟示，會使《南方中心公報》的讀者們很感興趣，特別因為這是您從一個正在崛起的舉足輕重的大國發出的大聲吶喊！」[4]因此決定把本長篇論文的核心內容（即第四部分，約7000字），以紙面版和電子版同時發表於該機關理論刊物，以擴大全球讀者受眾範圍，增強其學術影響。（見本章後附「來函選輯」C部分之（三））

日內瓦《世界投資與貿易學報》《日內瓦天下大事論壇》的編輯Jacgues Werner先生閱讀本篇論文後，於二〇〇六年一月和二月兩度來函，前函稱：「我們發現您的《南南聯合自強五十年的國際經濟立法反思》論文，對於當前WTO正在進行的談判磋商，作了很有創見和雄辯有力的評析，充分反映了您的見解，因此，我很樂於採用，並即將發表於本刊二〇〇六年四月這一期。」後函續稱：「我發現，您的這篇文章令人很感興趣，因此想要把它另行發表於我所編輯的另一種學刊，即《日內瓦天下大事論壇》季刊。這另一種學刊面向更加廣泛的讀者物件，包括聯合國各種機構中的公務人員、外交人員、國際公司中的高層執事等等。……我們認為，這是一個良好的機會，讓您的見解傳播給更加廣泛的公眾，因而期待您能同意我的上述建議。刊載您這篇文章的《日內瓦天下大事論壇》季刊預定於二〇〇六年四月二十六日出版。」（見本章後附「來函選輯」C部分之（一））

本文的中文版原稿曾刊登於《中國法學》二〇〇六年第二期，其責任編輯戚燕方副編審認為：「此文旗幟鮮明，站在國際弱勢群體的共同立場，以史為據，以史為師，史論結合，視角獨到，力排『眾議』，頗多創新，具有極強的現實針對性和學術理論性。其資料翔實全面，邏輯嚴謹，說理透澈，論證雄辯，是這一學術領域中不可多得的力作和佳作。」「據我們所知，中國法學家撰寫的長篇學術論文，能引起國際組織和國際性學刊如此重視、具有如此國際影響者，尚不多見。」（見本書第六編「陳安早期論著書評薈萃」第三章之十一）

隨著時間的推移，本長篇論文得到了國際學術界更多的關注。其修訂版已被翻譯成韓語，並於二〇〇六年六月發表在韓國重要的學術刊物*The Joural of Inha Law*第九卷第二期。翌年，本文修訂後的英文版又被收錄在Yong-Shik Lee教授主編的*Economic Law Through World Trade: A Developing World Perspective*一書，列為該學術專著的第二章，由國際知名的法學學術出版社Kluwer Law International出版。

二〇〇八年一月，前「南方中心」原秘書長Gosovic教授得知本篇長文的全文連續數度增訂並由多家國際性學刊發表或轉載，又滿懷同道熱情，特意附函寄來他撰寫的書評，對本文進一步加以推介。他認為：這篇長文所作的理論分析和雄辯論證，是「對第三世界思想體系的重大創新性貢獻」，其「重大意義就在於，它為當代全球弱小民族國家提供了用以抗衡強權和抵制霸權的理論利器和實踐工具」。他強調：「儘管關於WTO的故事隨著香港部長級會議的落幕而暫時告一段落，但是這並不會讓陳安教授的這篇論文顯得過時。恰恰相反，香港會議以後出現的種種事態發展，已經充分說明這篇論文依據歷史所闡明的有關主題主旨仍然合理有效，並且具有深遠的影響。因此，陳安教授的這篇論文不僅仍然可以作為學生和學者的標準讀物，而且對於許多決策者和參與WTO等談判磋商和日常活動的人士說來，也是可供參考的標準。同時，還可以指望它能對促進南南合作，加強南南合作的機制和組織機構，產生積極的影響。」（見本書第一卷卷首「前輩大師評論」之IV）

（三）對《晚近十年來美國單邊主義與WTO多邊主義交鋒的三大回合》〔5〕一文的評價

這篇英文論文長達六萬五千字，原先發表於美國天普大學《國際法與比較法學報》二〇〇三年第十七卷第二期。它援引十年來的大量事實，針對美國在加入WTO多邊主義國際協定後仍然頑固推行其傳統的經濟霸權政策和單邊主義立法，進行系統的理論分析和深入批判。本文發表後引起國際上有關人士廣泛關注。二〇〇四年六月，作者應國際組織「南方中心」要求，作了修訂、增補，於二〇〇四年七月由該中心將本文作為T. R. A. D. E.專題「第22號工作文件」重印發行，分發給世界各國或地區常駐日內瓦WTO總部的代表團，並刊登在該中心網站上，供讀者自由下載。（見本章後附「來函選輯」C部分之（二）（三））

「南方中心」是亞、非、拉美眾多發展中國家締約共同組建的政府間國際組織，總部設在日內瓦，發揮「國際思想庫」和「國際智囊團」作用，中國政府是其核心成員之一。中心的主要工作是向國際社會宣傳發展中國家的政治和經濟主張、思想觀點和理論文章，設計和論證發展中國家在各種南北談判中的共同立場，並提供給各國政府作為決策參考。

（四）對《「解決投資爭端國際中心」述評》[6]一書的評價

「解決投資爭端國際中心」（ICSID）是一個國際機構，根據一九六五年的《華盛頓公約》設立，是「世界銀行」的五大成員機構之一，總部設在美國華盛頓。該機構的業務與中國的對外開放和吸收外資國策關係密切。中國已於一九九〇年二月正式簽署參加《華盛頓公約》，並於一九九三年一月提交了締約批准書，同意接受ICSID體制。

陳安教授於一九八七年開始承擔和主持國家教委博士點基金專題科研專案，就中國是否應當參加《華盛頓公約》接受ICSID體制問題，為對外經貿部提供國策諮詢。其集體科研成果《「解決投資爭端國際中心」述評》一書於一九八九年十二月出版。

一九九〇年陳安教授受聘在美擔任客座教授期間，曾將上述著作一本連同全書目錄英文譯文一份寄贈設立在美國華盛頓的ICSID總部，該總部反應如下：

一、世界銀行副總裁、「中心」秘書長希哈塔（Shihata）委託「中心」法律顧問帕拉（Parra）來函表示「非常感謝」，並稱：「我們將在最近一期的《『中心』訊息》刊物上宣布您這部著作的出版消息，並將在下一版的《『中心』論著書目》中將這本書正式列人。」（Parra 1990年3月22日致陳安教授函）

二、一九九〇年《「中心」訊息》第七卷第一期宣告：「中國正式簽署參加《「中心」公約》(即《華盛頓公約》)」,同時,在《有關「中心」的近期最新論著》專欄中,列出世界各國近期出版的有關「中心」的新著六種,把陳安教授主持撰寫的上述專著列在首位。

三、一九九〇年八月,「中心」法律顧問帕拉寫信給陳安教授,附函寄贈上述刊物一份,並稱:「您論述『中心』的新書,已在本期的《『中心』訊息》上宣布了有關的出版消息。**根據本書內容目錄的英文譯文來判斷,這肯定是一部極其有益的著作。**」(見本章後附「來函選輯」C部分之(五))

中國政府有關主管部門對本書的出版也給予很大的鼓勵和良好的評價,認為:「該書的出版無疑會推動我國學術界對於《華盛頓公約》和『解決投資爭端國際中心』的理論研究,同時亦對我們研究加入該公約的工作具有積極的參考價值和借鑑作用。」「您的大作,對我們的立法工作幫助很大。」(見本章後附「來函選輯」B部分之(十)(十一))

(五)對《是重新閉關自守?還是擴大對外開放?——論中美兩國經濟上的互相依存以及「1989年政治風波」後在華外資的法律環境》[7]一文的評價

「1989年政治風波」發生後,美國某些政客掀起陣陣反華叫囂,誣衊中國對外開放政策即將「壽終正寢」,外資在華處境「惡化」,並一再威脅要中斷對華「最惠國待遇」,以示「懲罰」和「制裁」。美國社會上許多對華友好人士也因不明真相而產生各種疑慮和誤解。一九九〇年九月二十五日,時值陳安教授應聘在俄勒岡州擔任客座教授抵美不久，即應邀在路易士與克拉克西北法學院校友會和俄勒岡州律師集會上進行專題演講，並與美國「福特基金會」原駐北京官員馬克·賽德爾（Mark Sidel）教授展開辯論。陳安教授列舉大量事實，力排眾議，論證中國對外開放與吸收外資的基本國策不但未有改變，而且因「1989年政治風波」以後又相繼制定了許多新的法律、法規，而使外資在華的法律環境進一步改善，導致大量新的外資投入中國；並論證一旦取消對華「最惠國待遇」，美國經濟本身勢必首先受害。其後，陳安教授將上述演講稿整理成文，發表於俄勒岡州《律師》雜誌一九九一年第十卷第二期（中文版收輯於本書第三編「國際投資法」第十二章）。

美國俄勒岡州唐肯（Tonkon *et al*）律師事務所首席律師歐文·布朗克（Owen D. Blank）曾與會聆聽上述演講，後來又閱讀了上述論文。他致函陳安教授稱：您針對中國與美國經濟互利關係所作的分析，切合實際，令人耳目一新。您對於中國繼續實行開放政策所作的論證，很有必要加以廣泛、普及的宣傳，以促使美國的許多公司恢復信心——它們在『1989年政治風波』以前本來已經很好地確立了這種信心。」（見本章後附「來函選輯」C部分之（六））

中國駐美國西海岸舊金山總領館負責人朱又德先生收讀上述論文後，致函陳安教授稱：「很欣賞你的智慧、才幹和勇氣。此舉很有意義。由此，使我聯想到，如果我們的學者和學生中能有一批像你這樣的民間大使，對反駁美政壇對我國的非難，以及消除一些美國友人的疑慮和誤解，無疑將起到非同一般的影響和作

用。謝謝你利用講學、研究之餘，抽時間、尋機會為宣傳中國所做的工作。」（見本章後附「來函選輯」B部分之（九））

（六）對參加俄勒岡州「第三屆國際商法研討會」宣講中國投資法的評價

一九八八年十月底，陳安教授應邀參加美國俄勒岡州「第三屆國際商法研討會」，在會上做了專題學術報告《中國涉外投資法十年來的發展》，並印發了長篇演講文稿。

會議主持人美國路易士與克拉克西北法學院院長斯蒂芬・坎特教授（Stephen Kanter）會前（1988年9月12日）來函稱這個報告選題「極好」（perfect），「我們希望您在本屆研討會上做開幕演講」。會議通告將陳安教授列於八位在會發言人的首位。

研討會結束，陳安教授回國後，路易士與克拉克西北法學院「律師進修班」主任勞麗・梅普斯（Laurie B. Mapes）於一九八八年十一月二十九日來函稱：「我代表本法學院對您光臨參加『第三屆國際商法研討會』表示感謝。此次學術活動取得巨大成功。我們收到許多反映，誇獎讚揚此次研討會以及您的演講——《中國涉外投資法十年來的發展》。我們深切感謝您對本次出色活動所做的貢獻，它給我們法學院帶來了很高的榮譽和聲望。」（見本章後附「來函選輯」C部分之（七）

（七）對《是進一步開放？還是重新關門？——中國吸收外資政策法令述評》[8]一文的評價

一九八二年秋，中國政府在繼續對外開放的同時，大張旗鼓地打擊同吸收外資有關的一切經濟犯罪活動。國際上當時曾因此盛傳：中國對外開放的「風向」已經改變，即將恢復「教條主義」，重新實行「閉關自守」政策。陳安教授當時正在美國哈佛大學從事研究和講學，遂於一九八二年中國國慶日應邀在該校發表專題學術演講《是進一步開放？還是重新關門？》，旨在澄清美國、日本學者對中國吸收外資有關政策法令的疑慮、擔心或非難，答覆他們的詢問，並以事實為根據，從法學理論上說明中國今後既要繼續堅持對外開放政策，進一步積極吸收外資，保護合法外資和正當外商，又要繼續嚴肅認真地打擊同吸收外資有關的一切經濟犯罪行為，從而為建設具有中國特色的社會主義服務。事後，陳安教授將演講稿整理成文，發表在紐約法學院《國際法與比較法學報》一九八四年第六卷第一期上。

此次演講由哈佛大學法學院助理院長兼該校東亞法學研究所副所長斯奈德（Frederick E. Snyder）主持。事後他索贈文稿，並來函稱：「這次演說非常打動人心，很能發人深思，令人興趣盎然。您的文稿中對於保護外國投資的兩種不同做法的有關論述，也相當深刻周詳。我認為，您針對美國（保護海外投資）的立場得到（某些國家）追隨而又遭到（許多國家）挑戰這個問題所作的論述，是特別有意義的。我殷切地期待您能把這篇文章公開發表，從而使國際法學界有更多人可以從您的深刻見解中獲得教益。」（見本章後附「來函選輯」C部分之（八））

哈佛大學法學院權威老教授、該校東亞法學研究所所長亞瑟・馮・墨倫（Arthur von Mehren）在閱讀上述演講文稿以及陳安教授的另一篇文章〔9〕之後，來函稱：「我認為這兩篇文章對於有關主題所作的論述，都是很有教益和很有創見的。兩篇文章都寫得條理分明，行文妥善。每一篇都大大有助於促進美國的讀者加深理解您所論述的問題。我們東亞法學研究所的同事，大家都知道您在這裡的工作中，一向是幹勁充沛和專心致志的。您的兩篇論文就是令人欽佩的例證，說明您的研究工作的品質和成就。我們高興的是：如今您在美國幫助我們理解中國的法律和社會，日後回到中國，您有能力在那裡以同樣的方式向您的同事以及學生們闡明有關美國法律和美國社會的各個方面。」（見本章後附「來函選輯」C部分之（九））

日本訪美研究員、日本國家石油公司金融經濟專家杉原啟示先生於聽講後索要演講稿，並來函稱：「我認為，日前先生發表之高見對於日本國民理解中國之政策精神，頗具參考價值，故已將先生惠贈之講演原文（英文）稿件，迅即摘譯要旨，徑送日本國家石油公司參考。」（見本章後附「來函選輯」C部分之（十））

（八）對《是棒打鴛鴦嗎？——就「李爽案件」評〈紐約時報〉報導兼答美國法學界同行問》[10]一文的評價

一九八一年秋冬間，中國政府對中國公民李爽（女）與法國外交官貝耶華（Bellfroid，有婦之夫）在法國使館公開姘居一案作了嚴肅處理，將李爽收容勞教兩年。法國媒體借此攻擊中國當局，美國《紐約時報》也對此案作了錯誤報導。哈佛大學法學院曾將該報的兩篇報導列為參考教材，散發給研究生「學習」，引起在哈佛進修的各國學者議論紛紛，對中國的涉外政策法令、個人婚戀自由、知識份子政策、勞教條例以及案件審理程式等，頗有非議。陳安教授應邀在哈佛課堂上對近百名研究生及旁聽的日、澳、德等國的訪問學者做了專題演講，從法學理論、國際條約、國際慣例以及中國法令具體條文規定上，論證中國有關當局在處理此案時，不但維護了民族尊嚴和國格，而且嚴格依法辦事，做到合情、合理、合法，從而澄清問題，以正視聽。事後，陳安教授將演講稿整理成文，發表在紐約法學院《國際法與比較法學報》一九八一年第三卷第一期上（見本書第五編「國際經濟法熱點學術問題長、短評」第四章）。

該學報主編艾姆林・希加來函評論說：「您這篇論文的主題是評論刊載於《紐約時報》的克利斯托弗・雷恩所寫的兩篇報導。這些報導曾經引起人們對中華人民共和國政府當局處理李爽案件的做法，嘖有煩言，紛紛非難。您的文章提出了人們所殷切期待的答案。這種答案，來自中華人民共和國的一位公民，來自一位像您這樣卓越出色的中國法學學者，是再恰當不過的了。您的這篇論文從中國的風俗習慣、志向抱負、政治和社會的奮鬥目標的角度，從反映著這些因素的法律體制的角度，條理分明、令人信服地剖析了李爽案件。我不能設想有比這更加雄辯透澈的解釋說明。您對於美國和中國的刑事法制所作的比較分析是特別有教益和富有啟發性的。不過，我認為最能發人深思的還是您所使用的方法，即把李爽案件放置在中國的社會主義理論、社會主義實踐以及社會主義目標的背景之中，加以剖析。」（見本章後附「來函選輯」C部分之（十一））

美國波士頓大學法學院教授弗蘭克・K. 阿帕姆（Frank K. Upham）索贈上述論文後，來函表示感謝，並稱：「我認為，您的論文以一個中國法學學者的敏銳眼光，對這樁案件作了引人入勝的、相當精闢的闡述。您那精心細緻、沉著冷靜的分析，提出了一些重要的課題，它們將鄭重提醒美國的法學研究生們必須注意另外一種法學觀點，這種法學觀點往往同他們原有的觀點迥然相異，並且難得有人能夠妥善確切地加以論述闡明。我的研究專業雖是日本的法學，但我仍然打算今後要求我的研究生們閱讀您的這篇論文。因為這篇論文是如此妥帖完善地闡明了中國法制與美國法制之間的基本區別和某些相似之處，而這兩種法制對於日本法制的形成，向來是有促進作用的。」（見本章後附「來函選輯」C部分之（十二））

二、來函選輯

A　前輩大師來函

（一）武漢大學教授韓德培老先生致陳安教授函

陳安同志好友：

日前承惠贈大著兩卷，非常感謝！翻閱後不勝敬佩！我曾認為足下是閩南一位才子，短短二十餘年，竟有如此豐碩研究成果，實屬少見。

您在自序中說「古稀逾六，垂垂老矣」。其實，您還不能說「老」，在我的心目中，您還是在「奮發有為」時期，毫無老的跡象。我現在已九十五歲，真可說是一個「老人」或「老朽」。雖然學校不讓我退休，我還在帶些博士研究生，但也只能量力而為。

我在九十歲時，曾在一首詩中說「鞠躬盡餘熱，接力有來人」真的，只有寄希望於「來人」了。

廈大的許多老朋友，請代問候。

敬祝

冬安

韓德培　敬啟

二〇〇五年十一月三十日

（二）安徽大學教授朱學山老先生致陳安教授函

陳安同志：

新春好！敬祝您身體健康，闔家幸福！

返抵合肥後見到大著《芻言》，不勝欣喜！我已將其常置案頭，以供不時研讀，我一向以為您的文章是耐得百回讀的，何況這些文章全是中國國際經濟法學理論的奠基之作，應該反覆研讀。

關於「慶父不去，魯難未已」，我對您談過。現將談話底稿奉上，以供參考。在年會上我提交的短文《小問題》，您沒見到，現亦寄上，以便您了解一些情況，並祈教正！

專肅，即頌

著安！

朱學山再拜

二〇〇六年一月十五日

（三）中國人民大學教授郭壽康老先生致陳安教授函及附件

【評獎推薦書】陳安教授是中國國際經濟法的奠基人之一，也是中國國際經濟法這門前沿學科的領軍人物。我國傳統法學（包括中華人民共和國成立前和成立後）只講授國際公法與國際私法，沒有開設過國際經濟法課程。國外法學院系也大體如此。改革開放以來，陳安教授積極宣導建立中國國際經濟法這門課程與學科，逐步形成了中國國際經濟法的體系。萬事開頭難，陳安教授為創建中國國際經濟法，費盡心血，成績卓越，發表了大量的優秀論文、教材與專著，做出了重大的具有歷史意義的貢獻。二〇〇五年由北京大學出版社出版的《國際經濟法學芻言》（上、下兩卷，211萬字），是二十餘年來其著作的精華與代表，也是本學科發展中又一里程碑。

《國際經濟法學芻言》這部專著是國際經濟法學這門學科的扛鼎之作。不但顯示出作者知識淵博，深思熟慮，而且多有創新之見。二戰後，逐漸興起的國際經濟法學，陣地多為發達國家的作者、專家所占領，發展中國家聲音微弱，居於劣勢。陳安教授這部專著旗幟鮮明地站在國際弱勢群體即廣大發展中國家的立場，理直氣壯地闡明對國際經濟法學中的熱點問題觀點，持之有故、言之成理，為當代國際社會弱勢群體爭取經濟平權地位提供有力的理論武器。尤其是用英語發表的作品，在國際上影響很大，既體現出發展中國家的主張與立場，也擴大了我國的國際影響，為我國的國際經濟法學贏得了國際聲譽。

書中論證的螺旋式上升的「6C軌跡」論，無疑是作者多年研究的創新之論。

這部著作理論密切聯繫實際，對我國政府有關部門處理國際經濟法律問題，有重大參考價值。這從商務部條法司和我國常駐WTO使團團長孫振宇大使的有關函件裡，可以清楚地看到。

二〇〇七年六月七日

（四）對外經濟貿易大學教授沈達明老先生致陳安教授函

陳安同志：

謝謝你寄來的新著《美國對海外投資的法律保護及典型案例分析》。內容非常豐富，在近期內將細細拜讀。我國近年來出版的涉外法律書籍都是些簡論、淺說、基礎知識等科普性的書。科普很重要，但沒有專著，科普就缺乏基礎。你的大作在走向專著的道路上定能起帶頭作用。

世界銀行在成立「解決投資爭端國際中心」之後，又有成立「多邊投資擔保機構」的計畫。我手頭有草案的英文本。不知你有沒有這些材料。如需要，可告知，以便寄上。

再次謝謝來信，致

敬禮

沈達明

一九八五年九月十六日

（五）中山大學端木正教授致陳安教授函

陳安同志：

您好！

別來三個月，不知蘇州會議參加了沒有？

收到大著《美國對海外投資的法律保護及典型案例分析》一冊，喜出望外。近年國人自著如此專書，尚屬罕見，實為閣下對我國學術界一大貢獻，可喜可賀！

長春和北京之會又可面敘，謹先函謝，順頌

旅安

端木正上

一九八五年十一月三十日

※　※　※

B　中國政府官員來函

（一）中華人民共和國外交部條法司司長徐宏致陳安教授函

尊敬的陳安教授：

您好！

來信收悉。感謝惠贈專著！陳老耄耋之年仍筆耕不輟，著此大作，面向國際社會弘揚中華學術、發出中國聲音，您深厚的學術功底、嚴謹的治學態度、真摯的愛國熱情令人欽佩。專著內容豐富，不僅具有很高的學術和理論價值，對實務部門參加國際談判、解決實際問題也具有重要參考意義。

祝身體安康！

徐 宏

二〇一四年九月十二日

（二）中華人民共和國外交部美洲大洋洲司司長謝鋒致陳安教授函

尊敬的陳安教授：

你惠贈的《評「黃禍」論的本源、本質及其最新霸權「變種」:「中國威脅」論》一文我已拜讀。感謝你心繫國家發展，關心支援國家外交工作。

從「黃禍」論這一獨特歷史視角探究「中國威脅」論的根源，令人耳目一新。與幾百年前相比，今天的「中國威脅」論涉及因素更複雜，包括地緣政治、意識形態、歷史偏見等。這是實現中華民族偉大復興和中國和平發展必須破解的外部障礙。我堅信，正如「黃禍」論最終被歷史所唾棄，當代「中國威脅」論終將隨著中國的持續繁榮發展被丟入歷史的垃圾堆。

祝工作愉快，闔家幸福！

謝 鋒

二〇一二年八月六日

（三）中華人民共和國外交部條法司司長黃惠康致陳安教授函

尊敬的陳安教授：

七月五日您致楊潔篪部長和我本人的來函及附文敬悉。

我認真拜讀了《評「黃禍」論的本源、本質及其最新霸權「變種」：「中國威脅」論》一文，深感文中所列史料豐富、分析精闢、論述深刻，讀後啟發良多。我已請我司主管處認真研究此文，以冀從中擷取有益建議，為外交工作提供指導參考；並加強外交一線工作者特別是年青後輩對「中國威脅」論的歷史及現實聯繫的認識，踐行您在文中所提「以史為師、以史為鑒」的建議。

同時，您值耄耋高齡依然關心國家外交事業發展並為此筆耕不輟，我深感敬佩。我謹代表廣大外交工作者對您的關心和指導表示由衷感謝，也希望您能繼續為外交事業發展建言獻策、啟微發瀚。

順祝

安好！

黃惠康

二〇一二年七月三十日

（四）中華人民共和國常駐世界貿易組織代表團團長易小准大使致陳安教授批復函

紀文華學友並轉呈中國駐WTO使團團長易小准大使：

郵上拙作中、英文本各一份，討論熱點問題，直抒管見。謹請惠予批評指正。

英文本是在中文本基礎上增補改寫而成。

收到後，請簡複。謝謝！

感謝你多年來惠予的關注和支持。

順祝

健好

陳　安

二〇一一年三月三十日

陳會長：

我非常同意您的觀點，WTO作為一個重要的國際貿易法律體系，也需要與時俱進。這就是我和我的同事們在多哈談判中肩負的責任。

謝謝您對WTO問題的關注！

易小准

二〇一一年四月二十七日

（五）中華人民共和國商務部辦公廳主任姚堅致陳安教授函

尊敬的陳老，您好！

您寄來的論國際經濟法學叢書收悉，非常感謝！

作為中國國際經濟法學科的重要奠基人、領頭人，您始終立足於中國國情和廣大發展中國家的共同立場，致力於探索和開拓具有中國特色的國際經濟法學科。您潛心所著的《陳安論國際經濟法學》奠定了學科基礎，提出的學術理念和學術追求深受國內外學界的推崇。

拜觀「人過半百再出發」專輯，深為您抱持的「餘熱未盡，不息奮蹄」之精神所感動，您至今仍在教學和科研戰線上不懈耕耘，培養法學人才，推動學術研究。更為難能可貴的是，在教學科研任務繁重、領銜眾多學術團體的同時，仍緊密跟蹤國際學術界和實務界的最新動態，及時向國內實務部門反映並提出了大量深具價值的對應之策。前次您專程到商務部洽商工作，讓我們受益匪淺。作為商務戰線上的一員，我謹向您致以崇高的敬意。

敬祝

安康！

姚堅　謹覆

二〇〇九年五月十九日

（六）中華人民共和國商務部條法司楊秉勳致陳安教授文〔11〕

由於工作關係，前兩日到了一處仙鄉好所在——廈門大學，她周遭山清水秀，背靠南普陀，旁邊就是仙風道骨的南普陀寺，飛簷走角，藍色的寺廟屋頂和青山相得益彰；她面迎無際的大海，天光碧海，海風颯爽，有漁舟片片，當真治學樂土，人間仙境……

得益於一位有著綿綿學術追求的領導，組織了一場有眾多知名學者參加的研討會，諸如復旦的陳治東、董世忠兩位先生，人大的余勁松先生，教過我的車丕照先生等等，諸位先生縱談國際投資法、世界大勢、國家利益、國際法律原則，收益頗豐，先生們的治學態度和卓越風采令人起敬，然而給我印象最為深刻的是廈門大學的老先生陳安教授。

老先生，福建人，今年虛歲八十，著作等身，精神矍鑠。先生於二十世紀五〇年代畢業於廈門大學，修政治學於復旦大學，八〇年代在哈佛大學從事國際經濟法研究，兼部分講學，九〇年代以「亞洲傑出學者」名義應邀在美國俄勒岡州路易士與克拉克西北法學院擔任客座教授，曾任中國政府根據《華盛頓公約》遴選向「解決投資爭端國際中心」（ICSID）指派的首席國際仲裁員、中國國際法學會顧問等。

千金難買老來瘦，老先生很瘦，雖然襯衫塞在腰帶裡，舉手投足還是帶出了道道褶皺，似乎有學識之氣在隱隱流動。馬可·奧勒留說：「我們必須抓緊時間，這不僅是因為我們在一天天地接近死亡，而且因為對事物的理解力和消化力將先行消失。」我看到這句話時有點cry的衝動，然而老先生給了這句話相反的注解，他講話似乎不多，但是每句話都透露出覽勝高一層的睿智。老先生眼睛不大，但是講話時目光銳利，將真誠、平實的感覺凝聚到你的心裡。以前曾有人說某位學術巨擘是時代的號角、歲月的良心，老先生也表現出這樣的特徵，他擅用成語、平實的話語點綴出高潔之士的俊彩，他並不忌諱自己被人稱作「保守派」，他認為國際投資協定不宜走得太快，畢竟我國相當長一段時間內沒有改變投資東道國的身份，「走出去」戰略才剛剛開始；也用了「貽害無窮」「居安思危」「亡羊補牢」「陳述管見」……他又是一個尊重科學的人，他說：「知識份子說話雖然不一定中聽，但是知識分子說話都是有根據的，是科學的，也許你會認為它片面，但是一個個的片面加起來就是全面，……任何事情都是兼聽則明，偏聽則暗……」

也許我是一個懷舊的人，我喜歡吳經熊，喜歡梁任公，所以我也喜歡陳安先生的話語風格，其實比較一下就知道他們都是學貫東西的人，然而保留了中華民族的傳統話語風格，骨子中一以貫之的是對於國家的熱愛，對普通大眾的關懷，對真理的孜孜不倦。

這裡有一段陳安先生的趣事：

一九八一年春，哈佛大學法學院柯恩教授來廈大訪問。在一場座談會上，柯恩教授批評道：「外國人來中國投資有顧慮，因為中國政府不尊重外國人的財產，會隨便沒收。」儘管對方來自世界最著名的大學，又是全球知名的學術權威，還是哈佛大學法學院副院長，而陳安老師當時只是個副教授，但他根本沒想到「身份」的差別，立刻展開了辯論：「我認為你說錯話了。」陳安當時只會講點「蹩腳」英語，還好柯恩教授會一點中文。陳安就以夾雜著中文的英語，向柯恩教授詳解中國法律：「在中國，任何外商，只要遵紀守法，不觸犯刑法和海關法規，他的財產絕不會被沒收。」柯恩教授臉紅了，他辯道：「但是，中國政府還是有可能會將外國人的財產拿走呀！」陳安知道他講的是「徵收制度」。他反問道：「難道美國沒有徵收制度嗎？」他引用美國的許多例子，反問柯恩教授：「美國人在美國本國都不能保證財產在任何情況下絕對不被徵收，何以到中國來就要求享受絕對不被徵收的特權？」美國人素來堅持「在真理面前沒有權威」。柯恩教授對陳安老師產生了興趣。座談會一結束，他立刻走到陳安面前：「我打算邀請你到哈佛講學，講中國的法律，講你的思想。」

陳安教授初到哈佛，一度講的是中華人民共和國成立前的「山溝溝英語」，甚至連「中國式英語」都談不上，外國人經常聽不懂。在哈佛大學講壇上，一個旁聽的美國教授當眾嘲笑他。陳教授用英語反問他：「我能講英語，講一點美國式英語，儘管講不好，但是你能講中文，會講中國的北京話嗎？」那位教授臉紅了，他承認：「我不會。」後來，那位美國教授對陳安教授尊敬三分，路上見到老遠就打招呼：「嗨！陳教授，你好！」經過發奮圖強，到美國講學的第二年，陳安教授再站上哈佛的講臺時，英語已經非常流利。一九八二年秋，他做了一場演講：是進一步開放？還是重新關門？——評有關中國吸收外資政策法令的幾種議論》。他的雄辯說理、精闢闡析，緊緊地抓住了聽眾的心。演講結束後，全場響起了雷鳴般的聲音，一位臺灣地區留美研究生擠到陳教授身旁，說道：「佩服！佩服！外國人給你鼓掌，掌聲這麼響，作為中國人，我們也有份，覺得很體面。」

（七）中華人民共和國商務部條法司致陳安教授函（2005 年 9 月 27 日）

中華人民共和國商務部

尊敬的陳安教授：

籍第九屆中國國際投資貿易洽談會期間，我司與您領導下的廈門大學國際經濟法研究所再一次就國際投資協定問題進行了深入地研討和成功地交流，收到了很好的效果。多年來我司與廈大國際經濟法研究所緊密合作取得豐碩成果，離不開您的鼎力支持，我司特此，並代表商務部和雙邊投資保護協定的談判團隊，向您致以誠摯的感謝。

您是新中國國際經濟法學的奠基人之一，並在國內最早進行有關國際投資協定和國際投資爭議解決的開創性研究，著作等身，立言煌煌，為我國國際法學作出了重大貢獻。您在學術研究中始終將維護國家利益放在首位，把正義和法治作為不懈訴求，代表中國和廣大發展中國家法學界在國際上發出了建立國際經濟新秩序的強有力呼聲。近年來，您在教學科研任務繁重、領銜眾多學術團體的同時，仍緊密跟蹤國際學術界和實務界的最新動態，及時向國內實務部門反映並提出了有價值的應對之策。

另一方面，您一直嘔心瀝血，辛勤耕耘，以培育英才為己任，以教誨學生為樂事。春風化雨，暑去寒來，一批又一批的國際法人才在鷺城湧現、成長，成為中國國際法學界的新一代中堅。在您的啟發和指引下，廈門大學一批年輕學者投身國際投資法的研究，組成了充滿活力而富有鑽研精神的學術團隊，使國際投資法的研究欣欣向榮。市場經濟的大潮對法律人充滿誘惑，而您和您的團隊始終堅守著對學術的執著追求，在國際投資法這一片園地裡辛勤勞動、精耕細作。廈大國際經濟法研究所在這一領域內已擁有雄厚的研究力量和突出的研究成果。

我司與您和廈大國際經濟法研究所開展合作可以上溯至上世紀八十年代。改革開放之初，您和廈大國際經濟法研究所的學術梯隊成員就曾多次接受原外經貿部條法司的專題委託或專題諮詢，提供有關「解決投資爭端國際中心」（ICSID）體制和雙邊投資保護協定的專題委託或專題諮詢。為我國對外商簽雙邊投資保護協定和加入《華盛頓公約》、接受ICSID機制提供了重要的理論支援和決策依據。您與我司歷任司領導多次深入研討，廈大學術梯隊與我司談判團隊間也始終保持交流切磋，雙方間的合作堪稱學術研究機構與政府決策部門互相配合互相支持的典範。在我們的最新合作中，我們又一次感受到了您和這一學術梯隊的寬廣視野和深厚功底，以及您所立意營造的寬鬆和諧、鼓勵爭鳴的學術氛圍。目前，我國已與一一二個國家簽署了雙邊投資保護協定，對吸引外商來華投資、貫徹我「走出去」戰略發揮了越來越重要的作用，在這背後您和廈大學術梯隊的學術鋪墊和政策建言發揮了重要的作用。

最後，再次衷心感謝您在此次活動中的盛情款待，以及您對我國商務法律工作的長期支援和重大貢獻，並期盼在今後與您和廈門大學國際經濟法研究所繼續緊密合作。祝您身體健康，工作順利！

商务部条法司

2005 年 9 月 27 日

（八）中華人民共和國常駐世界貿易組織代表團團長孫振宇大使致陳安教授函

陳安同志：

您好！感謝您的來信及大量重要資料。

我反覆拜讀了您的學術報告《中國入世後海峽兩岸經貿問題「政治化」之防治》，受益匪淺，足見您對WTO規則研究功力之深，所提建議極具參考價值。

信中所提另一篇英文大作[12]我沒有收到，十分想了解您對美國以單邊主義對抗WTO多邊主義的見解與分析，如能寄來，將十分感激。

作為WTO中的新成員，我們對WTO規則的學習以及對WTO的認識還是十分膚淺的，急需國內有關的學術科研機構的協助與支持，如果貴學會能就中國作為一個新成員如何有效地應對由於廣泛的加入承諾與一些不利條款給我國帶來的挑戰，以及中國作為一個發展中的大國如何在新一輪談判中發揮應有的作用開展一些研究工作，將是對我團工作的重大支持。

我也會積極考慮選一些有一定分量的調研報告在貴會的學刊上發表，達到互相交流的目的。

順致謝意。

孫振宇

二〇〇四年四月十六日

（九）中國駐美國西海岸舊金山總領館負責人朱又德致陳安教授函

（中華人民共和國總領事館）

Consulate General of

the People's Republic of China

1450 Laguna Street

San Francisco, California 94115

(415) 563-1718

陳安老師：

你好！

來信並演講摘要已悉。很欣賞你的智慧、才幹和勇氣。此舉很有意義。由此，使我聯想到，如果我們的學者和學生中能有一批像你這樣的民間大使，對反駁美政壇對我國的非難，以及消除一些美國友人的疑慮和誤解，無疑將起到非同一般的影響和作用。謝謝你利用講學、研究之餘，抽時間、尋機會為宣傳中國所做的工作。

我已將你的演講摘要轉有關領導閱，並擬抄報國內有關部門及你的國內工作單位——廈門大學。

順致

安好。

朱又德

一九九一年五月二十三日

（十）中華人民共和國對外經貿部條法司致陳安教授函

陳教授：

您好！

來函收悉，十分感謝您對我們工作的關心與支持，您的大作，對我們的立法工作幫助很大，急盼早日得之，如果可能的話，我局有關同志共需約十本，冒昧相求，望諒解。

關於「ICSID」目前國務院已原則同意加入，正在做最後階段的準備工作，待我國一旦加入後，「實施條例」不久可望出籠，當然還要廣泛徵求意見，爭取一個比較好的立法，既利用了公約的好處，又不損我國權益，這點我與您也有同感。在這方面，還盼您及貴校大力支持。

此致

敬禮

經貿部條約法律司

一九八九年十二月十五日

（十一）中華人民共和國對外經貿部條法司致陳安教授函

廈大法學院並陳安院長：

欣聞貴院擬出版《「解決投資爭端國際中心」述評》，在此表示祝賀。

目前，我國政府正在研究加入「國際中心」的可能性，並進入了最後階段。該書的出版無疑會推動我國學術界對於《華盛頓公約》及「解決投資爭端國際中心」的理論研究，同時亦對我們研究加入該公約的工作具有積極的參考價值和借鑑作用。

我們感謝貴院對我司工作的支援並期待大作早日出版。

此致

敬禮

經貿部條約法律司

一九八九年八月二十九日

（十二）中華人民共和國對外經貿部條法局致陳安教授函

陳教授：

您好！

很高興收到您寄來的大作「國際經濟法系列專著」。對您的辛勤耕耘而結出的纍纍碩果，我們表示欽佩和祝賀。也對您為國際經濟法研究做出的貢獻表示感謝。

在實踐中，我們碰到過許多理論上的課題，而理論工作者也需了解實際工作的需求，並為實踐服務，在理論與實踐相結合的道路上，您和您領導的廈大法學院做了很出色的工作。「國際經濟法系列專著」對我們無疑是一套可以信賴的有價值的業務參考書和工具書。

過去，在我局的有關事務中，您給予了很大幫助，今後還希望廈大的法律工作者對我們的工作繼續給予支持。

國際經濟法與我局業務密切相連。我局辦公室願與貴院資料室建立聯繫，互換資料，以便更好地為國際經濟事業服務。

最後，再次向您表示謝意，並預祝您取得更大的成績。

此致

敬禮

經貿部條約法律局

一九八八年一月三十日

（十三）中華人民共和國對外經貿部條法局致陳安教授函

陳安教授：

您好！

關於我國是否加入《華盛頓公約》（ICSID）之事，徵求意見已初步結束，在這項工作中，得到了您及貴校法律系的大力支持，再次表示謝意。

加入公約是一項理論性和實踐性都很強的工作，既要有實際工作部門同志的研究，也要有理論方面的同志配合，這一點已從我們過去的工作中得到了充分的印證。

您對我國是否加入公約的意見，經過研究和討論，使我們受益很大，我們認為從下述幾方面對我們有啟示作用：

一、從國際法的角度，全面分析公約條文及產生的背景、機構和作用，由此分析我國加入的利弊；

二、重點提到了公約本身應引起重視的地方，如「法律適用」「同意的形式」「費用」等；

三、客觀地分析一旦加入公約後，我國可能提交中心仲裁的範圍；

四、提出研究公約案例的研究方法。

您的意見對我們做好這項工作幫助很大，還望今後繼續得到您及貴系的支持。

此致

敬禮

經貿部條約法律局

一九八七年三月一日

※ ※ ※

C 外國學界來函

（一）《世界投資與貿易學報》《日內瓦天下大事論壇》季刊主編致陳安教授函（摘譯，原文附後）

陳教授：

感謝您於二〇〇六年一月二十七日發來的電子郵件。我們發現您的《南南聯合自強五十年的國際經濟立法反思》論文，對於當前WTO正在進行的談判磋商，作了很有創見和雄辯有力的評析，充分反映了您的見解，因此，我很樂於採用，並即將發表於本刊二〇〇六年四月這一期。

…………

Jacgues Werner[3] 編輯

二〇〇六年一月三十一日

From: Werner & Associes

To: chenan

Sent: Tuesday, January 31, 2006 11:02 PM

Subject: contributing an article

Dear Prof. Chen,

Thank you for your email of last January 27. It was good to hear from you again. We found your article "A Reflection on the South-South Coalition in the Last Half Century from the Perspective of International Economic Law-making" a thoughtful and vigorous assessment of the current WTO negotiation, reflecting your views. I am pleased consequently to accept it for publication in our coming April 2006 issue.

Please confirm that, in accordance with our policy, we will have exclusive publishing rights.

Your article will need a lot of linguistic editing and you will hear in due time from my editorial assistant, Mr. Jim Boyce.

We provide authors with 50 off-prints of their article. You may order additional off-prints on your own account, in which case, please advise my editorial assistant within the coming three weeks. Please note that off-prints are usually dispatched four weeks after the issue has come out. Mr. Boyce will get in touch with you concerning your article.

Best regards,

Jacques Werner

Editor

陳安先生：

您的論文《南南聯合自強五十年的國際經濟立法反思》一文即將發表於《世界投資與貿易學報》四月這一期。我發現，您的這篇文章令人很感興趣，因此想要把它另行發表於我所編輯的另一種學刊，即《日內瓦天下大事論壇》季刊。這另一種學刊面向更加廣泛的讀者物件，包括聯合國各種機構中的公務人員、外交人員、國際公司中的高層執事等等。

…………

我們認為，這是一個良好的機會，讓您的見解傳播給更加廣泛的公眾，因而期待您能同意我的上述建議。刊載您這篇文章的《日內瓦天下大事論壇》季刊預定於二〇〇六年四月二十六日出版。

…………

Jacgues Werner編輯

二〇〇六年二月二十日

From: wernerp@iprolink.ch

To: chenan@xmu.edu.cn

Cc: james.e.boyce@wanadoo.fr; wernerp@iprolink.ch

Sent: Monday, February 20, 2006 10:38 PM

Subject: Your Recent Article on the South-South Coalition

Dear Mr. Chen,

I found your article "A Reflection on the South-South Coalition in the Last Half Century from the Perspective of International Economic Law-making", which we are going to publish in the coming April issue of the *Journal of World Investment and Trade*, so interesting that I would like to re-publish it in another Journal which I edit, called *The Geneva Post Quarterly—The Journal of World Affairs*. This Journal is aimed to a wider readership of civil servants in the United Nations Organization, diplomats, executives in international corporations, and the like.

The style of this Journal is along the line of the well known US-based publication Foreign Affairs, and has no footnotes. We have consequently made a new version of your article, incorporating footnotes in the text itself, as well as taking into consideration the final changes you made to your original article. This new version is enclosed.

We think it would be a good opportunity to have your views disseminated to a wider public and hope that you will consequently agree with my proposal.The date of publication of the issue of *The Geneva Post Quarterly* where your article is planed is April 26, 2006.

Please let me have your consent to the above.

Best regards,

Jacques Werner

Editor

（二）天普大學《國際法與比較法學報》學術論文編輯 L. K. Kolb 致陳安教授函（摘譯，原文附後）

陳安教授：

…………

我作為學術論文責任編輯，曾與本學報主編共同審閱全部來稿，並從中選擇我們認為當前最受關注、最引人入勝和最有創見的文章，儘快發表。

我們確實十分高興能在本學報二〇〇三年秋季這一卷發表你的這篇學術論文，題為《晚近十年來美國單邊主義與WTO多邊主義交鋒的三大回合》。這篇論文論證有理有據，主題緊扣時局，資料豐富翔實。同時，它針對當前特別重大和特別令人關注的爭端問題展開論述。簡言之，選用本文是由於我們認為它的論點論據雄辯犀利，發人深思，並且緊扣當前熱點話題，相信它會使國際法理論界和實務界都大感興趣。

…………

Laura K. Kolb

美國天普大學《國際法與比較法學報》學術論文編輯

二〇〇四年六月三日

From: Lkathkolb@aol.com

To: chenan@xmu.edu.cn

Sent: Thursday, June 03, 2004 8:43 AM

Subject: Re: your article

Hello,

…

As Articles Editor, I reviewed all submissions to the Journal and together with the Editor-in-Chief, facilitated the publication of those papers we found to be the most topical, interesting and original.

We were truly pleased to publish your article entitled "The Three Big Rounds of U.S. Unilateralism Versus WTO Multilateralism During the Latest Decade" in our Fall, 2003 issue. The thesis was well-developed and the topic both timely and informative. In addition, the article addressed issues that are of particular import and interest at the present time. In short, we chose the article because we found the argument provocative and topical and believed that it would be of interest to those involved in the study and practice of international law.

…

Best regards,

Laura K. Kolb

Articles Editor, *TICLJ*

（三） 日內瓦「南方中心」（South Center）秘書長B. Gosovic致陳安教授函（摘譯，原文附後）

陳安教授：

我從「南方中心」向您問候致意！

我極其欣賞您的這篇論文，閱讀時確實覺得是一種享受。我已建議我的同事們把這篇論文列為我們「南方中心」的出版物之一，納入我們的「貿易發展與公平」專題議程（Trade-Related Agenda, Development and Equity, T. R. A. D. E）作為系列工作文件之一印刷發行，以便使它能更廣泛傳播，為公眾所周知，特別是讓它在我們發展中國家的廣大讀者和各國政府中，能夠廣為傳播，普遍周知。

不知您是否同意這樣做，是否可以結合最近〔WTO〕針對美國「201條款」案件的裁斷情況，對本文加以修訂更新？特此徵求您的意見。

等候您的回音。

謹致問候！

Branislav Gosovic

「南方中心」秘書長

二〇〇四年六月二日

附言：我們還打算把您的這篇論文發表在「南方中心」的電子網站上。

From: gosovic@southcentre.org

To: chenan@xmu.edu.cn

Sent: Wednesday, June 02, 2004 12:26 AM

Subject: from south centre

Dear Professor An Chen,

Greetings from the Centre.

I was extremely pleased with your article and really enjoyed reading it. I have suggested to my colleagues that we print it as a South Centre publication in our T.R.A.D.E. working paper series and thus make it more widely known and accessible, in particular to our readers in the South, including especially the governments.

So, my question to you is whether you would agree with this and whether it would be possible for you to update the paper to take into account the recent ruling regarding the US.

...

Looking forward to your reply.

With best regards,

Branislav Gosovic

Head of the Secretariat

South Centre

PS: We would also like to place your article on our website.

陳安教授：

我剛讀到您的來信，謝謝！本星期以來我一直忙於參加「南方中心」的董事會會議和理事會會議。您的論文已於上星期四出版，並已在「中心」的理事會上分發；同時也已送交各國常駐世界貿易組織的代表團。我們將給您寄去一批（單行本）。

謹致問候！

Branislav Gosovic

二〇〇四年七月二十四日

From: gosovic@southcentre.org

To: chenan@xmu.edu.cn

Sent: Saturday, July 24, 2004 7:31 PM

Subject: Re: the new version

Dear Professor An Chen,

Thank you for your message, which I just read. I was busy all week with the meetings of the Board and the Council. It was ready last Tuesday and it was distributed at the Council and sent to Permanent Missions. I will send you a supply.

Best regards,

B.Gosovic

（四）「多邊投資擔保機構」（MIGA）首席法律顧問 L. Weisenfeld 致陳安教授函（摘譯，原文附後）

陳安教授：

上星期我在飛往南美多明尼加共和國的長途航程中，閱讀了你評論美國單邊主義的學術論文。這篇文章確實是具有頭等水準的佳作。它論證充分，雄辯有力，析理透澈，緊扣當前話題，引人關注。你發表了這樣一篇經過精心研究寫成的論文，請接受我的祝賀。

你的論文使我耳目一新，促使我更好地反思許多有關國際貿易的問題，更新觀念，過去我雖然知道這些問題，但從未認真深入探究。平日我閱讀的大多是英國和美國的資訊資料，一旦被迫從另一種迥然不同的角度觀察同類問題，就會感到面臨挑戰。……有時，我發現自己不得不重新思考長期以來我認為「理所當然」而未加探究的某些傳統觀念。

總的說來，我不得不同意你的雄辯論證。在我的職業生涯中，這麼遲才得出這樣的結論，未免使我感到慚愧，特別是因為我在東南亞各國工作過程中，長期以來聽到人們對美國的「301條款」抱怨連連，可是一直到我閱讀你的這篇論文以前，我始終沒有認真思考過全面的情況。因此，我認為，對於集中半年或一年時間研修國際貿易法的學生說來，認真閱讀你的這篇論文，諒必會受益不淺。

在當今布希當政時期，美國在各種國際場合的言行促使我反覆思考我自己這個國家在國際舞臺上的所作所為。理所當然，現在布希政府在有關環境條約、貿易制裁、國際刑事立法等方面所採取的立場，我一直是不能苟同的。而你在論文中所援引的各種事例，對於非專業人士而言雖較為生疏和不很熟悉，但卻是美國對待國際經濟法的「布希程式」的重要組成部分。

…………

總之，你的這篇論文是深思熟慮，催人猛醒的。我認為，它對於（國際法）這個學術領域做出了有益的貢獻。廈門大學法學院可以為寫出了如此高品質的論文感到自豪，你確實已經為這個學術機構增添了光彩。

…………

Lorin Weisenfeld

MIGA首席法律顧問

二〇〇四年五月十二日

From: Lweisenfeld@worldbank.org

To: chenan@xmu.edu.cn

Sent: Wednesday, May 12, 2004 4:26 AM

Subject: Warmest Congratulations

Dear Prof. Chen,

I went last week to the Dominican Republic, and your article on U.S. unilateralism kept me company on the long flight down. It was an absolutely first rate piece. The article was well-argued, well-written, timely and even interesting. Please accept my congratulations for having turned out such a well-researched piece.

Your article refreshed my memory, helped me to put into better focus issues that I have read about but not been forced to dwell on, and sharpened my thinking about these trade questions. Because so much of my reading is of Anglo-Saxon sources, it is challenging to be forced to look at certain familiar issues from quite a different perspective... Every once in a while, I found myself forced to rethink notions that I had long taken for granted without further examination.

By and large, I have to agree with your argument. I suppose that I should be embarrassed to be reaching this conclusion so late in my career, particularly since I have been hearing complaints in Southeast Asia over Sec. 301 for a long time, but I never really stopped to think long about the whole picture until I read your article. I can imagine, therefore, the benefits of reading your article that will acree to a student of international trade law, who is spending a concentrated semester or year trying to get a handle on the subject. Your article will be very helpful.

The behavior of the United States in international fora under this Bush administration has made me think about my own country's behavior on the international scene. Certainly, this Bush administration has taken positions — the environmental treaty, the trade sanctions, the international criminal code, etc. — with which I disagree. The instances that you cite, more arcane and less familiar to laymen, are part and parcel of the Bush approach to international economic law.

...

Of course, if one looks back over the history of the United States, one sees that our views of ourselves in the larger world have ebbed and flowed over time. In the middle of the last century, we were said to be "jingoistic", with our notions of Westward expansion, "manifest destiny", "54' 40" or fight", "Remember the Maine!", etc. Lord knows that Mexico has still not gotten over our attitudes of the last century. Then, in this century, we shifted to a proudly isolationist approach to international relations, safe behind "Fortress America". No matter how hard he tried, President Wilson could not bring the U.S. into the League of Nations. As a kid, I remember the bombastic Sen. Knowland of California with his isolationist dogmas. And now the pendulum has swung once again. Messrs. Bush, Cheney, et al. have found a doctrine of "preemptive war" somewhere and are quite happy operating from the position of what the French scornfully call a "hyperpower". History will judge the results.

...

Your paper, in sum, was thoughtful and provocative. I think that it has made a useful contribution to the field. Xiamen Law School can be proud that writing of this quality is produced within its halls. You have made the institution look good, indeed.

It turns out that, for a change, I have an enormous amount of news regarding MIGA. We had a significant change in management on May 3, resulting in the replacement of the executive vice president and two of the four senior managers. A new team has taken the reins, and the institution is in the process of a thorough reorganization. I believe, personally, that we had a number of managerial problems in recent years, and I sincerely hope that the changes being implemented will reinvigorate the organization. I support and welcome them. Yet, all change of this sort brings tensions and transitional issues, as well as temporary uncertainty. Our transition has been a bit rocky, but I assume that matters will settle down in due course. I will bring you up to date on these changes in MIGA when I see you in June.

One of the difficulties that we need to traverse at the moment is an increase in the work-load in the face of a diminished budget. This has affected all of us. I have had to postpone my trip to China from May to June because of more pressing difficulties affecting our clients, and now I am hoping, as we near the end of our fiscal year, that we have enough money left in the till to be able to afford the trip that I propose to take in June. In theory, I will arrive in Beijing on June 16. I hope to arrive in Xiamen on June 18. Regrettably, I will only be able to stay for a day. I will be able to confirm these arrangements when I return to the office in early June from Eastern Europe.

Prof. Chen Huiping has been a good friend and colleague and I will send her a copy of this e-mail, together with a separate note responding to her last two e-mails. I am without a secretary now, since Lucy has left for greener pastures and we are not in a position to replace her. That makes production more difficult than formerly.

I look forward to seeing you all in June.

Cordially,

Lorin Weisenfeld

Principal Counsel, MIGA

（五）「解決投資爭端國際中心」ICSID）法律顧問 A. Parra 致陳安教授函（中文摘譯見前「來函概述」之（四），原文附後）

March 22, 1990

Professor An Chen

Dean and Professor of Law

School of Politics and Law

Box 978

Xiamen University

Xiamen

Fujian, China

Dear Professor An Chen,

Further to Mr. Shihata's January 30 letter to you, I would like to renew our gratitude to you for so kindly sending us your article on whether an absolute immunity from nationalization for foreign investment should be enacted in China's law concerning the Special Economic Zones and Coastal Port Cities.

As Mr. Shihata is currently away on business, I would like to take this opportunity to thank you very much on his behalf for sending him the copy of your new book on ICSID. We will be announcing the book's publication in the upcoming new issue of News from ICSID, and plan also to list it in the next edition of the ICSID Bibliography.

The new issue of News from ICSID will also be reporting China's signature of the ICSID Convention on February 9, 1990. In case you would like to have a copy, I am pleased to enclose the news release that we issued on this important occasion.

With best regards,

Sincerely yours,
Antonio R. Parra
Managing Editor
ICSID Review

※ ※ ※

August 22, 1990
Professor An Chen
Visiting Professor
Northwestern School of Law
Lewis & Clark College
10015 S. W. Terwilliger Boulevard
Portland, Oregon 97219

Dear Professor An Chen,

On behalf of Mr. Shihata, I would like to thank you very much for your letter of July 12. I also am grateful for your separate letter to me. We are looking forward to reading your book that you kindly sent us on the legal aspects of foreign investment in China. I hope that we can have it reviewed for the ICSID Review.

…

The article that you also kindly sent to us on foreign investment laws of China is circulating amongst my colleagues in the Editorial Committee of the ICSID Review, and I will be writing to you again in due course on the possibility of our including it in a future issue.

Pursuant to your request, I am meanwhile pleased to enclose a copy of the issue of News from ICSID announcing the publication of your new book on the Centre. Judging from the translation of the table of contents of this book, it must be a most useful work.

I am looking forward to keeping in touch with you.

With best regards,

Sincerely yours,

Antonio R. Parra

Legal Adviser

（六）美國唐肯（Tonkon *et al.*）律師事務所首席律師 O. D. Blank 致陳安教授函（摘譯，原文附後）

陳安教授：

非常感謝您寄來最近發表在《律師》雜誌上的論文。您針對中國與美國經濟互利關係所作的分析，切合實際，令人耳目一新。您對於中國繼續實行開放政策所作的論證，很有必要加以廣泛、普及的宣傳，以促使美國的許多公司恢復信心——它們在「1989年政治風波」以前本來已經很好地確立了這種信心。

....

O. D. Blank

一九九一年七月五日

July 5, 1991

Professor An Chen

Northwestern School of Law

Lewis & Clark College

1015 S.W. Terwilliger Blvd.

Portland, Oregon 97219

Dear Professor Chen,

I greatly appreciate receiving the copy of your recent article in The Advocate. Your analysis of the mutual interests of China and the United States is refreshingly practical. The evidence regarding China's continued "open-door" policy needs to be widely disseminated in order for U.S. companies to regain the confidence that was building so well prior to the Tiananmen Event.

China and the United Stated both face complex political dilemmas. As China reaps the benefits of the open-door policy and of becoming a more significant "player" in the world, it must deal with the "burden" of having its external as well as internal policies subject to scrutiny by others. The world is getting smaller. As it does so, sovereignty is constantly being smaller. As it does so, sovereignty is constantly being redefined by the increased amount of political, cultural, economic and social interchange.

It is my hope and belief that by maintaining good relations between the United States and China, the peoples of both nations will benefit from the positive aspects of each nation and will learn that constructive criticism from friends is not intrusion. Rather, it is a way friends help each other.

I hope you are enjoying your visiting professorship at Lewis & Clark Law School. I look forward to seeing you in the near future.

Very truly yours,

Owen D. Blank

（七）美國路易士與克拉克西北法學院律師進修班主任 L. B. Mapes 致陳安教授函（中文摘譯見前「來函概述」之（六），原文附後）

November 29, 1988

Professor An Chen

P.O. Box 978

Xiamen University

Xiamen, Fujian

People's Republic of China

Dear Professor An Chen,

On behalf of the Law School, I thank you for your participation in our Third Annual International Business Law Seminar: Contract Negotiations with China in the 1990's, on October 28, 1988. The program was a tremendous success, as you know. We have received many compliments on the seminar and on your speech, "One Decade of Chinese Foreign Investment Laws." We are grateful to you for your contribution to a fine program that has brought great honor and prestige to the Law School.

Thank you also for participating in many activities with our faculty, students, and friends of the Law School. We are very grateful that you were able to spend some time here in Portland; we only wish you could have stayed longer. It was our pleasure to have you here with us.

I know that I speak for the entire Law School when I say that we are delighted that we have developed a close relationship with you and with the Xiamen University School of Law and Politics. We hope that our exchange will grow in the future.

I appreciated the opportunity to become acquainted with you. Thank you again for your beautiful gifts, which I will treasure and which will remind me of your visit here.

Copies of the videotapes of the seminar will arrive in a separate package. I hope that you will find them useful—perhaps your colleagues at Xiamen University School of Law would like to see them.

Again, thank you for traveling so far to participate in the Third

Annual International Business Law Seminar. Your presence at the seminar and at the Law School afterward enriched the lives of many people.

Sincerely,

Laurie B. Mapes, Director

Continuing Legal Education

（八）美國哈佛大學法學院助理院長、東亞法學研究所副所長 F. E. Snyder 致陳安教授函（中譯，原文附後）

陳安教授：

承贈送您在東亞法學研究所午餐會上學術演講文稿一份，非常感謝。正如我曾經對您說過[14]，這次演說非常打動人心，很能發人深思，令人興趣盎然。您的文稿中對於保護外國投資的兩種不同做法的有關論述，也相當深刻周詳。我認為，您針對美國（保護海外投資）的立場得到（某些國家）追隨而又遭到（許多國家）挑戰這個問題所作的論述，是特別有意義的。我殷切地期待您能把這篇文章公開發表，從而使國際法學界有更多人可以從您的深刻見解中獲得教益。

祝一切順利！

F. E. Snyder

哈佛大學法學院助理院長

哈佛大學東亞法學研究所副所長

一九八二年十月十九日

October 19, 1982

Professor An Chen

Pound 419

Dear An:

Many thanks for sending me a copy of your East Asian Legal Studies luncheon lecture. The talk was, as I mentioned to you, very stimulating, very provocative, very interesting. The discussion in your written text of the two different approaches to the protection of foreign investment is, similarly, very thoughtful. I found your discussion of the extent to which the American position has been followed and challenged to be especially helpful. It is my firm hope that you will be able to publish this piece so that more members of the international legal community will be able to benefit from your insights.

With all good wishes,

Sincerely,

Frederick E. Snyder

Assistant Dean and Associate Administrator

East Asian Legal Studies

（九）美國哈佛大學法學院斯托里講座教授[15]、東亞法學研究所所長 A. von Mehren 致陳安教授函（中譯，原文附後）

陳安教授：

您以訪問學者身份逗留哈佛大學法學院以來，即將屆滿一年。我的同事們以及我自己都非常高興有機會逐漸地親自了解和熟悉您，並且從您這裡學到了許多有關中華人民共和國法律規章和生活實際的知識。

我獲悉您曾在幾種場合對本院的學生和教員們做過演講。此外，我還閱讀了您寫的題為《是進一步開放？還是重新關門？》的文章，論述同中國吸收外國投資有關的各種認識問題和法律問題；也閱讀了您那篇將於十一月發表在紐約法學院《國際法與比較法學報》上評論李爽案件的文章。

我認為這兩篇文章對於有關主題所作的論述，都是很有教益和很有創見的。兩篇文章都寫得條理分明，行文妥善。每一篇都大大有助於促進美國的讀者加深理解您所論述的問題。

我們東亞法學研究所的同事，大家都知道您在這裡的工作中，一向是幹勁充沛和專心致志的。您的兩篇論文就是令人欽佩的例證，說明您的研究工作的品質和成就。我們高興的是：如今您在美國幫助我們理解中國的法律和社會，日後回到中國，您有能力在那裡以同樣的方式向您的同事以及學生們闡明有關美國法律和美國社會的各個方面。

您能同我們一起度過本學年剩下的時間，我們都感到高興。我們盼望：我們同您之間已經建立起來的個人接觸和學術聯繫，在您返回中國之後仍能繼續下去，並且欣欣向榮，開花結果。

謹致高度敬意。

Arthurvon Mehren

斯托裡法學講座教授

哈佛大學東亞法學研究所所長

一九八二年十月二十五日

October 25, 1982

Professor An Chen

Harvard Law School

Pound 523

Cambridge, Massachusetts 02138

Dear Professor An Chen,

It will soon be a year since you began your stay at Harvard Law School as a Visiting Scholar. My colleagues and myself have enjoyed greatly the opportunity to come to know you personally and have learned from you much about law and life in the people's Republic of China.

I have heard you speak on several occasions to student and faculty groups here. In addition, I have read your paper entitled "To Open Wider or to Close Again?" in which you discuss various of ideological and legal problems that arise in connection with China's approach to foreign investment, and your discussion of the Li Shuang case which will be published in November in the New York Law School's Journal of International and Comparative Law.

I found both of these papers instructive and thoughtful treatments of their respective subjects. Both papers are clearly and well written. Each advances significantly the understanding of an American audience with respect to the issues that you discuss.

All of us associated with the East Asian Legal Studies Program know the energy and devotion with which you have carried on your work here. Your two articles are admirable examples of the quality and success of your studies. We are delighted that when you return to China you will be in a position to explain to your colleagues and students there various aspects of American law and society in the same way as you have helped us to understand Chinese law and society.

We are delighted that you will be with us for the remainder of this academic year and we hope that the personal and intellectual contacts that we have established with you will continue and flourish after your return to China.

With high regard,

Yours sincerely,

Arthur von Mehren

Story Professor of Law and Director,

East Asian Legal Studies Program

（十）日本訪美研究員、金融經濟專家杉原啟示致陳安教授函（中譯，原文附後）

陳安教授閣下敬啟者：

一九八二年十月一日，適值中國革命紀念日之際，能聆聽教授閣下有關中國吸收外資政策之講演，深受教益。通過先生之講演，我得以加深理解當前中國一方面繼續堅持一貫奉行之自力更生路線，另一方面又利用外國技術與資本，旨在以中國獨特之方式方法，實現社會主義現代化。

我服務於日本國家石油公司。該公司係日本政府國營機構，目前已經以投資參加中日合作之方式，正在中國渤海灣以及鄂爾多斯地區積極推進石油開發事業。我認為，日前先生發表之高見對於日本國民理解中國之政策精神，頗具參考價值，故已將先生惠贈之講演原文（英文）稿件，迅即摘譯要旨，徑送日本國家石油公司參考。

我相信，就日中兩國關係而言，今後必將在經濟與文化兩個方面繼續通力合作，共謀發展。我得以在美國哈佛大學此地與先生邂逅相識，今後如能繼續交換意見，則不勝榮幸！先生善識日文，故今日謹以日文書寫此感謝信，特此表示謝忱。請恕草草。

杉原啟示　拜上

哈佛大學（日、美）交換研究員、

日本國家石油公司金融經濟專家

昭和五十七年（1982年）十月三十日

厦門大学法学部国際経済法研究科主任、
厦門大学学術委員会委員
陳安教授殿

拝啓 中国の革命記念日に当たる1982年10月1日に陳安教授より中国の外資導入政策についての講演を聞き、大変有益でした。先生の講演を通じて、現在の中国が従来の自力更生路線を続行しつつも、海外の技術と資本を利用し、中国独自の方法で社会主義の近代化を目ざしていることがわかりました。

私の会社が石油会社という日本政府機関で、現在既に渤海湾とオルドス地方で中日協力により石油開発事業を推進しておりますが、先生のご意見は日本側が中国の考え方を知るのに対して大変参考になると思っております。先生から頂いた原稿を早速要旨を書いて日本会社宛に送付しておりました。

今後も日中関係の経済? 文化両面での協力をしつつ、発展していくと思います。米国ハーバード大学でお知り合いになった上、今後も前向きに意見交換できる関係を継続していただければ幸甚で存じます。先生が日本語がお上手なので、本日は日本語でお礼の手紙を書かせていただきました。

草々をご了承いただけますようお願いします。

杉原啓示
ハーバード大学交換研究員、日本石油会社・金融エコノミスト
昭和五十七年10月30日

（十一）美國紐約法學院《國際法與比較法學報》主編 E. H. Higa 致陳安教授函（摘譯，原文附後）

陳安教授：

…………

您感到詫異，何以一家美國法學雜誌願意發表由一位中華人民共和國公民撰寫的文章，批評一家美國報紙的新聞報導。但是，事實上我們很高興採用這篇論文，並且引以為榮。

…………

您這篇論文的主題是評論刊載於《紐約時報》的克利斯托

弗・雷恩所寫的兩篇報導。這些報導曾經引起人們對中華人民共和國政府當局處理李爽案件的做法，嘖有煩言，紛紛非難。您的文章提出了人們所殷切期待的答案。這種答案，來自中華人民共和國的一位公民，來自一位像您這樣卓越出色的中國法學學者，是再恰當不過的了。

您的這篇論文從中國的風俗習慣、志向抱負、政治和社會的奮鬥目標的角度，從反映著這些因素的法律體制的角度，條理分明、令人信服地剖析了李爽案件。我不能設想有比這更加雄辯透澈的解釋說明。

您對於美國和中國的刑事法制所作的比較分析是特別有教益和富有啟發性的。不過，我認為最能發人深思的還是您所使用的方法，即把李爽案件放置在中國的社會主義理論、社會主義實踐以及社會主義目標的背景之中，加以剖析。

我簡要地說明了我對您這篇論文的看法，希望這能敦促您繼續向本刊投寄您的精闢論著，並且向您的同事們懇切說明我們美國人（特別是本刊同仁們）懷有重大的興趣，期待收到中華人民共和國這些飽學的法學教授們投寄具有創見的法學學術論文。

謹致最友好的敬意。

Emlyn H. Higa

紐約法學院《國際法與比較法學報》一九八一至一九八二年主編

一九八二年十一月十九日

November 19, 1982

Prof. An Chen

423 Pound Hall

Harvard Law School

Cambridge, Massachusetts 02138

Dear Prof. Chen,

…

This is in response to your inquiry, made on behalf of your colleagues in the People's Republic of China, regarding my reasons for accepting your article on the Li Shuang case for publication in the *New York Law School Journal of International and Comparative Law*. I am honored to have received the request and delighted to respond.

Although you expressed surprise that an American law journal would publish an article written by a citizen of the People's Republic of China that was critical of an American newspaper story, the fact is that we were pleased and honored to receive it.

…

The United States, as you well know, is a country born of rebellion and suckled on controversy, We are like a large, ill-mannered family whose members wranle loudly and sometimes violently with each other, seeming not to care that our neighbors may be disturbed by our domestic squabbling. But what binds us together is our common belief in the principle that for knowledge and wisdom and understanding to increase, debate must be open and free. Genuine doubts must always be voiced and responsible criticism is never improper.

We are a young nation. And with the restless enthusiasm and arrogant scepticism of youth, we are always greedy for new knowledge, straining to hear a new voice, or to see a new viewpoint. Therefore, when a charge is made, everyone waits and listens for the answer.

Christopher Wren's articles in the *New York Times*, which are the subject of your article, evoked much criticism of the way that the authorities in the People's Republic of China handled the Li Shuang Case. Your article provides the much awaited answer. An answer that can come from no one other than a citizen of the People's Republic of China and can come from no more appropriate citizen than such an eminent legal scholar as you.

Your article very clearly and responsibly explains the Li Shuang Case from the perspective of the customs, expectations, the political and social ambitions of the People's Republic of China, and the legal structure that expresses them. And I cannot imagine a more eloquent explanation.

Your comparative analysis of the criminal systems of the United States and of the People's Republic of China is particularly helpful and illuminating. But what I consider most thought-provoking is the way that you place the Li Shuang Case within the context of Chinese socialist doctrine, practice and purposes.

I hope that this abbreviated explanation of my attitude toward your article will encourage you to submit more of your excellent work to the Journal; and that you will urge upon your colleagues the great interest we in the United States, and particularly we at the Journal, have in receiving thoughtful, scholarly legal writing from such learned law professors in the People's Republic of China.

With much friendship and respect,

Emlyn H. Higa

Editor-in-Chief (1981-1982)

（十二）美國波士頓大學法學院教授、哈佛大學東亞法學研究所前副所長 F. K. Upham 教授致陳安教授函

陳安教授：

非常感謝您在一九八二年十一月四日寄來信件，並附贈有關李爽案件的論文清樣。

我認為，您的論文以一個中國法學學者的敏銳眼光，對這樁案件作了引人入勝的、相當精闢的闡述。您那精心細緻、沉著冷靜的分析，提出了一些重要的課題，它們將鄭重提醒美國的法學研究生們必須注意另外一種法學觀點，這種法學觀點往往同他們原有的觀點迥然相異，並且難得有人能夠妥善確切地加以論述闡明。我的研究專業雖是日本的法學，但我仍然打算今後要求我的研究生們閱讀您的這篇論文。因為這篇論文是如此妥帖完善地闡明了中國法制與美國法制之間的基本區別和某些相似之處，而這

兩種法制對日本法制的形成，向來是有促進作用的。

趁此寫信機會，讓我另外向您致謝，感謝您上學年（1981-1982）在我擔任哈佛東亞法學研究所副所長期間（Upham教授於1982年9月離開哈佛，應聘在波士頓大學執教）所給予我的支持幫助。您是一位優秀出色的同事，我盼望今後能繼續保持我們之間的友好關係。

謹致最良好的祝願。

Frank K. Upham

哈佛大學東亞法學研究所一九八一至一九八二年副所長

一九八二年十一月二十九日

November 29, 1982

Professor An Chen

East Asian Legal Studies

Harvard Law School

Cambridge, MA 02138

Dear An Chen:

Thank you very much for your letter of November 4, 1982, and for sending me the proofs of your article relating to the Li Shuang Case.

I found your article fascinating and an excellent presentation of the case from the perspective of a Chinese legal scholar. Your careful, calm analysis raises the important issues in a way that will alert American law students to a view of law often very different from theirs and seldom well articulated. Even though my specialty is Japanese law, I plan to have my students read your article in the future because it so well presents the underlying differences and similarities in the Chinese and American legal systems that have both helped form Japan's.

On a different topic, let me take this opportunity to thank you for your support last year (1981-1982) while I was Associate Director of East Asian Legal Studies. You were an excellent colleague, and I hope we can continue our relationship in the future.

With all best wishes,

Frank K. Upham

Visiting Professor

Associate Director, East Asian

Legal Studies, 1981-1982

注釋

〔1〕 這些函件的原件均收藏於廈門大學國際經濟法研究所資料室，存檔備考。

〔2〕 《國際經濟法學芻言》一書於二〇〇五年由北京大學出版社出版，上、下兩卷共約二一二萬字，二〇〇七年獲第五屆「吳玉章人文社會科學獎」一等獎。其大部分內容經進一步全面增訂更新，輯入《陳安論國際經濟法學》一書，該書篇幅約三一一萬字，由復旦大學出版社二〇〇八年出版，二〇〇九年獲「福建省第八屆社會科學優秀成果獎」一等獎；又於二〇一三獲「第六屆高等學校科學研究優秀成果獎（人文社會科學）」二等獎。

〔3〕 本文於二〇〇七年獲得「福建省第七屆社會科學優秀成果獎」一等獎。本文的中、英兩種文本已分別收輯於《陳安論國際經濟法學》（五卷本）第一編之XV、第七編之II，由復旦大學出版社二〇〇八年出版。兩種文本可資互相對照。

〔4〕 《南方中心秘書長Branislav Gosovic致陳安教授函（2006年2月1日）》，載陳安：《陳安論國際經濟法學》（第五卷），復旦大學出版社2008年版，第2591-2592頁。

〔5〕 本文及其「姊妹篇」中、英兩種文本，先後部分或全文分別發表於中外數種權威性學術刊物，因其引起國內外廣泛關注，具有較大學術影響，於二〇〇四至二〇〇六年相繼獲得第十二屆「安子介國際貿易研究獎」一等獎、「福建省第七屆社會科學優秀成果獎」一等獎、第二屆「全國法學教材與科研成果獎」一等獎，以及第四屆「中國高校人文社會科學研究優秀成果獎」二等獎（見本書第七編第四章「陳安教授論著、業績獲獎一覽（以倒計年為序/2016-1960）」）。本文的中、英兩種文本經再次綜合整理和增訂，已分別收輯於《陳安論國際經濟法學》（五卷本）第一編之X、第七編之I，由復旦大學出版社二〇〇八年出版。兩種文本可資互相對照。

〔6〕 陳安教授參撰並主編的這本書，約二十五萬字，是中國人針對《華盛頓公約》及其「解決投資爭端國際中心」（ICSID）機制開展系列研究的第一部創新成果，一九八九年十二月由鷺江出版社出版，一九九四年獲得「福建省第二屆社會科學優秀成果獎」一等獎。其後，在組織新的博士生學術團隊進一步深入研究的基礎上，陳安教授又參撰並主編了另外兩本「姊妹書」，即《國際投資爭端仲裁——「解決投資爭端國際中心」機制研究》與《國際投資爭端案例精選》，共約一一七萬字，二〇〇一年由復旦大學出版社出版，二〇〇二年先後獲得中國司法部頒發的「第一屆全國法學教材與科研成果獎」一等獎以及中宣部、國家新聞出版總署、中國出版工作者協會聯合頒發的「中國圖書獎」。以上三部專著中由陳安教授撰寫的部分，已經綜合整理和增訂，收輯於《陳安論國際經濟法學》五卷本）第三編之IV，題為《ICSID與中國：我們研究「解決投資爭端國際中心」的現實動因和待決問題》，由復旦大學出版社二〇〇八年出版。

〔7〕 本文的中、英兩種文本，已分別收輯於《陳安論國際經濟法學》（五

卷本）第三編之IX、第七編之XIII，由復旦大學出版社二〇〇八年出版。兩種文本可資互相對照。

〔8〕本文的英文文本已收輯於《陳安論國際經濟法學》（五卷本）第七編之XVII，由復旦大學出版社二〇〇八年出版。

〔9〕即《是棒打鴛鴦嗎？——就「李爽案件」評〈紐約時報〉報導兼答美國法學界同行問》，其中文、英文兩種文本已收輯於本書第五編第四章。

〔10〕本文的中、英文兩種文本，見本書第五編第四章。

〔11〕本文最初於二〇〇八年九月十二日發表在新浪博客（http: //blog. sina. com. cn/s/blog_4389bff20100w80s. html），原題為《說說廈大的那位老先生——陳安先生》，作者署名「Bethamyang」即楊秉勳。

〔12〕指英文稿 "The Three Big Rounds of U. S. Unilateralism Versus WTO Multilateralism During the Last Decade: A Combined Analysis of the Great 1994 Sovereignty Debate, Section 301 Disputes (1998-2000), and Section 201 Disputes (2002-2003)（《晚近十年來美國單邊主義與WTO多邊主義交鋒的三大回合：綜合剖析美國「主權大辯論」（1994）、「301條款」爭端（1998-2000）以及「201條款」爭端（2002-2003）》，全文約6.5萬字），發表於美國天普大學《國際法與比較法學報》2003年第17卷第2期（*Temple International & Comparative Law Journal*, Vol. 17, No. 2, 2003）。應孫振宇大使要求，陳安教授補寄了該長篇論文的單行本。事後獲悉：孫大使要求中國駐WTO代表團專業人員認真閱讀本文並開展討論。

〔13〕Jacques Werner先生是日內瓦著名的編輯兼出版人，主持編輯和出版四種國際性學術刊物。

〔14〕斯奈德助理院長當時是這場演講會的主席（主持人），他曾在演講結束時當場作過一些評論。

〔15〕在美國，「講座教授」是一種學術上的榮譽稱號。美國大學往往把這種稱號授予學術成就卓著的權威教授。斯托利（Joseph Sory），十九世紀中葉美國的法學權威，曾任美國最高法院大法官三十餘年，哈佛大學名教授。用他的姓氏命名講座，以示紀念。

陳安學術小傳及歷年主要論著目錄（以倒計年為序）

一、陳安學術小傳

陳安，福建人，廈門大學法學院前院長和國際經濟法研究所所長（1987-1998年），法學教授、博士生導師，國際知名的中國學者。主要學術兼職：中國國際經濟法學會榮譽會長（2011年至今），中國政府依據《華盛頓公約》於一九九三年、二〇〇四年、二〇一〇年三度遴選向「解決投資爭端國際中心」（ICSID）指派的國際仲裁員等。一九五〇年廈門大學法律系畢業，一九五七年復旦大學政治學理論研究生班畢業。

一九八一至一九八三年應邀在美國哈佛大學從事國際經濟法研究，並兼部分講學。一九九〇至一九九一年以「亞洲傑出學者」名義應聘擔任美國俄勒岡州路易士與克拉克西北法學院客座教授兼國際法研究學術顧問。先後多次應邀赴美、加、比（歐共體總部）、瑞士（聯合國歐洲總部）、德、英、澳、法、韓等國家和地區參加國際學術會議或講學。

在法律實務方面，陳安教授是兼職資深國際商務律師，跨國公司法律顧問；中國國際經貿仲裁委員會（CIETAC）仲裁員，國際商會（ICC）國際仲裁案件仲裁員，法國國際仲裁協會（IAI）仲裁員，美國國際仲裁員名冊（RIA）仲裁員等。

近四十年來，陳安教授立足於中國國情和國際弱勢群體即廣大發展中國家的共同立場，致力於探索和開拓具有中國特色的國際經濟法學這一新興邊緣學科。撰寫和主編的主要著作有《中國的吶喊：陳安論國際經濟法》《陳安論國際經濟法學》《國際經濟法學芻言》《美國對海外投資的法律保護及典型案例分析》《國際經濟立法的歷史和現狀》《國際經濟法總論》《國際經濟法學》《國際經濟法學專論》《國際投資法》《國際貿易法》《國際貨幣金融法》《國際稅法》《國際海事法》《國際投資爭端仲裁——「解決投資爭端國際中心」機制研究》《MIGA與中國：多邊投資擔保機構述評》等四十四種，合計約二五〇〇〇餘萬字。另在《中國社會科學》《中國法學》、國際政府間組織「南方中心」機關學刊《南方公報》（*South Bulletin*）、美國紐約法學院《國際法與比較法學報》、天普大學《國際法與比較法學報》《威拉梅特大學法律評論》、日內瓦《國際仲裁學刊》《世界投資與貿易學報》等國內外學術刊物上發表多篇論文。多項學術論著獲國家級、省部級科研優秀成果一等獎〔16〕或被指定為全國性高校本科生、研究生法學教材或教學參考書。

此外，陳安教授還兼任全國性的國際經濟法專業優秀學術論文的匯輯《國際經濟法學刊》的主編、《中國大百科全書・法學》修訂版）國際經濟法分支的主編。

陳安教授一九六〇年被評為福建省勞模，一九九二年獲國務院政府特殊津貼。一九八七、一九九四、二〇〇三、二〇〇六年先後四次獲得廈門大學最高榮譽獎「南強獎」一等獎；二〇〇八年又獲「南強獎」特等獎。

《人民日報》（海外版）、《光明日報》《法制日報》等報刊以及國務院學位委員會刊物《學位與研究生教育》先後多次報導他的學術觀點和有關事蹟。[17] 美國、英國多種《國際名人錄》均列有陳安教授的個人小傳。

二、陳安歷年主要論著

（一）書籍

1. 《美國霸權版「中國威脅」讕言的前世與今生》（專著），江蘇人民出版社2015年版。

2. *The Voice from China: An CHEN on International Economic Law*（英文版專著，中文名《中國的吶喊：陳安論國際經濟法》），德國Springer出版社2013年版。

3. 《陳安論國際經濟法學》（五卷本）（專著），復旦大學出版社2008年版。

4. 《國際經濟法學專論》（上、下兩卷）（主編），高等教育出版社2004年第一版、2007年第二版。

5. 《國際經濟法學學刊》（原名《國際經濟法學論叢》，2004年改用現名，第1-23卷）（主編），法律出版社、北京大學出版社1998-2017年版。

6. 《國際經濟法學》（第一版至第七版）（主編），北京大學出版社1994-2017年版。

7. 《國際經濟法學資料選萃》（主編），高等教育出版社2007年版。

8. 《國際投資法的新發展與中國雙邊投資條約的新實踐》（主編），復旦大學出版社2007年版。

9. 《國際經濟法》（主編），法律出版社1999年第一版、2007年第二版。

10.《國際經濟法學新論》（主編），高等教育出版社2007年版。

11.《國際經濟法學資料新編》（上、下兩卷）（主編），北京大學出版社2008年版。

12.《中國大百科全書・法學》（修訂版）之國際經濟法分支學科（主編），中國大百科全書出版社2006年版。

13.《國際經濟法學芻言》（上、下兩卷）（專著），北京大學出版社2005年版。

14《國際經濟法概論》（第一版至第四版）（主編），北京大學出版社1995-2010年版。

15.《國際投資爭端案例精選》（主編），復旦大學出版社2001年版。

16.《國際投資爭端仲裁——「解決投資爭端國際中心」機制研究》（主編），復旦大學出版社2001年版。

17.「國際經濟法學系列專著」（總主編，五卷），北京大學出版社1999-2001年版（含《國際投資法學》《國際貿易法學》《國際貨幣金融法學》《國際稅法學》《國際海事法學》）。

18.《海峽兩岸交往中的法律問題研究》（主編），北京大學出版社1997年版。

19.《臺灣法律大全》（主編），中國大百科全書出版社1998年版。

20.《MIGA與中國：多邊投資擔保機構述評》（主編），福建人民出版社1995年版。

21.《涉外經濟合同的理論與實務》（主編），中國政法大學出版社1994年版。

22.《國際經濟法資料選編》（主編），法律出版社1991年版。

23.《國際經濟法總論》（主編），法律出版社1991年版。

24.《臺灣涉外經濟法概要》（主編），鷺江出版社1990年版。

25.《「解決投資爭端國際中心」述評》（專著），鷺江出版社1989年版。

26.「國際經濟法系列專著」（主編，五卷），鷺江出版社1987-1989年版（含《國際投資法》《國際貿易法》《國際貨幣金融法》《國際稅法》《國際海事法》）。

27.《舌劍唇槍：國際投資糾紛五大著名案例》（主編），鷺江出版社1986年版。

28.《美國對海外投資的法律保護及典型案例分析》（專著），鷺江出版社1985年版。

29.《國際經濟立法的歷史和現狀》（日文、英文編譯），法律出版社1982年版。

30.《列寧對民族殖民地革命學說的重大發展》（專著），生活・讀書・新知三聯書店1981年版。

31.《印度特倫甘納人民的鬥爭及其經驗教訓》（英文譯

著），生活・讀書・新知三聯書店1977年版。

32.《修正主義反對無產階級專政學說》（俄文譯著），生活・讀書・新知三聯書店1962年版。

33.《反對修正主義》（俄文譯著），生活・讀書・新知三聯書店1961年版。

34.《現代資產階級社會學關於階級和階級鬥爭的各種反科學理論》（俄文譯著），上海人民出版社1958年版。

（二）論文

1. 《「左公柳」、中國魂與新絲路》。

2. 《建構中國特色國際法學理論》，載《人民日報》2017年5月8日第15版學術版。

3. 《向世界展現中國理念》，載《人民日報》2016年6月5日第5版學術版。

4. 《朝著合作共贏方向發展推動國際經濟法理念變革》，載《人民日報》2016年11月7日第16版學術版。

5. 《小議對外學術交流的三種「大忌」》，載《光明日報》2015年7月31日第2版評論・觀點版。

6. A Reflection on the South-South Coalition in the Last Half Century from the Perspective of International Economic Law-making: From Bandung, Doha and Cancún to Hong Kong，原發表於*The Journal of World Investment & Trade*（Geneva）2006年第7卷第2期。經增訂更新，被收輯於在海牙、紐約、倫敦同時推出的學術專著《從第三世界視角看通過貿易謀求經濟發展》（*Economic Development*

Through Trade：*A Third World Perpetive*），由Kluwer Law International於2007年12月出版。

7. 《區分兩類國家，實行差別互惠：再論ICSID體制賦予中國的四大「安全閥」不宜貿然全面拆除》，載《國際經濟法學刊》2007年第14卷第3期。

8. Distinguishing Two Kinds of Countries and Granting Differential Reciprocity: Re-comments on the Four Safeguards in Sino-Foreign BITs Not to Be Hastily and Completely Dismantled, *The Journal of World Investment &Trade* (Geneva), Vol. 7, No. 2, 2007.

9. Should the Four Great Safeguards in Sino-Foreign BITs Be Hastily Dismantled? *The Journal of World Investment & Trade* , Vol. 7 , Iss. 6, 2006.

10. Weak Versus Strong at the WTO, *The Geneva Post Quarterly*: *The Journal of World Affairs* , Vol. 1, No. 1, 2006.

11.《中外雙邊投資協定中的四大「安全閥」不宜貿然拆除》，載《國際經濟法學刊》2006年第13卷第1期。

12.《南南聯合自強五十年的國際經濟立法反思：從萬隆、多哈、坎昆到香港》，載《中國法學》2006年第2期。

13. Be Optimistic, or Be Pessimistic? The Fork Confronting DDR and WTO After Its Hong Kong Ministerial Conference, *South Buletin*, No 120, 2006 ·

14.《外商在華投資中的「空手道」融資：「一女兩婿」與「兩裁六審」》，載《國際經濟法學刊》2005年第12卷第3期。

15.《外貿代理合同糾紛中的當事人、管轄權、準據法、仲裁庭、債務人等問題剖析韓國C公司訴中國X市A、B兩公司案件述評》，載《國際經濟法學刊》2004年第9卷第2期。

16.《美國單邊主義對抗WTO多邊主義的第三回合——「201條款」爭端之法理探源和展望》，載《中國法學》2004年第2期。

17. The Three Big Rounds of U. S. Unilateralism Versus WTO Multilateralism During the Last Decade: A Combined Analysis of the Great 1994 Sovereignty Debate, Section 301 Disputes (1998-2000), and Section 201 Disputes (2002-2003), *Temple International and Comparative Law Journal*, Vol. 17, No. 2, 2003。後該文經修訂增補，由國際組織「南方中心」（South Centre）作為其「工作檔」第22號，於二〇〇四年七月以「單行本」形式發行，並全文公布於該中心的網站。

18.《論涉外仲裁個案中的越權管轄、越權解釋、草率斷結和有欠透明——CIETAC 2001-2002年個案評析》，載《國際經濟法論叢》2003年第7卷。

19.《中國「入世」後海峽兩岸經貿問題「政治化」之防治》（增訂本），載《國際經濟法論叢》2002年第6卷。

20.《中國「入世」後海峽兩岸經貿問題「政治化」之防治》，載《中國法學》2002年第2期。

21.《世紀之交圍繞經濟主權的新「攻防戰」——從美國的「主權大辯論」及其後續影響看當代「主權淡化」論之不可取》，載《國際經濟法論叢》2001年第4卷。

22.《美國「1994年主權大辯論」及其後續影響》，載《中國社會科學》2001年第5期。

23.《評對中國國際經濟法學科發展現狀的幾種誤解》，載《東南學術》1999年第3期。

24.《再論中國涉外仲裁的監督機制及其與國際慣例的接軌》（增訂本），載《國際經濟法論叢》1999年第2卷。

25.《指鹿為馬，枉法裁斷——評港英高等法院1994年的一項涉華判決》，載《升華與超越：大學生文化素質教育講座集錦3》高等教育出版社1998年版。

26.《論國際經濟法的邊緣性、綜合性和獨立性》，載《國際經濟法論叢》1998年第1卷。

27.《中國涉外仲裁監督機制申論》，載《中國社會科學》1998年第2期。

28.《英、美、法、德等國涉外仲裁監督機制辨析》，載《法學評論》1998年第5期。

29.《再論中國涉外仲裁的監督機制及其與國際慣例的接軌》，載《民商法論叢》1998年第10卷。

30.《論中國涉外仲裁的監督機制及其與國際慣例的接軌》（英文），載《國際仲裁學刊》（日內瓦）1997年第14卷第3期。

31.《一項判決　三點質疑》（中文增訂本），載《民商法論叢》1997年第8卷。

32.《一項判決　三點質疑：香港高等法院1993年第A8176號判決評析》（英文），載《國際仲裁學刊》（日內瓦）1996年第13卷第4期。

33.《臺商大陸投資保險可行途徑初探》，載《中國法學》1995年第5期。

34.《論中國涉外仲裁的監督機制及其與國際慣例的接軌》，載《比較法研究》1995年第4期。

35.《中國涉外仲裁監督機制評析》，載《中國社會科學》1995年第4期。

36.《論國際經濟法的涵義及其邊緣性》，載《中國國際法年刊》，中國對外翻譯出版公司1996年版。

37.《論適用國際慣例與有法必依的統一》，載《中國社會科學》1994年第4期。

38.《論有約必守原則在國際經濟法中的正確運用》，載《東亞法律・經濟・文化國際學術討論會論文集》，中國大百科全書出版社1993年版。

39.《「臺商大陸投資權益保障協定」初剖》，載《臺灣研究》1993年第4期。

40.《論國際經濟法中的公平互利原則》，載《中德經濟法研究所年刊》1992年卷。

41.《是重新閉關自守？還是擴大對外開放？——論中美兩國經濟上的互相依存以及「1989年政治風波」後在華外資的法律環境》（英文），載《律師》*Advocate*雜誌（美國俄勒岡州）1991年第2期。

42. Special Economic Zones and Coastal Port-Cities: Their Development and Legal Framework, *Chinese Foreign Economic Law: Analysis and Commentary*, International Law Institute, 1990.

43.《兩種「兩岸人民關係法」之對立與統一——兼談「閩臺自由貿易協定」之可行》，載《臺灣研究集刊》1990年第2、期。

44.《某些涉外經濟合同何以無效以及如何防止無效》（英文），載《威拉梅特大學法評論》美國）1987年第23卷。

45.《我國涉外經濟立法中可否規定對外資不實行國有化》，載《廈門大學學報》（哲學社會科學版）1986年第1期，其英譯本收輯於《在華投資的法律問題》，由香港中貿翻譯公司1988年出版。

46.《從海外私人投資公司的體制和案例看美國對海外投資的法律保護》，載《中國國際法年刊》，中國對外翻譯出版公司1986年版。

47. China and Foreign Capital: The Legal and Organizational Framework, in Harish Karpur (ed.), *The End of an Isolation: China After Mao*, Martinus Nijhoff Publishers, 1985.

48.《是進一步開放？還是重新關門？——中國吸收外資政策法令述評》（英文），載《國際法與比較法學報》（美國）1985年第1期。

49.《從海外私人投資公司的由來看美國對海外投資的法律保護》，載《中國國際法年刊》，中國對外翻譯出版公司1985年版。

50.《是「棒打鴛鴦」嗎？——就「李爽案件」評〈紐約時報〉報導兼答美國法學界同行問》（英文），載《國際法與比較法學報》（美國）1981年第3卷第1期。

51.《論社會帝國主義主權觀的一大思想淵源》，載《吉林大學社會科學學報》1981年第3期。

52.《試論和平共處與反帝鬥爭》，載《廈門大學學報》（哲學社會科學版）1960年第2期。

注釋

〔16〕詳見本書第七編第四章「陳安教授論著、業績獲獎一覽（以倒計年為序/2016-1960）」。

〔17〕例如，（一）《適應對外開放和發展外向型經濟需要，國際經濟法系列專著問世》，載《光明日報》1988年4月26日；（二）《就閩臺兩省結拜「姊妹」一事廈門大學法學教授發表看法》，載《人民日報》（海外版）1989年5月8日；（三）《為對外開放鋪路——記廈門大學法學教授陳安》，載《人民日報》（海外版）1992年7月7日；（四）《理性務實的學術交流盛會——1993年兩岸法學學術研討會綜述》，載《人民日報》（海外版）1993年8月27日；（五）《當代經濟主權問題縱橫談》，載《法制日報》1997年3月22日；（六）《第十二屆「安子介國際貿易研究獎」頒獎》，載《人民日報》（海外版）2004年12月21日。以上這些報導，均已收輯於《陳安論國際經濟法學》第八編之I「媒體報導」

第四章

陳安論著、業績獲獎一覽（以倒計年為序/ 2016-1960）

一、國家級、省部級一等獎

序號	獲獎論著/業績名稱	獎勵名稱及等級	獲獎時間
1	美國霸權版「中國威脅」讕言的前世與今生	全國社會科學普及工作組委會授予「優秀社會科學普及作品」榮譽稱號	2016年
2	批判「黃禍」論的美國霸權版變種：「中國威脅」論	福建省第十屆社會科學優秀成果獎一等獎	2013年
3	為中國法學理論體系建設和法治建設做出傑出貢獻	全國傑出資深法學家	2012年
4	論中國在建立國際經濟新秩序中的戰略定位	福建省第九屆社會科學優秀成果獎一等獎	2011年
5	中國加入WTO十年的法理斷想：簡論WTO的法治、立法、執法、守法與變法	重慶市第十一屆社會科學優秀成果獎一等獎	2011年
6	陳安論國際經濟法學（復旦大學出版社出版，五卷本）	福建省第八屆社會科學優秀成果獎榮譽一等獎	2009年
7	國際經濟法學芻言（北京大學出版社出版，兩卷本）	第五屆「吳玉章人文社會科學獎」一等獎	2007年
8	南南聯合自強五十年的國際經濟立法反思：從萬隆、多哈、坎昆到香港	福建省第七屆社會科學優秀成果獎一等獎	2007年

序號	獲獎論著/業績名稱	獎勵名稱及等級	獲獎時間
9	美國單邊主義對抗WTO多邊主義的第三回合——「201條款」爭端之法理探源和展望	司法部第二屆全國法學教材與科研成果獎一等獎	2006年
10	美國單邊主義對抗WTO多邊主義的第三回合——「201條款」爭端之法理探源和展望	福建省第六屆社會科學優秀成果獎一等獎	2005年
11	The Three Big Rounds of U. S. Unilateralism Versus WTO Multilateralism During the Last Decade	第十二屆「安子介國際貿易研究獎」一等獎	2004年
12	有關涉外仲裁監督機制的系列論文（共約22萬字）	第三屆中國高校人文社會科學研究優秀成果獎一等獎	2003年
13	國際投資爭端仲裁——「解決投資爭端國際中心」機制研究	司法部第一屆全國法學教材與科研成果獎一等獎	2003年
11	國際投資爭端仲裁——「解決投資爭端國際中心」機制研究	中國圖書獎	2002年
15	MIGA與中國：多邊投資擔保機構述評	福建省第三屆社會科學優秀成果獎一等獎	1998年
16	「解決投資爭端國際中心」述評	福建省第二屆社會科學優秀成果獎一等獎	1994年
17	國際經濟法學系列專著（五卷本）	福建省第一屆社會科學優秀成果獎一等獎	1988年
18	福建省文教戰線紅旗手	福建省省級勞動模範	1960年

二、國家級、省部級二等獎

序號	獲獎論著名稱	獎勵名稱及等級	獲獎時間
1	陳安論國際經濟法學（復旦大學出版社出版，五卷本）	第六屆高等學校科學研究優秀成果獎（人文社會科學）二等獎	2013年

序號	獲獎論著名稱	獎勵名稱及等級	獲獎時間
2	南南聯合自強五十年的國際經濟立法反思：從萬隆、多哈、坎昆到香港	司法部第三屆全國法學教材與科研成果二等獎	2009年
3	世紀之交圍繞經濟主權的新「攻防戰」——從美國的「主權大辯論」及其後續影響看當代「主權淡化」論之不可取	第四屆中國高校人文社會科學研究優秀成果獎二等獎	2006年
4	國際經濟法學專論（兩卷本）	福建省第五屆社會科學優秀成果獎二等獎	2003年
5	美國1991年「主權大辯論」及其後續影響	福建省第五屆社會科學優秀成果獎二等獎	2003年
6	臺灣法律大全	福建省第四屆社會科學優秀成果獎二等獎	2000年
7	論中國涉外仲裁監督機制及其與國際慣例的接軌	福建省第四屆社會科學優秀成果獎二等獎	2000年
8	國際經濟法學	福建省第三屆社會科學優秀成果獎二等獎	1998年
9	中國涉外仲裁監督機制評析	福建省第三屆社會科學優秀成果獎二等獎	1998年

三、國家級三等獎

序號	獲獎論著名稱	獎勵名稱及等級	獲獎時間
1	*The Voice from China: An CHEN on International Economic Law*（《中國的吶喊：陳安論國際經濟法》，英文版專著，德國Springer出版社出版，852頁，「國家社會科學基金中華學術外譯專案」重要成果）	第七屆高等學校科學研究優秀成果獎（人文社會科學）三等獎	2015年

序號	獲獎論著名稱	獎勵名稱及等級	獲獎時間
2	Weak Versus Strong at the WTO: The South- South Coalition from Bandung to Hong Kong（《世貿組織中群弱抗衡強權》，英文專論）	第五屆中國高校人文社會科學研究優秀成果獎三等獎	2009年

四、廈門大學最高榮譽獎

1	廈門大學南強傑出貢獻獎	廈門大學最高榮譽獎	2015年
2	南強獎特等獎（個人）	廈門大學最高榮譽獎	2008年
3	南強獎一等獎（個人）	廈門大學最高榮譽獎	2006年
4	南強獎一等獎（個人）	廈門大學最高榮譽獎	2003年
5	南強獎一等獎（個人）	廈門大學最高榮譽獎	1994年
6	南強獎一等獎（團隊集體）	廈門大學最高榮譽獎	1987年

以上合計：獲得國家級、省部級一等獎十八項；國家級、省部級二等獎九項；國家級三等獎二項；廈門大學最高榮譽獎六項。總共三十五項。其中三十三項均為一九八八至二〇一五年獲得。在這三十三項中，有二十六項是陳安教授一九九九年退休後獲得的。

（2016年12月12日整理）

後　記

一、本書第六編所輯書評薈萃數十篇，雖然並非本書作者所撰，但均是對本書作者近四十年來學術理念和學術追求的積極呼應和同氣相求，形成了對國際經濟法學領域「中國特色話語」的共鳴強音，在國際論壇上對共同構建「中國特色國際經濟法學理論新體系」，發揮了和發揮著積極的推動作用。把國內外高端同行學者所撰數十篇書評，薈萃輯入本書，以饗讀者，冀能從一個側面，證明國際經濟法學領域的「中國特色話語」，確實是「友聲四起，吾道不孤」；同時，也殷切期待從更多的國內外學者和讀者之中，獲得對「中國特色話語」更大的共鳴強音，共同參與構建「中國特色國際經濟法學理論新體系」的「理論長征」，共同推動國際經濟秩序和全球治理體系與時俱進的變革和創新。

二、把「大師評論」部分放在本書的開篇，旨在表達作者對他們（其中韓、朱兩師均在百歲後離世，郭師也在92歲高齡後離世）的真誠謝忱、緬懷紀念和由衷敬意。

三、本書總篇幅多達二九〇萬字。讀者乍讀，恐難掌握全書概貌以及其中論述主線、脈絡、重點。鑑此，把幾篇「學者導言」放在本書開篇，可以對許多青年讀者起到「導讀」作用。

四、本書各編各章雖已融為一體，但各章仍然具有相對獨立性，可以各自獨立成篇。同時，本書各章撰寫和發表時間前後跨度近四十年，各章論述主題常有承前啟後、與時俱進、互相交叉、彼此滲透之處，為便於讀者理解本書各章的論證邏輯和發展思路，有的後章必須適當複述或摘引前章部分內容。這樣處理，也便於日後向國外輸出版權、製作單篇「數位產品」、翻譯、轉載等等，酌情分割、剪裁，靈活使用。

五、本書第二編「國際經濟法基本理論（二）」、第三編「國際投資法」和第四編「國際貿易法」各章中，含有作者對親身經歷的二十幾個典型案件的理論剖析和是非臧否。在近四十年來的法律實務中，作者秉持公正公平原則，針對這些涉外經貿爭端個案的處斷，依法據理，祛邪扶正，分別以法學專家、兼職律師、涉外仲裁員的不同身份，撰文從理論上伸張正義，深入探討相關的法理問題，提出創新見解，**維護司法公正**。在這些「弘揚獬豸精神、觸不直者去之」的實錄中，含有大量原始附件和確鑿證據，限於本書篇幅，不得不割愛從略。有心**深入研究**這些典型案件的讀者，不妨前往具體辦案的司法機關和仲裁機關，查閱原始案卷文檔。因為，其中「獨角獸」所觸而去之者，既有中外不法奸商，也有外國「權威」法官和「御用大律師」，還有中國「權威」仲裁機構的高級仲裁員，另外還有個別見利忘義、泯滅良知的中國律師。顯然，這些枉法裁斷、褻瀆法律尊嚴的行徑和人員，都有待同道學友們**追蹤研究，深入質疑，口誅筆伐，徹底批判**。

陳　安

二〇一八年七月十六日

社科文庫．國際財金研究叢刊 AA101018

中國特色話語：陳安論國際經濟法學 第四卷 下冊

作　　者 陳　安
版權策畫 李煥芹
責任編輯 林以邠

發 行 人 陳滿銘
總 經 理 梁錦興
總 編 輯 陳滿銘
副總編輯 張晏瑞
編 輯 所 萬卷樓圖書股份有限公司
排　　版 菩薩蠻數位文化有限公司
印　　刷 百通科技股份有限公司
封面設計 菩薩蠻數位文化有限公司

出　　版 昌明文化有限公司
桃園市龜山區中原街 32 號
電話 (02)23216565
發　　行 萬卷樓圖書股份有限公司
臺北市羅斯福路二段 41 號 6 樓之 3
電話 (02)23216565
傳真 (02)23218698
電郵 SERVICE@WANJUAN.COM.TW
大陸經銷
廈門外圖臺灣書店有限公司
電郵 JKB188@188.COM

ISBN 978-986-496-536-6
2019 年 9 月初版
定價：新臺幣 560 元

如何購買本書：
1. 轉帳購書，請透過以下帳戶
合作金庫銀行 古亭分行
戶名：萬卷樓圖書股份有限公司
帳號：0877717092596
2. 網路購書，請透過萬卷樓網站
網址 WWW.WANJUAN.COM.TW
大量購書，請直接聯繫我們，將有專人為您服務。客服：(02)23216565 分機 610

國家圖書館出版品預行編目資料

中國特色話語 : 陳安論國際經濟法學. 第四卷 / 陳安著. -- 初版. -- 桃園市 : 昌明文化出版 ; 臺北市 : 萬卷樓發行, 2019. 09
冊 ; 公分
ISBN 978-986-496-536-6 (下冊 : 平裝)

1.經濟法學

553.4 108015601